MEDIA AND MONARCHY

MEDIA AND MONARCHY

J. MALLORY WOBER

Nova Science Publishers, Inc.
Huntington, New York

Library of Congress Cataloging-in-Publication Data

Wober, J.M. (J. Mallory)
    Media and monarchy / Mallory Wober.
            p.   cm.
    Includes bibliographical references and index.
    ISBN 1-56072-77-2
    1. Government publicity--Great Britain. 2. Monarchy--Great Britain. 3. Government publicity. 4.
Monarchy. I. Title.
    JN329.P8 W63   2000   99-087798
    352.23'32748'0941--dc21   CIP

Copyright 2000 by Nova Science Publishers, Inc.
    227 Main Street, Suite 100
    Huntington, New York 11743
    Tele. 631-424-6682   Fax 631-424-4666
    e-mail: Novascience@earthlink.net
    Web Site: http://www.nexusworld.com/nova

Printed in the United States of America

CONTENTS

PERSPECTIVES FROM THE PAST: WHERE ARE THERE MONARCHIES NOW, AND WHERE HAVE THEY EXISTED IN THE PAST?

Mention of monarchy in the English speaking world will very likely lead people to think about the British example[1]. Fewer would probably first bring to mind the current Danish or Monegasque monarchs, or think of the Dalai Lama let alone the Kabaka of Buganda, though some may want to consider what will be said about the other European monarchs (such as in Spain, Belgium, Netherlands, Luxembourg, Denmark, Norway and Sweden, not to ignore Monaco) the Saudi or other present Muslim Kings (there are several, from Morocco to Malaysia) and even the Mikado of Japan. In one way then this book will accept convention and focus mainly on the British monarchy.

Can we take it for granted that we know what defines monarchy? We shall see that at different ages and across the world there have been different varieties of monarchy - a composite word which means (or is drawn from parts that mean): rule (the 'arch' particle) by a single person or one (the 'mon' particle). Most have been hereditary - and perhaps this is a truly defining characteristic of a monarchy - though we shall see that some people called kings have been elected, in the two or three cases known the election being by an elite group of nobles or other leaders and not by the public at large. If being a monarch is something inherited, then often it is implied or even proclaimed that the inheritance is ultimately derived from Divine authority. Is a chieftain of a small national group or tribe, especially if his or hers is an inherited status, a monarch? The question will not be settled here by hard and fast rules; rather, the answer will be left to 'develop' through the exploration and discussion of examples.

---

[1] When we were on holiday in Yosemite National Park in California my wife and I took a ride in a bus in which many other tourists from the US, transPacific nations and possibly a few from Europe were shown notable locations including the splendid hotel. About this, the driver/guide said that some years previously "the Queen" had stayed there. Nobody asked "which Queen?".

What do we mean by "media"? The word is usually understood to refer to what I call the "mass message systems" of today - print (books, billboards, the press), radio and television. Generally, in these mass message systems there are few voices who gain access to large numbers of readers, viewers or listeners. A true discourse is not possible in any of these systems, though they often imply that this happens, not least by using the word communication to refer to what they facilitate. To some extent, by sales and audience research, letter pages, phone in times and such devices, the mass of users of these systems do reflect their ideas to those who essentially control the message inputs. The writers or broadcasters nevertheless are able to filter or choose a version of these ideas from among the mass, to play back to that mass; so "mass" media is certainly the mainstream of what we will be concerned with as regards today's society.

Like monarchy with supreme leadership, the notion of "mass media" is not a cut and dried one with which to represent the wider world of "media". Looking ahead, the situation is changing with the development of the internet and a gradual (and as yet slight) erosion of the gigantism of the press and broadcasting outlets of the twentieth century. Looking back - and at other examples of our own time - the notion of "media" can very usefully be broadened out by including all those ways in which ideas or statements or feelings are put into a public domain. This immediately includes the worlds of the arts and culture as examples of "media". Is painting a "medium"? Yes, in the sense accepted here. Theatre? Folk song and folk tale? Sculpture? Opera? Yes, they are all media as in the sense accepted here. We will come to the intriguing notion that monarchy itself may be a "medium" because, as an institution it exists as a channel or symbolisation of ideas and experiences in the past of a people or a nation, which are represented in its present, to be carried forward for the future - or to be ended. Does this idea of an institution being a medium apply further? Is the family a medium? Motherhood? Perhaps these are not, in the sense being developed here, as they are not channels for the expression of ideas and feelings that are public. So by using the idea of "media" we can interestingly and usefully look at many phenomena other than the mass message systems which the word "media" will first bring to mind. Again, as with the exploration of monarchy, this notion will develop through looking at and discussing examples.

How common or widespread are monarchies today? It is a matter for empirical verification but it may be true that if English speakers are asked whether they believe monarchy is a common contemporary institution, many, perhaps a majority may start by thinking that it is rare. Surveys have shown[2] that even in Britain many people think monarchies are in a minority among European nations whereas, until the recent expansion of the European Union to fifteen states, half of the previous twelve were (and remain) monarchies. Any underestimation of the proportion of states that are (still) monarchies is likely to be connected with the pre-eminence of the British one, and the comparatively low visibility of the other monarchies. The British monarchy is (still) shared by other countries such as Canada though some, such as Australia now contain strong republican movements. One of the arguments of Australian republicans is that the (British and thus foreign) monarchy is alien to Australian needs, but that leaves implied another question as to whether Australia might be well served by importing or appointing its own home-based monarch. Australian opposition to monarchy contains the notion that the institution is not modern, is an outmoded and quaint European form and out of place in twentieth century Pacific countries, even though some of these such as Brunei, Cambodia, Fiji, Laos, Japan, Malaysia and Thailand do retain forms of monarchy. On the Indian ocean, Mozambique has joined the Commonwealth and further north Yemen is a state which seeks to do so, thus even if they do not recognise the Queen as Head of this grouping, they have sought to come within the penumbra if not the full cover of a monarchy.

ANCIENT PRECURSORS OF EUROPEAN MONARCHIC FORMS: WHY DOES MONARCHY EXIST?

The considerations above suggest that an enquiry into how monarchies are made known within their own societies, and by their own societies for wider acquaintance is of very wide relevance. For practical reasons this book focuses on British research; nevertheless, the best point from which to start the study lies not in Britain but in the Middle East. I suggest we need to look first at the Bible, not because it tells us something about the Pharaoh or Nebuchadnezzar, or in the Apocrypha about Antiochus Epiphanes but because it presents a moral political science of the Israelite experience which establishes reservations about what a monarchy should or can be, and to whom it should be beholden and why. These ancient reservations are not remote fragments of social anthropology but are woven into the European and British experiences of monarchy in their histories of ways in which monarchs have asserted their authority or their standing, and in which they have managed their positions with regard to (Judaeo)Christian religion.

In Deuteronomy, where Moses sums up his history and prescriptions for Israel's development and polity he comes in Chapter 17 (verses 14 - 20) to his prophecies[3] on kingship. "When thou art come unto the land which the Lord thy God giveth thee ... and shall say, I will set a king over me, like as all the nations that are about me; thou shalt ... set him king over thee whom the Lord thy God shall choose: one from among thy brethren shalt thou set king over thee ... but he shall not multiply horses to himself ... neither shall he multiply wives to himself ... neither shall he multiply to himself silver and gold. And this shall be, when he sitteth upon the throne of his kingdom, that he shall write him a copy of this law in a book out of that which is before the priests the Levites. And it shall be with him, and he shall read therein all the days of his life: that he may

---

[2] See Chapter 5.

[3] I take this word to mean forthtelling (rather than the more prosaic notion, commonly attached to the term today, of foretelling).

learn to fear the Lord his God, to keep all the words of this law and these statutes, to do them: that his heart be not lifted up above his brethren, and that he turn not aside from the commandment, to the right hand, or to the left ...".

This anticipates what the prophet Samuel experienced (I Samuel, Chapter 8, verses 18 - 20) when he was old; he had made his sons judges (one would now say, some sort of republican leaders) but they "had taken bribes and perverted judgement. Then all the elders of Israel ... came to Samuel ... and said ... now make us a king to judge us like all the nations. But the thing displeased Samuel ... And Samuel prayed to the Lord. And the Lord said unto Samuel ... hearken unto their voice: howbeit ye protest solemnly unto them" (from verses 3 - 9). The Lord goes on to recount how the king will exploit the people "And ye shall cry out in that day because of your king which ye shall have chosen ...: and the Lord will not hear you in that day. Nevertheless the people refused to obey the voice of Samuel; and they said, Nay; but we will have a king over us; that we may be like all the nations...").

To interpret the Israelite demand for a king one has to examine the birth and evolution of their state. The Israelites were a "people" in Egypt and brought out from there as a multitude or a crowd; within this swarm there were well preserved lineages which enabled the people to be subdivided into tribes, each of which had elders, who in some cases were referred to as princes. After forty years they entered the promised land in which each tribe was allotted a particular area. The identity of the people transcended that of the tribes and focused on its law and history which were quite likely to have been inscribed in books of papyrus or scrolls of leather. The nomad economy gave way to one of cultivation and pastoralism, with a beginning made in industries of arts and crafts. Such a developing society accumulates wealth - not just in cattle on the hoof but in money, stored food and artefacts, and looks for symbolic and military leadership which protects this property; and the priesthood was not sufficiently worldly to supply this.

Neighbouring peoples had already developed kingships and the Israelites felt ready for the same role. Public opinion in effect demanded a monarchy. The idea exemplified in this demand, of a bottom up group of appointed or elected citizens as lawmakers came to European cultures from Greece, while the Israelite experience was of a top down dispensation of law. The early leadership system of judges was therefore replaced by what we may call a monarchy, because it was headed by a king; and evidently there was an implication that the monarchy, once installed, would be hereditary. However, the Mosaic and other texts (written down or probably more often spoken in oral lore) made it clear that the king was not a true mon-arch, a lone ruler - because the laws were ultimately made by God. Moreover, the performance of the first Israelite king, Saul, led to the representative of divine authority - at that time the prophet Samuel - revoking the hereditary privilege and restarting the institution with a new dynasty. The procedure of electing kings has not been a common one though in Poland, when the Jagiellonian dynasty had become extinct in 1572 the nobles insisted that the crown should be made elective; in the view of one historian (see Fisher, below, p. 729) the nobles refused any longer "to submit to the rule of strong government ... (and as a consequence) ... the condition of this country had been one of complete moral and political disintegration. The king was a cypher. He had no machinery for collecting taxes, no standing army, and since any member of the Polish Diet, ... might impose an absolute veto ... no means of effecting constitutional changes, or of procuring for his country any ordinary legislative progress"[4]. It may be a defining, or a useful condition of monarchy therefore, that it should embody history and represent it by being hereditary.

We are not concerned in this book about how republican democracies manage their public relations but with the parallel challenge, for monarchs in their societies. So it is important to note that in the model which gives rise to our modern forms, the Israelite king was expected (by Moses) to write down the law constraining his powers, and this expectation was itself written down. This text will not have been commonly available, but it will have been commonly known about. At the very start of the western European monarchic tradition therefore we see a parsimonious model of kingship expecting the monarch to be honest and modest and to implement principles which were not edicts and fads of his own but which were based on divinely given laws.

The Israelite model goes even further in tying the monarch's hands than merely expecting him to be honest and modest. The ideology makes it abundantly clear that it is God who is really King. The idea first emerges in Moses' song of exultation when the Israelites had escaped from Egypt and, having praised God for his miraculous power and strength, says "The Lord shall reign for ever and ever"[5]; the word for reign is from the same root as the word King. It was not necessary to underline God's Kingship during the years in the wilderness or indeed during those under Judges. The last verse in the book of Judges (Chapter 21, v 25) says, however, that "in those days there was no king in Israel: every man did that which was right in his own eyes". The next book, Samuel, tells of vicious local wars; on some occasions the Ark of the Covenant was used as a source of superhuman power in these struggles, and Samuel also tried to get Divine support by urging the people to accept God's authority[6] "If you do return to the Lord with all your hearts, then put away strange gods ... and prepare your hearts unto the Lord, and serve him only, he will deliver you out of the hand of the Philistines". Eventually Samuel made his own sons "judges over Israel" and they, clearly lacking his exceptional quality "turned aside after lucre, and took bribes and perverted judgement. Then all the elders of Israel ... said ... now make us a king to judge us like all the nations" (I Samuel, Chapter 8, vv3 - 5).

---

[4] Fisher, H.A.L. (1952) *A History of Europe From The Beginning of the 18th Century to 1957.* London: Eyre & Spottiswoode.

[5] Exodus Chapter 15, verse 18.

[6] Samuel Chapter 7, verse 3.

Samuel was not pleased with this request. Eventually however, he found in Saul a person who was not only "goodly" but also exceptionally tall, and anointed him with oil. He told Saul he would meet other prophets and "the Spirit of the Lord will come upon thee ... for God is with thee" (Chapter 10, vv 6-7). We now have several strands of authority in play. God is the ultimate power and King, his plans are detected and made known through Samuel, the prophet; there are the priests (of whom not much is said in this book) and there is the secular king, Saul. We may be tempted initially to think of the king as the one who makes rules and applies them; but it is soon made clear where the ultimate power lies. In Chapter 15 of his first book Samuel, who is the channel of God's plans into the community, tells the king to go to war. Saul does so and wins, but does not fully accomplish the command to annihilate the opponent. Disobedience to the ultimate King, God, is a fundamental crime (earning the 'red card' in modern footballing practice) and Samuel delivers the verdict (Chapter 15, vv 22-23) "to obey is better than sacrifice ... for rebellion is as the sin of witchcraft ... and idolatry. Because thou has rejected the word of the Lord he hath also rejected thee from being king".

Soon after this, Samuel finds Jesse's youngest son David, of whom "the Lord said, Arise, anoint him: for this is he. Then Samuel took the horn of oil and anointed him ... and the Spirit of the Lord came upon David from that day forward. ... but the Spirit of the Lord departed from Saul, and an evil spirit from the Lord troubled him" (Chapter 16, vv 12 - 14). Unsurprisingly, Saul descended into depression and hatred of David. David had a long and eventful kingship within which several aspects are relevant for this study. An early "media related" event occurred when David "returned from the slaughter of the Philistines, and the women came out of all the cities of Israel, singing and dancing ... with tabrets, with joy, and with instruments of musick ... and (sang) 'Saul hath slain his thousands, and David his ten thousands' ... and Saul was very wroth" (and tried to kill him! - (Chapter 18, vv 6 - 8).

David himself was a poet and musician and almost certainly Israel's most distinguished king. His distinction is established not least in his legacy of Psalms, one of the most important features of which is the frequent emphasis that the real and ultimate King of Israel is God, beside whom David can be only an insignificant official. Here are some examples of David's humility (or of the humility ascribed at that time to David - if we have to accept the view of some scholars that many of the Psalms were written centuries after David):

Thou O Lord art a shield for me; my glory and the lifter up of my head ...
Have mercy upon me O Lord: for I am weak ...
Judge me, O Lord, according to my righteousness ...
The Lord is my Rock and my fortress, and my deliverer ...
The Heavens declare the glory of God ... the law of the Lord is perfect ...
Who is this King of glory? The Lord of hosts, He is the King of glory ...
Thou art my King, O God ...
God is the King of all the earth ...
Because of thy temple at Jerusalem shall kings bring presents unto thee ...
... let us bow down: let us kneel before the Lord our maker ...

Not unto us, O Lord ... but unto thy name give glory ...
The Lord is gracious, and full of compassion; slow to anger and of great mercy ...
Praise ye the Lord ... praise him with the timbrel and dance: praise him
with stringed instruments and organs. Praise him upon the loud cymbals:
... let everything that hath breath praise the Lord. Praise ye the Lord[7].

These verses show quite clearly that though David was a national king, he totally recognised that his power, such as it was, and his earthly fortunes were drawn from God as a supreme King. David was a master of the message systems of his day; and through his psalms he has had an influence on western religion and liturgy across a distance of three thousand years. David's influence on Christendom and, to a lesser extent on Islam, and on the ways in which humankind seeks happiness within a superordinate order has been profound. In all societies humans try to live satisfying lives and perceive that this can best be done if there is an overarching, convincing moral order. Societies differ in whether they have top down views of whence this order emanates, or a bottom up idea in which the public generate their system of rule and appoint those who will apply it. The latter kind of society, which may be exemplified in the United States of North America, is not the direct focus of concern of this book[8].

King David's earthly monarchy was quite different from anything found in neighbouring countries of his time, or in their successors for a thousand years. The Pharaoh was considered divine. Nebuchadrezzar (II) and Belshazzar both met with trouble, the former for setting up idols he expected to be worshipped. In Daniel (Chapter 3 vv 1 - 26) it explains that Nebuchadrezzar "made an image of gold" and commanded "O people, nations and languages ... at the time ye hear the sound of the cornet, flute, harp, sackbut, psaltery, dulcimer and all kinds of musick ... fall down and worship the golden image". Resisting this order certain Jews who had been "set over the affairs of the province of Babylonia ... (namely) Shadrach, Meshach and Abed-nego" refused to adore the idol and were punished by being thrown into a "burning fiery furnace ... seven times more than it was wont to be heated". Nevertheless, they came forth uninjured. The monarch seems to have been one of the few to have been influenced by the Jewish example as he is quoted by Mackenzie as having composed a prayer similar in sentiment to some of David's psalms[9].

---

[7] These lines are, respectively, from psalms: 3v3; 6v2; 7v8; 18v2; 19vv1, 7; 24v10; 44v4; 47v7; 68v29; 95v6; 145v1; 150vv 4-6.

[8] It could be argued that in the US which has "In God We Trust" written on its banknotes, God is recognised as the ultimate single authority, and is in that sense a Monarch. It is difficult, however, to find any texts that use the term monarchy in describing the US and (nearly?) all Americans are ruffled if one suggests that their polity is a monarchy with God as Monarch.

[9] Donald A Mackenzie. *Myths of Babylonia and Assyria.* London: Gresham Publishing N.D. On p. 479 we read:

O eternal prince! Lord of all being!
As for the king whom thou lovest and whose name thou has proclaimed
As was pleasing to thee, do thou lead aright his life, guide him in a straight path
I am the prince, obedient to thee, the creature of thy hand;
Thou has created me, and with dominion over all people Thou has entrusted me.

Belshazzar did not show a similar open mindedness to this more parsimonious model of kingship. The prophet Daniel reports, (Chapter 5 vv 23-31) that because "thou knewest all this; but hast lifted up thyself against the Lord of heaven ... and thou has praised the gods of silver ... which see not, nor hear, nor know: and the God in whose hand thy breath is, and whose are all thy ways, hast thou not glorified ... in that night was Belshazzar the king of the Chaldeans slain. And Darius the Median took the kingdom ...". Not long after, Alexander of Macedon made a long detour on his march upon Persia, going down to Egypt to the oasis of Siwa where there was an oracle, to hear from it that he was himself of godly origin. It is likely that the oracle was aware of his military power and knew what Alexander wanted to hear, so was willing to oblige with a suitable message. After Alexander's death and the division of his empire Antiochus Epiphanes, his inheritor in Syria antagonised the Maccabees and most of the population of Israel by setting up a statue of himself in Jerusalem requiring it to be worshipped as an idol. Augustus Caesar did the same thing in Rome. The ancient Middle East is replete with examples of monarchs who put themselves across as divine; Mackenzie[10] notes that "the Assyrian king was regarded as an incarnation of his god, like the Egyptian Pharaoh" (p. 352) and continues "no images were made of him, but his symbols were carried aloft, as were the symbols of Indian gods ... in the *Mahabharata* epic".

Many European monarchies in recent centuries have reflected some of the pagan models in which the king has tried to convince his subjects that he has (quasi) divine status; Fisher (op. cit., p. 697) points out that even until the 19th century in Russia "The Tzar was the elect of God"; but there is also at work in Europe the Israelite monotheistic heritage in which the king acknowledges God as Monarch. This perforce removes the "-archy" from the role of the human king, whose status becomes ambiguous. On the one hand many or most of the subjects consider the king as effectively the source of top-down authority; on the other hand there is also a spiritual authority present, manifest before the Christian era in the roles of priesthood and prophets, and during it in the form of bishops and saints, who do a great deal to point out that the king is NOT the ultimate fount of authority, which is to be found above him and which not infrequently faults his behavior and to whom he is held to account. In biblical times Moses was punished (by not being allowed to enter the promised land) because he disobeyed God (by striking a water bearing rock). Saul was also punished for disobedience (by not having his descendants inherit his crown). David was punished for the sin of taking Bathsheba and sending her husband to the front to be killed. In modern times Charles I of England and Scotland was executed for various reasons including that he tended to think of his authority as divine, and Louis XVI of France was also executed amongst other things for a similar presumption.

According to thy grace, O Lord, which thou dost bestow on all people
Cause me to love thy supreme dominion, and create in my heart the worship of thy godhead
And grant whatever is pleasing to thee, because thou hast fashioned my life.

[10] *Myths of Babylonia and Assyria*. London: Gresham Publishing N.D.

MESSAGE SYSTEMS IN AND UNDER
ANCIENT MIDDLE EASTERN MONARCHIES

This brief sketch of the predicament of Kings (and Queens) in Europe and its heritage illustrates, in modern jargon, that such monarchs "have a PR problem". They tend to need, and sometimes to want to show glittering glory; if they do establish this they can extract tax revenue and build monuments to themselves (which they are sometimes tempted to turn into idols). On the one hand the cost of these monuments antagonises their own people; on the other hand, if skilfully handled, the monuments dazzle the populace whose loyalties can be deployed in armies which consolidate the regime and even protect ordinary people, (from the possible ravages of alien monarchies) which the public welcome provided the tax burdens are not too high. Many monuments of ancient times are nothing other than what would now be called "media" symbols. They are examples of messages under the control of the monarchs, a form of top-down "communication" (or what I have elsewhere labelled admunication).

The most spectacular of these ancient symbols demonstrating the power of monarchs are the Egyptian pyramids. Debate still thrives as to the complete functions of pyramids which may be giant graves, astronomical devices, or something else; but they must have evoked tremendous pride amongst their constructors even if these died in their thousands in slave labour, and also admiration for the kings who commissioned or who were buried in them. Undoubtedly the pyramids "told" the Egyptian people, and foreigners, that Pharaohs were powerful, even of divine connections. In the other middle eastern nexus of power, between the rivers Tigris and Euphrates there were also huge and impressive structures, the most lastingly famous of which was probably the Hanging Gardens of Babylon, erected by Nebuchadnezzar II. Mackenzie informs us (op. cit., p. 220) that the gardens "occupied a square which was more than a quarter of a mile in circumference. Great stone terraces, resting on arches, rose up like a giant stairway to a height of about three hundred and fifty feet ... on each terrace ... fruit trees were grown amidst ... luxuriant foliage ... Water ... was raised from the river by a mechanical contrivance to a great cistern situated on the highest terrace". This tremendous edifice no doubt cost a huge amount in human labor (including Judaeans: Nebuchadrezzar carried off "all the princes, and all the mighty men of valour, even ten thousand captives, and all the craftsmen and smiths"[11]) but equally did much to express the glory of the monarch whose enterprise this represented.

When Rome became paramount generals assumed supreme power and in some cases posed as (demi)gods. Many had coins struck bearing their portraits. Each coin is a message, or a "medium" by which a message is passed to the user that the ruler portrayed is a person from whom value emanates. If pyramids are "media" carrying messages some of which are extremely painful, coins are much less emotionally two-sided. As well as coins, successful Roman rulers constructed important symbolic buildings, including

---

[11] 2 Kings, xxiv, 8-15.

arches[12] and obelisks. These were largely theatrical statements; so an obelisk may have been a giant stone needle marvellously transported to Rome from a distant conquered state, while an arch carried surfaces upon which reliefs or sculptures showed stories of victories and conquered distant rulers and peoples. Arches also rubbed in the message of the local ruler's power when a procession could be held in which the said distant rulers and people, now captives, could be dragged through the building which now stood majestically above them, as they went to a colisseum where they were used as expendable entertainment for a bloodthirsty audience.

An interesting example of aggrandisement was reported in the *Times* (6 November 1998, p. 16) and concerns the emperor Nero who had an underground palace called the Domus Aurea (golden house) built beneath Trajan's Baths near the Colosseum and said to cover an area 25 times the size of that substantial building. Nero's palace contained an octagonal room covered by a dome; either the stage floor of the room, or the dome revolved like a giant carousel, propelled by hydraulic machinery; in any case Nero took the stage, viewed by audiences seated in side chambers (and was showered from above with rose petals dropped through holes in the roof, by slaves) and sang and recited his own compositions, all glorifying his own reign. The example illustrates that excessive indulgence in "media" opportunities could detract from other activities more essential to the prosperity of a regime, as Nero's rule did not last long.

THE MONARCHIES OF CHINA AND JAPAN, AND IN BALI

Over two thousand years ago any regime, whether a monarchy or something else faced tremendous problems of communication in trying to hold a large country together, let alone an empire. The nervous system of a nation consisted of messages sent (at their fastest) by relays of horse riders; though there were roads such as the King's Highway running north from Egypt to Syria, and the much longer Silk Road connecting ancient Persian systems with the far East, it would still take a long time for the centre to know what was going on everywhere else, and also to reach out and relate with a distant province, whether to levy and collect a tax, recruit soldiers, quell disturbance, parade glory, or whatever. The internal telecoms situation was crude and clumsy. The Roman empire had to put great energy into maintaining cohesion, and presently broke into two components, East and West. The Chinese empire faced the same problems.

In 211 BC a king Shih-huang-ti achieved effective control over most of the current land mass of China and proclaimed himself its first Emperor. His dynasty, called Chin or Ts'in has the same name as the country, and succeeded the Chou dynasty presiding over a feudal society. Shih-huang-ti saw the history of China as beginning with himself and issued a decree commanding that all existing literature be burned, except medical and agricultural books and those dealing with divination. Those disobeying this order were put to death. Nevertheless, some people surreptitiously preserved earlier classics which

---

[12] The Arch of Titus in Rome is possibly the most explicit and splendid example of these.

remain available to scholars. The Chin dynasty may have failed in its project of a totally fresh start to history - in itself an interesting case of lack of full control over the message systems of the day; but amongst other tremendous memorials it had built the Great Wall, which had several functions. One was to turn the hostilities of Mongols and others westwards, eventually having considerable impact on Western Asia and Europe. A second function was to foster greater internal cohesion, which would have been the condition necessary for the initial decree to have succeeded. A third outcome is something we now have to imply, or to allow contemporary texts to confirm, that the wall was seen as a great symbolic work in itself, a testament to the glory of its builders - who must have included the monarchs who presided over the project but including the engineers and labourers. The achievement of a massive edifice, with conspicuous military and social functions must have led people to think of the monarch as marvellous.

Chinese culture contained three main doctrines, teachings or systems we may liken to religions. Taoism, influenced by Lao Tze (who was born around 600 BC) overlapped with Confucianism (Confucius was born about 50 years after Lao Tze) and Buddhism. A statue of Lao Tze was taken into the palace of the Chin Emperor, with pomp and ceremony in the second century BC. A myth held that Lao Tze had assimilated with Shang Ti the Supreme and Divine Emperor in heaven; the term Shang Ti included the spirits of dead Emperors of China and was worshipped in temples and domestic shrines. Shang Ti thus, in some respects, was the divine father of the living monarch, not unlike the models in ancient Egypt and Babylon. We should therefore think of the temples and domestic shrines as counterparts to todays mass message systems since they carried the beliefs about the nature of rule in the world into the hearts and minds of the common populace.

China had another five major dynasties before arriving at the last one, the Manchu, which finally ran out of steam at the start of the 19th century. In 1860 Lord Elgin commanded that 200 pagodas in the then Peking be burned down, in retaliation for a hostile gesture the Chinese had made to British forces, a calamity that caused much distress at the time, and which is one of the injuries still in the minds of Chinese when contemplating their dignity and relations with the British. The episode is a kind of negative counterpart of the meanings symbolised by the building of great temples or palaces. Modern societies can demolish large office and apartment blocks found to be dysfunctional or which stand in the way of yet larger edifices, but the loss of these has nothing like the symbolic strength of meaning attached to the building of palaces and temples, and in an opposite way to their destruction.

In both China and Japan large "goddess portals" or "gateways" - not connected to walls or ushering roadways into desired locations were built. Some scholars[13] have held that these gates symbolised the 'gate of birth' and also of death, these transitions being supremely fascinating to and problematic for all of humanity. A "Mother Of All Things" was evidently discussed by Lao Tze and likened to water in its life giving essence. Some

---

[13] The material in this section is taken from D.A.Mackenzie (N.D.) *Myths of China and Japan.* London: Gresham Publishing.

goddess portals may thus stand in the water. One such gateway, at Miyajima, is considered to be one of the three most beautiful scenes of Japan.

The old Japanese 'religion' Shinto was and is a system of ceremonies and laws on which the whole social structure rested. Shinto dealt with the food supply, child-getting, preservation of health and protections against natural calamities and disasters. At the top of the system was (and still is, though some public repudiations have been made of his traditional 'divinity') the Mikado, called the Heavenly Grandchild, his heir being the "august child of the sun" and his residence the "august house of the sun". After the Mikado had ascended the throne an important food offering ceremony was performed, in which he received "auspicious" grain from the Gods of Heaven and therewith nourished the people. One of the sons of an early Mikado Kei-ko (died AD 130) was called Yamato-Take and is a famous legendary hero of Japan. He had martial and romantic adventures and challenges; a specially potent sword is part of the tale in which he dies eventually after being soaked in a rain sent by a goddess whom he had assailed when she was incarnated as a boar. The death is a kind of spiritual exhaustion and in some ways the whole story resembles that of Arthur, in England. The function of these stories is not just to tell of some element of truth they originally acquired, but to strike a chord in the minds of ordinary people, who yearn for benevolent authority, who have an aesthetic sense of appreciation of the beauty of nature and who feel awe at the mysteries of the human condition. Where a society has royal figures such as Yamato-Take or Arthur as central to its heroic and romantic myths, it is likely that the monarchic model is strengthened.

After World War II - whose ending with two atomic bombs had to achieve the recognition by the Mikado that his nation and society should accept defeat - the Mikado was decreed, on American insistence, not to be of divine origin. However, he continues to be a very venerated and important mouthpiece for expressing fundamental national thoughts and emotions and is still the titular head of the Shinto religion. Thus when the Mikado visited Britain a great deal of press attention in Britain and in Japan paid attention to what he would say along the lines of a humble apology, hoped for by some in Britain, for war crimes committed on British prisoners. The form of words expressing regret - but not apology - published in the most widely sold tabloid newspaper, *The Sun* was closely noted and debated; and this contrasts with the Mikado's full apology to the Korean people (in September 1998) for Japanese war crimes against Korean civilians - particularly women forced into prostitution. The Japanese will make what they will of the Korean feeling that even this apology was not enough. For our purposes here, it is an example of a society which is a monarchy, in which it is not the monarch who controls a vital decree disseminated by the most modern mass message systems of the day, but where the elected authority determines what is said. There is an element therefore of the Japanese system having evolved from a fully divine-monarch model to being more like a symbolic (secular) figurehead symbol such as is found in modern Europe; however, the fact that these decrees could not be effectively delivered (as far as the Japanese were concerned, not the British or the Koreans) by the Prime Minister, but had to be uttered by the Mikado suggests that perceptions of his status have not fully left behind a recognition of its more-than-secular nature.

A particularly interesting Asian monarchy, in the perspective of message system studies was that which no longer exists, in Bali. An island off the much larger and Muslim one of Java, Bali has a Hindu culture and at the end of the nineteenth century had a Hindu-style monarchy. An account of this institution has been reconstructed by the American anthropologist Clifford Geertz[14]. Geertz tried to explain what will be difficult for western readers to work themselves into understanding. He wrote (p. 13): "the expressive nature of the Balinese state was ... pointed not towards tyranny ... not even very methodically toward government ... but rather toward spectacle ... toward the public dramatisation of the ruling obsessions of Balinese culture: social inequality and status pride. ... Court ceremonialism was the driving force of court politics; and mass ritual was not a device to shore up the state, but rather the state ... was a device for the enactment of mass ritual. Power served pomp, not pomp power". Geertz used a term the "doctrine of the exemplary center" to describe a theory that the court-and-capital was "a ... microcosm of the supernatural order - an image of ... the universe on a smaller scale. The ritual life of the court ... is reflective of ... 'the timeless Indian world of the gods'".

Geertz provided a vivid report from a contemporary eyewitness of a funeral ceremony or a Rajah (king) in 1847, in which three of his concubines were sacrificed in the joint (and giant) funeral pyre. There were evidently over 40,000 spectators who experienced the proceedings as a carnival. All this appears to mean that in Bali the wider population was not seen as a target which a separate organism called the monarchy had to control, or persuade or reach with messages which would portray the monarchy in favourable terms. On the contrary, in this system the public were part and parcel of the same world of which the monarchy was in itself a particular and refined version. The more splendidly the monarchy played its part in being this 'icon' or representation of the view of how the world is, the better. In Geertz's words (p. 102) "the state cult was not a cult of the state. It was an argument, made over and over again in the insistent vocabulary of ritual, that ... hierarchy is the governing principle of the universe and that the arrangements of human life are but approximations ... to those of the divine".

Again, (p. 103) "the Balinese ... cast their most comprehensive ideas of the way things ultimately are ... into immediately apprehended sensual symbols ... carvings, flowers, dances, melodies, gestures, chants, ornaments, temples, postures and masks - rather than into a(n) ... ordered set of explicit beliefs ... the message here is ... deeply sunk in the medium". So all the art forms he mentions (and probably others), in which all the people partook, expressed - not just their vision - but also their feeling, their 'hearing' and all the other sense-modal apprehensions of the world in which they lived; and the monarchy and its embodiment in the court and its rituals was a splendid version of the universal experience. Monarchy did not *use* a medium - it *was* a (or the) medium.

---

[14] Geertz, C. (1986) *Negara. The Theatre State in Nineteenth Century Bali*. Princeton, N.J.: Princeton University Press.

MONARCHIES IN THE AMERICAS

Leaving aside for the moment the current monarchy in Canada and looking back historically, the two most prominent monarchies that have left a major imprint on their countries in America were those of the Aztecs in Mexico and the Incas in Peru. These lasted and indeed flourished until the sixteenth century, when the Spaniards brought them down. The stories of these two collapsed empires are well told in the Bernal Diaz Chronicles (first published in 1632 by a member of Cortes' military expedition) and in a major history by the American Prescott, compiled in 1843. Prescott's account has without doubt been amply expanded by subsequent scholarship but he does provide useful descriptions for our purposes here, and we can raise some questions about what he tells us, some of which may well have been filled in by later researchers[15].

Both these authors describe empires in which there was a "High God" and plenty of closer figures and substances (especially gold) imbued with divine power. The religions in both Aztec and Inca empires were heavily occupied with propitiating these intermediate divine powers; in both empires there were priestly castes and in both cases the monarch (referred to in each case by the same name as by which we know the people) played his part in supporting the system. Prescott relates (p. 748) that "when an Inca died or, to use his own language 'was called home to the mansions of his father, the Sun' ... the bowels were taken from the body and deposited in the temple ... plate and jewels was buried with them, and a number of his attendants and favorite concubines, amounting sometimes, it is said, to a thousand, were immolated on his tomb ... the body of the deceased Inca was skilfully embalmed (at) the great Temple of the Sun at Cuzco. There the Peruvian sovereign ... might behold the effigies of his royal ancestors, ranged in opposite files - the men on the right, and their queens on the left ... on certain festivals, the revered bodies of the sovereigns were brought out with great ceremony into the public square of the capital ... and 'such a display ... was there in the great square of Cuzco ... of gold and silver plate and jewels, as no other city in the world ever witnessed'".

The polygamous Inca sovereigns produced many 'royal' descendants who formed a class of the nobility who served as civil and military leaders. "The laws were few and exceedingly severe ... the laws emanated from the sovereign, and that sovereign held a divine commission ..." (p. 759). The central administration was very well informed, kept a register of all births and deaths throughout the country and regular ecological and economic surveys were made. Prescott explains that the Incas were constantly at war with neighbouring tribes. Their internal communications policy was successful in strengthening internal cohesion, which helped in winning most of the external conflicts. Internally, a major media measure was to insist on a common language. If there was a rebellious province, a substantial part of its population was moved to another part of the

---

[15] Diaz, B. (1956) *The True Story of the Conquest of Mexico*. Edited and Translated by A.Idell. New York: Doubleday and Prescott, W.H. (ND) *History of the Conquest of Mexico And History of the Conquest of Peru*. New York: Random House.

empire whence a similar number was returned to the first part. Great roads served as communication arteries ... along these routes were posts at which "*chasquis* or runners were stationed to carry forward the despatches of government ... the chasquis were dressed in a peculiar livery ... and selected for their speed and fidelity ... messages were carried ... at the rate of a hundred and fifty miles a day ... by these wise contrivances ... the most distant parts of the long-extended empire of Peru were brought into intimate relations with each other. ... so admirable was the machinery contrived by the American despots for maintaining tranquillity ... it may remind us of the similar institutions of ancient Rome when ... she was mistress of half the world" (pp. 766-7).

In both empires there were splendid temples and much golden ornament and these edifices served the religion but are not described by the invading Spaniards in terms by which we could think of them as being there simply to aggrandise the monarch. Thus although there were pyramids in Aztec Mexico (called 'cues' by Diaz) they were not tombs each for a given King; the same apparently was true in Inca Peru. In both cases the monarch was greatly respected by the nobles, the priesthood and the society but that respect was connected with their hereditary status and leadership. It was signified in both cases by splendid costume and in Peru, by the equivalent of Roman-style triumphal parades, "progresses" (as in Renaissance Europe), arches and by a role in presiding over - or at least witnessing from their positions of leadership - human sacrifice. By Diaz' account and also in Prescott's, the sacrificing was much more common and brutal among the Aztecs, and involved cannibalism there. In southern Mexico ancient Maya kings were said to have used eclipses to reinforce their authority by staging acts of communion with their gods; they drew sacrificial blood from their own genitals and from their queens' tongues with cactus thorns. The loss of blood is said to have induced visions in which divine messages that confirmed the monarchs' policies were received[16]. This is a rare example amongst world-wide cultures in which the monarch sets up a communication line with the divinity, with his or her own blood being the "medium" to generate messages which are then relayed, presumably by more orthodox means of public speech and via officials to the population at large.

The Inca and Aztec empires were brought down by extremely resolute though tiny Spanish armies, in campaigns in which division preceded collapse. Prescott explains that the penultimate Inca had - foolishly - divided his inheritance into two, with the result that the ensuing quarrel between the two was used by the Spaniards to their advantage. It so happens that the fall of the Inca Atahuallpa was precipitated by an incident involving a media artifact - a book, either a breviary or a Bible. This had been commended to the Inca by a Dominican, but Atahuallpa threw it down. For this insult to the vessel of the Christian doctrine the Spaniards (helped by their possession of firearms) attacked and captured Atahuallpa and after a trial, put him to death. Prescott observed "the Inca of Peru was its sovereign in a peculiar sense ... his authority reached to ... the thoughts of the individual ... He was not merely the head of the state, but the point to which all its institutions converged ... the keystone of the political fabric, which must fall to pieces of its own weight when that was withdrawn ... Gold and silver acquired an importance in the eyes of the Peruvian, when he saw the importance attached to them by his conquerors" (p. 982). In Mexico, the Spaniards had allied themselves with the enemies of the Aztecs and thus gained sufficient leverage with which to destroy the latter's empire.

The statecraft of the two empires differed considerably, but in both instances we see examples of societies where the monarchy had indeed command of its internal means and contents of communications; however, they had no idea what may have ensued when foreign powers developed different perceptions and attitudes towards their cultures, than they had of themselves. In particular, the practices of human sacrifices and cannibalism fitted in with the Christian motive to evangelise and thus to civilise in a Christian mould. Christian powers thus felt justified in demolishing such states as those of the Inca and Aztecs, if they could. Since they had guns and other cultures mostly did not, the evangelistic impulse successfully worked along with plain greed for gold. In today's societies we can see that the problem for the Aztec, Incas or other such societies when confronted by militarily superior and evangelistic invaders was first to get hold of guns; and with that, to get the invaders to perceive the monarchy and its culture as acceptable - a challenge for what we now call "public relations" practice which requires a command of the ways in which knowledge disperses into a hostile culture. No such command was held by the American monarchs, nor even an inkling that this is what would have helped them. The contrast between what happened to them, and an alternative which allowed a 'native' monarchy to survive mortal threats to its integrity, is found in a few instances in Africa, to which we now turn.

MONARCHIES IN AFRICA

A story of monarchy and gold provides a rare example in which outsiders' understanding of an indigenous culture allowed the two to co-exist, and comes from Ashanti in Ghana. It is said that early in the eighteenth century a magician named Anotchi announced that he was commissioned by the great god of the sky, to make Ashanti powerful. This he did by bringing down from heaven a gilded wooden stool, which he said contained the soul of the people, that with it was bound up their power, their honour, their welfare and that if ever it were captured or destroyed the nation would perish[17]. Ashanti did well in wars and rival kings were beaten, beheaded and their gold added to the stool, increasing its prestige. Presently, British forces tried to curtail Ashanti liberties and their capital Kumasi was occupied. The stool was carried off by its guardians, to be hidden in the forest.

---

[16] Fernandez-Armesto, F. (1999) *Truth: A History*. New York: Black Swan.
[17] Smith, E.H. (1927) *The Golden Stool. Some Asects of the Conflict of Cultures in Modern Africa*. London: Edinburgh House Press.

At the turn of the century the British tried to seize the stool, to deliver it to Queen Victoria and hopefully thus to demonstrate where the real power now lay. This provoked a war, which the British won; but the stool remained in hiding. Twenty years later a second attempt was made to obtain the stool, but the British this time forbore from extracting it by force. What had happened? An anthropologist, Captain Rattray had reported on the history and significance of the stool, which "holds the soul, not of any individual but of the nation ... the Government made it known that ... no attempt would be made in future to interfere ... (so) when the women of Ashanti wished to offer Princess Mary a wedding present their gift took the form of a Silver Stool ... their principal Queen Mother ... in her speech said: '... all we women of Ashanti thank the Governor exceedingly ... this stool ... does not contain our soul as our Golden Stool does, but it contains all the love of us Queen Mothers and of our women ...' (Smith, p. 14-15). In short, effective communication had taken place (Rattray could not have come to the understanding he achieved, had he not had frank and honest Ashanti informants).

At the other end of the continent a few years before the Ashanti war erupted British forces and missionaries approached the then Basutoland (modern Lesotho) part of which had been taken over by Boer migrants (Smith, p. 163). The Suto King Moshesh moved smartly to appeal to the British in the following terms:

"I will be under the Queen as her subject and my people will be her subjects but under me ... I wish to govern my own people by native law ... but if the Queen wish to introduce other laws ... I should wish such laws to be submitted to the Council of the Basuto ...".

In effect, this is what came about - and the British administered several African territories by such "Indirect Rule" conserving local institutions, including monarchies. The Basuto had a "Pitso, or National Assembly ... at this annual gathering all Basuto men enjoyed the rights of attendance and free utterance. The way in which not only the principal chiefs, but commoners expressed themselves was most impressive. Their eloquence, frankness and dignity would be creditable at Westminster ... No land troubles exist in Basutoland such as those which emerge elsewhere when Whites and Blacks come into contact" (pp. 164-5).

These two examples of well-managed information were not, however, the norm. European explorers including Bruce into Ethiopia, Baker, Burton, Cameron, Grant, Livingstone, Speke, Stanley, Thompson and others into Central Africa, and Barth, Clapperton, Lander and many others into West Africa all too often came back, if at all, with tales of considerable dangers. These were from the environment itself and added anxiety to those which arose from the reactions and the behavior of capricious monarchs - or chiefs of tribes or small nations - who sometimes helped the travellers, but on other occasions hindered them. Equally or more important were the tales of slavery - many of these explorers saw slave trains and knew that some had been obtained by war, but others by plain barter with their own overlords - and of wanton cruelty. At the first points of contact it may be supposed that the African kings had little idea of the societies from which the explorers came, and thus of their motives and intentions; but it did not take long before travels occurred in both directions.

An interesting example is given by the sister of one of the great missionaries, Mackay, of Uganda[18]. The Kabaka, or King whom most of the earlier explorers had known, Mutesa sent envoys to England, one of whom, Saabadu reported back in glowing terms of the powers and marvels he had seen. The latter included accounts of a British Royal palace, which precipitated a telling response from the Kabaka. Mackay tells it thus, quoting Saabadu (p. 209):

> "'The Queen's house is all made of looking glasses and gold and silver inside, and we sat on chairs made altogether of *ivory!*'. At this stage Mtesa said 'stop' and dismissed the court, telling Saabadu that he was to tell no one except himself what he had seen in England ... (then) Mtesa sent for his wives (their name is legion) and made Saabadu tell again in their presence all his marvellous story. All the women replied ... ('you have done well, sir; you have been victorious') ... this congratulations was to Mtesa, for having so successfully sent his men to such a great country. Mtesa then gave Saabadu (presents) ... and two women ... so that already he has returned, like the dog to his vomit, to the life of debauchery in which every big man lives here. this is, of course, part of Mtesa's acute policy, as much as saying to the man ...'you will enjoy yourself better here than in England'".

This anecdote raises several points. One is that an African king finds out about the powers that support explorers and missionaries, agents of change, who have come to his country, and can assess the extent to which he can afford to accept or reject what they are trying to do. A second is that such an African monarch had no control over the stories that spread in the powerful western country, about him, other than depended on his own behavior (and Mackay's attitudes toward wanton murder, which was common, polygamy and other crimes "too severe to mention") were clear enough to Mtesa. Thirdly, the African king tries to control the diffusion in his own society, of news about conditions of life elsewhere; but although Mackay('s wife) thought Mtesa was being clever in propitiating the envoy, he had surely made a mistake in spreading the news amongst his wives, who would likely leak the story. Public opinion in Buganda would thus move towards support for Mackay. Indeed, by his heroic efforts (he learned the language, Luganda, cut characters out of wood and printed translations of several books of the Bible) he eventually made many converts. This did not prevent Mtesa's successor Mwanga from spectacular relapses into cruelty, but such behavior created reputations both in Africa and in Europe that reinforced the eventual success of the missionaries; and with them came trade and the military and civil administrative power that established colonies and "protectorates".

Some African monarchs did try to influence the course of foreign imperial power, in a few cases by going themselves to Europe[19]. Parsons reports the trip of Khama, Sebele

---

[18] Mackay, J.W. (1890) *A.M. Mackay. Pioneer Missionary of the CMS to Uganda*. London: Hodder & Stoughton.

[19] Parsons, N. (1998) *King Khama, Emperor Joe and the Great White Queen*. Chicage: University

and Bathoen in 1895 and points out that the title king is merely how English represents a Setswana word which could also be translated great chief or paramount chief. The "three kings" - as the British press found it struck a romantic chord to term them - came to England with a London Missionary Society missionary with whom they shared the same puritan protestantism, spoke at many public meetings around the country and met the then colonial secretary ("Emperor" Joe Chamberlain). What was at issue was how to preserve autonomy by diplomatic means, to avoid a military confrontation (other groups had less successfully held off the intrusions of the expansionist Rhodes). Parsons demonstrates that these particular African rulers exercised leverage successfully, even pursuing their own expansionist agendas. The outcome of their efforts was that Bechuanaland became merely a Protectorate (today, Botswana) rather than being incorporated either into South Africa or Rhodesia.

It is sometimes argued that imperialist greed amongst European powers was the essence that motivated expansion into Africa (and the corresponding reduction of its monarchies). Alongside this it has already been pointed out that the missionary imperative to spread Christianity was an equal if not prior motive and with it, a desire to end slavery. Two strands of argument to support these other motives come from the cases of Ethiopia and of Muslim monarchies (stretching across Northern Africa). Ethiopia already had a marked Christian tradition and thus did not "need" evangelism; the slave trade was not that easily conducted from Ethiopia, if at all, in comparison with the rest of tropical Africa; so the Emperor of Ethiopia continued to rule (after clumsy fascist Italian efforts to grab his country - which the mass media of the decade in Europe, in the 1930s, did much to expose) until he was brought down by corruption, a massive famine (televised world-wide, to the monarchy's disgrace) and a Soviet-supported revolution in the 1970s. The Muslim monarchies were obviously not Christian, but their faith had prevailed through the Crusades and was perhaps a tougher nut to crack than was polytheism. There was nevertheless a variety of behind the throne military campaigns mounted by European powers, across northern Africa, designed to take control of each state with the Muslim monarchs (the Sultan of Morocco, Kings in Libya and Egypt, and lesser rulers as in the Southern Sahara) in vassal status.

Imperialist ambition, which we might call 'hypermonarchism' must not be denied, but the twin other motives of trade and evangelism must equally be recognised and the travellers tales whose effect was to shock European publics into support for intervention, played their part in intensifying these motives. Not only were those tales told during their time, but they rang down the following century in two mass-mediated forms. One of these was the mini-genre of Tarzan movies, in which a heroic white man outwits and brings under benevolent control various cruel enemies who were depicted as uncivilised cannibals. A less politically incorrect literary format was the documentary television series presenting the story of European exploration, often accompanied by well-illustrated coffee-table books. One such is the source of the following items:[20]

---

of Chicago Press.

[20] Anon.: (1973) *A History of Discovery and Exploration Africa and Asia: Mapping Two*

(following the campaigns of the warrior king Mzilikaze, when the Presbyterian missionary Campbell visited Botswana territory) "of Kaditshwene and the other large Hurutshe towns ... (which had hitherto been models of tranquility and order) ... nothing now remained but dilapidated walls ... and human skulls ... Mzilikaze turned out his regiments for a war dance ... 'They must conquer or die, and if one returns without his spear or shield, at the frown of his sovereign he is instantly dispatched". (p. 218).

(on Speke's visit to Kabaka Mutesa, when he had been mightily impressed by the 'gigantic grass huts') "'men, women, bulls, dogs and little pages ... everyone holding his skin-cloak tightly round him lest his naked legs by accident be shown'. Should such a breach of etiquette occur in Mutesa's presence, the offender was instantly executed ... Everyone grovelled face-downward in his presence and anyone who gave offence was dragged out and killed. Grant saw a man speared to death because he had spoken too loudly in Mutesa's presence ...". (pp. 254-255).

(when Speke went on, to the Kingdom of Bunyoro and found its King not too helpful) "Kamrasi was churlish, mean, suspicious and grasping. He told the travellers he had heard that white men drank rivers and ate mountains seasoned with the tender parts of human beings ... 'this horrid king' finally let them head down the Nile ... (p. 257); later, Samuel Baker visited Bunyoro where the "king insisted that Baker repair Speke's chronometer which had stopped when Kamrasi had prodded at its works to find the tick". (p. 263).

(in the upper Congo area), the naval Commander Verney Lovat Cameron "was camped at the village of a powerful despot named Kasongo (whose) retinue included men whose hands, lips, noses and ears had been cut off as a result of his bad temper. Despite this, the mutilated subjects followed him around like faithful dogs ... Cameron's ... rescuer was 'an old and ugly Negro' slave trader called Alvez ... on his way to Angola ... they moved off ... with 1, 500 yoked slaves". (p. 282).

(Further north, early in 1870 the German botanist Schweinfurth "set out for the dangerous but ivory-rich Niam-Niam cannibal country ... (under) the despotic King Manzu who ruled much in the style of Mutesa or Kamrasi. His village ... contained a hall 150 feet long and 50 feet wide. There King Manzu himself, attired in a black baboon headdress ... danced 'furiously' in a circle of 80 selected wives and massed ranks of armed warriors ... Manzu's tribe were cannibals. When Schweinfurth let it be known that he was looking for human skulls ... they poured in. Some were still warm from the cooking pot. But out of 200 skulls, only 40 were intact. The rest ... had been smashed to get at the brains ...". (pp. 298-299).

Such remarks made a great impact in Europe. They depicted (tropical) African monarchs as ill informed monsters of childlike intellect and emotions. Combined with the evidence of slavery these perceptions combined into a powerful case for intervention in the name of what are now labelled as human rights, at that time understood as accruing from an established Christian culture. It is very important to recognise that not all African monarchies could be described in these terms, nor were they. Credit was spoken for outstanding acts in support of human needs and rights, but these were perhaps more often recounted as coming from the ordinary people, sometimes liberated slaves,

Continents. London: Aldus and Jupiter Books.

rather than from the monarchs. Nevertheless, the combined impact of the feedback from Africa was to support intervention.

> When Stanley's expedition visited Buganda "the pleasing civility of Mutesa's well ordered kingdom rewarded them. ... 'either Mutesa is a very admirable man, or I am a very impressionable traveller, or Mutesa is so perfect in the art of duplicity ... that I became his dupe' ... for Stanley's benefit (Mutesa) laid on a naval review of 40 war canoes and about 1, 200 men commanded by an admiral in a crimson, gold-braided jacket. Impressed by the King's interest in Christianity, Stanley wrote ... to his newspapers appealing for missionaries .... within weeks (of receipt of the news, in Britain) £25,000 was subscribed for the dispatch of a mission to Buganda". (op. cit., p. 286).

> (another naval captain, George Lyon, travelling in Sahara territory) "joined a slave caravan to take them north ... Lyon was appalled by what he saw of the transsaharan slave trade and its brutalities ... many of the slaves believed they were being taken as cattle, to be slaughtered as meat for cannibals across the sea ... (a subsequent expedition led by Hugh Clapperton in 1822 went to Sokoto, the Fulani capital, whose ruler Mohammed Bello, was the most powerful man in the whole of the western Sudan ... received Clapperton kindly ... (and eventually) ... set him on the eastward road. He sent a letter to the British king ... expressing his willingness to cooperate in ending the slave trade ...". (p. 439).

In 1840 there was an anti-slavery convention, expressing and reinforcing the British Government's desire to suppress this practice. Combined with these motives were the adventurous ambitions to map the world and apply a benevolent scientifically ordered control upon it. So explorers such as Speke and Grant were greeted with triumph on their returns to England and their addresses to learned Royal societies produced a considerable impact. When the Scotsman David Livingstone came to Britain in 1856 the cities of London and Edinburgh conferred honours on him. Queen Victoria received him at court.

> "Most flattering of all, he was elected a Fellow of the Royal Geographical Society ... he wrote: 'I view the end of the geographical feat as the beginning of the missionary enterprise'; in an address at Cambridge University he concluded: 'I beg to direct your attention to Africa ... which is now open. Do not let it be shut again! I go back to Africa to try to make an open path for commerce and for Christianity". (p. 231).

MUSLIM MONARCHIES AND THEIR MESSAGE SYSTEMS

This massive topic would need more than a whole book to deal with it so here, the purpose is merely to open the door to some of the structures and issues which arise in their experience with the media for Muslim monarchies. Undoubtedly the first, and structural matter is that Islam focuses very clearly on a single high God Allah, who is the ultimate King. Under his shelter any earthly king is just that, in no way a demi-god or with any claim to divine authority. Islamic doctrine holds that all Muslims are equal brothers in their surrender - or submission - translators from the Arabic evidently run the risk of conveying the wrong impression - to a faith in the supremacy of Allah. This 'religious' brotherhood has obviously not stopped Muslim monarchs in many cases from being cruel despots, just as others were benevolent.

As in other societies, in Islam the issue of coins by a ruler indicated his royal authority. Inscribing the ruler's name on coins was a special privilege and sultans (in India) issued coins on their assumption of power, on victories and other occasions they deemed important. The first coins issued by Mahmud of Ghazni in 1007 AD featured the profession of Islamic faith in Arabic but by 1028 this was carried in Sanskrit translation, together with the monarch's name as *Nripati Mahamud* in Devnagari script on the obverse. One sultan in Bengal had a coin issued with the lengthy testimony *Al-Sultan al-fath al Kamaru wa Kamtah wa Jajnagar wa Urisa* (Sultan, conqueror over Kamaru, Kamta, Jajnagar and Orissa). The Mughal Emperor Akbar was one of several Muslim rulers who sought to communicate with their Hindu subjects through the coinage, in his case with coins carrying the figures of Ram and Sita with the words *Rama - Siya* in Nagari script; Akbar's son Jehangir issued coins bearing the sign of the zodiac of the month of issue, and his son Shah Jehan returned to the Islamic *Kalima* - profession of faith.[21]

Muslim monarchs have excelled in display. The famous Peacock Throne of Persia, the Harem of Istanbul, the Taj Mahal and numerous other dazzling buildings signified the aesthetic refinement of the rulers who paid for the creation of these edifices, and pointed to their wealth. The Taj Mahal expressed the sorrow of the Mogul Shah Jehan at the loss of his wife and did so at the cost of the hands of the artisans who decorated it, lest they work on any other similarly beautiful building. Notwithstanding the celestial palaces such as at Granada, built for royal comfort and to stand above the riches of others, and the names of sultans given to some of the finest mosques in Istanbul (Sultan Ahmet, Suleimaniye, and others) it is probably true that the greatest buildings of Islam are mosques, made to house worship of Allah and not principally to aggrandise their builders. Avoiding the danger of idolatry entailed in putting faces of rulers on coins, Turkish Sultans each had a *tugra* - which would now be called a logo - namely a calligraphed signature which appears on all manner of art work as well as on coins.

To make a start in the understanding of Muslim monarchies and how they interact with what we think of as separate institutions or mechanisms we call the media, one has to begin with the origins of Islam, and judge from their evolution whether a different way of thinking about media, or message systems is more apt for early Islamic societies. The question of the Khalifah (or successor) of Mohammad was (partially, and eventually schismatically) settled by recognition of Abu Bakr, Mohammad's father in law; after him the third caliph (as these successors are now referred to - in the following discussion[22] - was assassinated and replaced by Ali (Mohammad's son in law, and father of Hasan and Husayn). When Husayn was killed in AD 680, supporters of his line took to

---

[21] From an unsigned article in *Jetwings,* January 1999; the journal of Jet Airways, India.

[22] (1994) *New Encyclopaedia Britannia, 15th Edition.* Volume 22. Chicago: Encyclopaedia Britannica Incorporated.

demonstrations of emotional frenzy and self wounding, and the development of what the Encyclopaedia Britannica (p. 17) calls "passion plays ... 'taziyahs'. ... (in which) ... the figure of the political ruler (imam) was transformed into a metaphysical being, a manifestation of God; "this 'sectarian' concept recognising the role of imams developed in Afghanistan and India, and in Iran amongst the Shiahs, while the other main branch of Islam, the Sunnis (prominent in Arabia and in North African countries) put emphasis on the "ujma or consensus as the source of workable knowledge" (op. cit., p. 31).

The encyclopaedia tells us (p. 36) that "because Islam draws no distinction between the religious and the temporal spheres of life, the Muslim state is by definition religious". From this one might be tempted to see the caliph - successor of the Prophet Mohammad - as in some similar status to the Pope, but the encyclopaedia explicitly denies this simile - it suggests instead that the caliph be seen as a chief executive and though it does not make it explicit, evidently there was an assumption that the post was hereditary - unless derailed, as in western and other monarchies - by a coup. After some centuries we see the arrival of sultans (rulers) and "soon, the sultan was declared to be the 'shadow of God on earth'" (op. cit., p. 36). There seems to be a strong tendency therefore, for Muslim monarchs to claim or to be accorded at least part of their power or status because of a perceived connection with the Divine.

The encyclopaedia reports, however that "in literature, drama and pure fiction were not allowed - drama because it was a representational art and fiction because it was akin to lying ... story literature was tolerated" (p. 38); this led to a huge elaboration of poetry, hyperbole and metaphor. In the early centuries of Muslim monarchies therefore, anything we might term the media should be understood differently from the modern notion of a realm of discourse housed in a particular technical world - such as print and books, or pictures (and eventually, film and television). In the first place, the early Islamic media were part of a seamless institution of a religion-based society in which the monarch - or caliph was also a part; however, there was a vibrant folklore in which the stories and how they were told were neither generally scripted by or under control of the caliphate or sultanate. Nevertheless, the last of the "four righteous caliphs" (and the only dynasty to control the whole of the Islamic world) al Walid ibn Yazid, who died in Damascus in AD 744, was "famous not as a conqueror but as a poet who excelled in frivolous love verses and poetry in praise of wine ... His verses convey a sense of ease and gracious living" (op. cit., p. 50). This reveals a swift and major shift in cultural emphasis from the teetotal puritanism of the earliest followers emerging from the dryness of Arabia, to the more bibulous ease of prosperous city life. The next dynasty of caliphs, the Abbasids, were based in Baghdad and presided over a golden age of literature. "Grammarians ... standardised 'High Arabic' giving it an unchangeable structure once and for all ... the Kitab al-badi (Book of the Novel and Strange) by Ibn al-Mutazz (d. 908), caliph for one day, ... laid down rules for the use of metaphors, similes and verbal puns ..." (op. cit., p. 57).

Later than this the Turkish Sultan Selim I (otherwise known as "The Grim") composed quite elegant Persian ghazals ... and Babur (d. 1530 - the first Moghal entering India from Turkestan) wrote an autobiography, which was a comparatively rare form in Islam. In the time of the Ghaznavids - ruling in Afghanistan, the great poet Ferdowsi (d.1040) composed the Shah-nameh (Book of Kings) depicting the struggle between Iran and Turan (Central Asia). These tales about Persian Kings "contain between 35,000 and 60,000 verses in short rhyming couplets ... and the importance of the legitimate succession of kings, who are endowed with royal charisma, is reflected throughout the composition" (op. cit., p. 54). The encyclopaedia continues (op. cit., p. 57) "in the Iran of the Middle Ages ... not only professional poets but even the kings and princes contributed more or less successfully to the body of Persian poetry". This active part in shaping the discourse evidently touched not just upon its content but perhaps more importantly on its very structure and implements.

"Architecture is by far the most important expression of Islamic art, particularly the architecture of mosques ... the arabesque ... spiritually represents the infinite vastness of God ... (op. cit., p. 39). The encyclopaedia points to the Mausoleum of Timur at Samarkand (who, as part of a "language of cruelty" signified his power by having constructed towers made out of the heads of his victims), and to the great Masjed-e-Shah of Abbas I (the Great) at Isfahan, and says (op. cit., p. 94) that "architectural projects were well patronised by the Timurids as a means to commemorate their respective reigns ... Timurid princes also created mausoleums for themselves ...". Abbasid caliphs had developed the urban palace and the 'dar al-miarah' or centre of government, as at Samarra (now ruined). So Muslim monarchs worked through the ways of their religion to monumentalise their powers and their glory. This was not just mediated through architecture even though this was an important art, or medium by which impressions were conveyed; thus the Dome of the Rock (copied from the form of a Christian basilica in Mesopotamia) in Jerusalem was ordered by the early caliph Abd al-Malik to be built in "a major centre of non-Muslim population ... (he also) encouraged the use of Arabic as the language of government and had Islamised coins minted to replace the Byzantine and Sassanian-style coinage" (op. cit., p. 111).

This brief review of the roles of Muslim monarchs in interacting with what is said, performed or constructed, that reflects on and perhaps projects them may usefully bring in three further points, the first concerning carpets. In the Muslim world the carpet is more than just a comforting piece of furnishing; it is a pillow(case), a saddle or saddle-bag, but beyond this it is also a mat upon which the faithful person prays. The shape of an arch is seen in "prayer carpets" and is included as a decorative motif or icon in many reduced or incorporated versions in semi-abstract designs. Carpets made in city workshops, often of great size and equally of superb fineness, symbolise the leisure of gardens and some say the luxuries of paradise, and were and still are owned by rich and important people and the best, by monarchs.

Dilley[23] tells us that when Persia was invaded by Turkey its Sultan Suleyman the Magnificent (of whom the historian Stanley Lane Poole wrote 'the age which boasted of Charles V, the equal of Charlemagne in empire; of Francis I of France; of Henry VIII and Elizabeth; of Pope Leo X; of Vasilie Ivanovich, founder of the Russian power; of Sigismund of Poland; of Shah Ismail of Persia; and of the Mogul Emperor Akbar, could yet point to no greater sovereign ...') occupied the carpet-making centre of Tabriz and took away highly talented weavers (p. 153). Dilley reports again (p. 40) that the Persian Shah Tahmasp presented the Turkish Sultan Selim II on his accession to the throne with magnificent gifts amongst which "were silken carpets ... carried on forty four camels; among them twenty large silk carpets and numerous small ones, decorated with birds, beasts, flowers and embroidered with gold ..."; Tahmasp's grandson Shah Abbas was nevertheless again invaded by Turkey whose Sultan helped himself to a further substantial number of Tabrizian carpet weavers.

Nevertheless, Shah Abbas developed an artillery industry with the aid of a British envoy Sir Anthony Sherley and reasserted a Persian power and artistic renaissance. Sherley wrote that on one occasion he received "sixteen mules, each mule carrying four carpets ... four of silk and gold, six of clean silk ..." and on another occasion ... "eighteen Carpets curiously wrought with Golde" (Dilley, p. 43). Dilley continues that in 1599 "Shah Abbas, at the instigation of Sherley, sent the first mission of Persian ambassadors to the courts of Europe ... bearing important and now historic rugs as gifts ... (though) ... its thirty two heavy cases of presents were stolen in Archangel ... and later sold by English merchants in Muscovy" (p. 44). Again, (p. 46) "In the year 1607 the Persian embassy brought to the court of Phillip III of Spain two precious old carpets; the victories of Timurleng were represented on them". From such evidence it is plain that carpets were messages and carried messages from east to west; they were "media" - from the land of the Medes! These messages told of magnificence and power in the lands they came from; and in the west they were used to develop similar messages. European court painters continued an existing practice of showing royal or even just wealthy figures standing on magnificent oriental carpets, or seated at tables on which carpets were laid. Rich carpets from Muslim cultures were and still are used on the altar steps of great churches and cathedrals and featured in paintings of holy figures.

Lest it be thought that such silent symbols of prestige spoke in an orderly way of well ordered social institutions, we have occasionally been warned to beware of hyperbole, and that all was not always what it was made out to be. This is the second point one may bring out - it so happens, within this discussion of Muslim monarchies; but does it not also have to be remembered that the anecdote below is not only about their domains but is likely to be much more universal? A retired British diplomat invented a Persian character, Hajji Baba, whose adventures were intended to cast a wry perspective on Persian - and oriental society[24]. Hajji Baba relates that a (Persian Shah's) vizier (minister)

---

[23] Dilley, A.U. (1931) *Oriental Rugs And Carpets*. Philadelphia: Lippincott.

[24] Morier, J. (1925) *The Adventures of Hajji Baba of Ispahan*. London: Dulau.

"called to one of his mirzas or secretaries 'Here' said he, 'you must make out a fatteh nameh (a proclamation of victory), which must immediately be sent into the different provinces ... in order to overawe the rebel khans there: and let the account be suited to the dignity and character of our victorious monarch. We are in want of a victory just at present; but recollect, a good, substantial and bloody victory'. 'How many strong were the enemy?' inquired the mirza ... '*Bisyar, bisyar*, many, many' answered I ... 'Put down fifty thousand' said the vizier coolly. 'How many killed?' said the mirza ... 'write ten to fifteen thousand killed' answered the minister: 'remember these letters have to travel a great distance. It is beneath the dignity of the Shah to kill less than his thousands and tens of thousands. Would you have him less than Rustam ... No, our kings must be drinkers of blood, and slayers of men, to be held in estimation by their subjects, and surrounding nations. Well, have you written?' said the grand vizier'.
'Yes, ... I have written ... that the infidel dogs of Muscovites (whom may Allah in his mercy impale on stakes of living fires!) dared to appear in arms to the number of fifty thousand, flanked and supported by a hundred mouths spouting fire and brimstone; but that as soon as the all-victorious armies of the Shah appeared, ten to fifteen thousand of them gave up their souls; whilst prisoners poured in in such vast numbers, that the prices of slaves have diminished one hundred per cent ...'.
'*Barikullah*! Well done' said the grand vizier '... if the thing be not exactly so, yet by the good luck of the Shah, it will, and therefore it amounts to the same thing ...' and quoting a well-known passage in Saadi, 'Falsehood mixed with good intentions is preferable to truth tending to excite strife'. (Morier, p. 202-3).

A third and final - and probably unique - feature of Muslim monarchy is again recounted by Dilley (op. cit., p. 134) though it may not be intrinsically Muslim, rather than Indian. We hear through Dilley from a British envoy to the Moghal throne, Sir Thomas Roe that

"The first of September was the King's Birthday, and the solemnitie of his weighing, to which I went, carried me into a very large and beautiful Garden ... in the midst a Pinnacle, where was prepared the scales, being hung in large tressels, and a crosse beame plated with Gold thinne: the scales of massie Gold, the borders set with small stones, Rubies and Turkeys ... here attended the Nobilities, all sitting ... upon Carpets until the King came; who at last appeared clothed or rather loden with Diamonds, Rubies, Pearles, and other precious vanities ... his fingers every one, with at least two or three rings ... Suddenly he entered into the scales, sate like a woman on his legges and there was put in against him many bagges to fit his weight ... that I understood ... to be nine thousand rupiahs ...'.
later, when Shah Jehan was weighed 'bowls of costly gems were poured over him, and all these riches, to the value of a million and a half (pounds) were ordered to be distributed among the people'. He was the most popular of the great Moguls ...".

Lest we cast this anecdote into the realm of hyperbole under Morier's influence, it should be borne in mind that recent Aga Khans have followed the practice of being weighed against gold or silver and then distributing an equivalent amount of money to the needy. Strict economic accounting of these events has not been provided by our sources above, but it must be most likely that the (invisible) income to such potentates extracted from a more (or less) willing public must very far have exceeded what was so splendidly returned to them by such theatrical acts. The weighing must go down as an original media format or public relations initiative, found in the Muslim world but unfollowed (as yet - Presidents or Hollywood idols might wish to consider the option[25]) in the west, in which monarchs managed to aggrandise their reputations.

ANCIENT MONARCHIC MESSAGE SYSTEM
FORMATS TRANSPOSED INTO RECENT EUROPEAN TIMES

Roman triumphal processions were a model for major festivals mounted by Renaissance princes and monarchs throughout Europe, with a heyday of two centuries between 1450 and 1650. These festivals sometimes took the form of giant theatricals in a particular location, and other times as processions of entry into cities. Roy Strong[26] provides vivid descriptions and illustrations of these events; he focuses mostly on their structure and aesthetic content, but the accounts make it clear that the festivals were intended or in some cases may have served to unify diverse or divided dominions and to glorify rulers. Strong allows it to emerge that these enterprises did not always work - King Charles was executed shortly after the performance of a masque in which he had himself performed - Sir William Davenant's *Salmacida Spolia;* Strong tells us that Charles was aware of the gravity of the moment, and he played Philogenes, a king doomed to reign in adverse times. As Strong notes (p. 170) "his power is endurance and his chief virtue patience" though these merits were not called upon for long; so it must be said that the dramatic effort or "media format" was a failure.

Strong's book deserves considerable attention for our purpose. One element in his title namely "power" probably more usefully represents what I have referred to as Monarchy; and the other element "art" introduces the structure and content of the enterprises he describes, which seen from another angle are "media" through which meanings about rulers are, or are intended to be transmitted to the populace. Strong presents us with "three main types of festival form which the Renaissance era took over from the middle ages - the royal entry, the tournament and the indoor mascarade or entertainment" (p. 6) and starts with an account of the first form.

The royal entry "incorporated in one gigantic spectacle its judicial, economic, political, religious and aesthetic aspects in a format which reflected vividly not only the rise to prominence of the urban classes but also the increasing power of the prince" (p. 7). The ruler would arrive at a city gate where the leader of the citizens (those who live in a city) would hand over keys; in return the prince guaranteed the rights and privileges of the citizens. Note: Strong says citizens; but it could be argued or at least asked whether, by enacting such ceremonies of legitimacy the citizens transformed themselves into subjects. Strong underlines that these events included ingredients such as "biblical

---

[25] Prince Charles might consider having himself weighed against organic carrots, each one then to be auctioned and the proceeds given to charity; US Presidents could modify the procedure as and how their publicity managers suggest.

[26] *Art And Power*. Woodbridge: The Boydell Press, 1973.

and historical *exempla*" which "emphasised the legitimacy of the monarch, ... in terms of his own sanctity, due to the act of coronation and anointing with sacred oil"; as for underlying or implied meanings Strong says "the key reference becomes the king as Christ entering the new Jerusalem" (p. 8).

This interpretation could well be supported by reference to associated paintings and role players; for example, Strong tells us that Henry VI of England entered London (aged 15) after his coronation in Paris at an occasion when a pageant included a king, a fountain running wine, a genealogical tree including St Louis and Edward the Confessor as precursors, a depiction of the biblical Tree of Jesse and a "reminder of the divine nature of monarchy, set apart by anointing with holy oil and the ritual of crowning, in the form of a stupendous paradise in which the throne was surrounded by a heaven complete with hierarchies of angels and from which God the Father spoke to the king" (p. 9). Strong affirms that over half a century later the themes connected with Charles VIII's entry to Rouen were basically identical.

It emerges that there were two models of monarchy dramatised in these post-mediaeval festivals. One model can be considered that which Strong calls one of "empire" in which (mostly Catholic) monarchs saw themselves as quite closely connected with divine authority. This is more like the pagan models in antiquity in which Pharaohs and Caesars set themselves up as gods, requiring worship. The European houses of Habsburg, Medici, Valois and Stuart, all Catholics, were often projected in public pageants as versions of the Holy family. In contrast, emerging Protestant monarchs, such as Elizabeth of England connected with a different model. Elizabeth I's entry to London in 1559 included tableaux depicting her as Deborah, the 'judge and restorer of the house of Israel'; in Strong's words (p. 11) "Catholic cosmic apocalyptic visions gave way to monarchy cast as Old Testament kingship revived". It falls just outside the period described in his book but it is clear that the Hanoverian kings signalled a return to this Davidic modesty when Handel's Messiah set the lines from Psalm 24 (see above: "Who is the King of Glory - the Lord of Hosts ...") with such power that eventually, for a later chorus (Hallelujah) the then King George rose in respect to his feet.

Strong suggests that it is no coincidence that it was when new rulers of hitherto republican city states in Italy sought to establish their absolutist rule, that the pageants were developed "as expressions of a political reality that recognised monarchs and princes as a semi-divine race ... the fete enabled the ruler and his court to assimilate themselves momentarily to their heroic exemplars..."(p. 40). A splendid example of the phenomenon was Henri II's entry into Rouen in 1550, shortly after the surrender of Boulogne by the English. The processions started with a chariot with the figure of Death chained at the feet of Fame, followed by fifty seven of the king's ancestors in splendid robes followed by another chariot drawn by unicorns carrying Vesta, the goddess of religion. Models of forts captured by the king, and banners depicting Scottish lowland landscapes won from the English, elephants, captives in chains and finally a chariot with a representation of the King himself being offered an imperial diadem by a figure of Fortune, all filled out the pageant.

For our purpose, it is important to note that this street theatre must have been seen by a large number of people, not only townsfolk but also others who will have come in from the surrounding countryside to see the fun. More than that, woodcut prints of pictures of these events achieved a wider audience for them; this wider audience served the monarchy's purpose not only in supporting the ideas they depicted, but also in providing models for other monarchs and ceremonials to emulate and elaborate. A question Strong does not generally pose is whether, in possible over-elaboration some of the events may have been dysfunctional, going beyond what the populace could accept both in terms of cost and in plausibility. Nowadays we have audience research to give some bearings on whether a (political) campaign has worked in the way intended; not infrequently, parties and candidates will then amend either what they say or how they say it. In Renaissance times however, not only were such techniques unavailable, they did not accord with the top down ideology in which truth and knowledge were imparted from above downwards, and it was superfluous to ask, let alone to find out or pay attention to the bottom up perceptions and feelings of the ordinary population.

One example however (p. 51) however relates to a tournament held in honour of Queen Elizabeth I. Mentioning that "these were spectacles to which the public were, for a small sum, admitted" he goes on to quote from a German visitor in 1584 that "many thousands of spectators, men, women and girls, got places, not to speak of those who were within the barrier and paid nothing". Aside from assumptions one may make today, it is clear that such events reached a large public directly in the first place, before any secondary diffusion took place via hearsay and the sale of printed reports. Not infrequently, the monarch him or herself would be a principal actor in the proceedings, including tournaments, and Henri II of France was evidently killed at one of these.

One of the greatest Renaissance monarchs, the Emperor Charles V travelled widely and used festivals, pageants and entrances in themselves and supported by printed accounts extensively as "a central instrument of government" (Strong, p. 74). The most "significant" spectacle of the reign was Charles' coronation at Bologna in 1530, interesting in that it was his second such experience, having been crowned King of the Romans at Aix-en-Chapelle in 1520. Several thousand men in splendid armour provided the spectacle and then "imperial heralds casually tossed eight thousand ducats in gold and silver to the crowd" (p. 79). This is a reversal of what happens at most similar occasions nowadays, when it is the spectators who have to pay; it does resemble the Muslim idea of giving out wealth after a weighing. The pageantry involved symbols harking back to the glories of ancient Roman emperors and generals as well as to the contemporary church, whose support for the emperor was being dramatised. Involved in these events were not only historians, stage designers and playwrights but also musicians, architects, engineers to construct machinery by which clouds, floods and other natural phenomena were represented, scenery painters, woodcut makers and printers, a civilian army of media professionals of their day. It would be useful to know whether the monarchs involved in these occasions were usually their own impresarios or to what extent chief ministerial figures took the initiative. If the latter, the monarch could be thought of as somewhat less than as what they were portrayed as being, imbued with a divine authority.

Strong explains that from these performances in city and other open spaces stagings evolved that were to some extent closed; as the tournament and carnival died out the theatre was being born, in its early days including the form of the masque, whose rise and fall, Strong reports, was "exactly coincidental with the rise and fall of extreme claims to monarchical divinity" (p. 154). One who did not make such claims (for) herself was Elizabeth I whose "monarchy ... used alfresco shows ... to display the monarch to every rank in the kingdom ..."; in contrast under the Stuarts outdoor shows were phased out; the Order of Garter ceremonies were transferred to Windsor by Charles I while a Masquing Room was built in the Whitehall Banqueting House, in which court theatre developed. Strong does not underline the point but it is implied that in losing touch with the populace (even though they might not need always to be showered with cash) the monarch's theatrical enterprises were ineffective in their ultimate purpose of reinforcing recognition and loyalty throughout the society. Strong might also usefully have discussed the contrast with a practice in China where, when the emperor went to the Temple of Heaven once a year to pray for the granting of a good harvest for the year ahead, all doors and windows were closed so no-one should dare to peep at the Son of Heaven as he rode to his task. It seems likely that if and when a monarch communes with the divinity, his closeness to this power must be reinforced by separation from the common public; when a monarch communes with the public he might act the part of a demi-god but generally the contact with the public should be direct.

Strong's book impressively illustrates a substantial segment of our broader topic, of the ways in which monarchies have used the arts of communication. Several questions remain, however, about his material and one of these concerns the meanings which might underlie the ceremonial entrances which were so frequent. A Freudian interpretation for these could carry some force. In this, the city could be thought of as illustrating a female essence - nurturant, a haven or womb for its citizens, in mediaeval ages and for many years afterwards surrounded by walls in which there were only a few apertures, gates, guarded by force and open only to those whose entry was approved. When a monarch appeared, usually male, his figure set out to represent power and it was possible that he could simply force an entry; in that case the meaning of the event would be hostile like a rape and the citizens would be devastated, inclined to disloyalty and ready to give loyalty to another monarch who might be more considerate in his attentions. On the other hand, if the monarch promised to be benign the grandees of the city would "permit" entry, the whole contract - like a wedding - acted out in ceremonial form, and then not only could the monarch reign but the population would be more content to submit to or to accept the regime.

The metaphor of a wedding may not always be convincing (or at least in its possibility of carrying monogamous meaning) as we know that many monarchs made many ceremonial entries into many cities, and each would certainly know about the other ceremonial entries. Western kings were not supposed to be polygamous, so it would not suit their public relations if there were even a germ of an interpretation aroused that felt about the relationship as if it was unique. It would require a much more fine grained historical analysis than can be afforded here, to detect whether what may have been perceived as over-commitment may have stimulated cynical or disloyal attitudes. A different interpretation of the metaphor of civic entry is that it represented a sexual act. In that case the city would expect some metaphorical "offspring" and might even turn a blind eye to the relationships being cemented elsewhere. The offspring might take any one of several forms such as protection of trade, arts patronage or useful alliances.

A third aspect to the interpretation of meanings inherent in the act of ceremonial civic entry is to examine what it might mean where the monarch was a woman. Many of the examples concerned Elizabeth I, whose epithet the Virgin Queen appears to deny or at least postpone the potency of her personal sexuality[27]; although the underlying perceived or felt meaning of a ceremonial civic entry would not, in this case be considered corrupt, it would lack the same valency that would have occurred with a male monarch. Other Queens making entries in other continental cities will most likely have been perceived as proxies for their spouses. It might be held that all this is idle speculation, but it is certain that these events did occur, and it is widely agreed that they conveyed not only the superficial meanings entailed in amicable arrangements between civic dignitaries and monarchs but also a whole range of metaphorical and underlying meanings to which the accompanying theatricals, including historical and mythical referents were obviously intended as pointers. It is likely therefore that feelings beneath the surface may well have connected with patterns and structures based on experience of individual relationships, so ideas of this neo-Freudian kind may well be appropriate, especially where they point to possibilities of verification such as would be the outcome of studies of attitudes evoked by ceremonial entries with different socio-economic outcomes.

Roy Strong's book sweeps past Elizabethan times to end with the eruption of the Commonwealth in England. He develops an art historian's perspective rather than a literary or social anthropological one. The latter is the subject of a huge contribution by the recent Poet Laureate Ted Hughes[28] who deals not just with Shakespeare but with the underlying meanings grounded in ancient myth that the playwright has wrought into what are not, in Hughes' persuasive view 'just' a body of immortal plays but which functioned at a deeper level in helping England to deal with the cultural and constitutional changes of Elizabethan years.

---

[27] The term Virgin taken by the secular Queen was also important during an era when Roman Catholic allegiance, and its prominence for the Virgin Maary was being challenged in England; some may say that Elizabeth's decision to have her cousin (and potential successor) Mary executed may have had subconscious religious, as much as explicit political meaning.

[28] *Shakespeare and the Goddess of Complete Being.* New York:Farrar, Strauss, Giroux, 1992.

THE MONARCHY AS A "MEDIUM" - OF A NATION'S SENSIBILITY

Hughes' book is of interest not just in its content, but in itself as an unusual "media phenomenon" under the umbrella of the present monarchy. His position as Poet Laureate was under appointment to the monarch and recognised him as, or required him to be the most eminent poet of his day and also to write pieces at appropriate occasions in celebration of the monarchy or of its leading members. Many critics would agree about his eminence but few would know what to point to, let alone remember, of his poetic works that could be said to celebrate the monarchy. Unlike many other poets however, he has produced a work which is a composite of literary criticism and of social anthropological understanding of the circumstances of the times in which Shakespeare was at work. Hughes' thesis is important in what it says about the Elizabethan monarchy, and it also suggests a role for the monarch him or herself which dissolves the seeming separation inferred in the term "media and the monarchy". We will come to this new idea, presently.

Hughes said that Shakespeare built his plays upon the story-structures embodied in each of two ancient myths. One of these stories, elaborated in the early poem Venus and Adonis "operated as the 'myth' of Catholicism, while the myth behind Lucrece operated as that of Puritanism" (Hughes, p. 5). Catholicism was the religion of mainland European empire, associated with what the Stuarts in Britain called the Divine Right of Kings and underlining a notion of the monarch as connected with divine authority. What Hughes termed Puritanism is more generally the protestantism we have recognised above as having more Davidic roots in acknowledging that the monarch is human and him- or herself recognising the superior divine authority. Hughes believed (persuasively) that Shakespeare "creates dramas which, no matter how secular they seem ... embody and communicate a very particular 'mythic' dimension, which ... operates at mid-level in each work, as a controlling, patterned field of force, open internally to the 'divine', the 'demoniac', the 'supernatural' ... but externally to the profane, physical form ... ... the mythic ... appears in the finished work no more than the mathematics (without which it would have been unthinkable and impossible) appear in the nuclear reaction and flash of the bomb" (pp. 2, 3). As monarchs are very significant players in Shakespeare's scenarios, Hughes was telling us that the playwright was not only reflecting a revolutionary development of a new model of monarchy in Britain but to a considerable extent was also an architect of the ways in which a wide section of the population came to think and feel about what the monarchy should be, and eventually helped it to come about[29].

Hughes made it clear that though Shakespeare was not simply a spokesperson for the evolving monarchy he had to be careful not to offend its power; "if Shakespeare's manifest effort to record a few straightforward truths is to be taken seriously ... these

---

[29] Tony Blair's "New Labour" administration has said much about "modernising the monarchy" but in place of the engaged Shakespeare of old there are now "think tanks" paddling in the shallow waters of sociological detachment.

lines ... make a plain declaration of the burdensome subjective side of his life as a professional dramatic artist beleaguered by police-state censorship, by officious pedants ... and by a super-sophisticated elite" (pp. 460-461). "King Henry VIII's rejection of the Papal Authority was the act which begot (what Hughes called) the Tragic Equation[30] within the English psyche ... it seems understandable that ... Shakespeare should have a go at the historical event ... but even in 1611 (that is, even after Henry's daughter Elizabeth had died) it ran him headlong towards political quicksands, from which he deftly backed off ..." (p. 505). The playwright had long experience in articulating his material so as to keep alive, and in good business, as much earlier he had worked for "the powerful 3rd Earl of Southampton, Henry Wriothesley ... (whose guardian was) ... the great Lord Burghley, Queen Elizabeth's chief minister and the most powerful man in the land" (p. 51). These were times in which sufficiently careless or outrageous political dissidents could be put to death; Hughes pointed out that dissident (Roman) Catholics "including one of his own distant relatives were evidently ready to be half-hanged, castrated, disembowelled, quartered and to have their heads stuck on prominent spikes, all for taking this myth - of the sacrificed god and the Great Goddess - too seriously" (p. 56).

Shakespeare's early seminal work *Venus and Adonis* was written for Wriothesley and Hughes reported that it "struck a deep chord in Elizabethan readers. It was a best seller. It seems to have pleased and fascinated everybody. And it made Shakespeare famous in a way far beyond his reputation as a dramatist ... the theologian censor Whitgift must have read it, for ... it is clear that Shakespeare had not only appropriated this Catholic myth of the sacrificed God ... he had also updated it ... squarely centre stage, in the tragic theological conflict of the English Reformation" (pp. 55-56). Hughes explained that this long poem "seems to favour a Protestant (actually a Puritan) idealism. The new Christ, Adonis, seems to be rejecting the Catholic Church, personified in the poem by the Great Love Goddess as a whore ... (however) had Whitgift read it thirty years later, he might have thought again. In the context of the later tragedies ... Adonis's rejection of the Great Goddess of Divine Love turns out to be an error ... Eventually ... that brings down the kingdoms of both Heaven and Earth" (p. 57).

Hughes reminded his readers of the times during which Shakespeare was writing. "Between the Catholic regime (repressive terror, executions, martyrs) of Queen Mary, who died six years before Shakespeare was born, and the Puritan regime that executed Charles I thirty three years after Shakespeare died, England went through the final phase of its Reformation and was transformed ... events immediately preceding Mary's reign pushed her Catholic fanaticism to a ferocity beyond anything that England had ever suffered before, while the ... passions of the Civil War carried Cromwell's victorious

---

[30] Hughes' metaphor of an 'equation' drawn from algebra may be misleading. An equation in algebra usually means "this set of items *equals* this other set of items". Hughes appears to mean that "this set of components in a situation *leads to* that other configuration of items". The algebraic usage is static and can imply movement in either direction; Hughes' (mis)use of the term is clearly directional and implies that developments proceed in one direction only.

Puritans to a severity beyond what the country would ever tolerate again ... the decisive factor in England ... which perhaps more than any other determines the nature and evolution of Shakespeare's Tragic Equation - was that the process of religious change was arrested, or rather held in suspense by ... Elizabeth I. Those two savage competitors for the English soul ... the new Puritan spirit and the old Catholic spirit ... were deadlocked, ... by her deliberate policy ..." (p. 75).

Shakespeare wrote during the reigns of the Tudor Elizabeth and of her Stuart successor James I (of England) and VI (of Scotland). These monarchs either knew all about, or even attended Shakespeare's plays. Hughes suggested that the parade of future kings (in Macbeth) was watched by James who "found it a supportive salute to himself, in his role as a sacred king who might repair the terror of the Reformation nightmare" (p. 394). In greater detail (pp. 242-243), "Macbeth ... could well have been the first play after his acting company ... became the King's Men, and the senior members Grooms of the King's Chamber (they wore the King's livery). ... One motive for Shakespeare's choice of the theme of Macbeth, it has been supposed was to celebrate James's royal Scots ancestry ... and so salute the legitimacy of his claim to the English throne. But he seems to have been influenced too, by James's obsessive concern with witchcraft, on which the King had written a book ... and which was one of the best known things about him ... Shakespeare shaped his play under an arc-light awareness that this Scot was his principal audience".

In Hughes' opinion the late romances differ in their style from the tragedies, for several reasons including the use of a new theatre and the death of Shakespeare's (reputedly Catholic) mother but also that if the tragedies "are viewed as a suite of diagnostic variations on the result of the divisive religious policy of Henry VIII and his daughter Elizabeth, then the romances adapt equally well to the religious policy of James, which seemed potentially more fluid and even reconciliatory" (p. 330).

In all, we can draw out three major elements in the substance of Hughes' analysis. One concerns the extent to which the monarchy can influence what is said about it, by important artists. In the crudest case, they can build pyramids or other monuments of mute glorification, or have statues or even idols made. They can stage dramatic extravaganzas of the kind Roy Strong described, using characters and plots from mythic or historic sources, on which to model representations of their current real selves. Briefly, the monarch writes the scenario or designs the celebratory work. Hughes was not saying that anything of the kind applied in Shakespeare's case; but his contextualisations show that there were things and ways of saying or showing things that Shakespeare felt he could not risk expressing. In this situation the monarch is not the detailed censor, but with officials who do that work, and with the monarch's responses to witnessed or reported performances likely to place the author either in credit or in jeopardy, there is an effective secondary censorship that the monarch may exert, even upon the world's greatest playwright.

The second element in Hughes' exposition is somewhat more subtle. In many of Shakespeare's plays his leading roles are given to kings, queens and rulers, to monarchs;

these include, amongst others, Hamlet, Duncan and Macbeth, Leontes, Lear, Caesar (in Antony and Cleopatra) and finally Prospero. These characters invite identification with the audience's own current monarch (or with rival or enemy monarchs) so that the characters and actions set in the dramas can come close to being scrutinised as direct political comment and even criticism. The monarch's role in the development of the state is thus either being explained or defended, or taken to task by the artist who, in this case, has his work appreciated by effectively the whole of educated and much of the uneducated society during his lifetime, and by influential parts of the public in nearly all succeeding generations down to the present time. The creative artist thus adopts the role of a critical political scientist or historian[31].

The third point is yet more subtle. Shakespeare used two basic "plot situations" for his tragedies, set out in his early long poems, *Venus and Adonis*, and *Lucrece*. Hughes argued that the first structure expresses what is essentially a 'Catholic' pattern taken from the storehouse of Greek myth, the second expresses a 'Protestant' or Puritan pattern emerging from Roman folklore. In Shakespeare's earlier poems and tragedies the Catholic pattern seems to be repudiated in the development of the drama - thus favouring the protestant side in the drama of the nation's real evolution. This fits in with the period during which Elizabeth ruled and when the Catholic side of the nation's sensibility was being suppressed. In the later tragedies and the final play of resolution *The Tempest* Hughes detected an element of rejection of the sensibilities of Puritan rigor, rejection of female sexuality and some return to an expression of the more 'Catholic' sensibilities involved in accepting a drama of a Great Goddess figure, combining maternal and maidenly aspects.

Combining the second and third of these features of Hughes' thesis we can identify a notion of the monarch as a vessel of the country's developing history. The real live monarch's heritage and behavior express both what has happened in the past, and what is developing in the present. In this way we can think of the monarchy as a "medium" in itself, and not just as an object about which other media make representations.

---

[31] When Hughes died many critics (writing in broadsheet papers) were scathing about the idea of a poet laureate as it were "hired to glorify the monarchy". They failed to realise that Ted Hughes took his own time in allowing his stature as a great poet to emerge in its own way - and in finding another quite different means in which to realise the role of (royal) laureate, through his analysis of Shakespeare. Hughes nevertheless did write some "official" poems one of which is the following (the BBC which carried the item on its website kindly pointed out that the image in the last line refers to the coffin on the horse-drawn carriage in the funeral procession):

Mankind is many rivers
That only want to run.
Holy Tragedy and Loss
Make the many One.
Mankind is a Holy, crowned
Mother and her Son.
For worship, for mourning:
God is here, is gone.
Love is broken on the Cross.
The Flower on the Gun.

In the case of the United Kingdom we can see historically that the Catholic model, drawing upon pre-Christian mythical sources, was phased out. The last emphatically Catholic monarch, Mary, was succeeded by Protestant Elizabeth; and while Stuarts returned to a Catholic approach in which the monarch was seen as having a Divine Right, thus resembling the pre-Christian mythic model of a king as (demi)god, they were presently removed in favour of the Oranges and finally Hanoverians, all Protestant, for whom no Divine Right was recognised by their subjects and who found themselves perforce more in the cast of the biblical David, who explicitly and often repudiated any claims to quasi divine authority. Hughes told us that it was the work of the greatest playwright and poet, to articulate these tremendous changes, that is to say, to express them in a deep down position in his plays and to get across to his audiences that this was the course of history developing in the nation. Shakespeare is thus seen as beyond an analyst and critic, also a prophet and guide for the nation in its understanding and its construction of what it wanted to be and to become. England (and to a lesser extent Wales and Scotland, Hughes says less about the polities of these two other countries in the Union, though he has extensive footnotes about Welsh and Celtic myth and legend) was thus blessed in its greatest "media artist" of the turn of the sixteenth century.

It is not necessary for Hughes to have raised the matter, but a comparison with French theatre may reveal that France was less fortunate than Britain, in not having a Shakespeare, even though its great playwright Racine did draw upon classical mythical sources for many dramas through which contemporary developments could be understood. The French monarchy remained Catholic and in a more brittle condition less able to weather the pressures of eighteenth century urbanisation and incipient industrialisation, so it collapsed. The story of royal patronage of great composers such as Haydn and Mozart reflects at least some credit on the monarchs' discernment, even if their support of the former was not steadfast enough. Domenico Scarlatti was affectionately supported by the Princess of Portugal who married the King of Spain; and though the composer was a Neapolitan born, he produced over 600 jewels of keyboard work which distil essences of Spanish sensibility.

The careers of the other great central European nations, Germany and Italy were those of emerging coherence of the greater state rather than mainly of resolving problems between Catholic and Protestant social models. Each of these nations had copious and great "media" interacting with their monarchies in different ways, each of which deserves a book in itself and on which only a few questions may be thrown out here. Consider how Beethoven expressed central European feelings about his hero Napoleon overstretching himself - after the Eroica symphony exalting the conqueror, the ninth exalts the "common man"; Tschaikowsky, from a different perspective, celebrated the Tzarist regime's defeat of Napoleon. Verdi used opera to stir Italians in their emergence from Austrian domination and toward the short-lived monarchy of the house of Savoy. In none of these cases did the monarchy come remotely near influencing let alone manipulating the composer and thus the work that reverberated down the media-ways of the time.

A BRIEF SUMMARY OF THE FIRST CHAPTER

We have explored the idea and the phenomenon of monarchy and have found that it has occurred over many ages and in most parts of the world. Monarchy takes many forms, but two main strands of these can be made out; one of these is something we can call "constitutional", the other "quasi-divine". The constitutional form has roots in the 'Davidic' ideas of the ancient Israelites. This form denies any divinity in the monarch but accords it to the High God, and thus limits the monarch. This form was hit upon by the Protestant breakaway states of northern Europe and it had to be wrested violently from a Catholic historical context. The latter can be seen as having links with certain pre-Christian middle eastern, and with many non-European forms in the Americas and Asia, where the monarch puts himself forward and is perceived as being related to a divinity. One might argue that Muslim monarchies are a third kind, but it may also seem that they more closely resemble the Davidic than the quasi-divine cases.

It is a difficult idea to grasp and to impart, but one which emerges from the work of superior artists and analysts - such as the recent British Poet Laureate Ted Huges - that monarchy can be and sometimes is a "medium" in itself. It is a medium through which ideas, feelings, traditions, formative experiences of a nation's past can be embodied in the person of the monarch and in the way in which she or he supplies leadership. What the monarch is, and what the monarch does is seen, spoken about, heard and discussed throughout a realm - and beyond that in other realms; so what is being projected to the nation (in the best cases) is not just or only the whims and designs of the monarch, but the experience and the future aspirations of the nation. This, then, is the first (and possibly only) important idea that emerges from this chapter: the monarchy (sometimes) IS a medium, quite aside from the other more conventionally termed media "out there".

The second theme is that "media" are only narrowly understood as todays mass message systems. The arts and the cults and religions are also "media". They carry and deliver ideas and feelings. Thus not just newspapers and television but sculpture and architecture, poetry, pottery and carpet weaving and many other arts and crafts are all media.

Monarchs have tried to harness media; sometimes to use them, in other instances to muzzle others' uses of them. Monarchs need to use media not just to influence the life of their own society internally but also to influence how they are perceived and felt about externally. Thus we have examples of positive communication in which envoys take verbal messages or extravagant presents back to their own rulers; we also have many examples of negative communication in which explorers, envoys, missionaries or other visitors take home stories that will cultivate hostility. Sometimes such hostility is in what we may nowadays consider a good cause, such as an intention to end slavery; other times hostilities are based in greed or ambition. Whatever the reasons for hostilities, monarchs (just like other non-monarchist regimes) have it in their best interests to control their external reputations, and they have to control the message processes through which theses reputations are communicated. This may mean that we can see a homegoing missionary as a medium, or the messages he or she carries as media.

We have not yet discussed the development of INDEPENDENT "media" or arenas in which ideas and feelings are expressed about many matters, including the functioning of a state's leadership which may be a monarchy. This does seem to be less of a problem for and in what Marshall McLuhan called 'pre-print' societies; in them the oral traditions of storytelling predominated and whatever was said or sung in ancient homes or byways did not have that degree of common visibility (and audibility) that emerges with the spread of print, and then more so of electronic mass message systems. Here we come to the question "what is the public saying about the king?" and the further question of what, if anything, the king can do about it. If it is protested that this is a problem of "public relations" then the position taken here is that public relations is effectively a scenario within or upon the wider stage whose structure is commonly these days called "the media" and which I prefer to term a "message system". In later chapters we will come to the problem of whether the monarch can take a lead in shaping what is expressed about the monarchy within the message systems of the time, in societies where economics and technical achievements have made a mini-monarch of each and every adult, and a slightly-more-than-mini-monarch of many journalists.

Chapter 2

METAPHORS OF MONARCHY

INTRODUCTION: SIGNS OF MONARCHY, UNSOUGHT

Virginia, Carolina, Maryland, Georgia, Louisiana: five of the republican United States; but they derived their names, which they keep, from European royalty and hence monarchy[32]. If one looks about, in many republics as well as in realms there are many signs of the mark of monarchy. These five states' names were given at their inception to celebrate royal connections or to recognise royal existence or functioning. Many of such links have been abolished or they have been worn away so that the connections can not be noticed without some educated effort. Nevertheless other names remain whose royal nature is so explicit that they serve as reminders that monarchy has been, and still remains a widespread institution.

New York city has its Queens borough and upstate lies Kingston; several other states have their own Kingstons. Prince George is recalled just south of Washington DC, where Georgetown University might otherwise be thought to have got its name from some non-royal source. New Orleans, Charlotte and several Charlestons, Williamsburg and at least two Windsors and even Raleigh all have a ring, however muted, of royalty about them. Clearly, there are not a large number of American place names that have royal roots or resonances; but a number of states and places do retain reminders of monarchist times. Across the other side of the world - and who would have expected it even just a few months before it happened - the severely socialist Leningrad was renamed St Petersburg, with its undoubted connection not just to the saint but also to the city's founder Tsar Peter, while Ekaterinburg reappeared further east after another Russian monarch. A street directory of Paris contains some 5, 500 location names and amongst these 30 or somewhat more than one in two hundred are explicitly royal.

---

[32] Spaniards leaving their mark on the West Coast appear more to have venerated the Church and their religion (notice Santa Barbara, San Francisco, Los Angeles, Santa Cruz, San Luis Obispo, Santa Monica, Santa Rosa, San Pedro) though an occasional name (Monte-rey) suggests that the monarch back in Spain was being complimented.

It is awkward to claim that cities and places, or the other objects and phenomena discussed in this chapter are "media"; but the conventional conception of that term is too narrow. It is sensible to realise that meanings are at one time injected, via names of places and other items, into the substance of society and that these original meanings do not entirely disappear. In this short chapter I will look at a few different fields in which names and characters remind those who come upon them that monarchy has been and remains an option, one moreover which carries a certain stature and glamour. The fields I will look at include the names of public locations, particularly in the centre of high-profile monarchy, London; I will also look at the worlds of entertainment, games, tales and marketing terms.

PLACE NAMES IN LONDON: THE ROYAL PROPORTION

A street directory (Nicholson's, 1986) was chosen, whose index provided a convenient data base for study. There were an estimated 42, 500 entries in the book. It is not unusual for a street to have one or more entries in the index; this is because it is such a long street that it is shown across more than one page. In this way the number of entries gives a measure not just of existence but also of prominence. The simple procedure was next to identify those place names which directly label royal or monarchic roles (Kingsway, Queen's Square; Princes Gate) and then to cast the net wider to include those first names which are or were well known monarchs and other clearly royal associations. What we find in terms of the names, and how often they occur is shown in table 2.1

In all there were 1481 'royal named' locations, which comprise some 3.5 per cent of all entries in the directory. One might therefore say that 'London is six times as royal - in the flavour of its names - than is Paris' (for which city the same procedure was carried out revealing, as expected, far fewer - but still several - royal place names). It is clear that masculines (except for the name of Victoria) far exceed feminines; it may be unexpected that the Tudor dynasty outnumbers others. The proportion of all names that have royal associations could be thought to be rather small; but it does mean that out of every 30 place names one has a royal ring to it. This is similar to the number of locations that have churchly meanings but it is three times as many as apply to military origins, or to names of artists, writers and musicians; and the monarchist terms are nearly six times as many as the names which remind citizens (or subjects) of scientists, engineers and explorers. The further context of meaning in London names shows that there are huge numbers of descriptions of the land and its fauna, hill and vale, ash and sycamore, (but not so many animals) are all over the conurbation; and place names outside London and even beyond the British Isles are plentiful. It could seem that London is denying its city-like essence and even denying its parochiality while celebrating nature and the world beyond its borders. However, within its precincts the people who are most often named are members of the monarchic system.

Table 2.1: How often Names Occur

Roles	N	Families	N	Individuals	N
Kings	318	Tudor	51	Victoria	83
Queens	208	Windsor	41	Albert	62
Princes	93	Norman	24	Alexandra	52
Princess	8	Stuart	19	Georg/ian	27
Regent	28	Hanover	17	Edward	21
Dukes	37	Orange	5	Elizabeth	20
Duchess	3	Plantagenet	3	Bruce	14
				James	13
				Charles	13
Other References	**N**			Alfred	12
				Frederick	12
Crown	41			Caroline	10
Empire/imperial	27			Charlotte	10
Brunswick	27			Arthur	9
Palace	26			Beatrice	9
Lord	23			Boleyn	9
Sandringham	19			Glendower	3
Jubilee	16			Mountbatten	3
Balmoral	11				
Fitzroy	8				
Coronation	7				

Since roads are inefficiently provided with signs many British people point the way for strangers by using pub names as landmarks. The telephone business directory for 1997 revealed 1237 pub names and among these 16.4 per cent had royal identity. The word King (together with a name such as Alfred, Henry VIII or whomever) came up 38 times followed by Prince which occurred on 34 pubs. As in the case of streets, the female names were less often in place with Queen (Elizabeth, and others) naming 22 pubs and Princess another 10. Exotic cases were infrequent with one Empress of Russia and one Sultan as pub names. An exotic addition to the vocabulary of monarchy in London's place names is found among names of Indian restaurants several of whom include words such as Mogul or Rajah which even some less educated British customers are likely to recognise as royal designations, helped as they often are by decorative artwork incorporating crowns.

Overall, the signs of monarchy are ubiquitous in London and elsewhere in Britain. As we have pointed out such names even survive to a small extent in republican Paris and in the United States. These names do not reveal the monarchy consciously at work and have not been for the most part acts of influence by the monarchies over "the media"; rather the namings suggest that it is some sign of popular acceptance of monarchy within which it is thought to confer an element of glamour on a street or a premises if it is given a royal name.

It is not only in street and pub names that people nod respect to their royalty. Individuals' own names are sometimes given to reflect their royal use; one may have such a name for reasons quite other than a desire to copy royalty, but perceptions of the name will likely be coloured by perceptions of the royal person with that name. One large study of images of childrens' first names in Britain[33] included Elizabeth amongst eighteen girls names, and referred also to Charles along with seventeen other boys' names, for each of which associated ideas were recorded. Elizabeth had top score on strength of association of the name with the characteristics 'honest' and 'strong minded' and came second being considered 'clever'. Elizabeth was considered least 'boyish' of the names listed and overall came second in strength of association with five positive attributes. Charles came third amongst the list of eighteen boys' names in strength of association with five positive attributes, like Elizabeth being top in connection with 'strong minded' and with 'honest'. The name Charles was strongly dissociated from the adjective 'sexy' and had weak scores on 'handsome' and 'happy' which is why it achieved only third place out of eighteen. It is not possible to say to what particular extent the replies were influenced by people's associations of these two names with selfsame members of the royal family; however, it is not unlikely that there was some connection.

ROYAL PRESENCE IN FAIRY TALES

Fairy tales may not have the prominence in western societies that they once had; but there are reasons to think that they are still well known and will continue to be so. Any visit to a bookstore or library will reveal that there is a diverse mass of competing books for children which now follow "politically correct" real or imagined guidelines. Sexism and racism are not just avoided, they are supplanted by egalitarian content. By contrast, many or perhaps even most traditional fairy tales are in no way gender-neutral and several are sexist and racist. Nevertheless, modern stories and tales are likely to be time-bound; whether the next generation, let alone the next child will find it enchanting to be taken through tales of a decade or even of five years ago is perhaps less likely than it is that adults will want to tell their children stories they themselves had as children; this process is likely to be repeated which is why certain rather dated tales such as that of Peter Pan or of Babar the Elephant may survive.

---

[33] Wober, J.M. (1998) Names and Notions: Sight Bites As Cues to Girls' Character And the Attributes of Happiness. Paper given at the British Psychological Society's Psychology of Women Section Annual Conference, University of Birmingham, July.

I have considered it relevant to look at five collections of fairy tales[34] and to count among them the number of appearances of kings, queens and their offspring. The first point is to find out how common it is to be given a picture of a monarchist society, which happens when any royal person comes into the story. Further points are to begin to explore the relative occurrence of different royal role models in terms of their sex or seniority. This is what was found:

Numbers of:

Character	Kings	Queens	Princes	Princesses
Good	42	18	24	32
Not Good	21	6	3	1

In 94 out of 169 tales examined, there was a royal figure; this number represents 55 per cent of the total. It is clear too that the 116 good roles far outnumbered the 31 which were not good. This makes 147 roles among the 94 tales (which comprise 79 per cent, or four out of five of all the stories analysed) that contained royalty and indicates that several tales included a king and a prince or three, or a queen and a princess, and so on. Kings occurred much more often than did queens; but reversing this gender proportion there were more princesses in the stories that were found than there were princes. There is no typical tale but many themes stand out, such as of the commoner who discovers in herself or himself royal quality. The commoner might be a Cinders who is discovered and translated to palace life, or a low-born young man who succeeds in a series of adventures and marries a princess. Several stories deal with competition between sons of a king, in which usually the youngest (who, like the commoner, is initially the least likely contender) turns out to be the winner. There is no really prevailing stereotype of a bad queen (though certain tales, like Snow White may create a strong impression of that kind, cast over the generality) or of a bad king.

The impression that emerges from the treatment of monarchy in these tales is that it is an institution to be taken for granted, more often benevolent than not, and curiously enough an institution that can be joined, almost always by displays of merit. The young men show merit by prevailing in tests of strength, stamina, fearlessness, ingenuity and to some extent of compassionate character. The young women show merit by being beautiful, meek, though often also intelligent and sensitive; they are not, however, required to traipse over hill and dale to vanquish monsters and come back with treasures (whether of gold or gems, or of magical potions such as "waters of life"), as are the boys.

These ingredients are inconsistent with modern political correctness and are challenges to those who wish to re-present tales which have had narrative power in past

---

[34] Grimm, J.L.K. and Grimm, W.K. (1824) *Fairy Tales*. London: Baldwin.
Riordan, J. (1976) *Tales From Central Russia*. London: Kestrel.
Andersen, N.C. (ND) *Favourite Fairy Tales* London: Blackie.
Carruth, J. (1976) *My World of Fairy Tales* Maidenhead: Purnell.
Housman, L. (ND) *Stories From The Arabian Nights*. London: Hodder And Stoughton.

ages. It could be argued (not here) that such examples and patterns contributed to the competitive and destructive societies which indulged in so many wars until the present. It remains to be firmly shown that folk tales effectively influence personality development or social institutions or behavior, though at least one study (by Korten, in Ethiopia[35]) analysed 129 stories and suggested that they present life as a contest providing few opportunities for social co-operation, and moreover that these themes influenced patterns of behavior. Korten claimed that in Ethiopian societies each person would fend for him (or her?) self and would resort to deception or revenge to attain their goals.

Several of the movies of Walt Disney have included models of monarchy. These movies include the hand drawn fictions Snow White and Bambi, each of which would repay some attention. Snow White may include a malicious queen, but behind her is nevertheless a taken-for-granted monarchy from which ultimately, it is hoped, blessings would flow. In Bambi the young deer sees distant and tantalising visions of the King of the Forest - a great stag who turns out to be his father. This King deer has large antlers which resemble in form a crown, while mother deer have smaller crowns. The implication is that eventually Bambi will himself become a kingly deer with a crown of antlers (if he escapes being shot by wicked human hunters; these hunters are commoners and not led in the chase by an aristocrat let alone a king).

The Walt Disney studio made several fictions in the decades after World War II, which took up mediaeval themes such as Robin Hood, and in which monarchs - good or bad - appear. Robin Hood may be a rebel but even in American-made versions is not presented as a republican, rather than as a romantic reformist within the system, ready to be loyal to a Good King (the LionHearted Richard - absent Crusading and/or troubadoring in Europe - these movies do not present him as a homosexual he is said to have been, and as the killer of some thousands of civilian prisoners in Acre) however much he rejected the Bad King (John, who did at least, even under pressure from equally grim barons sign Magna Carta). Disney returned to monarchist content with *The Sword in the Stone* favorably portraying one of the very founts of British monarchy, the story of King Arthur.

Without for a moment pretending that American film studios made many films containing, let alone proclaiming monarchy, they not infrequently return to the theme. Many will remember the movie *Anna and the King of Siam* which glamorised a story of the Thai monarchy. On trying to remake the story in 1998 the American film entrepreneurs were not allowed to film in Thailand as the authorities considered the version disrespectful to their monarchy. The company clearly believed the story has wide appeal, presumably including in America, as they then proposed to shoot their material in Malaysia.

It is a question for Americans to consider, why Hollywood has not found figures in its own revolutionary history as fertile a source of heroic-romantic movies as has been discovered overseas. Perhaps they were alive so long ago that they achieve identification

---

[35] Korten, D.C. (1971) The life game: survival strategies in Ethiopian folk tales. *Journal of Cross Cultural Psychology*, 2, 209-224.

with too small fractions of modern American society for Hollywood to glamorise Tom Paine or George Washington as foci for admiration for the whole nation now. In going back to Europe and even Asia for its epic figures (consider *Conan the Barbarian*) the American movie industry can deal in the realm of myth that is seen to be safely foreign, but nevertheless deals with the questions of how a state should be constructed so as to establish order and what kind of authority such a state needs. It should be recognised too, that the treatment of such historic material is not always pro-monarchist.

The movie *Braveheart* is an example where there has quite possibly been an anti monarchist effect, in Britain. The story concerns the Scottish hero William Wallace, portrayed as a man of the common people. He fought the English led by their (wicked, oppressive to the Scots) King Edward, and lost. He was brutally killed by the English (monarchist) state, leaving the Scots then (and those who see the movie now) with a sense of oppression by the English. Omitted is the development that the Scots were led soon afterwards by Robert the Bruce who eventually defeated a large English army at Bannockburn, and who reigned as Scotland's King. Scotland thus remained a monarchy and does so to this day, albeit having lent its own King James VI to England where he reigned as James I, the two countries (with Wales) continuing as a joint monarchy. The lesson of the movie, as far as it goes (without having been demonstrated in systematic research) seems to be that a monarch-led state is oppressive over the feelings of a people; and this was made use of by the Scottish National Party in the run up to the elections for the new Scottish Parliament in 1999. SNP sentiment contributed to a muted royal role in the opening of that Parliament.

MONARCHY IN GAMES

Bell[36] reports that several kinds of games of strategy or conflict involve monarchs. We read of the Swedish naturalist Linnaeus' visit to Lapland where he found a game called Tablut played on a board of nine by nine squares; the central square was called the Konakis or Throne and only the Swedish King amongst the pieces could occupy the square. While that game is not so widespread, draughts is; and while draughts starts with a model of an egalitarian society of pieces which all have equally limited power, if one reaches the opposite end of the board it becomes a King and is crowned - when it enjoys greatly enhanced power. These royal terms appear to continue to be used even in republican societies.

The great conflict game is however chess. Bell reports that it may have originated in the Indian game Shatranj in which there are four armies, each under control of a Rajah (king). In the Persian poet Firdausi's book the Shahnameh (see Chapter 1) there is a story of how chess came to Persia. An ambassador from India brought the game to Emperor Chosroes; the latter was challenged to set his wise men to solve the mysteries of the game. If they succeeded the Indian King would pay the Persian emperor tribute as an

---

[36] Bell, R.C. (1979) *Board And Table Games From Many Civilizations*. New York: Dover.

overlord, but if the Persian sages failed it would show they were of lower intellect and tribute would be demanded from them to India. Naturally, according to the story the Persians succeeded.

The early game was not identical to the one now universal. Keene[37] reports (p. 6) that in the late fifteenth century "the queen switched from being a waddling cripple (the Arabic vizier) to the most powerfully mobile piece on the board ... the increased fire power of the queen surely reflects the introduction of battlefield artillery ... The sudden advances in chess as a whole must also be explicable in terms of the Renaissance dynamic ... the increasingly urgent perception of distance, space and perspective". The modern term 'rook' may derive from the Persian word 'rukh' for war chariot; or perhaps the Italian 'rocco' for a town. These suggestions indicate that there is no fixed account of how and where chess arose, other than that it evolved and prospered in Europe from the early middle ages onward; but in doing this it incorporated a picture of a monarchic society in which the greatest endeavour was to protect one's own king (who, incidentally, had virtually no autonomous power) while trying to trap an opponent's into surrender. Chess sets made in republican countries generally do not include Presidents or Dictators (who would expect to be powerful pieces) but are content to represent kings, queens and even - as witness the practice of some generations of superb Soviet chess players - bishops and knights. Whichever king is defeated then, in the world represented by the chess board, monarchy rules.

While (mostly) only one version of chess is played with the set, decks of cards allow people to play many different games. There are also many structures to the deck arising in various European traditions. All of these traditions however, include court cards usually called (in English) the King, Queen and Jack. These are nearly always colourfully illustrated. Mann[38] thinks it likely that the suits represent different factions in mediaeval life, for example the church, the army, merchants and peasantry. Among Spanish cards "the name of the reigning monarch was usually found in the ace of money ... and Spanish cards travelled with colonisation and are still used in South and Central America".

Mann reports (p. 123) that "England seems to have been the first country to have employed cards as political criticism or commentary. The first such packs may have been one lampooning the Commonwealth Government and the Rump Parliament, but the principal series of such packs directed its vituperation ... against one target - the Catholic Church". Here then is a "mass medium" in print, not in the shape of the book but in the unexpected form of playing cards. Mann does not say that it was a monarch who pulled the strings for in Great Britain at the time she describes there was a short-lived republic, and it was private enterprise which published its impatience in this way. The pack she refers to (p. 151) included an ace of clubs which "shows a private house being sacked and a lady being abducted, with the caption 'a free state or a toleration for all sort of Villainy'. The 10 of clubs shows Oliver Cromwell praying with an execution taking

---

[37] Keene, R. (1993) *Chess for Absolute Beginners*. London: Batsford.
[38] Mann, S. (1979) *Collecting Playing Cards* London: Howard Baker.

place in the background: 'Oliver seeking God while the K. is murdered by his order'. The Queen of Spades has the caption 'The Lady Lambert and Oliver under a strong Conflict' and shows the couple seated together on a bed".

An interesting question now is where, when and to what extent did republics ever decide to throw off the monarchist 'terms' of the card deck. The first instance in which to examine this question was the French revolution. Cardmakers on their own account, or urged on by local authorities began to remove royal insignia from designs. Sometimes kings would be shown with topless heads, or a Phrygian cap might be painted in. Presently new titles replaced the 'court' designations; Kings became the Geniuses of war, peace, arts and trade; Queens became the Freedoms of marriage, religion, profession and the press. Jacks became Equalities. Aces represented Law. In another revolutionary pack Kings were philosophers; eventually, though, Napoleon had enough of such demotic expression and commissioned the painter David to produce a design showing Napoleon as Julius Caesar as the King of Diamonds. Like Napoleon, the design did not last for very many years.

Another French Revolutionary pack replaced Kings with the philosophers Voltaire, La Fontaine, Moliere and Rousseau while Queens became Virtues of temperance, wisdom and strength. One reason why such symbols may have lacked staying power is that there is not enough "family cohesion" within a suit, say, to link Voltaire with temperance. After a short time the traditional Paris pattern depicting a full court in each suit returned to French cards. In America it was mainly during the civil war that cards began to speak of the constitution and a deck of Union Playing Cards was designed. At the top of this was a general, followed by Liberty and then a soldier, but as elsewhere, designs reverted to courtliness.

In 1917 however a deck of Freedom Playing Cards emerged with a joker with the statement 'No Kings or Queens for me'. The 'courts' had Uncle Sam, Liberty and Infantry. Next year saw a new deck with the slogan "Patriotic Americans Insist on Democracy Playing Cards in your home and club. Out with Kings and Queens. Four million brave American boys and girls willingly answered the call to put down autocracy. They did their work well and Democracy's banner has been unfurled to the world forever". Naval ratings appeared on jacks, nurses on queens and infantrymen on the kings. But, the court cards still carried the letters (and what might these have meant?) J.Q. and K. Recent decades have seen Presidents Kennedy and Reagan on some American cards, but the designations J.Q.K evidently continue.

Not all the examples of attempts to efface signs of monarchy have arisen in what are now considered democratic countries. In Russia after the revolution at first the standard cards were discontinued but again the authorities relented and the previous Paris pattern returned. The indices on Russian cards are the equivalent in the Cyrillic (Russian) alphabet of K, Q, and J. Wowk reports[39] that in Nazi Germany there was a soldiers pack in which courts showed officers, non-commissioned officers and women auxiliary members of the armed forces, and another propaganda pack with caricatures of monarchs and political leaders of the allied countries supposedly dropped on Britain from raiding aircraft. A Nazi pack featured the standard Rhineland pattern (in which all the kings and queens wore crowns while the jacks had hats) but the suit of clubs was replaced by a suit of swastikas and the eagle badge of the Nazis appeared on all aces. Reports indicate that German cards have reverted to older patterns.

In societies where gaming has moved on to screens the domestic playing card may have been left behind and forgotten; but where they exist, they still generally display monarchic symbols. On the American-made computer on which this text is being written the giant software company has provided a solitaire game and in this the court cards are traditionally royal. In the 1950s the then King of Egypt, Farouk, predicted that eventually there would be only five kings remaining - those of Diamonds, Hearts, Clubs and Spades - and of Great Britain. At the turn of the century these five monarchs seem still to be universally prominent.

THE KINGDOM OF HEAVEN

Not far north of the site of Megiddo in Israel (and where prophecy suggests the final world battle will occur) is Mount Tabor. This is the Mount upon which Jesus gave his sermon now known by that name. Amongst the blessings Jesus uttered was an early one for the "poor in spirit: for theirs is the kingdom of heaven" (Matthew 5:3). Soon after Jesus taught his disciples how to pray with words including "Thy kingdom come. Thy will be done, in earth as it is in heaven" (Matthew 6:10). In a number of Jesus' sayings the kingdom could be thought to be that of God the Father; but in some instances the kingship was something that inhered in the figure of the Son Jesus, while on others it characterised the Holy Spirit.

In John (18:36) we read "Jesus answered, 'My kingship is not of this world; if my kingship were of this world, my servants would fight ... but my kingship is not from the world'". John later tells us (19:19) "Pilate also wrote a title and put it on the cross; it read 'Jesus of Nazareth, the King of the Jews'. The chief priests of the Jews then said to Pilate, 'Do not write "The King of the Jews", but 'This man said, I am King of the Jews'". Later, an apostle writes (Hebrews 1:8) "But about the Son he says, 'Your throne O God will last for ever and ever, and righteousness will be the sceptre of your kingdom'". One apostle wrote "He (i.e. God the Father) has delivered us from the dominion of darkness and transferred us to the kingdom of his beloved Son ..." (Colossians 1:13). In other epistles we read "For the kingdom of God does not mean food and drink but righteousness and peace and joy in the Holy Spirit" (Romans 14:17); and "then the end will come: Christ will overcome all spiritual rulers, authorities and powers, and will hand over the Kingdom to God the Father" (1 Corinthians 15:24). Eventually there is some shared sovereignty in "The kingdom of the world has become the kingdom of our Lord and of his Christ, and he shall reign for ever and ever" (Revelation 11:15).

---

[39] Wowk, K. (1983) *Playing Cards of the World*. Guildford: Lutterworth Press.

The first point here is not to debate whether Christ (the Son) is truly or exclusively King, or whether God the Father is King or whether Kingship inheres in the Holy Spirit. The point is to demonstrate that where Christianity is preached and practised the language and terms and presumably some of the thought patterns of Israelite monarchic statehood are common. Plato the Greek wrote of The Republic, and if that particular strand of (Greek) statehood had gained the upper hand in the development of early Christianity, the language and terms of consuls and elected leaders may have been woven instead into epistles and texts, even of the Gospels themselves. This is not what happened, however; both Gospels and Epistles frequently use the terms King, Kingdom and Kingship to develop a picture of a (future) good society under supreme authority and guidance. These texts are very largely masculine and do not develop any idea of complementary "Queenship" or of any hereditary succession other than that there are a Father and a Son to each of whom the monarchic metaphor is given on different occasions.

Obviously Christianity made a major place for a feminine aspect to the Godhead, though not all Christians feel equally welcoming or comfortable about this. A great deal of religious power is developed from the dramatic contrast (in the same figure) between the most lowly form of creature imaginable, the sacrificial Lamb, and the triumphant emergent King; quite likely, this power could not be generated from a contrast between the lamb and a title implying a leader by popular (and thus not wholly admirable) support. In short, when we say Lamb we need also to say King - and President will not convey the same impact; especially as nowadays, when Presidents are impeachable for squalid crimes.

This comes to the second point in this section which is that it is nothing strange within a state such as the United Kingdom, which has a Queen and an established Christian Church, for the language of Christianity to include such strong images of monarchy. It is a different matter in an avowedly secular constitution such as that of the United States. Here, although rule is from and for the people, Christianity is the most widespread religion and an image it offers of statehood is that of a monarchy. The monarch in Christianity is not human, which may be a neat arrangement in which the secular and demotic authority is organised and cocooned within a larger sphere of a Divine (thus superhuman) Authority. Still, the same option was open to the Israelites, who (against prophetic advice) wanted to have a king "because everyone else round about has one".

What role may the abundant imagery of monarchy in Christian texts play, in the ways in which modern Americans think and feel about leadership of the state? An American cleric[40] has examined this question in some depth. Halcomb draws on writers as far back as Aristotle and as close to us as C.S. Lewis in asserting that metaphor is a powerful way of not just communicating to, but energising ideas in a reader or recipient. This effectiveness is often greater than that of propositional speech. Applied to our case

---

[40] Halcomb, M.P. (1982) *The Use of Metaphor in Preaching* Doctoral Thesis at Bethel Theological Seminary, Milwaukee.

this would suggest that all the potential messages latent in the heroes of movies, the glamour of playing card figures key in to notions of and feelings about kingship or hereditary leadership that exist subconsciously but which are currently denied in the American political system. It remains true that none of these associations are activated by anyone within the political system, for various perfectly good reasons. In Halcomb's case, the messages of preachers concern the ultimate leadership, of God, about whom it is not possible to speak truly effectively in propositional speech; so it is necessary to communicate using metaphors.

Halcomb carried out a study in which congregants rated each of thirty six excerpts from real sermons on each of seven scales. Half the excerpts were metaphorical and half were propositional statements. The two kinds of statement were not judged effectively differently in terms of clarity or appeal; however the metaphoric group of statements were considered more imaginative, beautiful and emotionally evocative. Halcomb pointed out that in order to make these metaphors effective in terms of establishing religious messages it works best if they are supported with more direct (propositional) statements.

We may say that the "medium" of religion, which is a system of discourse about the higher realities of the human predicament and of regulation of that predicament, has much to say that is in terms of monarchy. It might not be surprising then, if in a Republic which has a strong Christian tradition the notion of kingship crops up, and not just as a metaphor, in a variety of ways. Returning to the case of monarchist ideas evidently embedded in American movies and tales, it may be that they have potential to support developments along the lines they suggest, but nobody (as yet) picks up the opportunity (to use a sporting metaphor) to run with this ball.

One way in which such notions could be explored would be in a futurist movie. Such scenarios are in a way metaphors about the current design of society; so *Bladerunner* looks to a near future concentrating on interactions between advanced technomena[41] and social structures and behavior. *Star Wars* is also pre-occupied with gadgetry and morals, rather than with state structure. However, the movie issued in 1999 (ostensibly the first *Star Wars* story, making the first published issue really the fourth chronological episode in the eventual complete series) illustrates a time in which republics coexist with at least one starry world ruled by a Queen. Either this could be taken as a metaphor devised for sales and marketing purposes to dramatise to the British audience that there is a place for monarchy in the future, so not to be afraid of fables of this kind; or it could be experienced even by American viewers as reminding them that monarchy is an option even in a habitable future. One could indeed script a movie in which American society had evolved to settle down to some kind of ecological equilibrium and had sought

---

[41] I am reluctant to (mis)use the word 'technology' to refer to physical objects or systems, when its second component part (ology) refers to a degree of knowledge or wisdom - *about* - these items. If we do have and want to refer to that understanding of such phen*omena* we might sensibly use the word technology; but where we refer to the phenomena themselves without acknowledging any wisdom about them, perhaps we should use the term I have devised *technomena*.

structures (involving symbols of continuity such as hereditary monarchy) with which to underline this ideal.

Constitutional monarchy is one such state structure and in the American case could involve a Duke for each state, from Alabama to Wyoming and a King/Queen or Emperor/Empress over the whole. These officers, elected in the first place but then hereditary would simply replace elected state governors and the President, with non executive and relatively stable lines of symbolic leadership. State and Federal legislatures would of course continue to be elected, and executively run by party leaders as in many European and Asiatic countries without any loss of democratic accountability, but with a change in the metaphoric equipment of the state. The germs of such a situation are already evident in the kinds of treatment accorded the Kennedys and Bushes. What happens when two such Dukedoms intermarry (as with mighty commercial mergers) provides the stuff for endless political drama in movies and television serials and this could be drawn upon right now in the form of a huge soap opera of a monarchised American future.

MONARCHY IN MARKETING

We come finally to a variety of examples of the use of the terms monarch, king, queen, and sometimes prince(ss) to try to add glamour, appeal, saleability, bankability to some performer whether a person or a product. The message systems within which such terms appear include all kinds of print, screen and broadcasting, not just outside but also within the United States. One of the greatest concentrations and sources of images in the western world in this century has been Hollywood (now exceeded in some ways by Bollywood - or the cinema of the city which was called Bombay[42]).

Hollywood has a firmament of stars and these epithets or metaphors suggest that, in common with more ancient pantheons in which, where there were demigods there would also be a supreme god, so the cinema with its stars and starlets would also have such a figure. Who would be the person, and what would she or he be called? It so happens that the term King has indeed been used in Hollywood, rather more often than has Queen and the accolade has gone to John Wayne and Frank Sinatra. Possibly age is involved here, with Kingship not being afforded to a young star - and hence Queenship being an inappropriate image for a sexually alluring woman. Thus Marilyn Monroe was not spoken of as Queen; and nor, for all their charisma were the older stars Bette Grable or Gloria Swanson. Possibly Elizabeth Taylor nudges that status, though she herself and her public relations may prefer to avoid such an event.

Crossing from Tinseltown to the allied world of Tin Pan Alley many will acknowledge that King is a title that has not been linked with anyone other than Elvis Presley. This might be a shrewd and opportunistic piece of marketing, branding him as

---

[42] Now that the city has been (re)named Mumbay, perhaps the cinematic epithet will follow suit, to become "mollywood".

unassailably supreme; but it would not have been able to take root had not the product had the popular support that it did. In other words, his fans worshipped him. Since Christendom rules in America it would not have been good, or even possible marketing to project Elvis as God; so he has been styled (and in America, where the throne is vacant) and accepted as King. Again, as with filmworld, there is no parallel Queen figure (other than, in partly (self) satirical terms Freddy Mercury). One reason is that in real life the Queen is generally married to or mother of a King, and this relationship can not be paralleled in entertainment star-world; another reason is that, until very recently women as singers were not projected as successfully as were males - there was a shortage of candidates. Madonna obviously bid strongly for the title but with this quasi-religious self appointed name side-stepped the secular monarchy and probably established her quasi-superhuman brand identity.

Descending a rung or two in existential importance the case of televised Miss World contests deserves some comment. This is said to be the most widely watched regular outside broadcast world-wide, seen each year by some 1.5 billion people. The 1998 version featured 86 young women one of whom was chosen Miss World and duly crowned. Having been crowned (with an ornate, glittering tiara, substantially larger than that of the runner up which was in turn more elaborate than that of the third placed woman) she will still be a Miss (World, of her year) but will also now be a Beauty Queen. The physical crown and the word Queen set the seal on someone who has risen (almost) out of the ranks of normal human kind. The royal insignia stand for excellence, certainly physical and everyone hopes, as well, moral. Cases are known where, if an incumbent has been reported to have lapsed from some ideal standard their Queenship has been declared void (by the company which owns the operation and seeks to conserve the brand's value).

The crown is a widespread emblem of royal status. What it appears to be doing is to add to the height of its wearer (Napoleon and other short emperors notwithstanding, greater physical height is generally taken as a sign of power). The Pope on occasions has a three-tiered crown which is substantially higher than a human head, and bishops wear Mitres which fulfil a similar function to a noble metal crown. The noble metals are silver and, to a significantly more lustrous extent gold. If anyone is fashioning a crown for real regal or even for marketing use they will not think of using copper, nor even stainless steel. Tradition weighs heavily in this matter. The Reverend Sung Moon conducted a wedding ceremony recently and sported a substantial crown, with his wife wearing a smaller one.

In Britain television's Channel 5, which annually shows the Miss World contest, competed in 1998 against the BBC's *Eurovision Song Contest* with its own *A Thong For Europe*. This included eight male contestants from across Europe who stripped off in front of female judges who selected a winner designated King Thong. There was no coronation and the event may more properly be understood as an example of those role-reversal jokes which range from festivals in which people dress as the opposite sex and other incorrect behavior is temporarily not just allowed but evidently expected, to cross-dressing drag performers of all kinds.

Although then there are some examples of events and uses of the monarchic terms which intend to send them up (by dragging them low) it is much more common for marketers to use the terms conservatively. That is, the dignity implied in the terms (King, Crown, Queen, Princess, etc) is intended to win admiration for the superiority of a product or a service. The widespreadness of this phenomenon is such that it can be left as an exercise for readers to note as many cases as possible where a bed or hotel room is king (sized), a motor car is a monarch or a ship a princess.

Chapter 3

BRITISH MONARCHS MAKING USE OF "MEDIATION"

A monarch reading the previous chapter may be tempted to think he or she need not worry about how society feels about them. Perhaps they can rely on signs along the folkways and embedded in the language to set people's minds to believe that there is no other way of supervising society than by a monarchy. Monarchs have usually not, however, been complacent. For a thousand years of well-recorded history and another thousand of less firmly established record in Britain, it is clear that monarchs have taken active steps to put themselves across so that their subjects would respect, accept and even (the term is nowadays widely used, in what we can realise is a rather curious way) love them. Monarchs have been in the business of positive public relations work in a wide variety of ways, as we shall now see. After looking at evidence for this activity, and sometimes for evidence of how successful it may have been (or not), we will then have a chance to attend to evidence that there has also been opposition, not just to how a monarchy has operated, but in due course also to its very nature. We can conveniently call such ideological anti-monarchism by its more familiar term, republicanism.

It is a temptation nowadays to think of media just as the mass message systems of the press and broadcasting; however, in this book we are thinking of media more broadly as the principal routes along which a source gives out (and receives) information to others and from others. Accepting McLuhan's clarifications[43] a pivotal historical and cultural event was the development of print by Johannes Gutenberg (in Germany, followed rapidly by Caxton in England and by many others). Before then books had to be hand-written and literacy was rare; print promoted a wider degree of literacy. In pre-print days what McLuhan terms oral culture prevailed, in which people told each other about events and feelings. Telling did not mean just conversational speech but included storytelling (for entertainment) or singing in which it was common for better performers to fix on reasonably well known versions of ballads and tales. Symmetrical metre helps to memorise material and this undoubtedly meant that sagas were recited in verse. Sagas and tales would focus on heroic deeds and events and these would often concern the past,

---

[43] McLuhan, M. (1962) *The Gutenberg Galaxy.* Toronto: University of Toronto Press.

and a tribe's experiences in establishing and holding its identity (and territory). Important ceremonies and festivals could thus be good topics to recount; and among such impressive events would be coronations.

A recent volume[44] reports that a form of coronation involving consecration and anointing had been settled upon in England by the year 900. Another device to establish a king in the consciousness of the population was the circulation of coins, which in many cases bore the king's portrait and or insignia. Silver pennies were struck for King Offa of Mercia, in the late eighth century, and a few years later for King Alfred (The Great) whose head is shown crowned; such coins showing a crowned head also survive for King Aethelstan in the early tenth century (and his successors whom it is not now necessary to list). Both Charlemagne and Offa (who exchanged letters with each other) had their sons anointed by the Church authorities during their own lifetimes. These ceremonials were proclaimed, which we can take to mean that a centralised announcement backed up with hand-written scrolled texts was distributed around the realm, undoubtedly followed by round-the-hearth and marketplace recitations describing events. Queens could have their own separate coronations, especially when they were married after the ascension of a king, and where they may have come from different realms. When King Aethelwulf of Wessex married Judith princess of Francia she was consecrated by the Archbishop in Rheims

Aethelstan was the first English king to have coins showing him crowned. Not all such ceremonies went off smoothly however, and the modern profession of spin doctoring could be said to have had a precedent at the coronation of King Eadwig in 955, at Kingston-on-Thames. Having been "appointed ... by popular election"[45] and anointed, the new King dashed off to bed with two women. Despatched to fetch him back were an Abbot and a Bishop who found "the royal crown ... bound with wondrous metal, gold and silver gems, and shone with many-coloured lustre, carelessly thrown down on the floor ... and he ... wallowing ... as if in a vile sty". The king was dragged back with force to grace his nobles' banquet. Bards would have seized on these events (journalists were always keen on colourful stories, even then) which would have become well known rapidly enough.

By the time Dunstan, the Bishop who rescued Eadwig, had become Archbishop of Canterbury, it was his turn to devise a coronation for King Edgar, at Bath, in 973. They had some design ideas to follow from the example of the coronation of Edgar's relative, Otto the Great in Germany, in 952. While anointing gained the property of being a powerful quasi-magical spell which protected the (accordingly divinely appointed) monarch, to counterbalance thi s privilege and along with it went his own commitment by sacred promise, to uphold Christian society and principles. One way of doing this was to support the arts, learning and education and a succession of monarchs patronised monasteries and scholars and eventually founded colleges which are at the core of the

---

[44] Cannon, J. and Griffiths, R. (1998) *The Oxford Illustrated History of the British Monarchy.* Oxford: Oxford University Press.

[45] Cannon & Griffiths, op. cit., p. 29.

nation's oldest (and still leading) universities. Monarchs also issued laws, formulated with the advice of counsellors (as early precursors of opinion pollsters, as to how likely it was that such laws would be respected). Towards the end of this century the scholarly abbot Aelfric wrote that "no man can make himself king, but the people have the power to choose as king whom they please"[46].

These developments were preceded in the north by the career of Kenneth Mac Alpin, King of the Scots and Picts who similarly had popular support and Christian validation to his monarchy. Like other kings at his time and later, he was buried in a traditional special place, in his case on the island of Iona, where St Columba had based his sowing of Christianity on the mainland of Great Britain, centuries before. One of the ways in which these apparently harmonious designs of consensual authority could - and did - go wrong arose when there were quarrels over succession; purists intended that no sons born in adultery or from incest could inherit; Saxon and Scottish systems expected inheritance to be confined to males, but Picts accepted female succession. Losers in contested successions might often go into exile and plot from there against the established monarch. Any such plots inevitably required an information system by which contenders could gather support for their claims. This information system would have involved the oral culture of story telling and at specific points, of proclamations; and the established monarch would have been advised to support a story telling of their own deeds which they believed would justify their claims to power.

The scarcity of written records and the unavoidable corollary that reputations and public relations were couched in spoken forms unrecorded and now lost is certainly the reason why we are told[47] that from among the hundreds of these earliest identifiable kings in the British Isles (which configuration includes the largest island of Great Britain, the next largest, of Ireland, as well as tiny ones like Man and Wight), we know very little about most of them. Of Athelstan who died in 939, though a contemporary biography of him is lost, it is known that he was admired and recognised as king of a greater proportion of England than were earlier rulers, by other monarchs in these islands as well as in mainland Europe. He fought together with three Welsh kings, against the Scots where "one of the decisive battles of English history (was) celebrated in song and verse"[48]. Again, this will mostly have been part of the oral culture.

Surviving written information was much concerned with military history; but occasions also stand out of pilgrimages which must have been, in addition to their intrinsic purposes of worship and connection with sacred sources of strength, also occasions of social theatre. It would have been widely known that a monarch, with his or her retinue was on a journey and that will have had the effect of a statement about the monarch's good purpose. If it was thought that a pilgrimage was insincere that too would have been underlined in the communal storytelling. Journeys to Rome were made by Hywel Dda ('the good') king of the west Welsh, by Alfred of Wessex and later by Cnut

---

[46] *ibid.*, p. 36.
[47] Cannon & Griffiths, op. cit., p. 39.
[48] *ibid.*, p. 54.

of England and Norway. Hywel may be the ruler recognised on the only silver coin surviving thought to have been minted for a Welsh king.

Before the Norman conquest several means of communication were being developed to popularise the institution of monarchy. These ways included the establishment of origin-myths, ceremonial and magnificence, civil progresses and holy pilgrimages and the establishment of particularly revered (and decorated) burial sites, the issue of laws and of coinage which latter, in the absence of today's press and broadcasting, was the most widespread and valuable way of projecting the monarch's picture and name throughout the realm. The historian Bede wrote of King Edwin of Northumbria (two centuries before the time of King Alfred, this state embraced both Newcastle in today's England and as far north as Edwin'sburgh, now the capital of Scotland) that "not only were his banners borne before him in war, but even in time of peace his standard bearer always went before him as he rode between his cities, his residences and provinces with his thegns. Also, when he walked anywhere along the streets that sort of banner ... was usually borne before him"[49].

Evidently Anglo Saxon genealogies traced ancestries into an indistinct past where they merged eventually with Woden the god of war from whom all warrior kings were thought to descend. However, a heathen pedigree was not the chief asset for Christian kings whose symbiosis with the Church was promoted by those scholars, mainly in those days within the Church, who constructed a view of history which reinforced other notions of monarchy. King Alfred was projected as a latter-day David by a Welsh bishop Asser, in a biography which will have been read in Wales at the time and which would have reinforced respect there for the emerging English kingdom.

Shortly after the millennium England became the centre of an empire crossing the seas, under the rule of the king whose name is most commonly spelled nowadays Canute. More authentically called Cnut or Knud in some texts, he was baptised (in Germany, before invading England) and later made a Roman pilgrimage. His silver coins, which were minted in the Norse kingdom of Dublin had a wide currency. His memory survives to this day in the form of a tale which has radically altered in recent centuries and which is a minor "media event" that deserves some attention. The story as we generally receive it today says that Canute sat on the beach where his feet were made wet by the incoming waves. The spin usually put on the story now is that the tide (representing the unfolding future with its technical and social changes) is going to engulf us and that nobody (even including a king) can stop this; one of the messages taken from such a version is that new inventions (nuclear energy, cloning, whatever) are irresistibly going to change society and there is nothing we can do about it other than to adapt to, and preferably welcome what is upon us.

Another, and possibly more correct version of what Cnut really wanted to get across was that he showed his nobles that if one did not want to get wet, even as a King, one would put prudence before vanity and withdraw some distance up the beach. The third, and probably more correct account is that the king used the situation to reject flattery from his nobles - who may have suggested that a person of his power could halt the waves - to show them that he could not thus alter nature, and did allow his feet to get wet to demonstrate his virtue of Christian humility. The episode could be taken to illustrate the fluidity of meaning in a largely oral culture in which meanings are not rapidly and firmly fixed (as in photographs) in widely available print. However, even in today's print and broadcasting environment it is obvious that "factual events" are retold in new ways to serve new purposes.

Cnut's death in 1035 dissolved the trans-North Sea empire which was soon replaced by a cross-channel Norman one. The early Norman kings opened the way for major landowning in England by an imported aristocracy whose members, moreover, spoke a different language, French. Here was a monarchy implementing a huge media role insofar as the language of a country is a medium in which human experience is developed, experienced and recorded. The kings and their aristocracy could have chosen to speak Anglo-Saxon; they did not, but for several generations spoke Norman French. A process of adaptation was protracted and painful, but creative and useful and leaves many significant signs which are still with us. Anglo-Saxon had been a relatively simple and 'concrete' language, while the infusion of Norman French gave English a new intellectual dimension. Todays English language is half of Latin and half of Germanic parentage.

Popular heroes of Anglo-Saxon resistance to oppressive Norman rule are still the subject of books and films; to a smaller extent Hereward in East Anglia and later the much better known Robin in the East Midlands fought against Norman oppression; however there is no indication that they conceived of let alone favoured a state without a monarchy; their ideology was nationalist rather than republican. King John, whose constraints Robin resented, got the nickname Lackland and then, after he lost territories in France, Softsword. An illustration in a book by Matthew Paris shows John wearing a crown at a tilt and with a church behind him, signifying his excommunication. Many who resented the Norman king John would have preferred to have been ruled by the equally Norman king Richard, whose epithet Lion Heart stood for his reputed heroism as a Crusader and later in western Europe, where he spent more time than in England, being killed in battle in France. Legend has it that he was a good singer and was found, when imprisoned in a castle, by his servant Blondin hearing his voice from afar. Richard will not have been the only English king to have been remembered for his musical creativity; Henry VIII had a good reputation as both a performer and composer. The song Greensleeves is linked with Henry VIII as author and even if this is not true, for our purposes it is important that people thought of some of their monarchs as we now think of pop stars.

Another folk art, that of embroidery, was used to produce one of the greatest achievements in public relations of the early Norman kings. The Bayeux Tapestry was woven soon after the battle of Hastings to help justify the Norman claim to England and to publicise the victory. The tapestry is 230 feet long and will have been intended to be

---

[49] *ibid.*, p. 78.

put up in a major hall or church where many people will have seen it. Seeing such a work will have counted as a major lifetime experience for ordinary people of the day and they would in turn have told about it to spread its fame. Scenes show the funeral of Edward the Confessor, the occasion on which Harold went to Normandy and acknowledged William as the successor, and the outcome of the battle where Harold was killed.

While most books are intended to be read, William the Conqueror had another kind of book made, the Domesday survey. This can be thought of in today's terms as an early example of vanity publishing (where people of minor achievement are invited, for a price, to install their brief biographies in finely bound volumes). The Domesday survey was a comprehensive catalogue of habitations and possessions (mostly farming and livestock). We must recognise it as an artefact in which it was important to know that their existence or possessions were recorded and recognised, rather than as a good read. A more familiar kind of book was written by Geoffrey of Monmouth fifty years later in which the antique past was retold with a dignity intended to give lustre and depth to the monarchy.

In parallel with the publicity activities developed by Norman kings in England both the Scottish and Welsh kings issued charters of laws, written in the monasteries to which the monarchs had given grants. While Norman military power extended across South Wales and the Welsh kings could not display their own magnificence in costume and ceremony, they had a weapon of their own which was poetry and music. Rhys ap Gruffydd the last king of Deheubarth was reputedly lauded at an eisteddfod at Cardigan in 1176. One should think of such an occasion as having much more impact and historical durability for his own community than even the largest of concerts devised on globally-broadcast screens for the latter day king of music Michael Jackson can have for his realm - which is defined by age and taste rather than by territory and tribe, livelihood and legend.

* * *

Although in England the Domesday Book and the Bayeux Tapestry serve the reputations of the early Norman kings very well, Cannon and Griffiths in their history[50] consider that Henry I was really the first conscious propagandist for his realm, in which he considered that French and English subjects had an equal standing. For the English part of the realm a "cult" of Edward the Confessor was promoted; the old king's tomb was opened and a new revised biography was written. The next king, Henry II, promoted Edward's canonisation; nevertheless, the Franco-centric consciousness of the time still meant that his own tomb was in France, at Fontevrault where too the queen, Eleanor, and Henry's successor Richard the Lionheart were buried. We have already discussed the notion that the monarchs themselves are a medium through which important elements of the history of the nation are represented, and it is quite realistic to consider the mortal remains in their tombs as statements within such a medium by which these Plantagenet kings showed that they considered certain sites in their realms of particular importance. Incidentally, the name of the dynasty comes from the fact that these particular kings chose to wear ('plant') a sprig of broom (genet) in their helmets. This visible sign was what we might now call a logo in establishing a brand image of a product - in this case the product being the particular monarch and his brand the dynasty and their mission statement - which in today's terms might well have been "equal status for England and France".

As in the ancient ways of Egypt, China and many other monarchies British monarchs thought carefully about where and how they would be buried. For two hundred years Winchester (the site of a major cathedral) was where Anglo-Saxon kings were buried and the Danish Cnut was also interred there as a sign of his wish to establish his dynasty in the heart of England. Tombs were elaborately decorated as in the example of that of Edward the Confessor at Westminster, which carries several layers of monumental decoration. King John was buried at Worcester cathedral in between the tombs of two saints. Others of England's Norman and later kings were buried in France, including Henry II and Richard I at Fontevrault, William I himself having been buried in Caen, his Norman home. William's funeral was undignified as the corpse exploded as attendants were trying to get it into the coffin; others fared better, carried on biers in processions and with heads crowned.

The potency of the royal tomb and its contents are demonstrated not only in the veneration evoked among visitors but in the hostility vented by those who, at the dissolution of the monasteries in the mid-sixteenth century, desecrated the Confessor's tomb and by the destruction of William I's tomb and dispersal of his bones by French republican revolutionaries in the late eighteenth century. One hundred years later the French were reinterring their recent emperor Napoleon's remains in a hugely splendid mausoleum at Les Invalides. Tomb effigies of Kings and Queens were often supreme works of the arts of the time, and being placed in abbeys or cathedrals undoubtedly drew admirers and pilgrims in a mood of veneration. An extremely impressive tomb survives in Dijon of Fearless Jean the Duke of Burgundy (who died in 1419) and of his wife Marguerite; such a work would have been a spur to the artistry of others and a lifetime memorable experience in those undecorated days for anyone who saw it.

CORONATION AND ACKNOWLEDGEMENT

We have mentioned coronation as a striking ritual. From time to time modern writers wanting to disparage some of the ways, or even the whole institution of monarchy, have claimed that coronation in its current form is a recently concocted invention; some have pointed to slapstick mistakes that have occurred. The criticism of recency is clearly not wholly true; it is worth establishing both that this ceremony was in itself ancient and to a considerable extent emphasised its ancient element as the reigns and centuries

---

[50] *ibid.,* p. 165.

progressed. However, before looking at coronation itself, it is also worth considering the 'numinous' moment at which the new monarch is first recognised by an official, as such.

No name has as yet been applied to such occasions which amount to informal rehearsals of the ritualised elements of the subsequent grand public ceremonial coronation; but the term *Acknowledgement* is suggested here as appropriate, until a better one is put forward. An acknowledgement probably draws its powerful numinous quality from at least two features; the first is that the status of the recipient is radically altered, entailing that the nature of relationships between the person and all those around him or her is also at a stroke transmuted. The second feature (which expresses the first) rests in the body language and choreography of how subjects demonstrate the existence of this new centre, or pinnacle of the society, both to themselves, to others and to the new monarch her or himself.

A well received film about Elizabeth I dramatises the moment with great impact when the teenager, who has survived a spell in the (often fatal) Tower of London is told, in the most beautiful countryside setting imaginable thus evoking a notion of the best qualities of the realm, that "the (old) queen is dead - Long Live the Queen!". Queen Elizabeth II was given the news of her accession when she was in a remote beauty spot on tour in Kenya. George III was welcomed back to normal life as King in another impressive moment, recreated on a widely seen film, after he had been mentally incapacitated through porphyria and thus substituted as King by his son as Regent. It is not simply the contrived gestures of onlookers, who thereby acknowledge the new (or the renewed) monarch, that is worth noting but something that goes beyond their gestures and is contained in a new mode of regard that is remarkable. Anyone who doubts what is being said about the almost spiritual element of (at least some of) these Acknowledgements should see a portrayal in one of the films mentioned.

After the Acknowledgement, and sometimes even before the coronation, a monarch often faces a *test of his or her quality in the role.* Queen Elizabeth I was reminded by the Commons three months into her reign that she should marry to produce an heir; she replied that she would not marry to the detriment of the realm. The competence of her speech went far to establish her authority, reinforced on later important occasions such as on the eve of the arrival of the Spanish Armada. Queen Victoria was eighteen when she addressed the House of Lords: "there never was anything like the first impression she produced" wrote one witness, while the Duke of Wellington observed "she filled the room"[51]. George I, whose hereditary link justifying his accession was relatively distant and who also had less charisma than Victoria, reminded his first Parliament that "it had pleased God to call him to the throne of his ancestors"[52]. Later monarchs took successively less part in laying down policy and in late Victorian years did not even open the annual sessions of Parliament in person. This function was restarted by Edward VII, and continues to this day, with a speech written by the Prime Minister for the monarch to read.

---

[51] *ibid.,* p. 551.
[52] *ibid.,* p. 461.

Anointment at Queen Elizabeth II's coronation was connected to what was done for Ecgfrith son of Offa of Mercia in 787 and far beyond that to the procedure performed by the prophet Samuel in biblical times. Since the Norman conquest, the coronation ceremony has always been held in Westminster Abbey. During the Commonwealth (after the execution of Charles I) most of the regalia were destroyed or sold, excepting the anointing spoon and the ampulla for the oil, in the shape of an eagle. On the restoration of the monarchy, the regalia were remade with the crown intending to resemble that worn by Edward the Confessor; a new crown was made for Victoria in 1838. The anthem "Zadok the Priest" was sung at Edgar's coronation (pre-Norman, it took place in Bath) and a new setting written by Handel for George II is frequently performed not only at rare coronations nowadays but at concerts at St Martin-in-the-Fields where it is popular with tourists and has been more widely in evidence in the film *The Madness of George III*. The purpose, clearly, is to anchor current coronation in the spirituality of Old Testament times.

As some writers have pointed out, not all coronations have run smoothly. An unseemly scene erupted at George IV's coronation when his estranged wife Caroline, having decided to return from abroad tried noisily and unsuccessfully to push her way into the abbey. The reign continued as inauspiciously as it had started. In Victoria's case a Lord Rolles fell down the steps while attempting to pay homage, and jokers suggested to foreigners that he had to do what his name implied. After the anthem the queen went behind the screen to St Edward's Chapel where she found the altar covered with a picnic of wine and sandwiches. The Archbishop did not know she already had her Orb and put her ring on the wrong finger, from which it had to be painfully removed. In spite of these contretemps the public part of the day went well and the reign was hugely successful. George VI was shown an open book from which to read his oath - which was covered by the Archbishop's thumb; the monarch was unsure whether his crown was placed the right way round upon his head and when he stood up from the throne he nearly fell over, another bishop having stood on the edge of the robe. For a stammerer, he dealt remarkably well with these obstacles.

A coronation is clearly a once-in-a-lifetime event, but wearing the crown need not be. William I invented *crown-wearings* (at the feasts of Christmas, Easter and Pentecost) which were designed to show his regal self to his subjects in the major (cathedral) cities of Gloucester, Winchester and Westminster. Currently the monarch has worn her crown at the annual opening of Parliament, sitting on a throne in the house of Lords (though its sheer weight may lead to some modification of this procedure as the Queen gets older). The occasion is televised and its splendour is very widely seen. In Britain excerpts appear in news and current affairs programmes each of which delivers an audience of several million, not all of whom have seen all of such transmissions. A recent study[53] has found that substantial majorities of the public in each of England and Northern Ireland (especially) but also in Scotland and Wales (though to a slightly lesser extent) consider

---

[53] Coleman, S. (1999) *Electronic Media, Parliament and the People*. London: The Hansard Society.

that television should continue to show the annual Queen's speech from the Westminster Parliament.

What the effects of such transmissions are, must remain for conjecture. On one hand it may be said that to see such a spectacle in the home while people are doing everyday things is likely to "dilute" the awe in which the symbol might otherwise be perceived say, by the members of Parliament who do attend such a ceremony. On the other hand it may be true that the symbol of the crown has power even in prosaic settings and that for each of the millions who see it reinforces some respect. It is not known which of these processes, if either, is more likely. The question is similar to that sometimes linked with the respect with which the national flag is accorded in many countries. In America the flag is hung in a dignified way both inside and outside homes, offices and official buildings, so it is ubiquitous and commonplace. It is now illegal to burn the flag (as a political gesture - which is why enemies - usually foreign - do that) and it is severely disapproved to use it for demeaning purposes, such as for underwear. In the satire-laden sixties, and later, in Britain, it became daring or eventually a cliché of underfashion to make underwear of the flag; this behavior may be partly a cause and partly a symptom of the debasement of such symbols in modern Britain.

The crown is not merely a metaphor for the rule of the monarch, but is of course a physical object. There are several crowns in the British regalia, including the crown of St Edward - actually a recreation made for Charles II based on the previous model destroyed during the rule of Cromwell. The form of this crown is "closed" with four hoops meeting above the centre of the circlet at which point they carry a cross; the design symbolises the self contained sovereignty of a Christian monarch and was devised by or for Henry V and widely publicised at the time on coins. It may now be considered an abstruse piece of language but the difference between this closed - and Christian form, and other open-on-top forms is worth observing. The British crown jewels are a principal attraction to tourists in London, who go to experience their charismatic expression of a history in which glitter is felt to outshine the stains.

FUNERALS

Royal funerals have in some cases been almost as substantial ceremonial occasions as coronations; other occasions have been squalid. Richard III having been killed in battle was slung naked over a horse and buried at a small church near Leicester though the tomb there was broken into and the remains dispersed. Edward II, who had been murdered was denied burial by monks in Bristol but others at Gloucester stepped in and obliged. Their charity was repaid when the site became a shrine for a deposed king, with the religious tourism of the time contributing enough to the local economy to pay for a fine new choir to the abbey church.

Henry VIII had a splendid funeral, at Windsor. The carriage was drawn by eight black-draped horses and the procession was said to have been four miles long. Charles I had his head sewn back on after execution; the Parliament was concerned lest there be demonstrations were he to have been taken to Westminster, so he was more quietly interred at Windsor. William III who was perhaps more devoted to the Netherlands than to Britain was buried as quietly as possible, at midnight. While George III's funeral was said to have been solemn and impressive, that of George IV was spoiled when the coffin (made of lead) began to bulge, and had to be punctured. Queen Victoria had an impressive funeral procession through London before the coffin was taken for burial at Frogmore, alongside Windsor. Edward VII, George V and George VI were all buried in St George's Chapel, Windsor, though the abdicated Edward VIII was not. The opportunity for a funeral to allow the nation to show what it felt about a departed monarch or close member of the royal family was shown when Diana Princess of Wales died, about which (much) more is written in a later chapter.

THAUMATURGY

This word comes from Greek and means wonder-working, or magical powers and has been applied to supernatural healing powers said to be exercised by certain monarchs. The Capetian kings of France started the practice of "touching for the king's evil"; not to be outdone the English kings followed suit. The practice continued in France until the 1820s but was discontinued a century earlier in Britain, by the new Hanoverian dynasty. Queen Anne, the last to perform the act did so, among others, for the young, future literary giant Samuel Johnson. The procedure had been for the monarch to stroke the patient down their cheeks and throat, and was thought to cure scrofula and other ailments. Charles II was said to have thus treated as many as 90,000 people[54]; these came in hundreds at each organised ceremony and each person received a souvenir medallion.

A related ceremony is that of the Maundy on the Thursday before Easter. The English sovereign (from the fourth century onwards) used to wash the feet of the poor (recalling Christ's act, and establishing a quasi-divine role for the monarch); Charles II delegated the washing to one of his bishops and James II was the last to do actual washing. Since 1754 the washing has been replaced by a gift of Pennies which are still distributed, and Queen Elizabeth II does so for the number of people equal to her age, giving them a specially minted (but non negotiable) coin. The notion that a royal person transmitted supernatural power was reinforced by the mediaeval view that special holy oil (chrism) had been given by the Virgin Mary to Thomas Becket (who was murdered in Canterbury by knights believing they were doing the will of Henry II), which oil was used in subsequent coronations. Such oil itself is no longer at hand, but the ampulla or vessel used to pour it does survive and was used when anointing Elizabeth II. The idea of healing power cropped up anew when Diana Princess of Wales died, when many people reported that her touch was more than normally comforting; it was also said that her

---

[54]Cannon & Griffiths, p. 308.

ungloved hand (unlike the gloved ones thought to separate the "established royals" from the ordinary population) was part of this special dispensation (see Chapter 6).

DIVINE AEGIS: RELICS, SAINTS, AND SITES

In the middle ages it was useful, perhaps even necessary for an intruding king to claim that his arrival was backed by God. William the Conqueror asserted this, as did Henry Tudor in 1485; as we have seen, George I was invited merely by the British government to take the monarchy, but still mentioned divine backing when he arrived. A reputed fragment of the True Cross was taken by Edward I from Prince Llywelyn the last in Wales, as was the Stone of Scone from Scotland (said also to have come from the Holy Land), both these relics adding a divine aura first to the English, and later to the British monarchy.

Monarchy supported its status not only by relics but by ancestral claims as well. The English monarchy alleged that the Roman Emperor Constantine had been born at the royal city of York of an English woman who was herself said to have descended from Aeneas of Troy. The heroic Arthur, said to have ruled all Britain was related to this line, according to the early historian Geoffrey of Monmouth. The French monarchy focused on a mausoleum to the martyred Saint Denis (reputed to have carried his severed head under his arm to their last resting place) and the English kings, though without such an emotive story, wished to emulate its miraculous and saintly connections. Henry III established the shrine of Edward the Confessor (who had been canonised) at Westminster, and the devout and unworldly Henry VI tried to have King Alfred made a saint, himself becoming the focus of a cult for a generation or two.

Mediaeval English kings held that England was as well established a Christian realm as was France, as Christianity had been brought first to England by Joseph of Arimathea (who had taken Christ down from the Cross) and who had planted his staff at Glastonbury, where it had sprung into flower. Not only is the Glastonbury myth cultivated for today by the verses of William Blake, sung annually at the end of the BBC's series of Promenade Concerts, televised from the Albert Hall ("and did those feet in ancient time, walk upon England's mountains green; and was the Holy Lamb of God on England's pleasant pastures seen") but Glastonbury remains a focus for new age cultists and, not merely by happenstance the site of a noisy pop music festival.

Back to the English kings, they also argued their merit in that they had supported the pope in Rome at the schismatic time when the French had backed a rival (whose line soon disappeared) at Avignon. Before this schism popes had given primacy to the French king; the French people were "chosen by the Lord to carry out the orders of heaven" and their king was thus God's prime agent. English kings tried to leap frog this status, among other things feeling that God had favoured them in battle not only against the French, but also the Scots - whose kings had developed their own claims of roots in a divine antiquity, connected with the reputed arrival on their shores of an early apostle.

After Henry V's victory at Agincourt he was celebrated by his supporters at "the true elect of God" and his baby son (who became Henry VI and had been crowned King of France) was likened to the Christ-child as the saviour of "that special tribe the English, whose king was over all other Christian kings"[55]. Henry V followed Richard II's example in having himself called the "Most Christian King" but his son went further as "Most Christian of Christian Kings". Henry VII was flattered by the pope with three Blessed Swords and Hats and referred to by Caxton in a book printed in 1489 as "the highest and most Christian king and prince of all the world". The English were trying to emulate the titles conferred by the pope on the Spanish monarchy, and were only eventually successful - ironically - in the person of Henry VIII who was designated "Defender of the Faith". Though Henry threw off Roman papal authority he kept the title, which British monarchs retain to this day, the Latin abbreviation Fid Def appearing even now on coins. The religious status of the British monarchy is currently under discussion. Prince Charles has suggested that he might as King become a "Defender of Faith(s)" in what is now said to be a multifaith society rather than of The Faith.

ARTS AND MATERIAL CULTURE

It may seem superfluous to discuss art as though it is a separate category of expression, as it really overlaps into other areas of law, religion and military history. Nevertheless it may be a good thing to draw together an account of the artistic aspects of the many ways in which the monarchy stands itself at the head of the society.

Some of the earliest relics of British kings includes objects such as the "Alfred Jewel" of rock crystal and gold, which use the best application of human skill, taste and resources to go beyond making what is merely useful. Kings of the Dark and Mediaeval ages supported the church and the arts in the production of finely coloured and written manuscript books, as well as the buildings in which such crafts were practised. The church's validation of the monarch's ("divine") right of rule has just been discussed but on notable occasions "for popular consumption, poems and songs ... helped to persuade English subjects to accept the ideology of their king. When Henry V took Rouen ... the celebrations ... were ... expressed in execrable verse: 'And he is king ... that liveth here in earth - by right, but only unto God almighty' ..."[56].

King Richard II, while particularly keen on books was possibly also the first English king to have appointed a painter Laureate; the earliest painted portrait of a contemporary king is of a kneeling Richard II in the Wilton Diptych (now in the National Gallery) in which nine blue-robed angels wear Richard's emblem of the white hart. It can not be re-emphasised enough today that in these mediaeval times resplendent colour was expensive and rare, and so were pictures and sculptures. Ordinary people would have to walk miles to see such things and would be awed by wall paintings of English kings in

---

[55] *ibid.*, p. 272-3.
[56] *ibid.*, p. 204.

the abbots hall at Gloucester or on the roof of Beverly Minster. Many tomb effigies and other sculptures were lifelike, often finely robed and crowned and painted. Particularly splendid effigies were those of Edward the Black Prince, in knightly armour and of Eleanor of Castile, the first wife of Edward I, both in gilded bronze and intended to rival the effigies of French royal figures in Saint Denis. This Eleanor was so mourned by the king that the route of her cortege from Nottinghamshire where she died, to Westminster was marked by finely decorated stone Eleanor's Crosses. Three of these constructions survive, the best known of which is now called Charing Cross, just off Trafalgar Square in London.

Other images were in window glass, mainly seen in church buildings. Henry VI sent a portrait painter to Armagnac to make pictures of two daughters of the count so that he could choose the one he preferred as a wife, and made a successful choice in the redoubtable Margaret of Anjou. More widely known is the choice by Henry VIII of Hans Holbein the younger to produce a portrait which was remarkably successful not just in its time, but for centuries until the present. The idea was to project confidence and authority and the picture of the king with his feet apart, vastly shoulder-padded robes increasing his apparent chest width, bulging silk-hosed calves, rakishly floppy hat and bravely displayed decorative jewels, clenched fists and imperious gaze was not just a single oil painting seen by a few people at court but the template from which many copies were made; several were placed in country houses where they will have been widely seen while other copies appeared in print. In today's terms if a public relations company is commissioned to define and project a "brand" with an image that not just represents but also creates the meaning of its contents, it could not do better than Hans Holbein did for his royal client.

Holbein also painted a large fresco in the palace of Whitehall, depicting Henry, his mother and father and Jane Seymour. This painting was destroyed by fire, though copies survive. The Stuarts commissioned more elaborate work in a similar vein; Charles I was presented in elegant portraits by Van Dyck, and had Peter Paul Rubens paint the ceiling of the Banqueting House in Whitehall, with one major set piece showing the Benevolent Government of James I (south), another on the Union of England and Scotland and a centrepiece showing the Apotheosis of James I. Charles' involvement with the arts (he took a heroic part in a masque, shortly before he was executed) did not save him from his fate. However, he had recognised the political as well as artistic works of Rubens who, though a Belgian, was knighted for his work in England.

Rubens had previously received high decorations from the Spanish King Philip IV; his career not just as a painter but as an ambassador and worker for peace across a strife-torn Europe shows not just that monarchs used art, and artists, but in Rubens' case that one such genius used monarchs in his designs; unfortunately, paint and canvas and classical allegorical themes proved more tractable than did contemporary European grandees[57]. Trevor-Roper sheds much light on the mainland-European examples for

---

[57] Trevor-Roper, H. (1991) *Princes And Artists Patronage and Ideology At Four Habsburg Courts 1517-1633* New York: Thames And Hudson.

British kings, of Habsburg support for arts, artists, sciences and thinkers; thus Rudolf II in Prague attracted the astronomers Tycho Brahe and Kepler, the philosophers John Dee (from England) and Giordano Bruno - who was later burnt in Rome; Rudolf was also an avid collector of work by Durer and Titian, and supported the eccentric painter Arcimboldo).

Royal concerns with painting can be recognised down the ages in five forms. First as we have seen there were commissions to leading artists to produce thematic works. Following Charles I his son used the Italian Antonio Verrio who worked at Windsor and at Hampton Court, while Verrio's pupil James Thornhill (also knighted) painted his masterpiece at Greenwich Naval Hospital and other works for the late Stuarts and early Hanoverians. Benjamin West, an immigrant from America followed in this tradition with paintings at Windsor and in St Paul's cathedral[58]. A second though similar form of concern is where these artists succeeded in producing definitive portraits of their monarchs, and to Holbein and Van Dyck one should add the name of Nicholas Hilliard whose miniature portraits of Elizabeth I were similarly iconic. The definitive portrait is what in modern terms is achieved by a logo or a visual sign encapsulating the essential qualities it wants to get across to the viewer.

A third form of royal engagement with painting is that of the work some of them have done themselves. Victoria was an accomplished painter as was her husband Albert and so now is Prince Charles. Some of Victoria's work has been reproduced in artistic volumes; but a few of Prince Charles' water colours have been made into limited edition lithographic reproductions and sold with the money supporting charities.

Fourthly, the most ubiquitous form of royal images apart from their appearance on coins is that on postage stamps. British postage stamps not only led the world in their origination but had and continue to have a high artistic status, at first based upon and to some extent continuing a tradition of simple design. The first (Victorian) stamps (though Cannon and Griffiths claim stamps were first issued in George III's reign) showed merely a silhouette portrait of the monarch. Her image was sufficient to convey that the stamp was British, and no text was needed or provided. Other countries provided their names, such as United States on the stamp, but Britain continued without, and still observes this sign of uniqueness.

What can be claimed to be the apotheosis of postage stamp design, commemorating a monarch and all his world-wide domains was the set produced for the 25th anniversary of the reign of King George V. This, in landscape format was printed in photogravure, an expensive process producing a tangibly embossed feel to the image. The image itself was of the crowned king on the right of the stamp, looking towards a "window" on the left of the stamp and in the window was printed a picture of Windsor Castle. This castle appears solid and gives an impression of permanence and resistance to attack (by time, or other agents of change). The castle is also beautiful, so the image had several positive attributes. The set of four values of the stamp was produced for over sixty countries and

---

[58] Lloyd, C. (1998) *The Quest For Albion Monarchy and the Patronage of British Painting* London: Royal Collection Enterprises.

territories in the empire and is probably the one occasion in philatelic history when such a widespread and unifying design, of such high physical and artistic quality has been published. In fact the capital of the empire was experiencing a major economic depression, the king was to die in a year's time and a world war was to play a major part in the dissolution of the empire within the next two decades. Nevertheless, the set of stamps depicts the imperial reign as great in many ways, during the last year or so in which that was still true.

To a considerable extent in more recent years the British "brand" of philatelic - and monarchic leadership has been diluted by artists who produce "commemorative designs". In all the new designs to date there has not been any text saying United Kingdom (or other country designation) and there has been a (progressively smaller) silhouette portrait of the Queen. The Queen is still shown all new designs before they are issued and theoretically has an option to accept or reject, but towards the end of 1998 had to accept at least one example which it was reported she did not like, as millions had already been printed, ready for release. With the arrival of political assemblies for Scotland and Wales in 1999 it remains to be seen whether stamp design will reflect this diversity and if so, in what manner.

The final form of royal interest in pictures is by their own collecting and exhibition. Stuart Kings not only commissioned but also collected works by Italian masters. Charles I bought a collection of works that had belonged to the Gonzagas, dukes of Mantua, including items by Titian, Raphael and Correggio. Though the collection was dispersed during the Commonwealth much was bought back by Charles II who added a major collection of drawings by Leonardo da Vinci. Hanoverians continued to acquire major continentals' works but developed Buckingham palace and Windsor apartments more as places where they could put up work they admired for themselves, rather than devoting resources to palaces where artwork could be designed to impress and put a message across to the public.

A particularly interesting royal appointment, which did not serve the monarch's purpose in an intended way was that of William Hogarth (son in law of Sir James Thornhill) to the post of Serjeant Painter "an outmoded court position soon to fall into desuetude, with a derisory annual payment"[59]. Hogarth had an opportunity to paint some royal portraits but evidently this did not enthuse him. He opposed the creation of the Royal Academy of Arts (established under the presidency of Joshua Reynolds, who was later knighted) and was better known as a satiric artist more likely to attack pomposity and humbug and as an independent mind unlikely to work well for or within an "establishment". Indeed Hogarth lampooned John Wilkes, a writer accused by George III's ministers of sedition, even though the gesture is unlikely to have been motivated by art in the service of monarchy. George IV was passionately fond of the arts and as well as sponsoring construction of the orientalistic Brighton Pavilion he bought Rembrandts and Rubenses as well as paying for pictures by Stubbs and Gainsborough. Eventually the royal art collection has become a major resource within the nation and on occasion lends its pictures out for exhibition and otherwise shows them in small numbers at a time at the Queen's own gallery, within Buckingham Palace.

MUSIC

Music has thrived under royal patronage to varying degrees across the centuries. Henry VIII was a noted musician, singer and composer; Charles I was keen on masques, a form of total theatre in public involving music and dance, predating the work of Wagner. Many critics regard British music as of a second rank (after German music, and certainly there was nobody to surpass the "three Bs" in Britain); however, in their time Purcell and Tallis, Byrd and Boyce were the finest composers and were supported by their monarchs. Equalling the finest Germans and indeed arriving from there during the reign of Anne was Handel, who poured forth works for performance in public pleasure gardens, on the river, at the opera, in church and in the concert hall. While George II is said to have disliked poetry and painting he was a great admirer of Handel as were his father for whose coronation the anthem Zadok the Priest was arranged by the composer, and his son George III.

A note is appropriate here, on the British national anthem. The anthem was neither written by a monarch nor commissioned by one; nevertheless its arrival in Hanoverian times (its use was recorded in 1745 when the second Stewart rebellion was quashed, though it was not formally adopted until the early nineteenth century) and its use is something the monarch could have influenced either by approving what has evolved or by suggesting or requesting something else. What we have for the time being: "God Save the Queen" is not so much a national as a monarchist anthem; or it is only national inasmuch as the monarch is felt as embodying the nation. The tune of the British anthem is internationally very well known, having been harnessed by many great composers (including Beethoven) within their works and having cropped up in other nations with various different verses (America, 'Tis of Thee).

A remarkable aspect of the tune is that it is in a three-time rhythm (a slow 'waltz') and in this respect differs from most other national anthems, nearly all of which are in four time. The point is that four-time music is suitable for marching and evokes a physical response in terms of body movements that are walking or running steps, which lend themselves to going forwards and to doing so in large groups of people. In short, such music is militarist. A waltz (like a tango, samba or other more complex beats) demands a higher level of mental rather than just bodily engagement in order to embody it, or sing it. This simple structural feature of the anthem is not just something (accidentally?) unique, intellectually demanding - and unsuited to militaristic expression; it also has some bearing on what becomes of it at the end of the century.

Half way through the century, at the end of World War II the national anthem was a widely revered piece. It was played in British cinemas at the end of the day's screening,

---

[59] *ibid.*, p. 16.

accompanied by a short film (in colour, often contrasting with the more drab black-and-white of many movies then) and the audience stood to attention; when it finished, they went out. As years went by audiences became impatient and exited before the anthem finished (only standing in order to leave, rather than to respect the anthem, or the monarch); cinemas then developed a much shortened version and eventually dropped the procedure altogether. The anthem is now played at national ceremonies such as a royal jubilee or a major anniversary of the end of a war, and, crossing from one form of mass entertainment to another (though sport may be seen as war by other means, fortunately without death or even intent to injure), at football stadiums and athletic competitions if and when a British player or team has won something.

Since the four component British nations play against each other at soccer and rugby football, a division has been evolving in which Scotland and its supporters express their loyalties through the song Scotland the Brave, and the Welsh through Land of my Fathers. The cohesion and appeal evoked by God Save the Queen is thus breaking down, and with the arrival of political assemblies for each constituent nation, and with questions about the relation of each nation and of the whole United Kingdom with Europe (which is beating the drum for its own superordinate anthem) it is an area not just for research to note what evolves but leaving at least some option for the monarchy and the political authorities to offer alternatives and for the people to have some influence on what happens. The question is in the melting pot not just for the monarchy in Britain but also for other European countries such as France, where the Marsellaise will die hard and Belgium which may choose not to replace La Brabançonne

BUILDING AND SCULPTURE

Architecture and sculpture have been self-consciously harnessed by several British monarchs. Edward I had built not just a military work at Caernarvon Castle but an object of beauty - as well as of terror to some - to rival others on the continent; a statement of several meanings in his principality of Wales. The royal Scottish achievements in building castles, at Edinburgh and Stirling and the palaces at Holyrood, Linlithgow and Falkland are very fine. (Although the painting collection at Holyrood is modest, one in a series of portraits - not claimed to have been from life - of an early Scottish king called Grimus has an odd resemblance to Salman Rushdie, whose first novel has that title; could this have been one of his jests?). Henry VI had a close interest in the building of Eton College at Windsor and of King's College in Cambridge; in the chapel of the latter is fine woodwork in which the carved initials of HR (Henricus Rex - referring to Henry VIII) appear. Windsor Castle, begun by William the Conqueror has been reworked by various monarchs including Charles I and George IV.

George IV, when Prince Regent not only supervised the erection of the elaborate and orientally-influenced Brighton Pavilion but also encouraged the architect and urban planner John Nash to lay out a section of London leading from Regent Street, lined with elegant town houses, to Regent's Park, studded with elegant country houses. Much of this survives and Regent's Park still serves as a major asset for the city, of a central breathing space affording a vision of countryside beauty in the town and helping to circulate clean air.

Currently Prince Charles has taken a major interest in architecture, seeking to encourage its expression in ways which respect and harmonise with people and the natural environment. His views conflict with those who emphasise difference (from what has gone before) and whose materials (concrete, metals, glass) are transformed further from their natural mineral origins than are the more traditional building materials of wood, brick and tile. A vigorous debate is thus set up in which the future monarch's views probably come closer to what 'ordinary' people like and feel, than to the more refined opinions of experts and aesthetes.

BOOKS AND TEXTS

Cannon and Griffiths claim that the Tudor kings' development of an embryonic civil service with which to administer the England and Wales "was largely responsible for the emergence ... of a standard written English ... It amounted to an official written dialect sponsored by the king ... Efforts were consciously made to ensure its use as the language of administration even in dominions such as Ireland, Wales and Calais ... it helped to make the monarchy and its administrative machine the focus of an increasingly self-conscious and united English nation"[60].

Succeeding Henry VIII his young son Edward VI leaned towards Protestantism and religious reform. His guide the Duke of Somerset had a Book of Common Prayer in English, introduced. They first tried to impose the English service in Cornwall, which led to an uprising, followed soon after by another one in Norfolk. Though these disturbances were quelled, the Duke of Somerset (who was the king's own uncle) was overthrown and, as the young King noted in his journal "had his head cut off on Tower Hill". Catholicism continued to hold sway in Scotland and three reigns later Charles I who had used the Anglican forms of worship himself, decided to have a Scottish prayer book, based on the English one. The congregation who witnessed the first use, in Edinburgh in 1637, rioted, and an uprising which was forcefully put down, followed.

By this time the joint nation had acquired what Winston Churchill referred to as a "splendid and lasting monument ... to the genius of the English-speaking peoples". James VI of Scotland and I of England had convened a conference at which an Oxford academic asked if a new translation of the Bible should be produced. James was enthusiastic and scholars were assembled in various places, assigned to parts of the task. Churchill emphasises "in an age without an efficient postal service or mechanical means of copying and duplicating texts, the committees, though separated by considerable distances, finished their task in 1609 and ... in 1611 the Authorised Version ... was

---

[60] Cannon, J. and Griffiths, R. (1998) *The Oxford Illustrated History of the British Monarchy.* Oxford: Oxford University Press, p. 260.

produced by the King's Printer". Churchill pointed out that no new revision was called for for nearly three hundred years; most emigrants to America took a few books with them - usually including this Authorised Version of King James I, still the most popular version, thought by 1956 to have had ninety million copies made of it[61]. Churchill gives generous credit: "This may be deemed James's greatest achievement, for the impulse was largely his".

An occasional monarch has inspired poets and artists to celebrate him or her. This happened most notably with Elizabeth I, whom Ben Johnson wrote of as Queen and huntress, chaste and fair and whom Edmund Spenser celebrated in his *Faerie Queene* as Gloriana. Shakespeare made a heroic and likeable figure of Henry V. A genre of historical novels ranges from Walter Scott's Ivanhoe along to works by many modern writers and while some do their best to be realistic others tend to romanticise monarchs such as the chivalrous Richard I, the wicked John, as well as the glorious Elizabeth I. Monarchs have, however, less often been the subjects of quasi-fiction than they have been real life collectors of books.

George III's library, in which he had added to ancient and distinguished manuscripts newer works on music, botany and on the Civil War, was admired by the first American ambassador James Adams. The royal library at Buckingham House had been open to scholars, and George IV donated 65,000 books to the new British Library. The Windsor royal archives, considerably added to by Victoria and Albert are now open to scholars. Some monarchs had been writers themselves; James VI of Scotland, before he added the English crown to his collection had authored *Trew Law of Free Monarchies* and *Basilikon Doron* both works arguing the divine right of kings. His son Charles also produced *Eikon Basilikon* which Cannon and Griffiths[62] assert "became one of the most influential books of all time, and established, as he had hoped, Charles as a martyr for his people".

BODY LANGUAGE AND SYMBOLIC SIGNS OF HONOUR

Perhaps the most dramatic way in which bodily behavior could signal leadership was in battle. We can think of war as a medium through which statements are made and meanings are conveyed to subjects as well as to adversaries. A monarch whose side wins a battle transmits a clear message of successful leadership, or of where it has been missing. British kings (to include Welsh and Scottish with the English) provided many examples of this. Going no further back than the Norman conquest, the Anglo Saxon Harold had no sooner beaten off one invading army at Stamford Bridge in the north when he had to walk nearly 300 miles south and face the second invader - to whom he lost his

---

[61] Churchill, W.S. (1956) *A History of the English-Speaking Peoples Vol 2 The New World.* London: Cassell, pp. 119-120.

[62] Cannon, J. and Griffiths, R. (1998) *The Oxford Illustrated History of the British Monarchy.* Oxford: Oxford University Press, p. 386.

kingdom and his life. English Kings Edward I and III were great fighters, just as Edward II was an ineffective one; Edward II was beaten at Bannockburn by the Scottish King Robert (the Bruce) the former losing much of his charisma; eventually he was deposed and put to death in a grisly way that symbolised a horror of his perceived homosexuality. Homo- or bisexuality itself may not have been an insuperable difficulty in a king; Richard I was both married and greatly admired for his military prowess and James I (of England, VI of Scotland) though married, was thought also to have had particularly close friendship with a man whom he raised to the status of the Earl of Somerset. Henry VII was of Welsh descent and won his kingdom on the field of battle against Richard III. To win was taken as a sign of divine support while to lose did not necessarily indicate divine disapproval, though in the case of Richard III it was used to argue that his coronation had not been valid. Where there were no battles for the time being tournaments were arranged and these were dangerous. The English King Henry VIII had a narrow escape when jousting with an open visor and Henry II of France was killed in a similar way.

The last British king to lead his forces in battle was George II, who did so at Dettingen. On the continent similar feelings of admiration were fostered about monarchs who won in battle and amongst many others an equestrian portrait of the Emperor Charles V by Titian celebrates his victory over protestant armies as Muhlberg. Earlier, Joan of Arc had similarly won glory and is celebrated in sculpture wearing romantic armour today in a major Parisian square. Perhaps curiously, though several naval battles were turning points in international conflicts, hardly any featured a monarch or heir as a victorious admiral. This provides a question for future (arcane, though likely very interesting) research: the English have a Henry V whose land battle leadership is admired and celebrated in painting and verse; most other nations have their own similarly successful figures - why is there such a scarcity of monarchs who are victorious at sea? Especially amongst the seafaring nations of the north European littoral?

The institution of knighthood was celebrated by several romantic writers and poets who projected from mediaeval practice to its supposed origins in a Celtic Arthurian model of a Round Table. The idea of initiation by and after gallant deeds and a dedication of self to service of God and the monarch was pictured in the scene of the novice on his knees all night, and of his receiving a knightly title from the monarch (or senior representative) while on bended knee. The fifteenth century saw two dynastic revolutions in England and probably reflecting the need to underline their greatness kings encouraged courtly manners which would dramatise their exalted position. Thus Richard II insisted that his subjects approach him on bended knee, a custom which continued in the next century and Edward IV got people to say Majesty when addressing him.

One practice which has continued until the present and which now draws forth some satirical derision is for the monarch to refer to him or herself reflexively. An example is where Richard II legitimized bastard-born children of the Beaufort family referring to them as "our most dear kinsmen ... sprung from royal stock' ... he also said 'the more we bestow honours on wise and honourable men, the more our crown is adorned with gems and precious stones'[63]. The glamour of knighthood reached its peak in the creation of the Order of the Garter, with self-conscious reference to the Arthurian Round Table, whose "corporate headquarters" were at the chapel of St George at Windsor. Selection of new members, up to a quorum of twenty four is still at the Queen's discretion; they still wear blue mantles with the escutcheon of St George and a blue garter on the right leg.

Other orders of chivalry around the British monarchy include the order of the Thistle, originating in the fifteenth century, and revived by Scottish King James VII (English James II), with a green sash and restricted to the sovereign and sixteen Scottish knights. A more widely drawn Order of the Bath was started in 1725 by George I, after mediaeval antecedents, and has a civil as well as a military sector. More recently the Order of St Michael and St George was set up for diplomats and the Royal Victorian Order was founded by Victoria for members of her (and later the royal) household. Edward VII established an Order of Merit, in 1902 with membership allocated to supreme achievers in the worlds of art, literature and music. Thomas Hardy and Edward Elgar were early members, while Lord Yehudi Menuhin was a widely known more recent member. Much more widely given still are the five grades of the Order of the British Empire. However, though these "gongs" are awarded on the Prime Minster's advice toward the millennium and with the Empire receding into a past century modernisers are proposing not just reformulating such a system, but even abolishing it altogether. Since the reformers are drawn from the political class many of whose members did and would still gain such titles it remains to be seen whether ideological demoticism prevails over vanity. Such honours systems are not unique to Britain but most countries have their equivalents.

Over the centuries and still today these British orders of chivalry use costume and jewelry (including medals) and through ceremonial processions also gesture to show, by such body language that they are a part of, and do not just decorate but even help to support a monarchy. In being the ultimate giver of honours the monarch makes statements in public about who is important and valued, and in what ways. The monarch's generosity was not always reciprocated. At the time of William III and Mary, who had showered honours including a dukedom on the great general John Churchill and thus on his wife Sarah, the monarchs received only barbs from the latter, who, after her husband had been dismissed from his commandership in the Netherlands referred to the King as "Caliban, or the Dutch monster".

It may be assumed that a hereditary peerage system (contrasted with the orders of chivalry, none of which are hereditary) will eventually grow until it becomes unmanageable, or it is stopped by modernisers - assuming a contradiction between a hereditary principle and modernity[64]. There were some brakes on the process, as when

---

[63] *ibid.,* p. 252.

[64] In many western and thus (?) modern countries personal wealth is (largely) passed down to one's descendants; for most people, so is the paternal (sur)name. Thus in private terms a hereditary principle is acknowledged - in rare exceptions, as in Iceland, paternal name is not the automatic surname of all offspring. Some families in republican states (Kennedys, Rockefellers, Bushes,

George II was keen not to dilute the value of the peerage by profligate appointments, and granted fewer of these titles than did previous monarchs. It was said of George II in the memoirs of a courtier Lord Hervey that "he hated the English, looked upon them all as king-killers and republicans ... (and said that) he was forced to distribute his favours here very differently from the manner in which he bestowed them at Hanover; that there he rewarded people for doing their duty and serving him well, but that here he was obliged to enrich people for being rascals, and buy them not to cut his throat"[65]. The monarch must nevertheless have carried considerable clout since though he disliked his minister William Pitt, the latter was well known for his fawning to the extent that he bowed so low that his nose could be seen from behind between his bowed legs.

Although monarchs could have used the power to create peers to continue to support the monarchy this option was dramatically reduced during the reign of William IV. He had not expected to inherit the throne and had a naval life after which he settled down with (though he was not married to) an actress. He evidently did not take too readily to the accustomed manners of monarchy and a Mrs Arbuthnot wrote of him that "The King is somewhat *wild* and talks and shows himself too much. He walked up St James's Street the other day quite alone, the mob following him, and one of the common women threw her arms around him and kissed him. However, I hope he will soon go out of town and be quiet"[66]. One of the interesting elements of this observation is that a common woman should want to kiss or show affection to a person she has never seen before. The woman clearly has no real knowledge of the admired figure but, like those who follow entertainment stars of today, possibly feels a need to embrace the role (of glamour, fame, strength or beauty) within the (quite possibly frail and even disappointing) actual person.

Early in this century difficulties in passing a budget led the prime minister Asquith to propose to create (by getting the King, Edward VII to comply) enough new hereditary peers of the right political hue to be amenable to the power in the Commons. Asquith returned to the project soon, in the next reign, of George V who was very reluctant to allow such alterations. Queen Victoria had been strongly against an earlier attempt to emasculate the House of Lords, arguing that the hereditary peerage and hereditary monarchy went together. The same arguments have recurred in the last administration of the century, which has now done what Victoria had opposed, though without explicitly committing itself to destabilising the monarchy (indeed, while claiming that it merely wants to modernise it).

Alongside the slow erosion on powers of the Lords has been a continued support of pageantry using the very peers and palaces under threat of removal. A little known piece of royal drama once involved the King's Champion, which was an office hereditary in the Dymoke family of Lincolnshire. The champion was to fling down the gauntlet at the

---

Ghandhis in India) have non-automatically conferred a political advantage upon descendants, but it is generally argued that an automatic access to parental political privilege (and also duties) is objectionable.

[65] *ibid.*, p. 475.

[66] *ibid.*, p. 548.

coronation banquet and offer to fight any rival claimant (to the just crowned monarch). The challenge was of course never taken up and without any such reality test came to be taken not seriously to the extent that at the coronation of George IV (which we have seen, above, was not too orderly in any case) the new king behaved "very indecently: he was continually nodding and winking at Lady Conyngham and sighing and making eyes at her"[67]. George IV had scandalised people and made enemies while he was Prince Regent and did not get on much better when he became king.

The British monarchy continued to survive royal body language from the next king, which fell short of what were considered desirable standards. While George IV was grossly fat and the butt of cartoons and what might now be called fatism in abuse of human rights, though he compounded the impression he gave by indulging in behavior that was gross as well, his successor William IV was merely uncouth. The American author Washington Irving noted that "His Majesty has an easy and natural way of wiping his nose with the back of his forefinger"; the king also made inebriated speeches calling the new French king Louis Philippe an "infamous scoundrel" and the French as a whole "the natural enemies of England"[68]. Such behavior in a mediaeval king may not have prompted comment, though by the time of the Stuarts, who used to show themselves to the people (or at least some of them) by eating formally at the banqueting hall, their requirement that waiters should bow and walk backwards away from the royal presence suggests that a refinement of manners had by then become established, and an inelegant departure from such refinement would find criticism.

Standards of personal hygiene, given the technology of the times, have only relatively recently been improved, and not just in Britain. Queen Elizabeth I went on "progresses" or transfers of the court to locations around the country not just to be seen by a wider section of the people but because the palace they were staying in became smelly and had to be opened and aired to revive them. Patrick Suskind in a novel set in pre-revolutionary France dramatically describes the stench not just in outdoor public places but also in grand houses and even palaces, which the nobility dealt with by overlaying it with perfume[69]. Stuart monarchs spent a great deal of their lives in public - or in view of courtiers who could report what they had seen - and much formality surrounded events. They began then to use a withdrawing room to afford the sovereign some privacy, but it soon became a drawing room where he held interviews. A similar phenomenon is found in Muslim palaces ranging from the Saray (Seraglio) at Istanbul to the Mogul courts in North India where the *diwan-i-am* or room of the people (diwan being the same as divan, or couch on which the monarch sat, or sprawled) was supplemented by the *diwan-i-khas* or withdrawing room. There, of course, special arrangements were set up for a separation of sexes and for the harem which, though jealously guarded from prying eyes eventually became shown to western viewers in paintings by the Frenchman Ingres, and others.

---

[67] *ibid.*, p. 540.
[68] *ibid.*, p. 546.
[69] Suskind, P., *Perfume*.

Royal body language continued to change with the years, and personal circumstances. Victoria was bereft when her husband died and withdrew into black clothes and dark surroundings for many years. Her ministers came to believe that the monarchy was endangered by the protracted absence of the queen from visible symbolisation of the nation's life. She eventually thawed, not it is said, in response to political urgings but through the reassurance she gained in a deep friendship with her Scottish ghillie (hunting guide) William Brown. It is said that through his openness she came to understand something of the nature of life in another nation (Scotland) and at a level as distant as possible from the position of the aristocracy, a story which has been dramatised in a movie called *Mrs Brown*. Eventually she returned to visible regal duties and was succeeded by her son Edward VII, whose protracted and probably frustrating wait had made him a very different person. He had known mistresses - alongside a well liked queen - and took active part in society life, as did his grandson, the briefly-reigning Edward VIII who abdicated.

Two Kings George - V and VI offered a more dignified demeanour. George VI stayed with his wife Elizabeth in London during the bombing. The two had visited America and had made a cordial friendship with President Roosevelt, which may have been at least one element in eventually recruiting America into the Allied war effort. The monarch's behavior when the palace received a direct bomb hit was to be pictured in amongst the damage. When the Queen was asked whether it would be safer for the two princesses to be sent to one of the Dominions she replied "the children won't leave without me; I won't leave without the King; and the King will never leave"[70]. Such resolute speech has its counterpart in the physical gesture of residence among the people.

SOME PARALLEL INFORMATION FROM INDIA

Pre-Christian era texts in India include a textbook called the *Arthasastra* attributed to Kautilya, a minister of one of the Gupta kings, and which was concerned with statecraft. Another early work is the twelfth book of the epic, the *Mahabharata*, known as *Santi Parvan*, also dealing with statecraft. These books pick up on a legend in a Vedic text, the *Aitareya Brahmana* (perhaps of the 7th century BC, thus written not far away from the Biblical book of Chronicles, explaining the introduction of kings at the time of the prophet Samuel); the Vedic legend says that the gods and demons were at war, the former doing poorly. They appointed Soma as their king and the military tide soon swung their way. A parallel legend takes a different form in which the discomfited gods sacrificed to the high god Prajapati, who sent his son Indra (identified with Soma) to become king (of the gods). The king was thus explained and justified as a military leader, and suffused with divine authority. Later, in early Buddhist times (three and two hundred years before Christ) a more civilian notion arose, of the origin of kings. In this story

---

[70] Cannon, J. and Griffiths, R. (1998) *The Oxford Illustrated History of the British Monarchy.* Oxford: Oxford University Press., p. 612.

mankind originally lived in a sort of fairyland where there was no need for food, clothing, private property or laws. Presently, all manner of stratification developed involving private property and conflict and so "the people met together and decided to appoint one man from among them to maintain order in return for a share of the produce of their fields and herds. He ... received the title of *raja* because he pleased the people. The derivation ... from the verb *ranjayati* ("he pleases") is certainly a false one, but it was widely maintained ...".

Similar to the Israelite and western practice of Coronation, the pre-Buddhist kings in India were imbued with special powers through royal sacrifices and by a *Royal Consecration* (*Rajasuya*). This involved a series of sacrifices which might last a year and a gesture in which the king took three steps on a tiger's skin, thus matching the god Vishnu, whose three paces covered earth and heaven. "Implicit in the whole brahmanic ritual was the idea of the king's divine appointment, and though the rajasuya was replaced in later times by a simplified *abhiseka*, or anointment, the ceremony still had this magical flavour"[71]. In the more Buddhist model the head of government is the first social servant "ultimately dependent on the suffrage of his subjects".

There were thus two Indian models of kingship, and Bisham says the author of the Arthasastra was quite aware of kings' human nature, but "recognised that legends about the origin of kingship had propaganda value" (p. 84). This author advised that a king's agents should spread the story that the first king was elected; but also that, as the king fulfils the functions of the gods Indra and Yama (the god of death), all who slight him will be punished by heaven. He is advised to have his agents disguised as gods so that his simpler subjects may believe that he mixes with gods on equal terms. Asoka and other Mauryan kings took the title "Beloved of the Gods" and were looked on as semi-divine beings. Eventually the Asokan title of raja was expanded (where it might be justified) to labels of "great kings" (maharaja) and "king of kings" (rajatiraja).

There were periods between established dynasties (Mauryas and Guptas) in which mass lawlessness occurred and a dread of anarchy ("the way of fishes - where the stronger eat the weaker") developed. These experiences strengthened royal prestige where kings did establish themselves. Nevertheless the *Arthasastra* says that "the king's good is not that which pleases him, but that which pleases his subjects". The king was told that he must always be accessible to his people. The best of Indian kings at all times have made the public audience or darbar an important instrument of government. Visitors to Akbar's (abandoned) city of Fatehpur Sikri will see the splendid pavilion from which the Emperor displayed himself ("*darshan*" - the same word as used for "broadcasting", nowadays) and the chamber in which he (like other Muslim rulers) held audiences (the *diwan-i-am*). The British raj set up two occasions on which first Queen Victoria and then George V went to India to be seen in massive and glittering ceremonies, though these did not offer opportunities for audiences at which grievances might be heard and largesse given.

---

[71] This passage and the remaining Indian material are found in Basham, A.L. (1967) *The Wonder that Was India*. Calcutta: Rupa & Co.

One important figure in the traditional Indian royal entourage was the *suta* "who combined the functions of royal charioteer, herald and bard ... another ... was the *vidusaka* ... who corresponded approximately to the court jester of medieval Europe" (Bisham, p. 91). As in Europe where monarchs made their progresses, Indian kings were similarly constantly on the move. Business was combined with pleasure (mostly hunting, evidently) but going beyond European practices many inscriptions on stone and copper, from the days of Asoka onwards record the munificence of kings to religious charities. Many kings were good writers and one, Samudra Gupta was a famous musician on some of whose coins he is shown as playing the harp.

SUMMARY

British monarchs have made purposive use of whatever were the current means of establishing their presence and powers. The media thus used included oral communications of speech, verse and song, written communications in hand-written and then printed books; painted and sculpted images were and still are used in many ways, including commissioning new works, buying existing ones, and making them oneself in a few instances. There have been specifically appointed poets laureate, masters of the king's music and appointed painters. Dramas with classical themes were drawn upon (see the previous chapter) as masques and other open air forms of widespread public entertainment; and rituals and ceremonial occasions were organised to project the monarchy. Other theatrical forms include the establishment of orders of chivalry, the members of which now extend quite widely throughout society. Some of these ceremonials and institutions have not functioned as smoothly as intended and in a few cases have been avoided; but evidently more often than not they have been affirmations of support for the institution of monarchy.

It may be thought now, that the evidence is simple (even if copious), that the message has been well put across and that opposition to or erosion of the status of monarchy has thus been negligible. Such conclusions are not altogether true, and the next chapter looks as some of the opposition to monarchy that has been expressed in different ways, down the centuries.

Chapter 4

OPPOSITION TO MONARCHY

There has always been opposition to rulers and symbolic heads of state, and thus to monarchs, as individuals; and there has also often been opposition to monarchy, as an institution. This chapter explores how such opposition has been expressed and whether "media" have been harnessed in particular or interesting ways in order to make opposition effective. The first mental step required is to realise again that media does not mean just the big three mass message systems of today, print, sound and vision broadcasting, but includes some pathways of expression which opposition to monarchy may need to use because it is denied access to more customary channels.

The historian Dulcie Ashdown[72] has referred to "propaganda by deed" as one mode or medium by which opposition has been expressed and has given many examples from world-wide history which illustrate this category. To such deeds which are more normally recognisable as rebellion and revolution, we will add a very unusual and limited category of opposition, that of expression by the divine intermediary, and then come to look first at instances where opposition has been exerted through mass message systems in a less, and then in a more ideologically grounded fashion. The difference between expressions that are ideologically grounded and others which may be emotionally urgent but inchoate in terms of political theory is important and is likely to interact with the ways in which mass message systems have been used. It may be tempting to say that print is the system by which a politically and ideologically coherent opposition may best be mounted, but there is at least one example in modern times where audio cassette as much as print is said to have been instrumental in successfully dismantling a monarchy.

---

[72] Ashdown, D.M. (1998) *Royal Murders: Hatred, Revenge and the Seizing of Power*. London: Sutton.

TOP DOWN OPPOSITION

Before we come to look at examples of propaganda by deed we should look at the rare instances in which the divine intermediary has opposed a monarchic. The first instance is probably that in which the prophet Samuel, having albeit reluctantly anointed Saul as King of Israel, eventually came to transmit the divine judgement that Saul's line could not inherit the monarchy, because of Saul's own shortcomings (he disobeyed a - particularly ruthless divine commandment to slaughter women and children and livestock, as well as the men of an enemy kingdom). The medium in this case was the prophet and the line of communication was that between the divinity and the monarch. Samuel's move was effective, and the monarchy passed to the "stock of Jesse" in the person of David, with results that reverberate down three millennia in the Judaeo-Christian world. Note that it was just the monarch and not monarchy as an institution which came under attack in this instance.

From India comes a quasi-historical case in which a legendary king Vena erred in exaggerating his own divinity and forbade all sacrifices except those to himself, and confused society by enforcing inter-class marriages. Divine sages remonstrated with him and when he continued in his behavior slew him with blades of sacred grass which had miraculously turned into spears in their hands[73].

In what may be thought a relatively trivial further example, but one which is structurally similar to the judgement on Saul there is the case of the Papal effort to excommunicate not just the Doge but the whole polity of Venice at the beginning of the seventeenth century. Some may object that the Doge was not a king and that Venice was thus a republic, with an elected leader; however the term Doge is cognate with the title Duce for the (fascist) dictator Mussolini, or Duke; and a historian of Venice[74] points out (p. 19) that the elected ruler "was accepted by the princes of Europe as one of themselves". Indeed, he lived in a palace, presided over the "most Serene" Republic, and was celebrated by a good deal of pomp with golden staircases and trumpeters, arts and architecture putting him on a pedestal that may be thought to have been somewhat above that of other presidential leaders, who may try to put it across that they are still, even in office, of the common people.

When in 1605 Pope Paul V decided for various political reasons to excommunicate Venice (and thus outlaw its Doge) the latter, Leonardo Dona rejected the diktat and declared that he recognised no power except the Divine Majesty[75]. He intended to remain within the Catholic fold and essentially won this conflict. Two years later the Pope withdrew the edict. Here we have the case that God's Representative (the Pope) relayed fundamental opposition to what was evidently a polity not much different from a monarchy, but where that mediation was a failure.

---

[73] Basham, A.L. (1967) *The Wonder That Was India*. Calcutta: Rupa & Co, p. 58.

[74] Robbins Landon, H.C. & Norwich, J.J. (1991) *Five Centuries of Music in Venice*. New York: Schirmer.

[75] op. cit., p. 69.

A fourth case of quasi-divine intercession, in this case successful was that of the Ayatollah Khomeini's opposition to the Shah of Persia[76]. The Shah had tried to westernise his country, but also, in a effort to aggrandise his own status and that of his monarchy, by a giant festivity at the site of the ancient city of Persepolis, to demonstrate some connection between the then present and other famous monarchies of the long distant past. Khomeini had been banished and lived in Paris, where he became a focus for what are described as fundamentalist Islamic ideals. These do not exclude a place for monarchy, as the long history of Caliphates and Sultanates shows, but in this case the Ayatollah urged on a priestly leadership for the country (with himself as overall leader!). He achieved this end by recording messages on audio tape, which were mass produced and distributed through bazaar sales and personal contacts and which, together with eventual mass opposition to the oppression exerted by the secret police, Savak, evoked mass public demonstrations eventually leading to the deposition of the Shah and the new leadership of Khomeini[77].

BOTTOM UP OPPOSITION: PROPAGANDA BY DEED

Ashdown recites a list of cases where the opposition first comes from a very close subordinate to the monarch, in effect being a within-palace coup. Such coups were often pre-empted by the monarch's own counter-measures. Between 993 and 1058 five Scottish kings were murdered by cousins who succeeded them on the throne. In Russia in the 18th century Peter I had his own son killed, and Catherine II had her husband put to death. In India Shah Jehan's third son Aurangzeb despatched his two elder brothers so that he inherited the throne; and the Turkish Sultanate with its harem produced so many sons that internecine murder was rife before successors emerged on the throne, with their brothers in bags weighted down at the bottom of the Bosphorus.

These oppositions were by no means to the idea of monarchy, merely to its embodiment. This makes their case very different from those of the assassinations which occurred at the turn of the 19th century in Europe, when five kings and a consort queen and empress were killed. As Ashdown puts it, this was the culmination of a half-century of revolutionist murders in which the major success had been that of killing the Russian Tsar Alexander II in 1881. At that time it was common to refer to the assassins as anarchists, a catch-all term for every shade of extremist ideology including socialists (who should not really be termed anarchist) and nihilists (who may more properly earn that title). In contemporary times Queen Elizabeth II was shot at in public - albeit with blanks, which she could not have realised at the time - by an a-theoretical assailant; King

---

[76] Generally termed Persia, in the West, the name Iran was then preferred by the ecclesiastical leadership. Both names for the country continue to be used, in different contexts (Persia especially when referring to its arts and crafts).
[77] Kapuscinski, R. (1986) *Shah of Shahs*. London: Pan Books.

Hussein of Jordan was the target of several assassination attempts (his father Abdullah was killed by one) and plots were made on the life of the King of Spain.

Looking back at Indian history the *Mahabharata* allows revolt against a wicked king: the claims of kings on occasions were thus challenged. Buddhist stories which Basham says were "not historical but which reflected conditions in Northern India well before the beginning of the Christian Era, gave more than one instance of kings deposed by mass revolt" (op. cit., p. 89). In some cases monarchs bowed to popular pressure if they wanted to keep their thrones, as in the experience of the king of Vijayanagara, Krishna Deva Raya, who remitted a marriage tax because it was not popular. Basham explains that divinity was cheap in ancient India and godliness was seen in every brahman and respected ascetic; moreover the gods themselves were fallible and capable of sin. So harsh rule was not a reason for necessary rebellion on theological grounds but it could eventually evoke hostile reaction if it caused widespread suffering and grievance.

BRITISH GESTURES AGAINST MONARCHS

British histories (that is, in Scotland and Wales as well as in England, and then in the Union) include many examples of serious in-palace, and of popular disturbances against the monarch. The first set of such cases to be related are those where the action has not necessarily involved a clear view that monarchy itself could and should be replaced by another form of rule - presumably a republican democracy. Probably the best known of such stories of agitation is that involving the quasi-historical figure of Robin Hood. As many cinemagoers know, he fought against the harsh rule of the Bad King John, seizing royal assets (money, goods, animals protected for the royal hunt) and distributing them to needy ordinary people. The stories make it clear however, that there was admiration for the supposedly Good King Richard (who in fact kept himself away at Crusades, and later was a prisoner and adventurer on the European mainland); so Robin was not an ideological anti-monarchist.

Outside the realm of fiction Cannon and Griffiths (op. cit., pp. 205-6) point out that, just like the Indian case there was an obligation on English monarchs to rule considerately but, if they did not, there was "no recognised or earthly means by which a king could be corrected or removed if he failed to discharge his obligations at least passably well. But practical pressures could be exerted on him ... extreme violence could be offered against him, as happened on at least six occasions between 1327 and 1485" (and, as we know, in 1649, to which we will come). Before 1327 opposition to the king had been mediated primarily through nobles and had brought into being a Parliament containing at least some representation from lesser landowners, merchants and clergy. Rarely however did crises reach the point at which a monarch had to be deposed nor, in these centuries, at which the whole institution of monarchy was cast aside. Henry III was criticised for exploiting his subjects and benefiting his favorites to the extent that "the first attempt to wrest actual control ... from the king ... took place in 1258"[78]. The king "humbled himself ... and made solemn oath ... that he would fully and properly amend his old errors ..." (op. cit., p. 208). Edward II was felt by his nobles to be incompetent (beaten in battle by the Scots) and disliked for his homosexual friendship with Piers Gaveston and was dethroned in 1327 (though it was described as abdication) and eventually murdered. A century after this the Scots did something similar when barons assassinated James I whose rule, though benevolent in some aspects had made enemies amongst some of the aristocracy.

When kings died of natural causes there was an opportunity for the succession to be challenged. At a time when it could take a week to travel across the realm it took this long to carry the news of Edward IV's death to his son at Ludlow on the Welsh border. In the turbulent fourteenth and fifteenth centuries ruling monarchs did their best to command the channels of communication but opponents, such as the Yorkists during the wars of the Roses "were especially skilled at circulating newsletters and propaganda against their Lancastrian enemies" [79].

When Henry VIII was succeeded by Edward VI, aged nine, the boy's uncle was appointed Protector. Amongst the latter's deeds was to move towards Protestantism, including the introduction of an English language prayer book, in Cornwall in 1549. This led to one serious rising in which Exeter was besieged and to another led by Ket, in Norfolk, where sixteen thousand rebels twice occupied Norwich and were only put down by a major military campaign using foreign mercenaries, led by the earl of Warwick. By 1634 Charles I had felt confident enough to order the preparation of a new prayer book for Scotland, modelled on the English one. When it was tried out at St Giles Cathedral in Edinburgh in 1637 the congregation rioted; this was quelled but was followed by intensified opposition which had to be put down by severe force. Colloquial Bible translations and prayer books subsequently became considered jewels of the culture of English-speaking peoples, but not without severe initial opposition which focused hostility upon the monarch, even if it did not challenge the institution of monarchy itself.

Elizabeth I's reign saw at least four potentially lethal plots against her, not least of which was the attempt by the Catholic King Philip of Spain to support a rising of English Catholics urged on by the distribution of copies of Cardinal Allen's *Admonition to the Nobility and People of England* calling upon them to overthrow Elizabeth in favour of a successor of the true faith. This counter-regime propaganda did not succeed and, after initial successes in Ireland the Spanish-Catholic enterprise was finally defeated by Elizabeth's regime.

In only the second reign after the monarchy of Elizabeth seemed indestructible, the king, Charles I was beheaded. Had immediate grievances at last given way to an ideologically-based desire for a republic and thus a revolution against the institution rather than its incumbent? According to Cannon and Griffiths (op. cit., p. 388) "hardly

---

[78] Cannon, J. and Griffiths, R. (1998). *The Oxford Illustrated History of the British Monarchy.* Oxford: Oxford Univeristy Press.

[79] op. cit., p. 264.

one of his opponents denied the need for monarchy, and the brief republican movement was the result of his downfall, not the cause ... Charles was convinced that his opponents aimed to subvert monarchy, but this was merely one of his many over-simplificatioins. The truth is almost the reverse - that until ... after the second Civil War, hardly any man of property or rank could conceive how a stable and tolerable society could survive except on the basis of monarchy". Indeed, it has been said by more than one essayist on the 350th anniversary of Charles' execution - and the 400th of Cromwell's birth, that the latter had been considered as a king, himself, and had passed on his Protectorship, hereditarily, to his son Richard. This incumbent proving weak it was the leading anti-Carlist General Monk who, himself, supported the recall of the Stuart successor Charles II. So this regicidal war, though some may be tempted to see it as a republican revolution, may alternatively be considered a major disruption of popular acceptance of the particular king. So monarchy survived in Britain to the extent that when the accepted line gave no clear internal successor, on two subsequent occasions monarchs were brought in from mainland Europe rather than clearing a way for a republic.

One King in the second incoming dynasty, of Hanoverians, George II evidently had not forgotten his history. Though he reigned over a nation that was increasingly successful (from 1727 to 1760) a vice-chamberlain at his court wrote of him that "in truth, he hated the English, looked upon them all as king-killers and republicans ... was forced to distribute his favours here very differently from the manner in which he bestowed them at Hanover; ... here he was obliged to enrich people for being rascals, and buy them not to cut his throat"[80]. Historians do not commonly depict this reign as a seed-bed for republicanism and it seems more plausible to regard these reported perceptions of George II as an outcome of his personality and its limited ability to accommodate itself to a rumbustious Britain, in contrast with his greater inclination to fit in with the more disciplined and deferential society as he found it in Hanover.

George III was more acculturated as an Englishman than was his father. An end of one series of wars early in his reign led to financial crises, food shortages and riots. There was a great growth in newspapers and the distribution of political expression in pamphlets, and the two radicals Wilkes and Junius (thought to be the nom de plume of Sir Philip Francis, who had helped to impeach Warren Hastings, a leader of British rule in India) were prominent polemicists. They attacked not only his administration but also the king. Junius admonished George to "remember that a throne acquired by one revolution (he referred to what was known as the glorious revolution of 1688, when the main Catholic-leaning Stuart dynasty was removed to be replaced by the clearly Protestant William of Orange, with his Stuart-related Queen Anne) may be lost by another ... it is not, however, too late to correct the error of your education ... Discard those little, personal resentments, which have too long directed your public conduct"[81]. Thus although obviously an irritant, Junius was hardly as revolutionary a critic as were

---

[80] op. cit., p. 475.
[81] op. cit., p. 496.

his opposite numbers soon to arise in France, or as thoroughgoing and durable a theorist as his contemporary, the Englishman-turned-American-Frenchman Thomas Paine.

BRITISH REVOLUTIONISM AGAINST THE MONARCHY

With the emergence of Tom Paine - who deserves considerable attention - opposition to particular monarchs is transmuted by thoroughgoing intellectual endeavour, smelted in a furnace of real insurrection and revolution, into a real case in favour of a republic. These pressures were applied to both the American and French societies but perhaps Paine did not do enough to generalise his case to insist that it was the best form for all societies including the British one. He had, indeed, in his pamphlet *Common Sense* (though this was published in America) attacked the hereditary British monarchy as undermining the independence of the House of Commons and pilloried George III as the royal brute.

Paine was born in Norfolk and spent some years in the radical town of Lewes (which had supported Simon de Montfort[82], and the regicide Oliver Cromwell in the past) before educating himself in London where he came to know the leading intellectuals of the day, including Oliver Goldsmith and Benjamin Franklin. Poverty and the exercise of law were harsh and Paine was hurt that London had ten holidays in the year, Easter, Christmas and then eight "hanging days" at Tyburn where even minor offenders were cruelly killed. In a public demonstration supporting Wilkes twenty citizens were killed or injured, at which King George gave his "gracious approbation" to his troops saying "I don't delight in blood letting, but if it should be necessary to spill a little for the sake of the law, then spill away I say"[83]. In this climate Paine opposed not only the way in which rule was exercised but also its fundamental structure.

Crossing the Atlantic, Paine became Editor of the *Pennsylvania Magazine*, one of the papers in a thriving popular press. With *Common Sense*, which at a price of two shillings sold 120,000 copies in three months, Paine sought to undermine any loyalties remaining in the thirteen colonies, to British rule, and to attack monarchy as an institution. Paine was thoroughgoing in criticising not only tyranny which he saw as embodied in the person of the King, but also Aristocratical tyranny in the person of the Peers, and calling for a revived Commons "on whose virtue depends the freedom of England"[84]. Paine collaborated with Jefferson in writing the Virginian Declaration of Rights (issued twenty days before the Declaration of Independence) and asserted that "The Nation is essentially the source of all sovereignty; how can any individual, or any body of men be entitled to any authority which is not expressly derived from it". Paine joined the revolutionary

---

[82] This baron had played a leading part in curbing the powers of King John, and in producing Magna Carta, seen by some as an important step on the way to the Universal Declaration of Human Rights.

[83] Powell, D. (1985) *Tom Paine. The Greatest Exile*. London: Croom Helm, p. 31.

[84] op. cit., p. 66.

army and became a Brigadier, while also writing several of a series of pamphlets each called *Crisis*.

The opposition to British rule in America was probably infectious; in 1778 there had been 'troubles' in Ireland; in 1779 disorders in London followed the petition the previous year in which 25 counties supported the County of York which, after charging George III with great and unconstitutional influence which may soon prove fatal to the liberties of this country demanded a thorough reform of the Exchequer. The radical John Jebb called for secret ballots, universal (male) suffrage, annual Parliaments and equal constituencies. In all this two things may be noted. One is that the leading theorist of republic, Paine, was based in secessionist colonies against which not only Hanoverian mercenaries but also British soldiers were fighting and losing their lives; indeed, a friend advised Paine not to try to return to England at that time; so the philosophy he propounded may have to some extent been seen as alien(ating). The second point is that however scathing opposition was in Britain to the person of George III, there was little to compare at home with the weight and cohesion of the case mounted by Paine overseas, and as part of an "enemy" project.

King George had been severely ill, and vexed with complex political manoeuvres and shortly after the Commons carried a motion not to pursue the war in America, he drafted a declaration of his own, of abdication in favour of his son. This document was not, however, delivered. Instead, when the first American ambassador John Adams arrived, in 1785 George gave a speech saying "I will be free with you. I was the last to consent to the separation; but the separation ... having become inevitable I have always said, as I say now, that I would be the first to meet the friendship of the United States as an independent power"[85]. This ability to relate was doubtless influenced by ties of culture and kinship, but it also would have had the effect of fortifying the monarchy east of the Atlantic, even though the same could not be said to apply for France.

Paine returned to Europe, but concentrated on France where he played a leading role in their own revolution. He spoke up for the life of their king, when it came under threat and worked towards his great book *The Rights of Man*, Part I of which was eventually published in March 1791 (in England: he had returned with a project to have an iron bridge of his own design, made in the cradle of the industrial revolution, for the Schuylkill River in his new home of America). The book rapidly sold 25,000 copies, while an opposing text by the politician Edmund Burke, titled *Reflections* and supporting a monarchy and a peerage as part of a nation's historic identity, sold poorly.

In England strong opposing political forces were unleashed. Paine himself was invited to speak to a meeting of the Revolution Society held - without evidently noticing any irony - at the Crown and Anchor pub. The meeting was however cancelled, the landlord having been persuaded it would be unwise to have such a gathering on the anniversary of Bastille Day. At a rearranged meeting Paine drafted the main resolution - which evidently rejected a republican government for England but which nevertheless

---

[85] Cannon, J. and Griffiths, R. (1998) *The Oxford Illustrated History of the British Monarchy*. Oxford: Oxford Univeristy Press, p. 511.

argued for the sovereignty of the people[86]. By now, many strata of British society were wary of what they had seen take place in France, which was not just the deposition of the monarchy but a subsequent period of severe disorder, and it was possible to see the two phenomena as being connected. At the Revolution Society a song was sung:

> He comes - the great Reformer Comes!
> The joyful tidings spread around
> Monarchs tremble at the sound!
> Freedom, freedom, freedom, freedom -
> Rights of man, and Paine resound!

Part Two of the *Rights of Man* raced to become a British best seller with over 200,000 copies bought in the first year alone (in a country of 10 million, equivalent to a sale of well over a million today). The Deputy Adjutant General went on a tour to check troop morale and wrote that "'the most seditious doctrines of Paine and the factious doctrines of the people who were endeavouring to disturb the peace of the country had extended to a degree much beyond my conception' ... and from Durham a correspondent was noting that 'During the late disturbances of Shields and Sunderland General Lambton was thus addressed "Have you read this little work of Tom Paine's - we much like it" ... while North Wales was said to be 'infested by itinerant Methodist preachers who descant on the Rights of Man and attack Kingly Government'"[87].

Presently the Prime Minister Pitt moved away from earlier ideas of Parliamentary reform rejecting "a madness which has been called liberty in another country; a condition at war with true freedom and good order" and the King issued a Proclamation for Preventing Seditious Meetings and Writings. The government funded King and Country mobs (earlier, in 1791 such a mob had rampaged in Birmingham, sacking chapels and burning the laboratory of the radical scientist Joseph Priestley); in Lincoln, Paine was hung in effigy, in Yorkshire he replaced Guy Fawkes on Bonfire Night and a song was sung

> Old Satan had a darling boy
> Full equal he to Cain
> Born peace and order to destroy
> His name was - Thomas Paine

Government agents penetrated radical groups; in 1794 Habeas Corpus was suspended and shiploads of dissenters were sent off to Botany Bay (the precursor of Sydney, in Australia; given a population primed at the start with such a degree of republican sentiment it may be a surprise that Australia has remained a monarchy for a further two hundred years). Anti-Paine cartoons were drawn by Gillray and medallions

---

[86] Powell, D. (1985) *Tom Paine. The Greatest Exile*. London: Croom Helm, p. 198.
[87] op. cit., p. 207.

were cast showing Paine hanging in chains; Paine may have overlooked these products of free (?) expression but was more prudent concerning the distinct possibility of being arrested, a summons having accused him of "being a wicked, malicious, seditious and ill-disposed person and being greatly disaffected to our said Sovereign, the now King, and the happy constitution and government of this kingdom"[88]. Paine left the country just ahead of a search party and sailed for France.

In France Paine was a Member of the Chamber of Deputies, for the region of the Pas du Calais, considered by some (in the days before Passports defined the matter more precisely) as a citizen of France, was himself imprisoned, and released only with the help of American intervention, crossing the Atlantic returning to end his days there. In 1817 Paine's body was disinterred by the radical English journalist William Cobbett and sent back to England, but it is not conclusively known what became of all the remains. One version is that a part, at least, received a Christian burial, and this may be a last irony in that Paine had scandalised people in his last years by professing the beliefs of a Deist - that is, that there is simply a one God, uninvolved in human affairs, while earthly religions are institutions which oppress people.

Through his range of beliefs and sentiments, concerning ideas and living people, Paine not only generated an intellectual laser beam of widely appreciated opposition to monarchy, but also a great deal of fall out of animosity from others who considered him too proud, too alien from whichever country he was living in, too disruptive of moral and social order. He successfully contributed to the replacement of monarchy in America and in France, but partly because these operations could be perceived as alien, not in his country of origin. He remains a problematic figure not only in Britain, where he is not commemorated unambiguously with admiration through statues, scholarships, street names and the other paraphernalia of incorporation into a nation's history, but also in America, where one of his last gestures was a published letter accusing President Washington of perfidy[89]. It is a good question to ask why America, equipped with the world's most powerful film industry, has not found it profitable to market or even make a movie biography of this fascinating anti-monarchist founding father.

BRITISH OPPOSITION TO MONARCHY AFTER TOM PAINE

Paine clearly helped to inspire other British revolutionaries. Thus one William Godwin wrote the *Enquiry Concerning Political Justice* in which he condemned all kings as would-be despots. Monarchs were demonstrably expensive and in many cases not people to admire[90]. Nevertheless, it can be seen that many expressions of opposition, in the wake of Paine were not focused on the institution itself but on the incumbent. Thus

---

[88] op. cit., p. 210.

[89] op. cit., p. 252.

[90] Cannon, J. and Griffiths, R. (1998) *The Oxford Illustrated History of the British Monarchy.* Oxford: Oxford Univeristy Press, p. 534.

the politician Charles Fox said of King George III "provided that we can stay in long enough to deliver a good stout blow to the influence of the crown, I do not care how we go out ... (the king was a) blockhead (and) Satan ... and will die soon, and that will be the best of all"[91]. British society had become larger, more complex and much more richly equipped with the means of expressing all shades of opinion, in the century leading to the rule of George III. In 1700 there was no London newspaper or any provincial ones. At the accession of George III there were four London papers and thirty five provincial ones. While papers early in Hanoverian times sold in mere hundreds Cobbetts *Political Register* sold 44,000 for each edition in 1816. Cartoons common in the early press were followed with vitriolic invective; the *Examiner*, in 1812 wrote of the Prince Regent

"this delightful, blissful, wise, pleasurable, virtuous, true and immortal prince is a violator of his word, a libertine over head and heels in debt and disgrace, a despiser of domestic ties, the companion of gamblers and demireps, a man who has just closed half a century without one single claim on the gratitude of his country or the respect of posterity".[92]

The *Times'* obituary for George, after the short reign for which he had waited so long, said:

"there never was an individual less regretted by his fellow creatures than this deceased king ... What eye has wept for him? What heart has heaved one throb of unmercenary sorrow? ... Nothing more remains to be said about George IV but to pay, as pay we must, for his profusion; and to turn his bad conduct to some account by tying up the hands of those who come after him in what concerns the public money".[93]

All of this was hostile enough to the royal person, but lacked that ideological underpinning essential in Paine's work, which focused on the institution. It may be carrying stereotyping too far to suggest that it was largely men who read newspapers (but they are depicted in contemporary illustrations as being in a majority in coffee houses and certainly there were no women in parliament) while women read novels; but it may be true that then, as now, that novels were something of a domestic and thus women's world. It should be important therefore to examine the novels of the time, by Fielding, Austen, the Bronte sisters and others to see whether they attacked, merely accepted or supported monarchism. An impression from today would be that most such novels accepted the institution of monarchy, underpinned by a stratified social system within which it was an ambition for women to marry well and be upwardly socially mobile. Such themes were supported by vivid descriptions of poverty and oppression for those who did not enjoy such fortune, but there is a dearth or even absence of any thoroughgoing revolutionary fiction. Not even the earlier Gulliverian satires by Swift truly attacked the institution of monarchy, even if they ridiculed royal individuals.

---

[91] op. cit., p. 513.

[92] op. cit., p. 532.

[93] op. cit., p. 545.

The next crisis for British monarchy arose not from ideological sources but when Queen Victoria was bereaved and withdrew psychologically, socially and ritually. Prime Minister Disraeli in 1871 said, wishing to defend her, that the queen was "physically and morally incapacitated from performing her duties"; in today's jargon he may better have said that she suffered post traumatic stress syndrome. However, Disraeli's indiscretion was seized on by the politician Charles Bradlaugh who spoke to the newly founded London Republican Club on what the people ought now to do, and published a booklet *Impeachment of the House of Brunswick*. The politician Joseph Chamberlain declared in 1871 that "the Republic must come ... and it will be in our generation". This was the same minister who, in 1897 brought colonial premiers and troops to parade in Queen Victoria's Imperial Diamond Jubilee procession. Sir Charles Dilke said in a speech late in 1871 that the change to a republic was only a matter of education and time and that "if you can show me a fair chance that a republic here will be free from the political corruption that hangs about the monarchy, I say, for my part - and I believe that the middle classes in general will say - let it come"[94].

By chance, the next month the Prince of Wales (later Edward VII) took very seriously ill with typhoid. Popular response was of widespread dismay. As the Prince began to recover, his biographer reported that "an elemental surge of loyal emotion destroyed republicanism overnight as a significant factor in British radical politics"[95]. Three months later in March 1872 Dilke moved for an inquiry into the "civil list" (the money the exchequer granted the royal family), based on the notion that the expense was a major popular concern but his motion was defeated by 276 votes to 2. By 1880 none of the republican clubs that had sprung up earlier remained in existence. Thirty years later the Labour Party had begun to establish a significant presence in Parliament and its ideas were influenced at least to some extent by Marxist philosophy which was explicitly anti-monarchist. The Labour leader Ramsay MacDonald, however, wrote in 1911 that "socialism does not consider republicanism of essential importance" and a motion at a party conference in 1923, that the royal family was no longer necessary as part of the constitution was defeated by nearly ten to one. A few months later the Conservative government fell and the king decided that a (minority) Labour party should be given a chance to form an administration. MacDonald and the king readily made friends.[96]

In the next brief reign, of Edward VIII the furore over his intention to marry a twice-divorced woman stimulated another upsurge of republicanism. Cannon and Griffiths report that "it was widely presumed that the abdication had dealt a mortal blow to the institution of monarchy" and even Edward's successor the Duke of York wondered whether "the whole fabric" might crumble. James Maxton, a Member of the Commons belonging to the tiny Independent Labour Party declared that the monarchy had lost its usefulness (an argument based on pragmatic, rather than principled grounds) and

---

[94] op. cit., p. 565.

[95] Magnus, P. (1964) King Edward the Seventh. London, p. 114.

[96] op. cit., p. 597.

supported by a communist member Willie Gallacher spoke for a motion for a republic. It was lost by 403 votes to 5.[97]

Ben Pimlott, author of a weighty biography of Queen Elizabeth II suggests that it had been possible to smooth over the abdication trauma for several reasons. Press restraint was maintained until the last act of the drama, and when the news broke in Britain the next moves were swift. The next King was dignified, and there was little if any strife visible between members of the royal family; finally, the press rallied round and supported the new monarch and his ready made photogenic and attractive family[98].

BRITISH LATE TWENTIETH CENTURY IDEOLOGICAL REPUBLICANISM

In our day a contender for the mantle of Tom Paine is the Scotsman Tom Nairn[99]. His book was reissued in 1994 so that he was able to include an introduction in which he could reflect on changes he observed since his first edition had appeared in 1988. Reflecting on responses (in the press, which may have constructed public opinion) to the fire in Windsor Castle in 1992 Nairn wrote that in a nation which had "succumbed to cost effectiveness ... pricelessness was already history". In that year opposition to the royal entity (by which we may here combine the institution of monarchy with the personal qualities and behavior of its incumbents) had included scandalous revelations about the deteriorated relationship between Prince Charles and (the then) Princess Diana and the alleged rapaciousness towards tenants of the Duchy of Cornwall under Prince Charles' leadership. In the domain of cost effectiveness were the press stories of the alleged meanness of the Queen in presiding over an overgrown "civil list" (or wider royal family all receiving money from the state) and in not paying taxes, the alleged duty of the Queen to pay the cost of repairing "her" castle at Windsor severely damaged by fire and the alleged extravagance of the royal family in expecting the state to maintain a Royal Yacht, a Royal Train and a Queen's Flight of (Royal) aircraft all to facilitate elegant (and efficient) travel.

Nairn acutely observed that "the Queen made matters worse by opening Buckingham Palace to the public ... as with the previous decision that the Royal Family should start paying income tax. Both moves were thought of as modernisation, or 'opening up'. But in fact they could be opening down, levelling things monarchical into a society ... where greed had eclipsed class"[100]. Nairn argues however, that while in the "popular" (that is the press') view any empirical weakening of loyalty to the monarchy said to have come about was caused by the traumas of 1992-3, the real turning point is likely to have been earlier, by 1990. He suggests that Thatcherism (that is, an emphasis on self-reliance and

---

[97] op. cit., p. 606.

[98] Pimlott, B. (1998) *Monarchy and the Message*. in The Political Quarterly. Oxford: Blackwell.

[99] Nairn, T. (1994) *The Enchanted Glass*. London: Vintage Books.

[100] op. cit., p. xi.

on the market rather than on paternalist institutions and policy in government) was the cause. The monarchy was the keystone of the arch of British society and of the identity associated with it. By undermining or changing British identity by a series of moves, including inflicting the poll tax first on the Scots, but including an ambiguous opening of the "door to European identity" (Mrs Thatcher signed the Treaty of Rome in 1986) Nairn suggests that the need or the place for the keystone - the centrality of the monarchy as symbol of British identity - had been radically (though not at first particularly visibly) altered.

The notion of British identity has been explored by Nairn's friend Neal Ascherson[101] a fellow Scot. Both are acutely aware of the question of whether or to what extent British and English identity were congruent, and to what extent either identity was built around an implicit model of a state organised in a particularly hierarchical way, with the monarchy at the top. Ascherson mentions that the German novelist Robert Musil nicknamed the Austro-Hungarian Empire, about whose decline he wrote, Kakania after the letters K.u.K short for Imperial and Royal; reflecting this, Nairn has been referring to Britain as Ukania. Both authors note that the Hapsburg Empire was a multi-nation state with overlapping Austrian, Hungarian and even German identities. That empire collapsed (they do not seem to notice, after the catastrophic defeat in the first world war) but Nairn and Ascherson imply a parallel with the British Empire (which has been dismissed, rather than defeated) and hint that with the passing of the imperial identities would also go the royal superstructure.

The book within which Ascherson writes is a collection of chapters including several by writers associated with a group calling itself Charter 88. This group was so named, on its foundation in 1988 marking the 300th anniversary of the Glorious Revolution (which dismissed the Stuart monarchs from Britain and introduced the House of Orange, with much reduced powers for the monarchy and an enhanced role for Parliament). Members of this group often express republican views. Including "My Vision For Britain" by the incoming Prime Minster Tony Blair, a contribution on "A People's Europe" and a conclusion on "A New Agenda" by the book's editor, there is however no mention in any of these chapters, nor in the Index of the terms Monarchy or Republic(anism). Many of the changes envisaged in the book, including the pooling of British sovereignty and identity within a Europe whose eventual parameters of a larger sovereignty and identity remain as yet to be fully clear, imply at least a dilution of the role of the British monarchy, if not its complete removal. Yet for the time being, Blair has not called for a republic and indeed has celebrated the Queen (whatever he may mean by this) as "the best of British".

Nairn's analysis is voluble, and curious. It may be that he has fallen foul of a risk taken by anthropologists who, when they study a society which practices evidently harsh actions such as elongating the necks of women, plugging their lips, binding their feet or crudely excising their sexual organs, come up with an explanation that such constraints

---

[101] Ascherson, N. (1996) National Identity in Radice, G. (Ed.) *What Needs To Change. New Visions For Britain* London: Harper Collins.

on human identity are really part of the way each society has devised for making the best of its niche in nature, and as such are quite acceptable. In short, home-based intellectuals have often taken field anthropologists to task for having "gone native". Tom Nairn, in observing and analysing the way in which monarchy works in Britain seems to start off as a revolutionary critic but presently gives the impression that he admires the institution, finds its relationship with the people an agreeable compound of the mysterious and the amusing and in general undercuts the force of what seems at first to be his political case, by experiencing the charms of the evidence he has collected and chooses to cite.

Early in his book Nairn (p. xxv) refers to "the decisive indicator (which) is the unstoppable slide of the Monarchy in both popular and political estimation ... It is ... leaving behind a vacuum which only some kind of ideological civil war can fill". He ends his book (p. 391) with "the break-up of Britain ... its Countries will no doubt go their own way at last ... I hope at least they are Republics". The metaphor of his book's title is explored (p. xxix) saying "identity-breakage - the shattering of the glass - is so far unaccompanied by a process of consciously national identity-reformation". The metaphor crops up later (p. 215) in discussing "The Glamour of Backwardness" thus "as decline and failure have corroded this antique liberality ... the Monarchical glass of national identity has constantly brightened and extended its radiant appeal". Though in one place Nairn believes that "a glass" (in which the nation sees itself) has already been shattered the book cover itself seems to side with a conclusion of indestructibility showing the title The *Enchanted* GLASS with the adjective elegantly written, with the author's name, over an unbroken *royal* purple background. Nairn is very sensitive to symbolic meanings so perhaps Enchanted suggests that the monarchy has a magical power of survival? What does he say about how it works? His first chapter - The Mystery - deals with this question.

We soon meet what seems a paradox (p. 45) "The inner meaning of the belief that 'They're just like us' ... is the certainty that they are not ... what's marvellous about them being like us is that it shows they aren't just like us - each new glimpse ... can only reinforce the glamour ... forever sharpening the appetite for more". Nairn uses the word Glamour to recall "the old Scottish word for magical enchantment, the spell cast upon humans by fairies, or witches. It was brought into modern English by Sir Walter Scott who also thought up and organised ... George IV's descent upon Scotland in 1822 ... bekilted, be-sporraned, be-tartaned ... to the roaring cheers of the loyal Scots. Glamour ... had become part of modernity"[102].

Nairn has earlier told the anecdote of the Thames Flood Barrier, a vast project of socialist engineering designed to do something that the King Knut was supposed to have said, a thousand years before, could not be done. The "socialist leadership had at first wanted to stage a new, anti-official opening ceremony ... but this radical notion was subverted by the workers themselves. They wanted the Queen. She came. Ken Livingstone (the firebrand leader of the Greater London Council) ... declared ... 'I have always thought ... that the Queen is a very nice person indeed. Today confirmed that view'. ... What is endorsed is the symbolic, cult idea of Royal niceness ... never stronger than when casually endorsed from the Left. There is something deeply ... English about the performance ... a ... rather important aspect of national identity ... the Monarchistic trance is automatic repulsion of inquiry from the overflowing cup of darling details and throbbing personalized emotion"[103].

Hostile emotion also exists but Nairn continues to say that "those who oppose Monarchy ... (presumably excluding himself) ... tend to founder into inarticulate rage. This hatred unable to speak its name boils over internally, uselessly (he gives an example of an intellectual who hates Princess Anne, whose 'fingers quiver as he points at her haircut, his lips go pale as he rails at her coat, her hat, even at her shoes. And this is a man who ... sees fit to lecture the British people for taking the Monarchy too seriously'). Such incoherent fury is in its own way merely another tribute to the taboo and so to the radiance of the Crown"[104] (Nairn pp. 50-51). Nairn considers whether public "stupidity is manufactured by media barons ... in the interests of making money" but rejects the notion that the mass is a passive, wholly manipulated entity; instead "the awkward fact which pseudo-Republicanism tries to exorcise ... is of course that popular Royalism is visibly not passive and mindless. It has something highly positive about it - an apparently inexhaustible electric charge. This is what makes media and Regime exploitation so easy and effective ... People enjoy ... the weird mixture of cheap fun, exalted moments and great spectacles, and come back for more. Whatever it all means ... is sustained ... by a genuine, positive will more significant than any amount of peevish grousing about cost"[105].

Nairn's ambivalent text selects several other aspects of monarchism as targets; kitsch taste is assailed, in the form of Pietro Annigoni's portrait of the Queen, and many tourist souvenir mugs and other paraphernalia; the honours system is ostensibly attacked, but every rhetorical campaign of Nairn's seems to be undercut with his own deflection of his own argument. Thus (p. 311) we read that "The national bending spine also has a familiar corset to help its curve stay in place: the Honours System ... (BUT, then he writes) As well as the daily media spectacle and nightly communion, Monarchy also refracts a more direct beam of ennoblement into every sector of the social body through it ... Twice yearly the refulgence is distributed ...".

Nairn turns elsewhere for a symbol that might reveal monarchism as decrepit or deserving termination; he alights upon the Mace "a five-foot-long ornamental club in lieu of a State - a piece of fetishized Monarchy instead of the humdrum bourgeois abstraction informing the governmental affairs of so many other societies" (p. 357). This mace rests on the desk in front of the Speaker's throne in the House of Commons, and symbolises (so long as it is at rest on its brackets) the presence of the monarch in Parliament. Nairn quotes a critic, Richard Rose as observing that "the idea of the state ... can be found in

---

[102] Nairn, T. (1994). *The Enchanted Glass*. London: Vintage Books, p. 214.

[103] op. cit., pp. 47-48.

[104] op. cit., pp. 50-51.

[105] op. cit., p. 53.

most parts of Europe ... but it is alien to British political thinking ..."; Nairn sees the symbolism of the Mace as "this conjuring trick ... substitutes mysticism for meaning - and yet the mystic surrogate works". Another potential weapon against the monarchy is thus brought to bite the dust.

Although in my view Nairn's "quiet republicanism" too often undermines itself by being beguiled by the institution it says it wants to replace, his friends and their colleagues may be somewhat more resolute. Ascherson reports that "the Tory years ended in an upsurge of criticism aimed at the royal family, leaving behind it an impressive number of people who declared themselves recruits to 'republicanism'. But most of these recruits imagined that a republic was simply a state that had dismissed its monarchy. They had no idea of the democratic revolution that is required to establish republican institutions on the basis of popular sovereignty"[106]. Here, Ascherson pinpoints a feature of "British" (actually English) thinking and tradition in which it is not *the people* who are Sovereign, (nor indeed the monarch) but *Parliament* which is. The Scottish tradition in contrast considers the people as sovereign. When the Scottish Parliament came into being these distinctions were highlighted and one consequence may well be a destabilisation of the position of the monarchy in Scotland.

Several other forms of mini-anti-monarchism are currently abroad in Britain. One takes the form of refusal of honours. The poet Tony Harrison revealed his self-centredness in a piece entitled Laureate's Block that appeared in the *Guardian* on 9 February 1999. He began with two verses saying how appalled he was to see a newspaper suggest he might be a next poet laureate, especially as it was the same *Guardian* in which he had written about the "abdication of King Charles III in the hope of a republic in Great Britain". Harrison quoted from Thomas Gray (author of the Elegy in a Country Churchyard) who had belittled the idea of accepting the post of laureate - except that Gray did eventually take it. Harrison says there should be no successor to Ted Hughes - acclaimed as a great poet, who had shed lustre on the post; we may agree with Harrison that the greatness was not in terms of the verse he wrote for it, but add, as explained in an earlier chapter, but of which idea Harrison seems unaware, that the merit lies in the light Hughes shone upon the roles of Shakespeare and Queen Elizabeth I, in his analysis of the interaction between the two. Harrison wants to be "free to ... write an ode on Charles I's beheading and regret the restoration of his heir". There is a wrestling with the prospect and meanings of one's own prominence, here; but apart from simple expressions of dislike, no deeper explanation of why republicanism might be preferable in Britain, or in England, to a monarchy.

There has been no shortage in Britain of other emotive cries against monarchy. Journalists in the daily papers the *Guardian*, and the *Independent*, in their Sunday versions and in the left wing weekly the *New Statesman* frequently rail against the institution. Thus John-Paul Flintoff (in the *Statesman*) we are told "wants to give up royalty. But the Queen is everywhere, even if you are lost at sea". In this semi-humorous piece Flintoff rails at all the institutions which have a 'Royal' prefix to their names, from the Royal Institution of Chartered Surveyors to the (more oddly styled, given its often iconoclastic preoccupations) Royal Court Theatre. He looks ahead to the "prospect of an altogether new currency in which the paper money will be devoid of royalist idolatry". Apart, however, from the embedded opposition to idolatry (which does not prevent many orthodox Jews and Muslims from being loyal monarchists) Flintoff gives little away as to why he opposes monarchy.

On another occasion Anthony Holden[107], an embittered "royal reporter" (see Chapter 8) lets readers know about the Prime Minister that "we all know that Blair, deep down, is a republican ... long time friends ... recall Tony chortling merrily as (his wife) Cherie trashed the royals over their pre-Downing Street dinner table ... 'You're the man who wants me to abolish the monarchy ...' he said to me ... about a year before the election. 'Yes' I replied, 'but not until your third term'. It is not explained why the republican Holden, who had just had part in the launch of the republican pressure group Common Sense (Paine's title for his early American tracts) wants to wait so long, especially when it is a rarity for Prime Ministers to achieve third terms in office; but the disclosure of a disaffected group is frank enough.

David Jenkins, the former Bishop of Durham is known as a serious thinker within the Church of England. He has pointed out that "we are beginning a process of unravelling constitutional arrangements that have developed over a millennium ... all is an interwoven fabric of custom, law and symbolism".[108] The ex-Bishop asserted that an established church is not fitting in "our pluralistic and multicultural society" and that it would be better for the Church to be free of entanglement with the state. The next reign might better be begun not by a coronation but by a secular "installation ... to which contributions were made from the traditions of all faiths". Jenkins rejected the Samuelite model in writing that "the days when it was assumed that states could exist under a sacred canopy within which the religious authorities are responsible under God for legitimating power, morality and civil order have long passed (but) ... how are we to recover and develop the Christian vision of a universal God with a universal purpose?".

In these thoughts (ex) Bishop Jenkins appears to accept a next reign, but one in which there would be no hereditary house of Lords to act as an example to the principle of hereditary access to the throne, and no clear divine sanction for a new monarch to enter his or her reign. The destabilisation of the role of such a monarch (leaving aside for a moment the greater integration of the British countries into the European Union) is not exactly a republicanist manifesto, but could be regarded as an attempt to reach such a position by stealth rather than by explicit action of a kind which might - or would - excite opposition. Other serious contemporary writings that alert readers to republicanism include a volume about what in monarchist times has been called "the Protectorate" but

[106] Ascherson, N. (1999) The Indispensable Englishman. *New Statesman*, 29 January 25 - 27.

[107] Holden, A. (1999) Diary in the *New Statesman*, 5 March, p. 7.

[108] Jenkins, D. (1999) The end of establishment. The secular state is coming. *Independent on Sunday*, 17 January, p. 25.

which the Scot Norbrook prefers to term "the English Republic"[109]. "While royalists believed in beauty, concord, unity, puritan republicans believed in sublimity, free speech and a turbulent iconoclasm". Milton is quoted as a prophet of the republic, albeit one who feared that Cromwell might, through the dynamics of ruling, find himself adopting the form of a new monarchy. Such books as Norbrook's, and their reception into the current debate may act as solvents eroding the currently deep-laid matrix of monarchy.

While exploring the range of anti-monarchist expression one might well expect to find a few telling blows cast from the ranks of Marxists. A search in the far-left literature then reveals curiously little on this matter. Most of any iconoclasm that there is to be found must be read into Marx's own writings. Marx wrote one book for which he is strongly remembered, *Capital*, as well as *The Communist Manifesto* and collected papers under the title *Grundrisse*; indexes in these volumes point to little that specifically undermines the institution of monarchy. In one passage Marx wrote "Communism is the positive abolition of private property and thus of human self-alienation ...". With his colleague (and funder) Friedrich Engels they asserted that a communist revolution was imminent in Europe; but they had different expectations of how soon this would happen in Germany, France, Britain and Russia (oddly enough expecting the slowest development in the latter)[110]. Vera Zasulich, a revolutionary with impeccable credentials (she shot the Governor of St Petersburg) asked Marx whether "history moves too slowly - it needs a push"; Marx's reply lacked an element of urgency: "... special research ... which I obtained from original sources, has convinced me that (the rural community) is the mainspring of Russia's social regeneration, but in order that it might function as such one would first have to eliminate the deleterious influences which assail it from every quarter and then to ensure conditions normal to spontaneous development"[111].

Lenin's elder brother performed a piece of propaganda by deed, joining a conspiracy to assassinate the Tsar, and was hanged for this. At the turn of the century there was a massacre in St Petersburg in which several hundred demonstrators were killed by soldiers in front of the Winter Palace. This drama of (dysfunctional) propaganda by deed saw the image of the Tsar as the "little father of his people" shattered for ever. Leaving physical conflict to others, Lenin expressed himself through writing and personal contacts and speeches. Oratory has to be recognised here as a most effective form, for readings of some of Marx's writings do not immediately suggest he would have been a leader but those who heard him fell under his spell. Lenin too, especially immediately on his return to Russia in 1917 (after the Tsar had been deposed, but before he and his family were killed) dramatically influenced events by speeches, as did Trotsky.

The question of why these quintessential revolutionaries may have said so little explicitly about removal of monarchy is not the main focus here, but just to check that

---

[109] Norbrook, D. (1999) *Writing the English Republic: Poetry, Rhetoric and Politics 1627 - 1660*. Cambridge: Cambridge University Press.

[110] McLellan, D. (1983) *Karl Marx the Legacy* London: BBC Books.

[111] op. cit., pp. 61-62.

nothing has been missed we may note that an analyst of the school, Giddens[112], refers to "extraordinary blank spots in social theory" in particular of their lack of attention to violence and war so that "with certain particular exceptions, the works of Marxist authors ... usually only touch upon violence as revolutionary ...". Giddens says that "Marx had no elaborated theory of the capitalist state ... still less did he work out an analysis of the bases of the nation state or of nationalism ..." and Nairn wrote "the theory of nationalism represents Marxism's great historical failure". These gaps are important, for Giddens points out that "wars conducted by the absolute monarchs shaped the map of Europe ..." so that while in 1500 there were around 500 autonomous political units by 1900 these had coalesced to around 25. Nationalism is in substantial part a psychological phenomenon, and monarchy is a psychologically important symbol. Thus it falls to social anthropologists and historians to grasp the importance of monarchy, while Marx and his followers had sociological and economic perspectives.

If Trotsky can be included as a Marxist, he can be considered to have made their thinking a little more concrete in so far as it concerned monarchies. Contrasting Britain and Germany shortly after the first world war Trotsky gave the former's advantages as "high technique, science, etc" but against them listed "monarchy, aristocracy, House of Lords, power of religious prejudices over people's minds". Trotsky considered that the upper strata of the British working class had at least some privileges and that this blunted class antagonisms; thus the development of the British proletariat was retarded[113]. "More than anything else the British bourgeoisie is proud that it has not destroyed old buildings and old beliefs, but has gradually adapted the old royal and noble castle to the requirements of the business firm". Nevertheless, though British "technique" was good, "the British monarchy, hypocritical British conservatism, religiosity, servility, sanctimoniousness - all this is old rags, rubbish, the refuse of centuries ..."[114].

In a speech in 1918 Trotsky said "the Englishman ... has a 'devil inside him'. There have been repeated occasions when the Englishman has taken up the cudgel against his oppressor, and there is no doubt that the time is near when he will take up his cudgel against the King, against his lords and against the cruel, cunning, clever and perfidious British bourgeoisie. And the first thunderclaps of the great storm can already be heard from the island of Great Britain"[115]. Six years later Trotsky was still immediately hopeful "we will venture to predict that in the not so distant future two bronze figures will be erected side by side in London, say in Trafalgar Square, those of Karl Marx and Vladimir Lenin ..."[116]. In Chapter 6 of his History of the Russian Revolution, published in 1931 Trotsky wrote "only a blind man could fail to see that Great Britain is headed for

---

[112] Giddens, A. (1981) *A Contemporary Critique of Historical Materialism* London: Macmillan, pp. 177 - 193.

[113] Chappell, R. and Clinton, S. (Eds. 1974) *Trotsky's Writings on Britain*. London: New Park Books pp. 19-20.

[114] op. cit., p. 24.

[115] op. cit., p. 171.

[116] op. cit., p. 193.

gigantic revolutionary earthquake shocks, in which the last fragments of her conservatism ... will go down without a trace ...".

Trotsky had despised Britain's first Labour Prime Minister Ramsay MacDonald and amused a gathering of Russian railwaymen with these thoughts on British politics: "suppose MacDonald said ... our country has ... a kind of august dynasty that stands above democracy and for which we have no need ... sitting in the House of Lords ... were all the titled heirs of bloodsuckers and robbers and that it was necessary to sweep them out ... wouldn't the hearts of British workers quicken with joy? What if he added, 'we are going to take their lands, mines, and railways, and nationalize their banks ...' he would unleash tremendous enthusiasm ... Britain would be unrecognizable in two weeks. MacDonald would receive an overwhelming majority in any election ... But MacDonald will not do that. He is conservative, in favour of the monarchy, private property and the church"[117].

Trotsky saw beyond sociology those elements of culture and attitude of which social anthropologists are aware, and of which revolutionaries should be aware if they are to stand the best chance of success, and recognised reasons - religion, conservatism, a sense of history, even of humour - why the classes and forces expected by a more mechanistic sociological analysis to produce a ferment and explosion, might not in the end do so. Trotsky also recognised that " formal democracy is higher than Asiatic despotism, higher than the power of the Shah of Persia or the King of England. (Furthermore) The dictatorship of the proletariat is higher than formal democracy. Those who accuse us of dictatorship have explained to us the advantages and sacred values of democracy ... (but) it emerged that democracy was only opposed to the working class and not the power of the House of Lords and the British monarchy"[118]. It should not be forgotten that Trotsky fought successfully against British (and other foreign) armies trying to put down the Red revolution; but he was himself hounded out of Russia and he began to work for world-wide revolution rather than specific changes in Britain, until he was murdered by an assassin working for Stalin.

One may have to say then, for them, that republicans of various hues reject monarchy for several reasons. We are not including for serious consideration here those utterances which arise from personal dislike of the behavior of individual members of the royal family, or even of all of them. The more structural reasons include that a monarchy seems to some to be a more juvenile or regressive form than a republic - acceptance of parental-style authority among adults who should look to themselves for the bases on which to form a good society. Other objections include that monarchy ties Britain to its past, and in particular to its family of commonwealth countries (seen as an advantage by others), and stands for a privilege derived from hereditary accident (rather than from individual struggle; though again, here, most republicans will probably be found to benefit from inheriting their own parents' material and social wealth); and some

---

[117] op. cit., p. 194.
[118] op. cit., p. 202.

republicans may dislike the glare or glamour of monarchy in a similar way to that in which some people prefer black and white to colour photography.

INEXPLICIT AND UNINTENDED DEVELOPMENTS POSSIBLY UNDERMINING MONARCHY

When the Canadian media guru Marshall McLuhan wrote that the medium is the message he undoubtedly meant that the ways in which information and feeling are carried (the media) may in themselves have more effect or impact than the actual content of such messages. McLuhan meant that to say I love or I hate by telephone would convey different meanings than to say either thing in person, or on paper, or by a gift of chocolates (where confectionery is a medium of expression) or a poison pen expression. We may be wise therefore to look for developments in society in which meanings may indeed be conveyed, along with the arrival of certain forms of social activity which nobody had intended to convey when promoting such developments.

Consider first the supermarket. In this institution the shopper can be said to be sovereign. One wanders the aisles, picking goods off shelves in a way similar to the experience of Sinbad the sailor in one of the jewel-encrusted caves he comes across on one of his more blessed journeys. These goods are taken past a counter at which a piece of plastic is waved - a magic spell. The whole experience is likely to be gratifying not only to the need to do one's shopping but also to an underlying assumption or feeling that one is behaving as a monarch, even if it is over a relatively small domain. The shopper who is dissatisfied with any part of their experience is encouraged to complain and a manager will appear like a jack-in-the-box to put right the offence. Since many people indulge in this experience weekly or even more often, and by now many have done so as adults from their childhood, the habit of self-gratification may have scored deeply into whatever is the modern equivalent of the soul. The consumer model is increasingly applied to the student in the college and to the patient in the clinic. Everywhere in a commercialised society the person who can afford its benefits is treated as a mini-monarch.

People increasingly have moved about by car. In the car the driver is king or queen of the small space he or she inhabits. Other people inside the car are allies or co-nationals but those outside are all too often a threat or a nuisance. The rules of traffic are like international law, and have a great deal of success in keeping the peace. But importantly, though these external rules, and road engineering increasingly limit the driver's freedoms, the ideal still exists, in fact it probably prevails - and advertising has much to do with this - that an important reward of driving is the exercise of power. If then one becomes, however briefly and in however limited a world, something like a petty monarch oneself, one's focus on some other distant national monarch may be diluted. As in the supermarket - "I am king - or queen" - how can someone else also be sovereign above one? Now, in Britain, the New Labour administration has adopted as law the European Charter of Human Rights which is another way in which the supremacy of the monarch's throne is sidelined while the - much smaller - sovereignty of every individual's throne, alongside every other individual's throne is given its due recognition.

What else may undermine those elements in a culture that sustain monarchy, which we are told in the writings of Trotsky and others, above, include the power of religion? One change may then be those changes in science and its application which have undermined religion. Birth control fuels a culture of unfettered sexual indulgence, the women's movement challenges those who oppose abortion, and sciences from astronomy and the new perspective on the heavens from satellites, to biology and the emerging power to construct and manipulate embryonic life, all either do, or are asked to empower the individual. Man (and woman) has become a god to him and herself. Movement of peoples has introduced large minorities in European states, hitherto only Christian, which must now make cultural room for Islam, other Eastern and Mediterranean creeds, so it is politically dysfunctional to consider any one religion as supreme, which undercuts the position of the previously dominant creed.

Along with the erosion of older religious cohesions in western European countries, there is a change of perspective in the teaching of history. Whereas some decades ago history was taught as a story of events tightly contained in a structure of dynasties, wars and a development and justification of national states and identities, more recently history is taught with more attention to the lives of the people in various times. Much focus on recent wars underlines not a jingoistic justification of nationalism but a shame and regret about the waste of life, and hence the wrong doing of those agents and institutions which brought this about.

One of the developments of modern life in states with sophisticated and open communication systems is that entertainment industries overlap into the news arenas, and both activities in their competition for readership and audiences need stars which they use in various ways. One phase of a star's life, as in astronomy, is when it waxes - the cinema or music artist, even the politician or other celebrity is placed in the limelight and helped to shine. It would not avail the media at all if such figures were dull; accordingly, any achievements or merit of figures who move into fame (sports people are included) can at first be magnified. The resulting glow or charisma or star quality is similar in some ways to that attached to royalty. There is then a phase in which a star is destroyed, if possible, by the very media which helped create them; often the destruction is not permanent and they are enabled to come back.

Career phases of movie stars in which they betray their partners or have falsities revealed (sexual affairs, plastic surgery) are wanes but, with artful public relations management can be transformed by tomorrow's successes. Such adventures within the mass message systems could be said to intensify the lustre of members of a lower rung of stardom and this leaves room which a few rarefied beings may inhabit, from which they may preside over a higher realm of such stardom. Thus the allegedly insatiable demand of or within the mass message systems for demigods may help sustain the ultimate charisma experienced and then radiated by a limited few at a higher level. This may be the worldwide realm within which but a few monarchies exist - the British, Japanese, Saudi and Thai institutions being examples.

It is likely that one way in which to reinforce or retain such supra-stellar status would be for incumbents to behave admirably and continue to do so. Another element in sustaining supreme starship arises from a hereditary position; in this, lustre from the past is available for the present, but also the knowledge that a descendant will carry today's starship on adds to the momentum with which today's brightness glows. It is not the actual personal merit or achievements of past occupancy of the monarchy that reinforce what is experienced today; rather, it is the nation's history itself, embedded into the royal line that has this power. It is also likely that a considerable element of restraint and controlled favourable exposure will enhance current super-star status. We have seen several cases where mistakes have been made by a monarch (George IV, Edward VIII, Marie Antoinette ...) and will come in a later chapter to others. However, it may be more subtly argued, with use of the failed impeachment of President Clinton (in his short-term quasi-monarchic role) as an example, that stratospheric stars may, like the gods of the Greek pantheon suffer no lasting loss of esteem even when they behave very badly; indeed, suitably communicated, the presentation of bad behavior may even enhance the monarch's (or president's) status by convincing the public that such figures require to be judged by criteria beyond those used for assessing ordinary mortals.

SUMMARY

There has been a wide range of ways in which people have opposed monarchs in particular, or monarchy in general. To do the former requires a certain level of offence by or frustration attributable to the monarch, and that has clearly often occurred. To do the latter calls for intellectual and emotional activity, an ideology or theory of state, and these have also been developed by many writers and activists. Curiously enough the most radical theorists within the last century, on the far left, whom one might expect to have had the most that is effective to say in opposition to monarchy have focused relatively little on it, though their revolutions have indeed deposed several monarchs, and killed some. Dictatorships on the right may be tempted to adopt the trappings of monarchism (some in tropical Africa - that of Bokassa in particular - exemplify this) and some absolute monarchies such as in Muslim states may seem dictatorial; but one dictatorship, that of Franco in Spain chose to succeed itself with a constitutional monarchy.

Various processes of change in modern society probably have an effect of altering subjects' disposition to monarchies, even if such effects are not intended. It is less easy to posit processes which might increase loyalties to monarchs, though some such processes may indeed exist. It is not easy to know how systematic research could be done to examine the notions put forward in the preceding paragraphs, but such studies might be stimulated by this discussion.

Chapter 5

CHANGING PUBLIC OPINION: 1980S AND 1990S

A respected broadcaster and print journalist Libby Purves told her readers[119] that her favorite birthday present was a copy of the BBC's Variety Programmes (that is, radio comedy) Policy Guide for 1948. This included an "Absolute Ban on jokes about: Lavatories, Effeminacy in men; Immorality of any kind. Suggestive reference to: Honeymoon couples; Chambermaids; Fig leaves; Prostitution; Ladies' underwear, e.g. winter draws on; Animal habits, e.g. rabbits; Lodgers; Commercial travellers" (capitals as given in the original). Conspicuous in this list was the absence of anything to do with satirising the royal family, or the monarchy. It was unthinkable in those early post war days that such an institution might be a target for scabrous humor. As we will presently see, the position on that had changed considerably by the 1980s.

Purves explained that since the abandonment of censorship over much of stage and broadcast expression "we have lost the true pleasures of baiting sacred cows because the only sacred cows now are PC ideologies, whose ascendancy can be challenged only by being nasty about the vulnerable". We shall see, in a later chapter, that this may have been one reason why some people may have found pleasure in being unpleasant about Princess Diana, and indeed other members of the royal family who, by tradition and by holding to the principle that it is absolutely necessary for them to be above the fray of public disputation, refrain from answering back and are thus vulnerable to being hurt.

Early in 1977 planning for a drama series eventually televised by Independent (commercial) Television as *Edward And Mrs Simpson* had begun[120]. The press took an interest in the project and the *Sunday Mirror* wrote (18 June 1978) that a "moving cry for help" was made on behalf of the former Mrs Simpson who "fears that the exact truth about the man who gave up the Throne for her may be distorted by television". The same report judged that it would be "impossible for any member of the Royal Family to intervene in such a matter". A television critic (Martin Jackson in the *Daily Mail*, 4

---

[119] Purves, L. (1999) No Laughing Matter. *The Times*, February.

[120] Wober, J.M. (1979) *Edward And Mrs Simpson. Explorations Of The Significance Of The Series For The Public*. London: Independent Broadcasting Authority Research Department.

November 1978) wrote "to watch an actor playing the Queen's uncle romping behind a bush ... or pelting the present Queen Mother with jazz records ... is quite extraordinary ... it ... bares the skeleton that has lain in a cupboard in Buckingham Palace ... an as yet unfinished personal tragedy of real people, still alive and not simply the make-believe of a script-writer's mind".

Audrey Whiting, styled by her paper (the *Sunday Mirror*, 3 December 1978) as an expert on the Royal Family stated "ALL members of the Royal Family ... regret that it has been screened not only in the lifetime of the Duchess ... but in the lifetime of other members of the Royal Family[121] who were closely involved". It was realised that the possibility of embarrassment could extend to producing damage to the esteem in which the royal family was held. The program company (Thames Television) spokesperson replied "at no point does the script suggest they made love before their marriage, and we certainly don't set out to make the Duchess look like a scheming bitch". The *Sunday Times* quoted the program's director[122] as saying "programme makers are fully entitled to make a comment on a woman who took a king from the throne of England ... As far as Mrs Simpson was concerned she was a woman who wanted power and did not get it".

Research on public perceptions of the broadcast took the form of a survey after the last episode had been shown, in December 1978, in the London region. Questions explored whether viewers felt they had been persuaded by the version of events shown in the dramatisation, that it was truthful, what they felt about respecting privacy (even over two decades after the events portrayed) of the participants, several of whom were still alive, and what viewers felt about the royal family and the effects that showing the program might have on them. As to what was then termed a possible "reality shift" having been brought about in viewers' perceptions, twice as many respondents denied being able to assess the reality of the drama, as who considered the two main characters were exact portrayals of their originals. There was a strong degree of concern for the privacy of the royal family, but four times as many people felt that public respect for the Royal Family would be stronger as a result of seeing this series as who felt that it would be weakened as a result. Of course, it was clearly realised that respondents' guesses about possible effects are not necessarily a valid indicator of what would really happen, on which we have extensive evidence to examine, below.

By the mid-1980s it was reported at a conference in Philadelphia[123] that the newspaper TV critic Herbert Kretzmer wrote (in 1980) "the impersonation of royalty is by its very nature a subversive act which so far, at least, stops this side of the throne. Not even Pamela Stephenson (then a well known satirical comedienne, by the late 1990s practising as a therapist in California) would dare to impersonate the Queen whose

---

[121] Note the capitals in which it was customary at that time to refer to the Royal Family.

[122] Then Jeremy Isaacs, later knighted (by the Queen, though not necessarily chosen by her for the honour). As a Glaswegian Scotsman, it would be unthinkable two decades later for him to refer to the throne of "England" (rather than of the United Kingdon thus including Scotland).

[123] Wober, J.M. (1986) Television And Politics In the UK *Annual Conference on Culture & Communication*, Temple University, Philadelphia.

Christmas afternoon message, this year devoted to the themes of service and sacrifice, fulfilled its traditional function of assembling families in a brief act of homage and remembrance". Soon after this was written a satirical comedy series using rubber puppets, *Spitting Image*, did impersonate the Queen. The program's portrayals, of a wide cast of characters in the public eye were remorselessly unkind to all of them in the grossness of their exaggerated images and sloppy behavior. Many public figures were drawn to claim, perhaps as an attempt to outflank the targeting, that they found their portrayals funny. The royal family were not afforded this luxury.

The 1980s witnessed other challenges to restraint in public speech. A theatre critic Kenneth Tynan had urged that because anglo-saxon words for private bodily functions were commonly used by ordinary people, as intensives, and eventually as meaningless punctuation, this should be reflected in theatres and in screened entertainment. He "led" the way by using such words in broadcast speech, and "four letter" expletives are now not infrequent on British screens (especially after 9 pm). There had been an office of the Lord Chamberlain who censored plays, and this practice came under attack as did restraint of publishing works such as D.H. Lawrence's *Lady Chatterley's Lover*, the subject of celebrated court case. Although public opinion surveys published annually by the broadcasting regulator the Independent Broadcasting Authority, continued to show that bad language was unwelcome to substantial sections of the population, it became increasingly commonly broadcast.

Together with a celebration of what had in previous decades been repressed as bad language, under arguments favoring frankness and a return to the scatological openness and ribaldry of writers such as Chaucer and Rabelais, came an insistence, in Britain, that there was no good reason to cultivate a correct form of spoken English. Described as the Queen's (previously the King's) English, it was developed in fee-paying boarding schools and ivy-league universities, and was spoken by broadcast news-readers and thought to give an unfair advantage in careers to those who used it. The Queen herself speaks a sharpened version of this accent, to make fun of which was seen as having some demotic force, by political radicals. Hitherto what was seen as an element in uniting national life (as no one regional accent could thereby gain dominance or prevail) had been re-characterised as divisive, by focussing on its hierarchically distinctive function.

One political event in the mid-1980s illustrates some of the arms-length awe with which the Head of State was regarded. The Republic of South Africa then still practised apartheid, and was pressed by many commonwealth nations and groups in Britain either to abolish this practice or come under an economic and cultural blockade; for example, official national cricket teams were not allowed to play against South Africa and one unofficial attempt to evade this sporting exclusion led to the players concerned being ostracised. The British government, then led by the Conservative Margaret Thatcher, opposed economic sanctions; eventually *The Times* released what it said was an insider's report that the Queen herself sided with the oppositional desire for blockade, against the behavior of the elected government in power. *The Times* then ran a piece by a contributor with the headline "Who Speaks This Treason" - referring to the act of revealing the

Queen's political preference, breaching the practice of maintaining the image of the Head of State as above political involvement. To have printed the suggestion that the Queen was herself partisan was seen as creating a very deep embarrassment for her.

The treason charge (and treason still carries the death penalty) reverberated for a short time, but what put it all aside was the wedding of the Queen's second son Prince Andrew to Sarah Ferguson. One indicator of popular opinion then was to be sensed within the crowd lining the processional route. The Queen received a direct ovation from her subjects, an implicit sign that the quasi-constitutional controversy was not a popular extension of inter-party differences on foreign policy. The royal wedding was televised and received vastly greater audiences during the day than who normally watched in such non prime time hours. Television had not thawed the political impasse on purpose, but this may have been how it had functioned. Hardly anyone in Britain at the time will have been as cynical as observation had become in the 1990s when it was widely charged that major US military actions, against Afghanistani, Somalian and Iraqi targets were public relations escapades designed to distract derision from a President threatened with impeachment. There are signs that during the 1990s, observers in Britain also imputed cynical explanations for actions of the Palace at a time when members of the royal family had clearly lost ground in respect for their personal behavior.

COLLOQUIAL TALK ABOUT THE MONARCHY: LATE '80s

Billig[124] in an amusing and perceptive book draws on interviews carried out with families in 1989 and on a wealth of press and broadcast material up until 1990. These fieldwork dates are important, as we will come across claims that the situation began to change considerably in the 1990s, with 1992 named by the Queen herself in her Christmas message as her "annus horribilis". Thus it is possible for Billig early on to discuss "Imagining the Unimaginable", by which he means that the question was raised in the family interviews as to whether Britain should, or might come to be without its monarchy, to which most people initially had little to say; when they did say something, they rejected both notions.

Having noted that tabloid newspapers often ran pictures upending royal dignity (quintessentially, an occasion when Princess Anne was shown, bottom up, being thrown from her horse) together with joking banter that might be taken as derogatory, Billig wrote (p. 14) that "it is a theme of the present book that the mockery and the lack of deference do not indicate a lack of ideology ... they represent contemporary ideological forms, by which the unprivileged accept their position of ordinariness in relation to extraordinary wealth ... The very existence of monarchy ... in outwardly egalitarian times (in which) the tabloid press hints that 'You The Jury' should decide the official visit of the Queen's husband to Japan and the wardrobe of her younger daughter in law ... is as if

---

[124] Billig, M. (1992) *Talking Of The Royal Family*. London: Routledge.

the ordinary subject occupies the superior position, and royalty awaits the jury's decision. Symbols of inequity are being reversed".

It is not immediately (or even later) clear exactly what Billig meant by "ideology"; perhaps it means that unprivileged people decide not to make revolutionary demands because one can "send up" and occasionally express pressure on royal figures to do certain things that will be popular. This corresponds with the Israelite and ancient Indian models of kingship in which the monarch has to please the public - and with many later acknowledgements especially by British kings and queens to the same effect. Billig then ran through several themes that arose in his conversations, most of which provide reasons for accepting, even celebrating monarchy. First there is the notion that the institution symbolises nationality. Billig's interviews were all with English and none with Scottish families, and he accepted that British nationality and identity, celebrated in imperial history (much of which was established by Scots and Welsh) has been co-opted in particular by the English; he also drew on Nairn's seismic awareness of the rift opening up between English and Scottish identities, in which the latter rejects the British superordinate element. By the late 1980s Prime Minister Thatcher's administration, with its abandonment of smokestack industries (much as Reagan's administration had done in the US) had greatly vexed Scots; but feelings had not yet had time to develop to the extent that it might seem, at least to some eager journalists, that monarchy could be in question in Scotland.

After a section on "the tourist defence of the realm" (monarchy must be a valid and good institution, because tourists admire it; people the world over can name the Queen of England but not the Queen of Spain) Billig discussed deflections of doubts. By this he meant arguments by which ordinary people counter objections that the monarchy may be too expensive an institution, or too outdated. He detected feelings that people think other nations envy Britain, at least its monarchy, in particular that America does so. This is especially important in that in several other ways Britain fears American power and envies it; it is useful then for British people to assume that Americans admire the monarchy.

At this point it can be said that Billig did not rest his analyses on surveys representing the whole of British public opinion. He has drawn themes from discussion with 175 people within 63 families; nevertheless, he wrote in terms of broader generalisations of a sort that can only be confirmed (or dismissed) by careful survey studies. Thus "is one dealing with an institution whose mass appeal is firmly rooted in the times of today? ... present times are producing states of mind which are drawn to the appearances of tradition. Monarchy, thus, fits today's modern, perhaps post modern times"[125].

Much of what Billig distilled from his material can be seen to set the scene for the jolts to public opinion in the 1990s. He quoted from a leader in *The Times* in December 1859 to mark the coming of age of the then Prince of Wales (later King Edward VII)[126];

---

[125] op. cit., p. 56.
[126] op. cit., p. 90.

the advice given to the future King was "to set his people an example of domestic life". Billig quoted the Victorian political scientist Walter Bagehot who wrote that "a family on the throne is an interesting idea ... (and) ... A princely marriage is the brilliant edition of a universal fact, and, as such, it rivets mankind" [127]. The heritage of this notion and its requirements was evident in people's expectations reported to Billig, in which they considered that the royal family should be models of probity in family life. They should respect other people, including ordinary subjects and any departures from such respect, either in terms of remoteness or worse still, of rudeness, caused discomfort. Billig said "the notion of 'image' kept recurring" [128]. Royalty could be seen as a 'job' in which the duties included the setting of a good example - synonymous with 'image', which is what the public sees. Billig did not draw it out immediately that the image is what is carried on a message system, and that most message systems actively influence the content they carry - but that is evident in much else of his book.

This (implicitly) raises the question of how the royal family use, or are used by the mass message systems. Billig quoted the Elizabethan thinker Francis Bacon who realised that people do not envy their monarchs, because monarchs are so elevated - beyond the circle of relevant comparison; Bacon put it that "Kings are not envied but by Kings" [129]. This implies that it would be wise to retain a substantial degree of remoteness if there is any prospect that people might start making comparisons between what they see as royals' behavior and what they expect it to be. However, as Billig pointed out not only did the royal family admit cameras to their private leisure, in a ground breaking documentary shown on BBC in 1969 but younger members of the family appeared in the television game show *It's a (Royal) Knockout* in 1987 [130]. The result of such appearances was to show the royal family as ordinary people, disturbing what Billig finds is their expected function, which is to be something like ideal examples of ordinariness (thus exceptional people), for ordinary people. It would not matter if their real behavior was not ideal - it must only seem (convincingly) to be so. Possibly to help in keeping up such appearances, Billig reported [131] that not only his own interviewees but also several representative poll results indicated that there was a strong feeling that the press (and by implication this also means television - and that is shown as well in my own surveys reported below) should leave a great deal of privacy for the royal family [132].

It may be taking a liberty to suggest an unexpected interpretation for such a desire for reticence: one simple explanation would be that people are being kind in offering someone else a privacy they would like for themselves; another less obvious explanation

---

[127] op. cit., p. 175.

[128] op. cit., p. 99.

[129] op. cit., p. 118.

[130] op. cit., p. 6.

[131] op. cit., p. 146.

[132] This notion that "we don't want to know what The President/The Queen ... is doing privately" became much more familiar to Americans in 1998 when President Clinton was nearly impeached.

may be that people subconsciously want to shield themselves from knowledge that would disturb their ideals or preconceptions. Billig said that many of his interviewees say that much of what is in the press about the royal family is untrue - the media lie[133]. A similar case may exist in America where, when President Clinton was threatened with impeachment there was a great deal of interrogation of Monica Lewinsky. Although audiences were high for such interviews, and her book sold well, this remained material that people did not want to know, and which many would rather they had not had to confront seemingly as part of their citizenly duties.

Billig suggested that monarchism is an institution with elements of "post-modernism" to it. Why we should bother with this seemingly abstruse notion is that Billig and others have theorised that the mass message systems of today have had something to do with producing a state that makes "modernism", paradoxically, obsolete. In this view, modernism is a state in which architecture, engineering, even social institutions are designed to exemplify logical and mechanically correct notions about how such structures would and do work. Modernism seen this way expresses the rationality connected with the period of the enlightenment in which science began to displace religion, thinkers set up logically coherent schemes (like Thomas Paine's *Common Sense*, and the ensuing *Rights of Man*) on which to build constitutions - most famously embodied in the Republics of America and France. Modernism replaced a pre-modernism in which less logical, well constructed social and physical structures were standard.

One of the conditions of "pre-modernism", altered during the reign of modernism was that public and private spaces (and what happened in them) overlapped. In modernism, so such scholars imply, the public and the private were kept more neatly separate. Billig quoted one scholar Urry who wrote that, leaving this modernism behind, "in the post-modernist age the media have also undermined what is to be thought of as properly backstage, what could be made public and what can be kept private. As Jean Baudrillard writes, the distinction between public and private space is lost"[134]. Billig cited on the same page the anecdote that in the 1953 Coronation seven coaches were borrowed from a film studio so "what could be more post modern than an audience watching the appearance of real film props in the film of the historic event?".

In contemplating the new intrusiveness of the media Billig observed that "reporters would be hard put to compete with the salacious details broadcast about Princess Caroline ... (George IV's wife) ... servants were called before Parliament to give evidence whether the Princess's bed-linen bore the tell-tale stains of adultery ... what was said in Parliament was repeated in the broad-sheets of the street. ... the more the Princess was exposed to public inspection, the more the public sympathised with her, condemning the King as her persecutor"[135]. This episode may be more correctly interpreted as a pre-modern piece of behavior, corresponding with procedures in Europe before

---

[133] Billig, M. (1992) *Talking Of The Royal Family*. London: Routledge. p. 158.
[134] op. cit., p. 207.
[135] op. cit., p. 209.

enlightenment days - and still to be found today in some of what are called tribal societies; it also suggests that there was a feeling that even then people did not want to know (or at least did not want to have broadcast) such intimate details, and would side with the victim of such intrusions.

Billig was cautious about accepting the notion, too readily, that post modernity is a real and pervasive replacement of modernity in society. For this to be true he would expect to find signs of a post modern consciousness in the thoughts of his interviewees. What is a post modern consciousness? One sign of it is that it "recognises images as mere images, whilst accepting the image as the reality ... this style is marked by self-reference, for it demystifies the image by revealing how it is produced"[136]. Billig says that quite a number of such signs were there in his interviews - people were "wised up" to the differences between reality and image, and in some cases wanted to take the latter as the important (social and political, rather than biological) reality. He leaves us with the thought that monarchism is a post-modern kind of institution - much as it was also a pre-modern format, leaving (by implication) the idea that republicanism is a paradoxically outdated modernist institution. Life today (one should not label it modern life) is not a clean-cut example of either modernity or of pre/post-modernity; rather, there is much overlapping of forms (and that overlapping has itself been claimed as a post-modern characteristic).

PUBLIC DISCOURSE IN THE EARLY 1990S

All this leaves us analytically prepared to tackle the turmoil of the 1990s. The decade opened with many stories of marital disharmony in the royal family. Prince Charles was accused of alienating Princess Diana, cold-heartedly driving her to bulimia and misery and callously yearning for his real love, Camilla (who had been married to an army officer). Prince Andrew's wife Sarah, Duchess of York was dallying with one or more unappealing figures. Princess Anne's marriage was in trouble. Prince Edward's first career in the military had been abandoned and he wanted to become a television program maker (this could be seen as a post-modern development, where it might be claimed that the privacy-seeker joins the profession of privacy-breakers. He, no doubt had his own version of this move, and an early product of his, about his namesake King Edward VIII could well be seen as a modernist attempt to put the public record straight, in accord with what had been the private experience). All these developments, many presented by the mass message systems of society in salacious, unsympathetic, prurient and hurtful terms, posed a tremendous challenge to the sensibility depicted in Billig's book. It would be difficult in these circumstances still to see the royal family as actors who project an image of family propriety. This being so, one would expect to find a reduction in expressed figures of loyalty to, and belief in the durability of the monarchy. What, then, were poll findings?

---

[136] op. cit., p. 206.

There are two major polling organisations whose findings are regularly published by newspapers - Gallup, and Market Opinion Research International (MORI) as well as many others; but the one which will be drawn upon most here, of these other organisations is the Television Opinion Panel, owned by and run for the main broadcasters, the BBC, the Independent Television Companies, Channel 4 (until recently) and latterly Channel 5. The public pollsters generally obtain samples of 1000 or 2000 adults representing the British public on a quota system, and interview them face to face or by telephone. The contact is personal. The TOP sends self completion booklets week by week to people on a panel (who are also quota-ed to represent the adult public) and generally around 3000 completed sets of questionnaires are returned each week. The contact here is not openly personal, and the difference is likely to be important when measuring opinion on topics that are fiercely reported in a partisan way in the press.

MORI publishes a report on British Public Opinion from which the figures in the following two tables have been drawn (these results will have been published in the press, at the time they were first measured):

Table 5.1: Public Predictions of Continuity of Monarchy

Q Looking to the future, do you think Britain will or will not have a monarchy?

	Jan 1990 %	Feb 1991 %	May 1992 %	Dec 1992 %	Feb 1996 %	Aug 1997 %	Aug 1998 %
in ten years?							
Will	95	90	85	76	76	80	79
Will not	2	5	8	**18**	17	15	16
NET 'will'	93	85	77	**58**	59	65	63

The crucial element in this sequence of results is that in the second half of 1992 (and it is important to note, just after the fire at Windsor Castle) the proportion doubled, who thought that the monarchy would be replaced within the next decade. In saying this, it is likely that respondents were reflecting what they were given to believe (in the mass message system contents) was likely to happen. Another polling organisation[137] found, in October 1997 in answer to the question "Do you think the Monarchy and the Royal Family will still exist in the next century?" that 71 per cent said yes and 23 per cent said no (six per cent offered no answer); this margin of 48 per cent seeing the monarchy continue "in the next century" lies somewhere between the MORI positive surplus of 65 per cent in August 1997 - for "the next ten years" and MORI's *negative* margin of 38 per cent who, in the same survey thought the monarchy would not last for a further one hundred years.

It is important then to put the results on the question reported next, into the perspective of what has first been shown. It is also important to realise that the polling result depends considerably on the exact terms of the question, and its outcome is in itself an ingredient of the climate within which people revise their guesses about the future. Some people at least, especially when speaking to an interviewer, may be reluctant to say they personally favor something which they may just have said will not exist.

Table 5.2: Preferences for Republic or Monarchy: 'Public" Polling
Q Would you favour Britain becoming a republic or remaining a monarchy?

	Apr 1993	Jan 1994	Dec 1994	Sep 1997	Mar 1998	Aug 1998
	%	%	%	%	%	%
Republic	18	17	20	18	19	16
Monarchy	69	73	71	73	74	75
NET: Monarchy	**51**	56	51	**55**	55	59

The outcome of this is that there has 'always' been a plurality of over half the public, who prefer the monarchy *over and above* those who want a republic. The figure reduced to 51 in the survey shortly after the *annus horribilis*, but it appears not to have been shifted by the events surrounding the death of Diana Princess of Wales (shown in the measurement in September 1997); more recently it has risen to closer to sixty percent. Those preferring a republic (who may also have said they believe a monarchy will not survive - the requisite cross tables are not provided, nor even ever discussed by the newspapers which report these matters) have been falling slightly since 1994 while the monarchist group have consolidated their position around three quarters of the public.

Another comparison across the years has been made with a question carried by the Television Opinion Panel (see below) first in 1986 and then again in March 1991. Results from the two surveys were as follows:

Table 5.3: Preferences for Republic or Monarchy: 'Private' Polling

		All %	Young %	Medium %	Old %
The powers of the British Sovereign should remain as they are now, for the foreseeable future	(1991)	60	42	62	68
	(1986)	67	56	71	77
The position of the British Sovereign should rapidly be scaled down to make Britain a republic like most other countries	(1991)	8	11	9	7
	(1986)	6	11	5	2
NET: Monarchy	(1991)	52	31	53	61
	(1986)	61	45	66	75

---

[137] Gallup - personal communication.

There was a small reduction in overall support for monarchy, similar to the extent suggested by MORI's personal interview polls. It must be pointed out that in 1986 the 'young' grouping was restricted to those aged 16 - 24 and the medium aged from 25 - 44 with the old being 45 and over. In 1991 the youngest subgroup were defined as being 16 - 35 and the medium aged as 36 - 54. Those aged between 16 and 24 in 1986, fifteen years later were aged 31 - 39, somewhat younger than those in the later survey aged 36 - 54. In general, older people in both surveys were much more inclined to support the monarchy; however, the result that the middle aged group in 1991 included 62 per cent who supported the monarchy (who sample from the young set among whom 'only' 56 per cent supported the monarchy in 1986) suggests quite strongly that as people get older they do not just take their youthful attitudes with them but change their attitudes towards those held by older people in an earlier decade.

MORI have asked another question in many of their polls, the results of which should be examined alongside the *personal* preference items, above. This other question asks for some kind of *detached* assessment.

Table 5.4: Public Assessment of Effects of Republicanism

Q On balance, do you think Britain would be better off or worse off if the monarchy was abolished, or do you think it would make no difference?

	Apr 1984 %	Feb 1987 %	Oct 1987 %	Jan 1989 %	Jan 1990 %	May 1992 %	Dec 1992 %	Jan 1994 %
Better off	5	5	5	7	6	14	17	14
Worse off	77	73	63	57	63	50	37	47
No difference	16	20	29	34	28	32	42	35
NET: worse minus better:	72	68	58	50	57	36	20	33

	Dec 1994 %	Feb 1996 %	Aug 1996 %	Jul 1997 %	Aug 1997 %	Sep (a) 1997 %	Sep (b) 1997 %	Sep (c) 1997 %
Better off	17	17	16	12	16	18	16	11
Worse off	40	34	42	39	50	48	53	45
No difference	38	42	39	43	31	27	28	39
NET: worse minus better:	33	17	26	27	34	30	37	34

Many comments are worth making about the results in Table 5.4. One is that the difference between those who think the country would be worse off (monarchists), offset by those believing the country would be better off (republicans) is in every measurement positive. Secondly, there have been immense changes across time, from a plurality of over 70 per cent down to a plurality on one occasion of only seventeen percent. Thirdly, the republicanist proportion which has varied from 5 to 18 per cent has on no occasion reached let alone risen above 20 per cent - or one in five people. What has been happening then is a softening of certainty about monarchism. Figures have been shown in bold, where they signify a substantial difference from what had gone before. Thus there had been an important reduction in the monarchist surplus, in 1987, and again in 1992 (the *annus horribilis*); and thirdly, there was another reduction in the monarchist surplus, to its lowest point, in February 1996. Since then, the monarchist surplus has increased somewhat; this was true in the (a) measure in September 1997 - which was immediately after the death of Diana Princess of Wales, and even more so in the (b) measure - taken on 6-7 September when the tabloid newspapers put forth the greatest weight of disaffection in the post-death week (see the next chapter) though there was no further gain in the monarchist surplus in the (c) measure, early in the week after the funeral.

Such figures embody a multi-faceted truth about public perceptions, and the structure of public opinion can be viewed from different angles and described in different ways. One republicanist is Polly Toynbee, who in 1995 was the BBC's Social Affairs correspondent, writing a weekly column in the mass circulation *Radio Times* and contributing articles to the *Independent* (though on balance republicanist) daily newspaper. Soon after the television broadcast in which Diana Princess of Wales gave an interview in which she revealed her dismay at the breakdown of her marriage, three contrasting perceptions of the interview and of what it disclosed appeared in that paper. Toynbee's was the most republicanist and she noted that "the latest MORI poll shows more people (55 per cent) think the country would be better off, or no different, without a monarchy"[138]. This is similar to the benchmark in February 1996 when 42 per cent said "no difference" and 17 per cent said "better off", making 59 per cent in all. It is a moot point whether this allocation of those noting no difference to the republicanist camp is the most valid way of describing matters, especially when twice as many said "worse off" than who said "better off" under a republic. Moreover, the more personal preferential question fielded by MORI all along showed that there was over 50 per cent plurality for a monarchy.

Toynbee's argument, a strong one, asked "what does monarchy stand for? It is the apex of a hierarchy and that is not a fitting model for a pluralistic democracy. The royal insignia stamps a notion of absolute sovereignty on all that politicians do in the name of the Queen. It diminishes us, turning us all into subjects"[139]. Later in her article Toynbee

---

[138] Polly Toynbee in *The Independent*, 22 November 1995.

[139] idem; it is worth noting that the way in which the word subject is understood, in the grammar of Latin-derived languages indicates that the subject is the person in a statement who has the initiative. The object is the person or thing upon whom action devolves. The anti-monarchist interpretation of the word subject in which it is presumed that the word describes a person as an object has meanwhile prevailed, at least in the rules of the British Psychological Society, in

asks "What must we do? Alas ... Her Majesty's Loyal Opposition bends in the deepest bow to the throne. ... Labour promises to ... giving Scotland a parliament - satisfaction to the 8 per cent who live there. What of the 92 per cent of the rest of us yearning to breathe free of the Westminster autocracy symbolised by the Crown?". If this means anything it presumably implies that all 92 per cent of the United Kingdom population not living in Scotland oppose the "autocracy symbolised by the Crown" - but neither of the polling questions whose results are given by MORI would give any support to such an opinion. Toynbee's republicanism has run away with itself here. It is nevertheless, an ingredient in the public discourse and one element in the nexus within which real changes in sentiment have, as shown above, occurred.

Toynbee's remarks appeared in 1995, during one of those "nodes" or surges of attention involving matters royal, following the interview with the late Princess Diana screened on television. As has been emphasised above another such node occurred in 1992, the "annus horribilis" when royal family broken marriages were followed by the fire in Windsor Castle. A small correspondence after this event may be instructive as regards the role of the BBC, widely regarded (not least by itself) as Britain's prime broadcaster and one whose existence is expressed in the provisions of a Royal Charter. How the BBC reported the aftermath of the fire is thus important in contributing to the shape and temper of the discourse.

AN ARGUMENT WITH THE BBC:
EARLY REACTIONS TO THE WINDSOR FIRE

In November 1998 a major fire broke out in Windsor Castle. The Castle is a historic building, begun in Norman times nearly 1000 years ago and maintained and modified as a royal palace and an emblem symbolic not just of English monarchy but of British monarchy and of the wider national achievement in establishing a world wide empire. During the fire helicopter pictures dramatically showed the destruction going on and all the newspapers the next day ran huge pictures and major stories on the event. It seemed that a superhuman power had struck at the vital centre of the monarchy - an image with a huge unspoken resonance towards the end of an extremely difficult year for the royal family.

Speaking on the *Today* program on 21 November, a flagship regular on Radio 4 - the principal station for news and discussion - the well known presenter Sue McGregor interviewed David Mellor, a cabinet minister with responsibility for Culture and Heritage. As I put it in a letter dated 23 November, to Mr Marmaduke Hussey, the Chairman of the Governors of the BBC, "McGregor based a question on the stated

---

whose publications it is forbidden to refer to people who take part in surveys or who have their opinions or reactions measured in other situations, as subjects, supposedly implying that they have thus been demeaned. We have to refer to people in experiments and surveys - even when they have had no part in designing these - as participants.

premise that the Royal Family are now in a state of reduced esteem amongst the British public (and so, it was implied, the people would be unhappy if the Government were to pay to restore the castle). Ms McGregor had repeated what a number of journalists had said before (e.g., Polly Toynbee, in the Radio Times). However, neither Toynbee nor McGregor cited any actual evidence showing lowered public esteem".

The letter continued "if these journalists actually had recourse to systematic evidence on public opinion, this would show that there has been no effective change, in 1992, despite a furious assault upon the role and performance of the monarchy ... of any reduced support for monarchism as a system. To restate such an ill-founded notion ... might eventually bring about some such development, and it would be most regrettable if the BBC was guilty of taking part in bringing about such an effect". The letter ended with a hope for reassurance that steps would be taken urgently within the BBC to appraise journalists with knowledge of the real state of public opinion, and to make sure that such knowledge is correctly used in discussions and interviews.

Over a month later, there had been neither reply to nor even acknowledgement of this letter. What has to be done in such situations, to induce a reply, is to write a reminder, together with a copy to one's Member of Parliament. The Members of the House of Commons at that time took an oath of loyalty to the Sovereign (the Queen) whose sovereignty is expressed in the presence of the Mace, on a desk in front of the Speaker of the said House. Until the reforms of Mr Blair's administration which was elected in 1997, Sovereignty in Britain was an idea embodied in Parliament rather than in the people. The Member of Parliament thus has some symbolic - and it may be added spiritual leverage. Accordingly I wrote again to Mr Hussey (30 December 1992) with a copy of the correspondence, to the local MP. The MP's acknowledgement (dated 5 January) of receipt of the letter, and a note that she had written to Mr Hussey herself preceded an acknowledgement from an official responsible for Viewer and Listener Correspondence at the BBC, saying "I am writing on behalf of the Chairman to thank you for your letter of 23 November, and to say that we have taken note of its contents".

This is a manoeuvre intended to close off most excepting the most persistent correspondents. However, in this case I was not just corresponding or complaining, I was carrying out an experiment, exploring ways in which what is a Public Service broadcasting organisation dealt with what was a quintessentially historic and current public matter. Aside from the official mentioned above there followed a note from the Editor of News and Current Affairs; he said (dated 15th January) "I thought Sue MacGregor's[140] question was rather precisely phrased. The future role of the Royal Family (sic - not the monarchy) in this country is under a lot of scrutiny at the moment and not just from the tabloid press. As you will be aware many MPs have also raised the matter and it clearly is a topic over which public debate will continue. We shall try to reflect (sic) that debate accurately and fairly". There was also a card, franked 28 January

---

[140] Mr Harding the (then) News Editor spelled the name of his interviewer differently from how the Chairman rendered it. I have copied what they wrote.

saying the Chairman thanked me for my letter (written over two months previously) "to which you will be receiving a reply as soon as possible".

The Chairman's letter, dated 14 January, arrived first as a photocopy in an enclosure from the Member of Parliament. He had obtained the transcript of the broadcast and reported that "Sue McGregor's question ... was 'I have to put a rather awkward point to you. One excepts the Queen from this, but the Royal Family is not held in very high esteem at the moment. Is there a national mood to foot an enormous bill when they don't have proper fire precautions in the palace?". Mr Hussey went on to say that "...support for the monarchy as an institution ... was not at issue in the interview". He says "the best regarded series of survey figures is that of the MORI organisation ... I understand Sue McGregor's remarks were consistent with their findings ...".

At this point it is appropriate to look back at the results of one of MORI's many questions, repeated at several occasions. This shows a large drop in (monarchist) opinion that the country would be worse off if the monarchy were abolished, had indeed occurred in the first half of 1992; it continued to fall, in the measurement at the end of 1992, after the Windsor fire and the discourse about it in the press and which was to some extent reflected in broadcasting. It is important to recognise however, (as Hussey and the editor Harding avoided doing) that discussion within broadcasts is not realistically seen as merely reflective; it may well also to have a formative role.

At the end of 1992 I was nearing the end of employment within the Independent Television Commission. I had, nevertheless, written to the BBC in my role as citizen and listener. From the start of 1993 I was no longer employed at the ITC (where I had access to certain BBC research studies, as well as having initiated several studies of my own, on perceptions of the monarchy, especially as these may have related to broadcasting, its particular programs and its overall culture). I therefore continued the experiment with a letter to Mr Hussey (21 January 1993). I underlined the question of "what steps are being taken within the BBC to appraise its journalists with knowledge of the real state of public opinion concerning the monarchy in general and of HM the Queen in particular". I returned to the notion raised by MacGregor that "the Royal Family were in a state of reduced esteem ... and so, it was implied, the people would be unhappy if the Government were to pay to restore the castle". I drew attention to the existence of the Television Opinion Panel - of which the News Editor Philip Harding had made no mention - and redefined my previous observations now as *complaints* (something which has a separate administrative existence!); there had been a "likely breach of 'impartiality' ... in failing to identify with the (true) fulcrum of public opinion concerning the monarchy" and a "lapse of accuracy" in using MORI (and other published) survey results while passing over copious internal (proprietary) survey data available to the broadcasters.

A further month later (though now without recourse to the MP), a reply arrived from Mr Hussey. He assured me that "a Fire Brigade report ... criticised fire precautions at Windsor. Since Windsor Castle is owned and managed by the state, not the Queen, I do not believe Sue MacGregor's reference to this report reflected on the competence of the

Queen in any way". He repeated the insiders' defence of occlusion of results from the Television Opinion Panel "the figures are often sensitive and are restricted to the programme-makers who have commissioned the research. Journalists can therefore hardly be encouraged to consider (the Television Opinion Panel) as a source on non-broadcasting matters".

Let us recall what Sue MacGregor is said to have said: "... the Royal Family is not held in very high esteem at the moment ... is there a national mood to foot an enormous bill when they (sic) don't have proper fire precautions in the palace?". I now pointed out to Mr Hussey (letter, 1 March) that "it is not only the intrinsic meaning of words, but also the extrinsic setting in which they occur that has to be attended to by those who are wardens of fairness on the airwaves ... when so much else in public speech at that time implied that the Queen was personally responsible for (mal)administration of a national asset, namely the security of Windsor Castle ... makes it seem that MacGregor was indeed not 'excepting' the Queen but implicating her". I suggested that one approach could have been to have said to the Minister, Mr Mellor "will this property tragedy ... prompt the nation to rally round and support Her Majesty after an event which is our loss as much as it is hers? ... Instead ... the question was ... directed ... towards a base emotion: she is rich, let her pay".

The theme of the Queen's wealth had been discussed extensively in the press in the months immediately before the fire. The *Times Education Supplement* (August 14 1992, p. 26) declared that "the wealth of the present Queen is currently estimated at around £1 billion"; the piece, by Ann McFerran offered links between money and lack of appeal: "fiscal privileges ... have allowed a kind of canker into the very heart and soul of British monarchy ... Mori reports how support for the Royals (sic) has dropped from 77 per cent to 55 per cent. 80 per cent ... think the Queen should pay tax and no less than half consider the monarchy a luxury we can no longer afford".

The *TV Times* commented on an episode in an ITV six part series on *The Monarchy* "if we assume (sic) that she had £30m invested 20 years ago ... adding on personal estates (etc) her private wealth could be (sic) £1 billion"; together with these conjectures it was explained that "the Queen's fortune as Head of State is £5-7 billion. The riches include art treasures, the Crown Estates and Buckingham Palace. These national treasures aren't hers to sell ...". The *Times* followed up (28 September 1992) reporting a *Business Age* magazine estimate that the Queen was tenth in the list of the fifty richest women in Britain (headed by Christina Goulandris); Her Majesty's wealth was given here as £100m, which is one tenth of the (American) one billion value given elsewhere.

The BBC's social affairs correspondent Polly Toynbee, writing in the *Radio Times* welcomed "Sue Townsend's new book ... to be serialised on Radio 4, ... a splendidly comic republican fantasy about the deposition of the Royals and their removal to a nasty Midlands council estate ... The timing of this book couldn't be luckier, arriving when, in the first time for more than 50 years, republicanism is starting to be seriously discussed ... the Royal Family appears to have become the Royal Broken Home, an embarrassment for the Defender of the Faith ... the undermining effect on public attitudes to royalty is already apparent in the opinion polls ... the Queen is being pressed to pay her taxes ...".

Not only was the press interested in the Queen's wealth; they were also deeply engaged with the affairs of the Duchy of Cornwall, an institution run by or for Prince Charles, who is also the Duke of Cornwall[141]. Under the headline "GIVE AND TAKE (We're giving, the royals are taking") the *Today* newspaper reported that "The coffers of Prince Charles and the Royal Family were overflowing ... Heritage Secretary ... pledged £80 million of taxpayer's money to repair ...Windsor Castle, the favourite home of the world's richest woman. Then Prince Charles ... put up the rents of the impoverished pensioners whose homes are run-down cottages ... by a crippling FIFTY percent. Letters ... dropped on their doormats while the prince was pheasant-shooting at Sandringham". Pictures of a rugged pensioner, in front of his unheated cottage and of Prince Charles being handed a dead pheasant by the Duke of Westminster accompanied the story.

Today was a paper owned by the American citizen (and reputed republican enthusiast) Rupert Murdoch; though it went out of business, he also owns the *Sun*, the market-leading tabloid; the *Sun* chose not to be openly hostile, but belittling. The lead picture was of a workman wearing a wide grin and his trousers round his ankles, seated on a huge urn, with the comment: "What a pot he's got - the Queen's rare malachite vase urns no respect from a cheeky repairman ...". Other photographs showed workmen enjoying mock swordplay with antique weapons. The limping tabloid the *Daily Star* carried a headline "Flaming Cheek. As we cough up for Windsor blaze: Charles puts rents 50% up, Queen bans guide dog from Palace". Inside the paper a main columnist Brian Hitchen explained "I don't believe the Queen should have to foot the entire bill for rebuilding Windsor Castle. Because she doesn't own it. ... It's our heritage we are talking about ... Her castle is our castle ... If it had been (insured) somebody would have bitched about the massive premiums ... Sadly, the Queen is surrounded by courtiers who don't understand the thoughts and feelings of ordinary people ... if she had good people around her, she wouldn't apply for grants for her fences ... allow Prince Charles to increase the rents of his tenants, and she certainly wouldn't ban guide dogs for the blind from ceremonies at Buckingham Palace ...". Several other cost cutting suggestions followed.

The *Daily Mirror*, second in circulation to the Sun ran a headline "UNFAIR, MA'AM" with a picture of the Queen looking serious and the text "This little old lady's home was wrecked by a fire. She was not insured. So taxpayers are going to pay £60m to fix it up again". Next to this was an equal sized picture of a man with the text "This old man is 84, lives in a cottage which floods, is riddled with damp and eats up his pension in heating bills. The Royals want to up his rent by 50%". The paper's editorial column was headed "Windsor wallies" followed by: "Hardly a day goes by without the House of Windsor sowing more seeds of its own destruction ... Meanness, greed and blinkered disregard for the feelings of the people are the mark of a dying, not a lasting dynasty ...". The *Mirror* had asked readers to telephone in to say whether they thought the Queen

---

[141] All the extracts in this and the next two paragraphs were from issues of papers on November 24th 1992.

should pay, herself, for the Windsor Castle repairs - 40,000 called in evidently, with only 5 per cent considering the taxpayer should pay the bill.

Two papers, the conservative *Sunday Telegraph* (on 22 November) and the *Daily Express* (24 November) were supportive in different ways, of the monarchy. The former offered a Page One Comment including " ... Windsor is more than a museum. It is the home of the reigning Queen and it lends its name to the ruling dynasty. Damage to the fabric serves as a metaphor for damage to the royal family and for the threat to the constitution ... Edmund Burke ... 200 years ago ... believed 'As long as the British monarchy ... like the proud Keep of Windsor, girt with the double belt of its kindred and coeval towers ... endure ... we are all safe together, the high from the blights of envy ... the low from the iron hand of oppression' ... There will be some, like the Labour MPs already calling on the Queen to pay for the repairs herself, who have no imagination ... but most people surely do mind ...".

The *Express* ran an opinion piece by Christopher Wilson which, though strongly critical of leading royal family members and senior courtiers equally admired Prince Andrew who, in an impromptu televised press conference presented a display of "calm, charm and quick wittedness ... a model of efficiency and decorum ... He had undoubtedly braved the flames, and came to tell the world about it. 'Her majesty is absolutely devastated ... she is inside the building, helping to take stuff out as a precaution' ... over his ill-starred marriage ... Andrew never put a foot wrong ... compare this with the behavior of his elder brother ... who finds it impossible to keep his agonies private ... Public decorum sits well on Andrew: When urgent journalists were quizzing him about 'Your Mother' he corrected them, without giving the smallest offence, by referring to 'Her Majesty' ... Andrew must remain on standby just in case greatness is thrust upon him".

Returning to the correspondence with the BBC, I explained that the Opinion Panel had been asked their views on the monarchy several times during 1992. The question was a stringent one asking them whether they agreed (or disagreed) that there was "no longer any need for monarchy". It is usually easier for compliant people to say they agree with statements and it takers more initiative to feel one has to disagree. This being said, on the proposition that there is no longer any need for a monarchy,

6 - 12 January	67% disagreed
22 - 29 June	67% disagreed
28 Sept - 4 October	66% disagreed
28 Dec - 3 January	62% disagreed

These results resemble one from Gallup which reported that 64 per cent agreed that "the monarchy is a national institution of which we can still be proud". They also suggest that there had not been much erosion (unlike what MORI found) during 1992 right until its end, after the Windsor fire and the sour opposition to the costs of restoration. I suggested "it would have been useful ... had the journalistic community known more widely, past the milestones of Andrew Morton's book, the Ferguson and phone-tapping scandals, that support for the Monarchy had been so firm in 1992 ... there is another fact, agreed upon by MORI and the TOP that support for the Monarchy fell between 1986 and 1992; but that can not have been due to the press-orchestrated climate of 1992".

One month later (30 March 1993) the Deputy Secretary of the BBC replied on behalf of Mr Hussey who had "noted your further observations on opinion polls". This repeats the diplomatic "closure" formula designed to end correspondence, but to which I decided to give one last turn. I wrote on 9 April to Mr Hussey on the Need for Operational Intelligence (Hussey had been a high ranking military officer during World War II) to maintain Quality in BBC Output. The MP David Blunkett had just written to The Times emphasising the need for the BBC to aim for high quality in its output; this connected with my concern on reading that Polly Toybee had written in *The Radio Times* (3 - 9 April) that "a moral panic grips the nation". I assured Hussey that there was no evidence of any moral panic; concern, about terrorism, crime, unemployment, yes; but not panic. A BBC newscaster Nick Clarke had implied that there would be an outcry if even one British life was lost through peacekeeping duties in Bosnia - but the Television Opinion Panel in a survey had found that 40 per cent *rejected* "the arguments of those who say that Britain should keep soldiers out of Bosnia". Mr Clarke could have been better informed through access to TOP findings - a lapse similar to that which detracted from Sue MacGregor's interview. Mr Hussey did not reply, but Mr Blunkett - to whom a copy had been sent - did; he explained that "part of the problem is that very young journalists ... are now brought in to edit and produce current affairs and news programmes. Most of them are frankly wet behind the ears and haven't the foggiest idea about the issues they are dealing with".

Several points emerge from this story of the BBC correspondence. The mass message systems in Britain carry a great deal of news or factual information, reported without much selectivity or what is now call "spined"; however there is also a great deal of comment. Some of the comment is bylined, but some comment takes the form of an attitude woven into a headline in print or into a question in a broadcast interview. The BBC has a duty to be impartial in matters of political controversy, and what is more, is governed under the aegis of a Royal Charter. It is extremely disinclined to admit any wrongdoing and is very skilled at fending off critics and their criticism. What is not visible to the outsider who takes the trouble to press through a series of letters is that inwardly the episode does reinforce a degree of caution. Many broadcasting journalists, even possibly including the Court correspondent may have republican sympathies; but working in an institution like the BBC they respond to outward pressure to some extent, to try to restrain subjectivity[142].

---

[142] In 1997 a controversy erupted over whether reporting of wars should be objective and somehow neutral, or committed - and hence partisan. Sites and episodes such as former Yugoslavia, Afghanistan, Central Africa, East Timor - and more problematic for Britain, Northern Ireland were examples in fierce debate. In war the traumatic experiences of reporters and urgency of need for political resolutions or change are more immediate than in the debate over monarchy,

The Aftermath of the Windsor Fire:
Sophisticated Audience Research in 1992

Within a few days of the fire the Queen made a speech at the City of London's Guildhall in which she reviewed the hardships her family had experienced in the year past, and used the now familiar term "annus horribilis" to describe it all. The *Sun* proclaimed "The Queen pays tax and it's victory for people power". A very different paper[143] suggested " In the Queen's mind ... there was no doubt that her troubles had been compounded by the efforts of several tabloid newspapers ... there is a popular theory that her troubles lie at the door of Rupert Murdoch ... It was the *Sun* that 'revealed' details of a taped telephone call between what was claimed to be the Princess of Wales and a male admirer. ... *Today* ... has strongly criticised the Queen over tax, and the *Sunday Times* ... recently serialised Andrew Morton's book on the marriage of the Prince and Princess of Wales, and which claimed the Princess had made several suicide attempts. Whether driven by the proprietor's republicanism or the fact that royal stories have given them an edge in circulation wars, the Murdoch stable has been in the van of royal exposure".

Langton and Elliott provided a brief history of the Palace's relationships with the mass message systems, which agrees in most details with similar accounts provided elsewhere. The story was taken back to 1936 when the British press were very reticent about Edward VIII's affairs with women and eventually with his wife-to-be the divorcée Wallis Simpson, and it was disclosure in the American press which finally brought the story to Britain, prompting political hostility and presently precipitating abdication. The British press were then prepared to take an initiative should a marital scandal erupt again. World War II provided an interlude in which George VI and Queen Elizabeth exemplified rock solid stability. The new Queen Elizabeth II overrode Prime Minister Winston Churchill's opposition and allowed television cameras into Westminster Abbey for her Coronation (prompting the sale of 3 million new television sets and establishing the BBC, with their ace commentator Richard Dimbleby as lead broadcasters of national heritage events).

A trace of sourness emerged when Prince Philip was vexed by intrusion of cameras into the life of Prince Charles at his boarding school, Gordonstoun (which, on the northernmost tip of Scotland was as far away as could be managed, in the British Isles, from London, the mass message system centre). A royal press officer denied that the "tired" Queen was pregnant in 1959 when, seven months later Prince Andrew was born - "how could the press ever trust Buckingham Palace again?"[144]. We will return to Prince

---

where in Britain change has proceeded for several hundred years, and individual events are not (so) traumatic. The professional options for journalists are nevertheless similar.

[143] James Langton and Valerie Elliott. Triumph of the Fourth Estate. *Sunday Telegraph*, 29 November 1992, p. 21.

[144] op. cit., a non-member of the press might expect trust to return if and when intrusive questioning abated and, perhaps, when a new and more adept press officer might be installed.

Andrew and the theme of trust, below. In 1973 however the then editor of the *Sunday Mirror* said he was asked to run a story ending speculation about a relationship between Princess Anne and Captain Mark Phillips. The paper agreed, but a few weeks later an engagement was announced. Then in 1981 the *Sunday Mirror* reported that Prince Charles and the then Diana Spencer has met secretly overnight on the Royal Train; the Palace repudiated the story, but the paper - and the rest of the press corps believed there was substance in the report.

Other royal family stories which bordered on showbiz chit chat at a pole opposite to that of the decorum of George VI's household included Prince Andrew's friendship with a Miss Koo Stark, understood once to have taken part in a soft porn movie; Princess Margaret's relationship with a playboy Roddy Llewellyn; Prince Edward's resignation from the Royal Marines; the collapse of the marriage of the Queen's daughter Princess Anne with Captain Mark Phillips, and that of Prince Andrew; the publication of intimate photographs of the Duchess of York, and the participation of "younger royals" in a television game show *It's A Royal Knockout*, in 1987.

On the positive side of the public relations equation there was a broadcast of the investiture of Charles as Prince of Wales, at a ceremony designed to amalgamate the needs of modern television, with ancient resonances, held in Caernarvon Castle. In the 1960s the Palace Press Secretary was the Australian William Heseltine, who believed in openness and who supported a television documentary on royal family life, shown in 1969. This has led to many comments leading from the Victorian theorist Walter Bagehot who warned that too much light shed on the inner (and ordinary human) nature of the royal family would destroy its magic. The weddings of both Prince Charles and Princess Diana, and of Prince Andrew and Sarah Ferguson were huge television successes, prompting much public support in the streets.

It could be argued from these examples that the mass message systems have in certain ways helped stimulate support for the monarchy. On the other hand, they continue their invasive interest even during normal times when incidents that are not "news" when they concern anyone else are played as such, and this intrusiveness can and does destabilise individuals and relationships under such scrutiny; the experience of most of those in show biz is testimony to this turbulence. Michael Shea, the Queen's former press secretary wrote to *The Times* (just before the Windsor fire) in 1992 arguing that the tabloid papers were "a cancer in the soft underbelly of the nation" damaging individuals and institutions with their mixture of "sexual innuendo, hypocrisy and lies".

There is a paradox involved in the centre of this nexus of conflicting forces. The press want to delve; the royal family (like other celebrities) want to moderate intrusion - or accept it mostly when it is felt to be useful to them; the public on their part have said in different ways and on repeated occasions in many opinion polls that they favor self restraint by the press, or even upon them by some appointed body. The paradox arises if one has to explain that when intrusion does occur into some royal affair then one has to explain what is claimed to be a substantial increase in sales of a paper (or in broadcasting terms, in audience for a program). The answers to this may include that there are not indeed such great increments in newspaper purchases or television audiences, and evidence on this will appear in Chapter Six. For the present, it will be useful to look at the results of a survey[145] which includes several questions relevant to intrusiveness.

Table 5.5: Attitudes Concerning Need for Restraint in Reporting Royalty

	Agree %	Disagree %
The number of reporters following a royal tour should be kept to a reasonable number so as not to inconvenience them	77	7
Reporting should deal with official royal visits abroad and leave alone Royal holidays in skiing/other resorts	66	14
Reporters should not get too far into the details of the Royals' private lives	63	14
There has been too much press coverage of minor misdeeds of younger members of the Royal family	56	17
Sometimes they make more fun than they should do of the Royal family	38	28

Those who did not reply as above, said they were not sure; people replied by self-completion of items in a booklet and over 2800 took part - in March 1991. The make-up of the responding panel was multiplied by factors so as to balance the proportions of answers correctly, to result in a sample that accurately reflected social composition and hence the opinions of the British population. It is clear that people supported a greater degree of reticence than they had been provided - and were to encounter six years later when Princess Diana died. In this same survey measures were taken of the degree of support for the monarchy, and of frequency of viewing of royal stories on television, of reading them in the press, and of overall amount of viewing of television. Support for the monarchy - in terms of agreeing that "the powers of the British Sovereign should remain as they are now, for the foreseeable future" came from 52 per cent of respondents but, taking account of those 14 per cent who did not answer this question, amounted to over 60 per cent of those who did offer an opinion.

An important purpose of the survey was to explore whether viewing (or press reading) experience had any connection with support for the monarchy. In fact there was no correlation between the measures - those who supported the monarchy were not either more, or less frequent viewers and readers of reporting of the topic. One could not say, from this, that there was any sign, by early 1991, that consumption of the avalanche of material influenced, let alone undermined support for the monarchy. There was another reason for this particular survey and that was to act as a benchmark for studies that were to follow.

---

[145] Wober, J.M. (1991 May) *Television And The Monarchy. Patterns of Viewing and Attitudes.* London: Independent Television Commission Research Reference Paper.

Amongst the blows to the royal family in early 1992 was the publication of Andrew Morton's book *Diana: Her True Story*. The *Sunday Times* lead story of 7 June introduced its serialisation as by "the royal biographer" with the words "it was anger at the lie of their publicly paraded 'happy marriage' that first prompted friends of the Princess to waive all royal protocol and talk to Andrew Morton". Here we have the accusation of lying, imputed to the Palace by the paper then edited by Andrew Neil; the palace's concern may well have been one of trying to maintain a calm appearance - for the sake of a possible modus vivendi in the marriage and importantly, for a climate in which the two young sons could experience a healthier public environment.

Neil returned to his accusations years later[146]. He wrote "as Britain became a less deferential society from the Sixties onwards, it was inevitable that the media would start reporting on the monarchy in ways which did not have the royal seal of approval. The arrival of Rupert the Republican (he means Murdoch) as a major force in Fleet Street reinforced the trend ...". It is worth noting that Murdoch's own (ex-) employee attributes at least some of the turning climate to a foreign republican. Neil considers that the Windsor family could not "muster the discipline and dedication to behave in ways that the British people expected of its royal folk ... so ... it started to lie when embarrassing stories appeared ... you do not have to take my word for this. No less ... than Prince Andrew has recently confessed that for the past 20 years the royal family - or at least those paid to do its bidding - has lied to the media ...".

Neil recalled the 1986 crisis when he had run the headline story exposing what were supposed to be the Queen's political opinions. He accused Michael Shea, then the Queen's press secretary, of first "feeding" the story out "confidentially" and then denying it when it was in print. Although this kind of thing is common in the British political world Neil perhaps expected a greater privilege when dealing with the Palace. Not receiving this, he believes "the Palace organised a lynch mob that was baying for blood - mine ... pressure was put on the directors of *Times* newspapers to have me sacked. ... if I (was) ... forced to resign then perhaps the Palace would be prepared to orchestrate the resignations of Shea and Heseltine ... fortunately ... Murdoch was disinclined to agree to such a deal ... years later, Lord St John of Fawsley admitted 'It was more true, Andrew, than you'll ever know' he confided ...". Neil also lists as "lies" Palace evasions of the stories about Princess Diana's eating disorders and the disintegrating royal marriage.

Two points to take from this include that Neil eventually betrays what he himself calls a confidence from a lordly informant; and that Neil, who remained in editorial positions of considerable influence became embittered with and unlikely to be friendly towards the monarchy. At the least, the Neil story is a cautionary tale in the thorny topic of how best to conduct press relations on behalf of a monarchy, when the iconic figures are not behaving in an ideal manner. Neil's verdict is that "denying what one knows to be true is a dangerous, self defeating strategy" and he is open enough to acknowledge that "the Palace's current lack of credibility undermines its pursuit of the many legitimate grievances it has against the press ... telling the truth is a noble, even a royal aspiration".

Returning now to events in 1992 (and pre-dating the Windsor fire) the *Sunday Times'* scoop with Andrew Morton's book unleashed something of a feeding frenzy - or a squabble. The *Evening Standard* (Editorial, 12 June, p. 9) reported that "last night on the BBC's *Question Time* John Smith[147] launched a savage attack on the press on the back of the controversy on the Royal marriage revelations". On 9 June Melinda Wittstock in the *Times* (p. 2) referred to "the tensions and rivalries ... between tabloids and broadsheets, and broadsheets and broadcasters ... until ITN stunned royal observers last month by broadcasting pictures of the Princess swimming during her trip to Cairo ...". *Today* (9 June p. 5) commented that "in the past few days every television and radio bulletin has included a lengthy report ... but have any of the editors ... followed their high moral principles by stopping their own Royal coverage? Curiously, they have not".

Anthony Holden (*Independent On Sunday*, 7 June p. 20) listed television's attacks on the performance of royal family members: "another rough passage for the Queen began with her mother paying dubious homage to 'Bomber' Harris and ends with her son and heir's marriage back on the rocks ... *Dispatches* (Channel 4) ... set out to prove the Queen's misuse of public funds for private gain ... why should the Royal Household ... be spared the legal responsibilities of ordinary employers towards women and minorities ... Why should the Queen scoop more than £1m a year from Lancastrians who happen to die intestate? ... *Dispatches'* timely tirade follows hard upon a gritty *This Week* wondering why the Head of the Commonwealth has so few if any, non white faces among her thousands of employees. BBC2's *Behind The Headlines* and *Public Eye* have also recently reflected growing public disenchantment with the monarchy".

One interesting element in this frenzy is that in calling shame upon the Royal family there appeared to have been no love lost between members of the press, and broadcasters. John Naughton in *The Observer* (5 May 1991, p. 12) referred to a "weekly three-sick-bag job called *Royal Appointment* (BBC1), and you begin to wonder whether the corporation is not just a rest home for monarchical sycophants". One can find other articles (e.g., by Anthony Holden) that report television's showing of material critical of royal behavior but it is not so common to find any articles that praise such broadcasts. Likewise, it was uncommon to find broadcasters praising the press for disparaging the royal figures. One implication may be that it may be a bad thing for others to disparage royalty (while reserving the right, or the luxury to do so oneself).

To examine the possible role of publication of the Morton book, and of other programs as they may have influenced loyalty to the monarchy, a TOP survey was carried out in June 1992, gaining nearly 3000 replies[148]. One measure was a set of items

[146] Neil, A. (1999) How To Strike A Happy Media. *Spectator*, 20 March pp. 44-45.

[147] Then the leader of the Labour party. He died not long after and was succeeded by Tony Blair.

[148] Wober, J.M. (1992 July) *No Menace To Monarchism. Stable Attitudes After Discussion of a Widely Publicised Book.* London: Independent Television Commission Research Reference Paper.

which, individually - and summed as a group - measures support for Monarchy. Among results on this measure were the following:

Table 5.6: A Cluster of Beliefs Concerning the Monarchy: 1992

	Agree %	Disagree %
The Queen fulfils an important role	73	0
Britain should firmly keep the monarchy	67	11
The press in Britain should not publish details of the Royal Family's private lives without their permission	67	9
There is no longer any need for a monarchy in this country	16	67
TV and the press in Britain are not critical enough of the Royal Family	12	67

These results indicated strong majority support for the monarchy; and the question then was whether such an attitude had any connection with evidence that people had seen certain programs, or had followed discussion of Andrew Morton's book either in the press or on television. As in the study previously reported, sophisticated statistical analysis was carried out that allows one to detect whether any relationship that may exist between two measures is a coincidence of their both being connected with some other measure, or whether any such relationship is "independent". The outcome was that the extent to which people heard discussion of Andrew Morton's book either on television or on the radio was not in either case linked with a person's degree of support for the monarchy. Contrary to what may have been expected, amount of reading about the book in the press was associated with **greater** support for the monarchy.

Having seen a program shown nearly six months previously, called *Elizabeth R* (shown by BBC 1) was linked with a greater degree of support for the monarchy. Experience of having seen a sympathetic program about Prince Charles (made by a friend of his, Selina Scott), or of having seen the hostile one about the Queen (*Dispatches*) was in neither case associated with more, or less support for the monarchy. There is a contrast between the coolness of these actual research findings, and the heat of the journalistic accounts. We saw that Anthony Holden expected that two critical programs he named "reflected growing public disenchantment with the monarchy"; what we found is that disenchantment with the monarchy was not really the correct way of describing majority opinion, which was generally satisfied; nor was disenchantment growing dramatically at all. Contrary to the conjecture of Holden, a supply of scandalous or disparaging information does not automatically have an immediate effect in the obvious direction, in this case, of undercutting support for the monarchy.

In discussing these findings I suggested that support for the monarchy was (and remains) a deep down structure that stands as a rock against being buffeted by storms and corrosive attacks. It is possible that where people cling to such an attitude, but seeing that criticism comes from a particular source, they deflect some of the disappointment which could logically be attached to the disparaged body (in this case the royal family, or the monarchy) and apply it instead to the source. The result may be that respect for the press (or for broadcasting, if it is seen as the originator of hostilities) may be damaged[149].

Aside from factual reporting of bad relationships and unhappiness (which has the possibility of provoking sympathy alongside disrespect) broadcasting indulged in two sharp satires in which royal family figures were made fun of. In *Spitting Image* the royal figures shared their targethood with many political and showbiz figures; nevertheless, extremely unkind rubber puppets of royal family members were shown behaving badly and ludicrously and it could be understandable if viewers came to disrespect these people and the institution they carried on their shoulders. To put it simply, did people who saw more of *Spitting Image* tend also to have less time for the monarchy and for Royalty?

To that research question one could add a similar one involving the program *Pallas*. *Pallas* was a short-run serial first shown at Christmas-tide 1991. It came up again in December 1992. Channel 4's own publicity said: "The first series (attracted) over 18 million viewers. It was hailed by ... the *Sun* as 'the only thing worth watching on TV this Christmas' and was bought by the Japanese, the Germans, the Canadians and the Swedes. This controversial ... spoof soap opera depicts the Royal family as never seen before ... (it) uses over 100 hours of genuine Royal footage ... the fictitious comedy storyline ... adds the voices of Royal soundalike actors ... Today's first episode sees the Queen slip off on holiday ... As Charles stands by ... storm clouds of foreboding gather. ... Charles is forced to appeal to the fabulous Diana for help in running the country ... Diana agrees - but insists that Fergie is re-instated in the nobility. Royal popularity soars. In the third, and final episode ... as Fergie and Diana open a Euro House of Windsor in Switzerland, the Queen puts the final touches to her outrageous publicity counter-coup ...".

It can be argued that elements of the story in *Pallas* might reinforce acceptance of - if not exactly respect for the monarchy. The simplest view is that frequent viewing of satires that puncture royal dignity or which go beyond that to suggest stupidity, cupidity and arrogance would presumably influence people towards a reduced esteem for royalty. Another possibility is more subtle, that the reiteration of such satires could reinforce monarchism by implying the importance of the figures whom these satires more explicitly derogate; but if viewers do not really believe that royal figures are in fact inadequate, irresponsible and misbehave, the programs would pass by as innocent, if somewhat daring fun. A third possibility is that viewing satire programs may have no effect on attitudes towards the monarchy, or on esteem for the royal family, which may

---

[149] It is not the business of this study to chart perceptions of the press, but MORI has been releasing continuous measurements of esteem for various professions, and that for journalism has been reducing over the years. In 1993 MORI asked whether people would "generally trust" (each of fifteen professions) "to tell the truth or not". In 1983 journalists were fourth from bottom with only 19 per cent willing to trust them; in 1993 they had descended to bottom position with only 10 per cent willing to trust them. Television news readers by contrast, trusted by 63 percent in 1983 improved their position to 72 per cent offering trust, in 1993.

be determined by developing attitudes towards the nation's evolving role in Europe and the wider world.

The research method devised to examine these possibilities was elaborate, and in two parts. Questions were put to the TOP in the first week of 1992 and included measures of whether people had seen *Pallas*, but not just *Pallas*, also *Spitting Image* and other satirical programs which had nothing direct to do with the monarchy, including *Drop The Dead Donkey, Saturday Night Clive* and *KYTV*. Results from the earlier survey run in March 1991 were available for amalgamation with the new information. The first question then, was, were those who watched more of *Spitting Image* people who were previously in favor of, or against the monarchy, or was there no connection between previous attitude and viewing? Nearly two thousand replies were available for comparison of the attitudes in March 1991 and viewing of satire at the turn of the year[150]. It emerged clearly that there was no connection between how monarchist people were earlier, and their later viewing of satire. There was a connection between another attitude (less support for the notion that reporting of royal matters should be restrained) and viewing: those who were more permissive on the measure nine months earlier, tended to watch more satire.

The second question was, was there any connection between watching satire at the end of 1991 and the degree of loyalty to monarchy measured on this second occasion? This took into account the extent of loyalty to the monarchy measured nine months earlier. The outcome was that certainly, one could tell who was monarchist in December by knowing their attitude towards monarchy in the previous March. Over and above that, those who had seen some of *Spitting Image* (who, remember, were not particularly prior monarchists - or anti-monarchists) tended now to show greater support for the monarchy. Whether or not people had seen *Pallas*, and three other programs containing satire (*KYTV, Saturday Night Clive and Drop The Dead Donkey*) had no connection with support for monarchy at the end of the year.

Amongst the many important results of this research was the finding that those who would want to protect royalty from scrutiny (measured in March 1991) watched satire less (in December 1991), and so those who accepted intense press scrutiny watched satire more. However, accepting scrutiny was not the same as republicanism or of lack of acceptance for monarchy; so this may reinforce the evidence that the feeling for the monarchy not only exists and is widespread, but evidently resists the corrosion applied by the acid of satire.

It has already been mentioned that the BBC program *Elizabeth R* (first) screened on 9 February 1992 reinforced monarchist feelings. This was discovered from research done at the Independent Television Commission, using the TOP. The BBC had done its own research on the program[151] and the outcome was similar to what was found by the ITC,

---

[150] Wober, J.M. (1992 February) *Television Satire And The Monarchy. No Evidence for Inter-Effects*. London: Independent Television Commission Research Department Reference Paper.

[151] The BBC's research report is labelled 'Not For Publication'; however, its results are important both as a research and a social document and some of them are reported here.

partly perhaps because some of the benchmark results used to measure attitudes before seeing the program were drawn from the same questions used by the ITC. The program had an exceptionally large audience of nearly 18 million (out of a population of 44 million adults) and they accorded it an exceptionally high Appreciation Index score. Several items measuring how people perceived the Queen herself (her hard work, sense of humor, likeability) showed a greater increase in positivity among those who had watched the program than amongst others who had not seen it. Those who disagreed that "there is no longer any need for a monarchy in this country" (that is, who were monarchists) were more common within the audience than outside it, but the proportion of pro-monarchism did not increase after having seen the program.

In all, both ITC and BBC detailed audience studies in 1992 both before and after the fire at Windsor indicated strong support for the monarchy and reinforcement, when provided by emphatic programs, of positive perceptions concerning the Queen. Viewing satires did not undercut monarchism, nor did encounters with reports of the book detailing the collapse of Princess Diana's marriage with Prince Charles. These results notwithstanding, it does not seem that the concerns driving reporters and commentators, particularly in the press, were for orthodox loyalty - rather, they appeared to be looking for trouble and willing to find and to run scurrilous stories.

SOPHISTICATED PUBLIC OPINION STUDIES IN THE MID-1990S

Many opinion polls are done in which a simple percentage figure is offered of the proportion of the public who agree or disagree with some statement. Sometimes, these figures are split into subcategories for those who are women and for the men; or by socio economic status or even, more rarely, by nation (Scots separate from English). Assumptions are then made by journalists that some small change from the previous measurement has been caused by some event. In 1995 the BBC broadcast a three-part series called *Monarchy* and we shall see that it tempted some to suppose that this program will have had an effect on people's perceptions and attitudes. But did it? To tackle this question in a more sophisticated way it is necessary to check who saw one or more episodes in the series and to search for a link, if it exists, between viewing and attitudes; then the thorny problem has to be tackled whether any connection that may be found could have predisposed choice to view the series, in which case it may not be an effect of having seen it.

The research to examine these questions used the Television Opinion Panel and consisted of a survey after the last episode of *Monarchy* had been shown. Two reports describe what was found[152]. The context then was that there were many social pressures

---

[152] Wober, J.M. (1996a) *Support For The Monarchy After the TV Programme Monarchy. Part I The Profiles of Public Attitudes Towards the Monarchy in the Context of Europe, The Commonwealth and the Church.* Bournemouth University, School of Media Arts & Communication, August.
Wober, J.M. (1996b) *Support For The Monarchy After The TV Programme Monarchy Part II*

that could undermine support for the monarchy, some coincidental, and some intended. Other forces might underpin the institution. A principal stage upon which these forces were displayed was television, though some sophisticated studies (described above) indicated that an overarching truth was of a continuity of support. Such systematic evidence remained within broadcasters' libraries and did not reach journalists making programs; or some few journalists might have sought out such material but it did not deter them from assuming that television had a powerful influence and had tended to subvert respect for the monarchy. Sometimes writers in the press made no distinction between attitudes towards the monarchy and those towards individual members of the royal family; but few if any writers held that television had helped sustain respect and affection for the monarchy.

The producer of the series, David Dickinson sent me a Fax noting that "the Monarchy is facing its most serious crisis of the 20th century. At the heart of British life for centuries, support for a once-revered institution is now at an all-time low, its reputation, some claim, reduced to little more than that of a soap opera or tourist attraction ... this three part series ... asks what can be done to restore the British public's affections for the Royal Family - and what would happen to Britain without it ... the first programme ... looks at the present collapse in respect for the monarchy ... the final programme (asks) is the crisis of confidence merely a reflection of the crisis of identity sweeping the nation?". While this appears stringent though potentially supportive of monarchy and of national identity, in the view of at least one other significant writer - whom we have met already, the BBC's social affairs columnist Polly Toynbee, the scrutiny may have been part of, and have contributed to a republican, or at least an evolutionary tide of opinion.

Introducing the series, in the *Radio Times* (22-28 July, 1995, p. 16) Toynbee wrote "not so long ago ... the Royal Family (her capitals) was immensely popular ... But now ... the institution of monarchy is in crisis ... people (are) starting to tell the pollsters that ... maybe the Royal Family would not be missed after all ... In an absorbing three part series ... William Shawcross examines their plight". Toynbee cited at least four processes she believed affected attitudes towards the monarchy:

- the Royal Family has imploded ... washing its most intimate and far from clean linen in public ...
- the Labour Party promises constitutional reform ... it would remove the voting rights of hereditary peers ... where does that leave the monarch?
- so few now bother to attend the Church of England that the ancient title Defender of the Faith ... cuts little mustard ... (and)
- people are starting to view the Crown ... as something that is stopping us from modernising.

Demographic And National Differences In The Structure Of Attitudes Unaffected By Viewing The Series. Bournemouth University, School of Media Arts & Communication, October.

Toynbee believed "we British tend to be a backward-looking lot, full of regret for lost empire" and she implied causes by asking "how far does the monarchy ... stop us from taking a place in Europe". She asserted "it's not (the Queen's) fault, but the monarchy does symbolise things we have to shed". Stepping up on her populist pulpit the concluded "I am inclined to let the monarchy have one last chance ... she pulpit she concluded Queen needs to put herself and her son in the vanguard of constitutional reform".

Toynbee's text illustrates how she, alongside many in the press, speak as though from an Areopagiticus, looking down from a height upon the rest of society (now including the royal family) and analysing and prescribing. It also suggests that empirical assertions made by such writers were not always as well informed as they might have been. It can be seen from the table early in the chapter that MORI's findings showed that the nadir of support had been passed in December 1992, and the values recorded in 1994 indicated some hardening of monarchist support.

A specialist survey carried out at the London College of Printing amongst 726 journalists and reported briefly (*Guardian*, 16 October 1995) found a marked leftward skew; 57 per cent of respondents intended to vote Labour while only 6 per cent said they would vote Conservative; three quarters were in favor of the European Union and fewer than half were in favor of monarchy. This last finding is a crucial one and one on which the author declined to elaborate, when asked. The balance of opinions amongst journalists indicates a marked difference between those who report and express what purports to be the current culture, and the public itself. Journalists included 49 per cent supporting the monarchy while the public still then included two thirds who did so.

When, in the week beginning 13 November 1995 it became known that Princess Diana had given an interview to the BBC's *Panorama* current affairs program, the whole press became tremendously excited. Tabloids splashed huge headlines and broadsheets took up the theme that the Palace was greatly dismayed. Many writers used the combative term revenge for Princess Diana's reply to Prince Charles' own account of his life's work and difficulties - and his admission of adultery when the marriage had irretrievably broken down - in his televised interview with the well known journalist Jonathan Dimbleby, which had been shown in June 1994.

As well as series such as *Monarchy* and the shocks of the televised royal admissions of adultery, some believed that other televised materials may have reinforced feelings for British nationhood and for its central institution of the monarchy. 1995 saw the anniversaries of the end of World War II in Europe and in Asia, two occasions which were cohesively commemorated and in which the royal family played a leading part. Even David Aaronovitch, a radical journalist asked (in the *Independent*, Section 2, 16 November 1995, p. 3) whether the Princess was "in danger (sic) of further discrediting the monarchy, just as it was hauling itself back into public esteem? Had it not been established through past experience that television is bad for royalty?".

This is clearly a poorly specified assertion: some television may reinforce support for the monarchy while other elements may erode it. Most theories suppose that manifest content may have some direct influence - thus *Elizabeth R* and the victory commemorations might have increased loyalty while televised accusations of greed and of other shameful behavior (such as had been made about the costs of the Royal Yacht Britannia, and the pay to less immediate members of the Windsor family) could reduce loyalty. In the few days preceding Princess Diana's Panorama interview news of the Queen Mother's hip replacement, and her redoubtable spirit of recovery were very widely and positively reported, serving as a metaphor for underlying loyalty to the institution.

Within and reflecting elements of this dense context the survey carried questions on the monarchy, Europe, the Commonwealth and the Church, on what people had seen of the particular series *Monarchy* and on respondents' estimates of the proportions of those in the public at large, and among journalists who supported the monarchy. The first simple level of results showed that 13 per cent (of well over 3000 respondents) had seen at least one episode of the series; and amongst viewers, 63 per cent agreed that "the programs overall seemed to support a continuation of the Monarchy".

Table 5.7: Two Clusters of Beliefs Concerning the Monarchy: 1995

	Agree %	Disagree %
A Monarchism Cluster of Opinions		
What with developments in the EU Britain should firmly keep the Monarchy	65 (59)	6 (13)
There is no longer any need for a Monarchy in this country	18 (16)	64 (66)*
The press in Britain should not publish details of the Royal Family's lives without their permission	66	21
Britain's links to the Commonwealth are very important for our future as a country	58	15
the Monarchy is one way of keeping up strong links between Britain and the Commonwealth	64	13
A Problems with Monarchy Cluster		
The Monarchy should be cut back to a few members of the Royal Family	62	18
The main problem with the Monarchy is its cost	54	28
The main problem with the Monarchy is that it ties people's thoughts and feelings to the past	21	53
The Monarchy should be separate from the church	53	16

*the figures in parentheses show what was found in 1994

Complex statistical treatment showed that opinions formed into clusters, and this clustering is thematic rather than depending on outright levels of support. For example Table 5.7 shows that two thirds supported the monarchy, somewhat more in 1995 than the previous year. Similar numbers supported continuing links between Britain and the Commonwealth. There was certainly support for economic cutbacks; but Toynbee's assertion that the institution thus impedes modernisation ("ties people's thoughts and feelings to the past") was rejected by over twice as many as who agreed with that view. It may at first seem strange to note the difference between **level** of support for some idea, and how it **connects** with other ideas; the example of the important idea that monarchy may tie culture to the past is a good one: a large plurality disagreed, but those who agreed tended to be the ones who agree with the other ideas in the cluster. So the **idea** of possible backwardness in the monarchy is part of a package of ideas bearing on problems with the institution and though the other items in the group have majorities supporting them, this one on backwardness had a majority who rejected it.

This survey included a set of questions which other polls have not asked. It asked people to estimate support for the monarchy, among different sets of the public.

Table 5.8: Public Estimates of Support Amongst Others for Monarchy

| | | Estimates chosen | | | | |
		70% or more	60-69%	50-59%	40-49%	less than 40%
What proportion of ... do	the British public	14	**33**	31	15	7
you believe now supports	print journalists	2	11	27	**29**	31
the Monarchy?	TV program makers	5	18	37	**24**	16
What proportion of EU states do you think are Monarchies?		1	6	18	**24**	51

correct figures are given in **bold**

It is clear that the public did not have an accurate view of the truth; and the error was in a direction diminishing the standing of monarchy. In fact we know from numerous surveys that between 60 and 69 per cent of the public do support the monarchy; but over half the public (53 per cent) thought that fewer people were monarchists while only 14 per cent thought that more were monarchist. The London College of Printing survey reported that 49 per cent of its journalists sample supported the monarchy; 40 per cent of the public thought that more than this proportion of print journalists were on their side and 60 per cent of the public thought (wrongly again) that television journalists were on their side - supporting monarchy. At the time of the survey seven out of fifteen EU states were monarchies, that is between 40 and 49 per cent; but only a quarter of the public represented here understood this fact rightly; over half the sample thought there were fewer EU monarchies.

The situation is similar to one which has been described by an eminent theorist of public opinion as a "spiral of silence"[153]. If it is dramatised in public that the tide of

---

[153] Noelle-Neumann, E. (1974) "The Spiral of Silence" A Theory Of Public Opinion. *Journal of Communication*, 24(2), 43-51.

opinion is moving strongly in a given direction (in this case, becoming fed up with the monarchy), people who do not want that to come about begin to feel isolated. They become less likely to voice their opinions in ordinary conversation; and when approached by pollsters some may tend to hide their real views or even claim as their opinion what they believe to be the fashionable (though not in some sense their own real) opinion. In contrast with much of the opinions polled in public, when members of a panel deal in private, as in a polling booth, with a question on a piece of paper, individuals who may otherwise be susceptible to the pressure of what they believe is the tide of opinion are more likely to report what is their own truer preference.

Calculations showed that on the cluster of monarchist items there was a clearly positive score amongst the English section of the sample; so too was there amongst the Scottish section, though it was to a small though significant extent less than in the English sample. The Welsh sub-sample was like the English and the Northern Ireland sub-sample was like the Scottish one. Even more complex calculations indicated that whether or not people had seen one or more episodes of the series *Monarchy* had no connection with their feelings on the first monarchy cluster of items. It can not be argued from this evidence therefore that watching the series had any unidirectional effect on loyalty to the monarchy. However, watching the series did have a connection with the second cluster of items - dealing with problems with the monarchy. The result indicated that people who had seen *more* of the series were *less* likely to perceive problems with the Monarchy.

There are several processes that influence the formation of public opinion, of which four are important here. First there is what has been called the **hostile media phenomenon**[154]. In this, people on both sides of an issue think the content in the mass message systems is biased against them. In the current results people who supported the monarchy tended to believe that press and television professionals were less likely to support the institution.

Another notion has been called the **false consensus effect**[155]. In this, people tend to think that others think similarly to oneself. Here, amongst the English section of the whole sample those who were stronger monarchists also thought the British public contained more monarchists. This incidentally is not a false consensus but a valid one, so it is evidence of a more general consensus effect.

The third of the relevant phenomena has been called **pluralistic ignorance** in which people feel that their own attitudes differ from those of the majority, when in fact this is not the case. Here, it was reported that people on average substantially underestimated the extent of public support for the monarchy, when their own opinions when totalled up revealed that a majority did in fact support the institution. This discrepancy may be the

---

[154] Vallone, R.P., Ross, N. and Lepper, M.R. (1985) The hostile media phenomenon: Biased perception and perception of media bias in coverage of the Beirut massacre. *Journal of Personality and Social Psychology*, 49, p. 577-585.

[155] Marks, G., and Miller, N. (1987) Ten years of research on the false consensus effect. An empirical and theoretical review. *Psychological Bulletin*, 102 (1), p. 72 - 90.

outcome of reading or hearing discussion of the many newspaper polls that appeared to point to an erosion of support for the monarchy.

How might one reconcile the press polls suggesting a collapse of monarchism with the present results indicating its continued existence? A fourth phenomenon, the **spiral of silence** may be at work. This holds that people who think their opinion is not shared by the majority are shy of disclosing their real feelings to others such as pollsters. In the present study, carried out by self-completion of questionnaire booklets in the privacy of one's home there was no such public exposure and thus a spiral of silence might not have been in operation (what is more, we saw there was a connection here between one's own monarchism and thinking that other people shared such views). So the spiral of silence may have tainted the poll results produced by face to face or telephone interviews - none of the polls published regularly in newspapers or on television are done by self-completion of papers in private.

Few, if any journalists or politicians deal with complexities of these kinds when reporting or dealing with something as epoch-changing as a supposed collapse in the British monarchy. Though as we have seen this is still a robust institution, it is one which has perhaps had less done by the mass message systems in order to support or strengthen it, than what may, either on purpose or unwittingly tend to erode or damage it. Without question the greatest "discourse event" affecting the monarchy in the late 1990s has been the aftermath of the death of Diana Princess of Wales, and that will be examined in following chapters. Before them, however, there are some other important events and developments to consider.

BEYOND 1995: POINTERS FOR PUBLIC OPINION ON THE MONARCHY

One year after the fieldwork for the study described above, Buckingham Palace had publicised ideas on how the monarchy might be reformed. While some commentators wrote of the move as a sign that the institution might be strengthened, others appeared to see it as part of a weakening process. In August 1996 Channel 4 television broadcast a program *Power And The People* on the process of deliberative polling in which the topic was Queen and Country. Individuals in a nationally representative sample were brought together for a weekend of discussion, before, during and after which they provided their opinions on the merits of the monarchy. The outcome of this was a continuing support for the institution, albeit in a modified form.

At the end of August 1996 the BBC returned to the topic with a program chaired by its star presenter Jeremy Paxman. Before the broadcast viewers had been encouraged to telephone in to vote on a proposition that Queen Elizabeth II should be Britain's last monarch. 'Yes' meant a republican opinion and one had to say 'no' to show adherence to the monarchy. In these circumstances out of over 40,000 calls received 52 per cent opted for an end to monarchy - before the program. The broadcast itself therefore took the form of a discussion of an already established republican position and another vote took place towards the end of the proceedings (with broadcasters waiting with excitement to reveal what would be found). This time, around 30,000 calls were received amongst which 63 per cent said 'NO' to the end of monarchy, thus reversing the pre-program position.

It is by no means clear that Jeremy Paxman's program had changed opinions to the extent of the reversal just reported, or whether the difference was partly or wholly attributable to a selective process in which anti-monarchists (or, if the distinction is a real one, those who opposed Prince Charles' accession but who might be willing to see Prince William become King - an option which is not entertained by any of the royal family) might have been more likely to provide their opinions on the first occasion. To some extent, the vote before the program may have reflected a feeling of disappointment or worry about the heir. On the other hand, the program will have focused more specifically on the monarchy as an institution, underlining that much of its function is independent of its incumbent, and that several European states remain loyal to their monarchies, even though these appear somewhat dilute compared with the British model. If all this is true, then the post program calls may have brought in people who had not found time to vote before but who felt they had to rally to the flag once it had been dramatised that the beliefs of their side had been put to the test. Unfortunately, there seems to have been no research done by the broadcaster that may have examined the complex question of whether opinion change could be attributable to what was communicated by the program; or, if such research was done, it was not published and remains inaccessible.

Aside from television and the press, the most important real event since 1995 which may affect the future of the monarchy was the arrival in power of Mr Tony Blair and his New Labour administration, in 1997. They had promised to remove the rights of the hereditary peers and by 2000 had achieved this aim; they had not been opposed in this purpose by the Conservative party and it seems very likely, in 1999, that within a few years there would be an "upper" chamber either elected or appointed, and with no automatic presence of hereditary peers (and bishops) with voting rights. This has been taken widely as undermining the notion that the monarchy itself should be inherited, and even that it should exist, after the present Queen dies.

There have been divergent opinions on what may be Labour's true intentions. One analyst[156] points out that The Queen Mother's 100th birthday will occur in August 2000, likely to be an occasion for celebration and that would be followed by a greater occasion, the golden jubilee of the Queen's accession, in 2002. Hardman points to the downbeat political atmosphere before the 25th jubilee in 1977, when unexpectedly "the eventual public response took everyone by surprise ... millions of people had found themselves drawn into a benign and reassuring national celebration ... the majority of participants had been young people ... there will have to be a general election by May 2002 ... whenever Tony Blair does go to the polls, the last thing he will want is any suggestions that a second-term Labour government might turn its guns on the monarch about to celebrate 50 years on the throne". There is already a Buckingham Palace committee

---

[156] Robert Hardman. (1999) A Millennial Silver Lining? *Spectator*, 20 March, p. 58-59.

discussing plans for the jubilee and the government is the driving force, via the Home Office.

Although Hardman sees that some commonwealth countries where the Queen is still head of state will want to become republics; "if there is a run on the Crown abroad ... 'if these other countries don't want the new king, why should we?' will be the republican line at home ... As the death of Diana ... showed ... public opinion can fluctuate suddenly, passionately and divisively". A quite different opinion is contributed by Peter Hitchens[157]. He believes most Labour activists are still republicans in their hearts "not to mention all those glinting, efficient think-tankists ... with their 'rational' plans for a 'modern' constitution, who don't have hearts. And now, at last, they may be about to get what they want, for the patriotic working-class Labour voters who frustrated them for decades are now almost gone. ... astute republicans such as Anthony Holden ... tended to think that Mr Blair would eventually abolish the throne ... (he runs through episodes when abolition was discussed in Labour policy making but when, on all occasions up to now the idea was postponed) ... But ... that time may well be approaching at last".

---

[157] Hitchens, P. (1999) Mr Blair's Battle Royal Draws Near. *Spectator*, 20 March, p. 54 - 55.

Chapter 6

THE DEATH OF DIANA, PRINCESS OF WALES

The death of Diana Princess of Wales has provided a complex and deep-reaching experience not just for British society, but internationally. It is in Britain however that the mixture of connection with myth and stereotype is richest and most intense. The reason for the difference in experience of the event as between Britain and the rest of the world is simply in the first place because she was British; but Diana's British identity keyed in with intricate connections and meanings that may and quite evidently do interest and involve readers in other countries. To construct a portrait of the connotational background to the simpler and superficial meanings of the event it will be relevant to refer to myths and stories that exist in the history and folklore of the country. Many of these are shared with other societies, which may have added to the potency of Diana's own myth; but some have a particularly British flavour - or at least had until recently.

This chapter and the next one will try to tease out how some of the ways in which people thought and felt about the death and how they were represented as feeling about the death, may have been brought to bear upon what people think and feel about the monarchy itself. There are two routes by which such an influence might occur; one is a direct way and the other is mediated - that is, individuals' thoughts and feelings throughout the population may be influenced by how they see and hear or are told that others are thinking and feeling. This mediated channel can itself be either direct through one's friends and relatives, or indirect through the work of the mass message systems of the press and broadcasting.

Where possible, empirical hard fact kinds of evidence will be sought that may either support or undermine theories and assertions about the impact of the death on the monarchy. All too often, printed or broadcast statements are made in the form of assertions (which appear not to realise that they may require corroboration or proof, but where the assertion and the proof seem to be combined), while it would have been much more prudent to offer such thoughts in the form of theories or hypotheses. Such propositions include the notions that:

a press pictures of Princess Diana would significantly increase sales of a periodical

b broadcast material about Princess Diana would attract enlarged audiences

c Princess Diana was desperately seeking to mend her life which had been damaged, by:

    1 divorce, in which she was largely the victim

    2 enemies at the Palace who were (perhaps)

       (i) the courtiers/Palace bureaucracy

       (ii) the Royal Family itself, or leading members of it

d Princes Diana had a personal charisma which she could and did use, to:

    1 solace, and even heal people in physical sickness or distress

    2 produce institutional change - as in abolishing landmines

e Princess Diana's manner was a modern one, contrasted with an outmoded demeanour of the other members of the Royal Family

f because of the popularity of Diana's ways, the other members of the Royal Family would have to behave similarly

g Princess Diana's life, and more especially her death would at the very least mean that the monarchy would have to change - to modernise itself; some even indicated that they felt that the monarchy should end

h initial shock at Diana's death was widespread, perhaps universal

i grief, and even a feeling of bereavement were widespread, perhaps even universal

j Princess Diana's example of warmth and spontaneity in relationships has changed the previously cool and dispassionate British (or English) in their essential personality, making them warm and reactive.

FOUR WAYS OF EXAMINING THE PHENOMENON OF REACTIONS TO DIANA'S DEATH

This chapter and the next one will use four ways of going about their exploration. One way is from the science of social anthropology; in this case one seeks out, describes and tries to understand the significance of the fables and stories that are formative and familiar in a culture and which may be relevant to some current phenomenon one is examining. This procedure may be called just literary criticism, and it would not be unfair to apply the term; but to suggest that ancient tales might influence how one feels and acts in the present is to work as an applied social psychologist; this needs systematically sought evidence with which to assess the ideas being tested.

A second procedure is to use industry data on the sales and readership of newspapers, and on the viewing of broadcast programmes, to assess whether there is any truth in hypotheses a) and b), and if so, to what extent. A third source of data is the narrative material in the press and broadcasting. Print is more readily stored and examined than are broadcast programs, so newspapers in the week following the death of

Princess Diana have been closely read and kept and the ideas and themes that have arisen therein have been noted down and sorted out into categories. Some television programmes have been recorded and examined likewise, but there is also a source of reflection on these programmes in the press, where critics regularly describe and give views on what has been broadcast. This material has been used - with caution - to reflect on the role played by broadcasting in mediating the public's response - not just to the death of Princess Diana but more so to their thoughts, feelings and expectations about the monarchy.

A fourth way of study is to ask people systematically about their experiences, actions and feelings. A custom-built questionnaire has accordingly been fielded, and this brings in fresh information which bears upon a number of the hypotheses listed above, and will be examined in some depth - in Chapter 8.

It was not possible, for financial reasons, to achieve a questionnaire respondent sample that would accurately represent the socio-economic composition of the whole public. (Ideally, one questions a random sample, less ideally a quota sample; it is debatable whether face to face or telephone interviewing would be best in this instance, or whether self completion and mail back of a postal questionnaire - known to reduce response yields, but quite likely to elicit more honest accounts of personal feelings would be better). It is not the purpose therefore, for the questionnaire used below to show precisely that x per cent of the nation grieved after the death or that y per cent thought the monarchy should remain while z per cent considered it should end. On the other hand it is possible and, quite likely valid, to use this information to explore the *structure* of experience and of attitudes; thus one would be able to say that 'people who report more religious practice' (or some other way of describing a section of the respondents) were more (or less) likely to attribute blame for the accident to one or more of the role players in Princess Diana's life.

There are over seventy quantifiable items in the questionnaire and the combinations between these can lead to well over two hundred hypotheses being set down. Each hypothesis examines whether a pair of measures are connected, positively, or negatively or not at all. We will not seek to be exhaustive about this; it is more efficient to rely on well established statistical methods, to detect which items form into clusters; in this way we can reduce the number of measures that can then be examined in pairs to see whether they run together in people's feelings or experiences.

MYTHS THAT MAY INFLUENCE RESPONSES TO PRINCESS DIANA'S DEATH, AND FEELINGS ABOUT THE MONARCHY

The myths to which I will refer (some may question the term; I do not use it to mean untruth, rather to refer to plot or dramatic model or script) begin with themes both in the New and the Old Testaments of the Bible; they add the story of King Arthur, and from European folklore the fables of Cinderella, Snow White and Beauty and the Beast; and one contribution from recent fiction that may well be relevant is the story of Peter Pan.

The suggestion is that anyone who has been familiar with the stories in these texts and who has at one time or another felt strongly about the characters in them and their struggles, triumphs and disasters, has thus acquired models for feelings which may, when a new story comes along, provide ready-made courses for new emotions. These new feelings, such as were evoked after Diana's death could be understood at one level as reactions only to her own life, actions, personality, thwarted prospects and death; or they could be understood in part at least as replays and quite likely intensifications of a person's reactions to stories experienced in earlier years.

The Biblical models have been the most obviously relevant; the American sociologist Camille Paglia has claimed that she had already noticed several years ago that Diana was being described as a saint. Such accounts were not just in writing about many examples of compassionate behavior but were also pictorial; some photographs struck viewers as resembling a modern Madonna. We thus come to the first and most potent model for feelings about Diana - a human connected with a mystically rich mine of love; such a saintly power bestows love and potentially healing power on the suffering. Even if limblessness and other forms of incurable disease or damage are not reversed or healed by Diana's agency, the experience of such sufferers is dramatically alleviated by her presence. The theme of Diana as a saint has cropped up in numerous messages written by mourners and journalists in the week after her death and before the funeral.

Technically, saints are recognised after rigorous checking by the Papal authorities, through the achievement of miracles ascribed to their agency, or by exceptional compassionate good works and charisma; but other saints have died for their faith, and are martyrs. Diana's death can not logically be cast in the latter mould; however there may be a psychological meaning in which the proximity of the death and of the telling of hundreds of first-hand tales spur thoughts that, like a saint she died in the midst of her good works.

The death of an almost supernaturally compassionate human, as Diana was sometimes described as being, evokes the image of Christ himself. He was a martyr of such exalted nature as was and is believed to be fully divine. Diana died - as presented by the mass message systems in which the public, their truths and beliefs are now immersed - in the full spate of her humanitarian mission. She had just visited Bosnia to publicise the need to abolish landmines; news reports had underlined that in Angola she had walked through a real minefield, implying that she has exposed herself to mortal danger.

These similarities between Diana and the Holy Family should not be dismissed as irrelevant because of the disparities between them. The disparities are fundamental; however much people may respect Prince William as a future King, nobody sees Diana as a mother of God; so the similarity between Diana and the Virgin Mary is only a very limited one. Diana did not challenge the forces opposing her mission and die at their hands while exemplifying a divine mission of compassion on earth; so the similarity between Diana and Jesus Christ is also a very limited one. So nobody has written of Diana as a saviour of mankind, or as the mother of a saviour. Nevertheless, there is enough in the similarities to provide a starting point to enter the labyrinth of ideas and feelings laid down in a Christian culture, no matter how tenuous its members' connection has become with the roots of this tradition, so that the ways in which people reacted to Diana's death can better be understood.

The scenario of the Gospels contains important characters whose roles, with no great transformation can be subconsciously connected with people close to Diana, and which may then reinforce at least a minor identification of Diana with the Holy Family. Just after the birth of Christ three Kings came to pay their homage to the seemingly unlikely recipient of their attention; even though heads of state did not attend her funeral, several of them sent their deep-felt condolences. Many will feel that Diana's royalty was not held in question by the public; rather, her value may have been seen as transcending the class boundaries which run so deeply within British society. The model for that universality was also dramatised in a Gospel first in the homage paid by the shepherds at Jesus' birth, and then in the support given by the multitudes who flocked to witness the last days of his ministry. The public were too late to show her their support fully in Diana's life, but their partial neglect of her mission may have been all the more poignant a reason for underlining their testimony to her posthumously.

We come now to the roles in the gospels of the principals of the Herodian state vis a vis the saviour of mankind, and ask whether anyone in the British state actually was, or was subconsciously being manoeuvred into similar roles vis a vis Diana. Caiaphas the biblical high priest was portrayed in the gospels as a dry legalist who feared the popularity of Jesus and his challenge to rabbinical ways. Rightly or wrongly, most likely the latter, more than one newspaper portrayed the royal courtiers as sticking to an unsympathetic dry legalism, implying that the Queen, Prince Philip and Prince Charles wanted to remain inhumanely distant from the scene and site of the "passion" (now located in central London, around the royal palaces and parks). Something of the role of the procurator Pontius Pilate, who washed his hands of responsibility for the crucifixion might also have been assimilated into the portrayal of the royal family, whose reasons for remaining in their Scottish home were neither understood or accepted by many who purported to speak for the public in London[158].

In the middle of the pre-funeral week many newspapers published pictures of the flagpole above Buckingham Palace, asking why no flag flew there, as in so many other public places, at half mast. The reason given for this by formalists[159], was simply not

---

[158]It seems to have escaped the London-based "national" press that the Queen is Queen of Scotland and that she and her family were in fact at home in Balmoral and did not need to return to Buckingham Palace in order to be at home. The fact that Balmoral has a nearby private or family church made that an even more homely place for a Christian family, than Buckingham Palace, from which a visit to Church would have been a most public excursion.

[159]The Royal flag, or Standard flies at the top of the mast wherever the monarch is in residence, and not at all where she is not. The option of the Royal Standard being flown at half mast at Balmoral - and photographed to create an impact for the nation, was neither discussed nor at first put into effect. The royal household evidently rejected the notion of flying a Union Jack at half mast at Buckingham Palace until the day before the funeral.

accepted by the press or by those of the public whose words they chose to print. The result was a stark image of an isolated needle adorning a high place upon which, metaphorically, the reputation of the monarch and her immediate family were impaled. In an emotional displacement of images this notional skewering of the Queen added energy to the felt quasi-crucifixion of Diana.

We turn now to the Old Testament for an image that may be relevant to the way in which many people perceived Diana; this image connects with a very similar one in the nursery folklore of Europe and with an element of the Arthur story. The selection of David the shepherd boy, to accomplish a hazardous task of national service (to fight and beat Goliath, when accredited warriors were daunted by the task) focused on the most unlikely candidate within the family for such a heroic role. The fact that David succeeded in his immediate task shows how fallible formal executive selection procedures may be; but the selection process brings to mind the choice of the young Diana Spencer as Prince Charles' fiancée. The fact that both David and Diana came from families of aristocratic pedigree was not uppermost in public perception of both figures at the time of their emergence, for which the publicity concentrated on the evidently humble nature of the future heroine.

A very similar selection procedure was experienced by Cinderella, dragged out of obscurity to become a princess. Her tale makes much of the high glamour of the ball, followed by a precipitous fall from such grace via a pumpkinised carriage, back to scrubbing a kitchen grate. However, she was elevated again by the Prince. Importantly, this fairy tale does not extend to a book two in which the complexities of real life are examined[160]. Elements of the theme are there not only in Diana Spencer's life, but also in how it has sometimes been described (without conscious reference to the fairy tale model) with mentions of the fairy tale princess. King Arthur's story also begins with the magical recognition of star quality in an unlikely lad, who easily draws the sword Excalibur from the anvil when several recognised champions failed to do so. Though this test was performed by a man and not a woman, this may not be an important difference from Diana's selection which, like Arthur's included an intention to use his or her qualities to consolidate the realm - and as a monarchy.

Fairy tales - at least in Europe - often contain beautiful and virtuous princesses. Something happens to them, however, when they become queens - jealousy and bitterness take over in their portrayals. The Queen in Snow White is not preoccupied with a challenge from her own daughter-in-law but from an outsider-beauty; the roles are deeply drawn between good and evil, and people may have subconsciously felt a resemblance between Diana and Snow White when it is underlined that the Princess "has had her HRH removed". A third important tale gives us the models of Beauty and the Beast; we recognise the first easily as the princess, and the latter as the initially unlikely

---

[160]Rossini's opera the Barber of Seville gives us a romantic tale of a Count and his beloved who emerge from daunting (and comic) escapades to get married - and do they live "happily ever after"? The sequel appears in Mozart's "anti-royalist" Marriage of Figaro, in which our erstwhile hero is seen to stray.

contender for her affection, Dodi al Fayed - either more crudely in the original tale because he is described there as ugly, or more subtly in our day because, notwithstanding his comeliness he is of another religion which has contended with the established one. It is all the more poignant then, that the symbolic kiss, or process of plighting and cementing a troth, by which the princess may have transmuted the beast into a beautiful prince was annihilated before it could be fulfilled.

The images I have discussed up to now had likely played their part in structuring people's reactions during Diana's life and just after she died. One other image, moreover, may have come into play shortly before her burial. This is the scene of the Lady of the Lake in the Arthurian legend, whose arm arose from the centre of a lake set in what Shakespeare called "this demi-paradise" to receive the sword (a symbol of manly enterprise) back into the womb of the nation for what the legend seems to indicate is merely a deferred period after which the realm would, with or without the aid of the sword, live abundantly again. Diana's burial on an island kept away from the demotic horde of tourist-buses speaks of the mythical conservation for its regeneration of a nation's essential powers. The meaning in a society pervaded by modern technomena will remain to be seen.

All the tales discussed so far have been anonymously written, hundreds of years ago; they have been re-presented by known authors, read by some in our time, told verbally to children, but increasingly purveyed by films and even pantomime. The biblical tales may well be fading fast, in spite of occasional revisitation by Hollywood, in epics which are nowadays shown on little-viewed cable channels or at off-peak hours. Nevertheless, elements of these tales are still present in the culture and many people will have them stored away in the subconscious, where they offer connection with new scripts that are developing out of real contemporary events. One well known tale, written by an author in our own century, remains to be referred to, which may have some resonance to offer in understanding our reactions to Diana's death.

Peter Pan's statue stands in London's Kensington gardens, not far from Princess Diana's home. She could hardly have been unaware of it, especially since her pre-marital role as a child carer had been physically and socially close to where those upper middle class families' children typified in the tale were taken care of by "nannies" and played in these selfsame gardens. Peter's mischievous and mobile (and seemingly androgynous) self is portrayed in the actual statue in a face that even has some resemblance to Diana's. The heroine of the story is not Mrs Darling but Wendy, the young and compassionate earth mother. Possibly Princess Diana's life evokes something of our solace in Wendy's protection of her boys; but with the addition of all that we have been told about her infectious laugh, there may have been something of Tinker Bell in her, too; and now, as many messages have tried to establish, Diana is undying in people's affections, in a still-youthful form, somewhat as Peter Pan himself never fully grew up.

It may be not just interesting but it is perhaps even plausible to draw together myths and tales and simply to assert that resonances between them and the themes in Princess Diana's life mean that we think and feel about the latter in ways that may have been influenced by the former. This kind of plausibility is not enough. We need evidence that these are ways in which people did indeed feel about Diana, and such evidence is sought in the press, after the next section.

In the sections which follow, after statistics on contents of the press, it will be argued that two "Grand Narratives" can be found which touch upon some of the themes described above and which organise the discourse about Diana and about events after her death. There is no single author or place where a whole and coherent account of either one of the grand narratives is to be found. Instead, many different authors and points of view are to be found which can be seen to contain either one of two main patterns. When all the components of each pattern are put together a "Grand Narrative" emerges. The two grand narratives can conveniently be seen in the following "diagram".

Grand Narratives	**Republican**	**Royalist**
The First Ascent	Dangerous Fantasy?	Disneyism
	Cynical Royal choice of "breeding mare"	Aristocratic pedigree/ Cinderella come true
Souring the Dream	Bad Faith Amongst the Royal Family	Inherent Weaknesses of Diana's character
Emergence from Victimhood/from Entanglement	Diana as Saint	Diana as Loose Cannon
	Wickedness, Dysfunction and	Diana as King's Mother
	Obsolescence in the Palace	Innocent Princes
	"Dianism"/People Power	Christian Country
	Healing Touch	
Death	Constitutional Turning point	Retrenchment
Minor Narratives	Market Justification	
	False Inference Syndrome	
	Universalism/"Feeling Fascism"	

All these themes will be illustrated in examples from press content collected in the funeral week immediately after Diana's death.

EFFECTS OF THE EVENT OF PRINCESS DIANA'S DEATH ON AMOUNTS OF PRESS AND TV USE

Newspaper sales figures are produced by the Audit Bureau of Circulation and published monthly in several newspapers. Several papers have cut price editions (such as the *Times*, which for many months was sold on Mondays for 10p, a price that barely covered the cost of production and of retailing; later, the Monday price rose to 30p, still not in itself enough to generate profit) and other forms of subsidised circulation. The figures below are the gross ones. It should be remembered that it is believed that there are approximately three readers per copy of a paper sold.

Princess Diana died on the night of 31 August, a month in which there had been substantial reporting of her affair with Mr Dodi al Fayed. Some of the Sunday papers (1

September) were already out with partly critical opinions about her behavior, but also with early coverage of her death. On Monday however, enlarged papers with massive coverage in pictures and text emerged as an avalanche, and this was sustained at least until and including the day after her funeral (Sunday 8 September). Attention did not tail off entirely for another week, when the next major concern was the trial in Massachusetts of Louise Woodward. To some extent therefore, September can be characterised as a month in which the story of the deadly accident, the funeral and the supposed constitutional aftermath loomed extremely large.

Table 6.1: Newspaper Sales in the Months Surrounding the Death of Diana

	August	sales (in '000) in the months of:: September	October
Dailies	13, 911	14, 341	13, 788
% change		+3.0%	-3.9%
Sundays	14, 892	15, 827	14, 819
% change		+6.3%	-6.4%

A summary of the situation is that there was indeed an increase in sales, twice that of the weekdays' gain, in the Sundays. What is at stake is approximately half a million papers a day among the dailies and about a million for the Sundays. The crude notion that "pictures of Diana sell papers" is borne out on this evidence; but the increment is not a huge one. We are examining one of the largest newspaper stories since the end of World War II and the unprecedented barrage of intense journalistic offer produced a six per cent gain in sales, at most. Nowhere is there any sign of an increase in sales of a half again, or even a third beyond the usual which is the kind of impression one might get from some of the rhetoric about the influence of Diana-content on sales[161].

The real figures may be taken to imply that for a single newspaper title that obtains a scoop, which it exploits for two or maybe three days, a sales increment of between 3 and 5 per cent is likely. For the *Sun*, selling some 3.9 million copies a day this amounts to some 150,000 copies; at 28 p per copy cover price (of which around 20p will go in production and distribution costs, but which may be augmented by raised advertising rates bringing in up to another 20p per copy[162]) this gives an approximate figure of

---

[161] The *Times'* media analyst Brian MacArthur reported (20 August 1999) that on the day after the eclipse of the sun visible in much of Britain total newspaper sales were up by over 440,000, a gain of over 3 per cent, without ludicrous prices being paid to photographers. Increases were much greater, up to over a third to even 50 per cent more for certain papers in the south west, where the eclipse was total. The hypothesis arising from these results is that where there is a once-in-a-lifetime event, of a positive nature, in which people want to be involved, more of them will buy a paper to have the story "immortalised" in their possession.

[162] Roy Greenslade, (When The Price Isn't Right - in *The Guardian* of 10 November 1997), reports that it costs "about 26 p. to publish each copy (of the *Times*): 19 p. for production and 7 p. for the retailer. This is offset by advertising revenue of around 11 p". It may be that "scoop"

£60,000 "prize" yield for a scoop, per day, which if it can be spun out to three days might bring in £150,000. George Walden, a columnist in *The Evening Standard* reported on 3 September that "*The Sun* put on an extra 175,000 copies the day it published those hazy pictures of Dodi and Diana embracing"; he also lamented that "one of the most depressing developments in the past few years has been the extent to which, when it came to royalty, the so-called 'qualities' have aped their inferiors ... as the competition between titles heated up, all ... were drawn into the royal hunt of The Sun".

Given these calculations and this evidence it is not convincing on purely immediate financial grounds that editorial cultures seem willing or even enthusiastic to pay larger sums than this for the most costly paparazzi products. The fact that editors did or may continue to pay sums which are unlikely to yield any, let alone huge net short term profits suggests that they are caught up in a **spending frenzy** which they believe is necessary with which to fight the longer-term battle for circulation, which is certainly a grim one[163].

One noteworthy feature of the overall sales increase that might be attributable to coverage of the story of Princess Diana's death and its aftermath is that not all papers showed equal gains.

Table 6.2: Change in Sales per Title, into the Month after Princess Diana's Death

	September increment over August sales, for:		
Dailies	%	Sundays	%
Sun	0.6	News of the World	3.0
Mirror + Record	2.3	S. Mirror	5.3
Mail	5.6	Mail on S.	4.7
Express	2.1	People	4.9
Telegraph	4.0	S. Times	11.5
Times	7.1	Express on S.	10.1
Star	-0.3	S. Telegraph	6.8
Guardian	10.6	Observer	19.7
Financial Times	5.8	Independent on S.	13.0
Independent	11.9		

One reading of the results in Table 6.2 is that the republican papers won the largest percentage gains; even if they are not characterised as overtly republican, the *Guardian*, its sister paper the *Observer* and the two *Independent* titles are where some republican sentiments are certainly to be found (as we will see, below), and where probably the

---

editions can be sold for much higher advertising rates, so the revenue estimates made above are generous ones.

[163] Greenslade reports (in *The Guardian*: Red Sales In The Sunset, 17 November 1997) that dailies have suffered a market drop in sales of properly priced sales of 14.8 per cent over the past five years.

most acerbic criticism of the monarchy as it operates, and of the courtiers and of the royal family is ventilated. However, the base level of sales means that the largest proportional gain, for the *Observer*, of nearly 20 per cent consists of some 82,000 copies, while the *News of the World*, with "only" a gain of 3.9 per cent added 172,000 sales, and was not editorially as republican as the up market broadsheets.

Any notion that a public disenchanted with the monarchy flocked to experience the trauma through the more disaffected papers needs therefore to be taken with some caution. One other circumstance has to be noted, which is that there is an inverse correlation between sales volume and gain over the month - the titles with smaller sales (and larger cover prices) tended to enjoy the greatest gains. One way of explaining this may be that a penumbra of occasional readers for these broadsheets exists, who enter the buying public on special occasions; the closet republicans may have come out for the occasion. Another possibility, suggested by the *Guardian* columnist Roy Greenslade (13 October, G2: p. 8) is that it may be that at a time of national tragedy people choose broadsheet credibility. (A similar notion arises in interpreting what happens with television viewing, when people move to follow a story on BBC rather than on commercial channels).

By far the most important aspect of all these figures, however, is the undercurrent of stability in purchasing patterns that they display. People who bought one title appeared to continue to do so, since the sales volumes are so similar. It would be extraordinary with sales patterns of this kind had there been a pattern of drift from usually monarchist or less critical, to usually republican or more critical newspapers. The *Independent* and *Guardian* did not gain readers at the expenses of other titles. All titles (except the *Star*) put on sales; but this was only to a modest extent and was immediately wiped out in the next month's return to normal news fare.

On television the news of Diana's death was broadcast from early on in the morning of Sunday August 31st. Data on amounts and patterns of viewing are obtained for the Broadcasters' Audience Research Board by a company called Taylor Nelson AGB which keeps up a panel of over 4000 homes in each of which all the sets are fitted with electronic meters; all individuals in these households are asked to press a button on a handset whenever they enter and exit a room with a television switched on, in it. Figures are published for what is referred to as "viewing" - but which should more accurately be termed "presence in the room with the set switched on". Whatever the social psychological reality behind the figures, they are published in outline in several newspapers and are available in greater detail in the library of the Independent Television Commission. Figures are given in different ways, for example, of millions watching each programme, but for an effective comparison here it will be convenient to look at average hours and minutes of viewing per panellist (and hence, presumably per person across the population).

Table 6.3: Television Viewing in Hours Per Person Before and After Diana's Death

	Increases in Hours of Viewing*, per person:			Gains in %		
On channel;	Sunday 31/8	Saturday 6/9	Week - 7/9	Sun	Sat	Week
BBC 1	0.26	**1.48**	**2.53**	42	169	44
BBC 2	0.01	-0.06	-0.07	4	-30	-4
ITV	0.29	**1.01**	**2.21**	40	107	34
C4	-0.03	0.03	-0.10	-12	16	-7
C5	0.02	0.02	0.03	40	25	7
Others	0.01	0.04	0.14	3	15	9
Total	0.57	**2.55**	**5.13**	26	91	24

*the comparison is between the amount recorded for the day shown, and the same day of the week in the week ending 24 August

Viewing television increased substantially during the week ending with the day after the funeral (see Table 6.3). BBC 1 received the greatest increases for the Sunday in which the death was announced, for the funeral day itself and across the week at large. ITV also recorded large increases, though not quite to the same extent as occurred for BBC 1. Channel 4 and BBC 2 which to some extent provided complementary programming not focussed largely around Princess Diana and the impact of her death showed scant change and in some comparisons (for example, for BBC 2 on the day of the funeral itself) recorded less viewing than for the same day on the week before the death. Channel 5 appears to have had large increases in percentage of viewing, but these figures are not very reliable since the base figures of amounts of viewing are very small; the same applies for the others (satellite channels).

Audience size figures (in percentage of the population aged 12 and over said to be watching during a programme, or more truthfully: present in a room with the set switched on) show that normal programming remained well patronised. In the week ending 24 August (that is, before Diana died) ITV's most widely viewed programmes on the Sunday were *Coronation Street* (22%) *Wycliff* (14%) and the *News* (13%); on the Sunday on which the death was announced ITV's top audience sizes were still *Coronation Street* (25%) followed by *Heartbeat* (25%) and the *News Special* (19%). On BBC 1 in the week before the death the most widely viewed programmes were *Open All Hours* (16%) *The Beggar Bride* (16%) and *Ronnie Barker* (13%) but for the Sunday after the death this pattern changed completely so that the greatest viewing was to the *Nine O'clock News* (15%), the *Six O'clock News* (13%) and the *News at 1* (11%). The religious programme *Songs of Praise* attracted 7 per cent of viewers on the 17th of August and 8 per cent on the 24th but this increased to 12 per cent on the day after the funeral and was still at an increased level of 11 per cent on the week afterwards.

Another way to describe viewing behavior is to look at the numbers of people who were said to have been viewing (rather than those numbers as percentages of the whole population). On Sunday 31 August at 8 am 1.8 million people were tuned to the BBC, by 10 am this had increased to 3.7 million and the audience reached 6.8 million by 1 pm. On the rival ITV channel the morning peak reached 3.6 million; however, the laws of inheritance (though they may be challenged in the House of Lords and even within the monarchy, they rule effectively in television audience behavior) operated so that ITV took the lead in the evening when 13 million watched the homecoming of the coffin on ITV (following as it did the appropriately named *Coronation Street* and *Heartbeat*) while just under 6 million watched similar coverage on BBC 1. During the "long afternoon hours ... the BBC's coverage began to shift perceptibly away from the politicians and the talking heads towards the grieving public - the tone of coverage has remained the same ..." - at least until their media correspondent Maggie Brown wrote these words in the *Evening Standard* of Wednesday 3rd.

Overall, we see increased viewing of news (though news programmes still did not attract anywhere near the size of audience drawn to a soap opera on another channel), increased viewing of a religious programme (there are not many of these), again, not to a huge extent, and increased viewing overall, especially to the two mainstream channels, both of which focussed heavily on the life and death of Princess Diana. The compensatory channels offering an alternative to the main story and essentially normal programming, fared normally in the amounts of viewing they attracted, or in some comparisons recorded small reductions in patronage.

The pattern of patronage is therefore in one respect similar for television and the press - both provided huge amounts of coverage of the story and both were rewarded with increased patronage, though this was to a far greater extent for television than the press. In another respect the press and broadcasting patterns were different inasmuch as the papers which expressed less attachment to the monarchy and its well being gained the largest percentage increases in numbers purchased while the television channels that stuck more to business as usual and ignored the trauma for the monarchy were not rewarded with increased patronage.

PHOTOJOURNALISM: SOME COUNTS OF CONTENT

What did the newspapers contain during this unusual week? Pictures, and words. The themes in the words ranged from admiration and love for Diana, her children and sometimes even some sympathy for Prince Charles and other members of the royal family, including romantic evocation of the past and shock and grief at the present, to analysis of the range of Princess Diana's behavior, from the abundantly emerging evidence of her sustained and genuine compassion for many kinds of suffering people, to her own sufferings and pain. There was a good deal of advice, particularly for the monarchy and the royal family, and some of this was extremely negative and even hostile. Pictures are said by some often to "say" more than words, and indeed some of the pictures were expressive. Many of the pictures were implicit invitations to become involved, and many of the words explicitly encouraged people to do so, if only by writing to the newspapers and by taking part in phone-in polls

The huge mass of material available in just one week poses problems for any attempt to analyse and make sense of it. One frame of reference for analysis would suppose that there might be differences in thematic content as the week progressed, and also differences between newspapers reflecting both their ideological positions as well as their resources and their assumptions about what they thought their readers wanted. What will be done here is first to report statistical evidence on the amount and kinds of pictures published; and then to quote from the written material to try and discern a developmental account of elements of the story as it unfolded, not just in one newspaper but (if such an entity has any coherent meaning) in the national press.

Table 6.4 describes the pictorial contents of five major newspapers, the *Express*, the *Sun*, the *Mirror*, the *Mail* and the *Star*. The major broadsheets were left out partly because pictures play a somewhat lesser role in these papers (though the *Independent* had recently been basing many of its front pages on evocative pictures) and partly because they account for a smaller proportion of the overall circulation. A picture has been defined as a photograph (thus omitting drawings and cartoons) showing a news story (rather than a teller of one - as several by-lines are now accompanied by portrait pictures of journalists; on this occasion the temptation to deal with journalists-as-news as been resisted). Also omitted are photographs as advertisements (of which there were many). The essence of the material counted below is therefore the photojournalism on offer. The procedure included double counting thus if Princess Diana appeared with one or both of her sons, or Prince Charles, each major role-player was counted.

Table 6.4: Pictures in the Press - the Week after Princess Diana's death

			Portrayals of:				
				Others			
Number of pictures	Princess Diana	Prince Charles	Young Princes	Royal Family	People In Story	Things, Places	Day
731 %	**61**	14	9	2	21	6	Monday
281 %	24	5	4	2	**35**	30	Wed.
588 %	15	4	6	2	32	10	Friday
Number of pictures	606	138	111	37	441		
"Tone"	%	%	%	%	%		
Positive	**80**	51	65	38	52		
Neutral	13	25	24	22	23		
Negative	7	24	11	**41**	47		

On the Monday 731 pictures were counted in the five newspapers, of which 61 per cent showed Diana Princess of Wales; together with pictures on the Wednesday and

Friday this amounted to 606 pictures and in four fifths of these she was shown in a positive mood - radiant, happy, amused, compassionate. In fewer than one in ten pictures was the Princess clearly shown in a depressed, unhappy, tense or otherwise negative mood. The greatest number of pictures of Princess Diana appeared in the Monday editions, with far fewer appearing during the middle and towards the end of the week. The emerging category of portrayals was of other people in the story - that is, politicians from far and near, celebrities, friends of Princess Diana, the al Fayed family and friends, and members of the public. The final column shows instances of things such as the mangled car and places such as the accident site and then later in the week the sites of memorial such as outside the London palaces (but also at Holyrood and other public places where people were gathered and privately or communally expressing - or sometimes perhaps looking for - their feelings).

Prince Charles appeared in around one seventh of the pictures; half of his appearances were positive but the other half were evenly divided between those that could be clearly recognised as negative (sad, unhappy, perplexed) and those which were indeterminate. There were fewer pictures overall of the two young princes, but two thirds of their appearances were positive (smiling shyly or showing glee on some outing). Other members of the royal family were shown in remarkably few photographs, and more of those that appeared (by a small margin) were recognisably negative than positive.

This evidence suggests that an effect of the pictures may have been to reinforce positive feelings about Princess Diana and, to some extent, to reflect or reinforce a variety of positive and negative feelings about Prince Charles and other members of the royal family. Also likely to be reinforced was self-esteem amongst the ordinary members of the public, seeing oneselves as represented in a wide variety of ages and statuses, but in all cases behaving in a cohesive and humanely affirmative way. That is, if they were shown as positive in the table it may have been when they had been cheerful with, or remembering some episode with Princess Diana, but even if they were classified as negative it will have been in showing sorrow after her death. This raises the possibility that negative here has a range of directional meanings: it may entail a picture of the Queen looking sombre or morose, and that could be interpreted not as showing grief (a "positive negativity" as might be read into the expressions of many ordinary people) but as revealing some mixture of guilt or remorse concerning alleged disposition towards Princess Diana while she was alive.

A major caution to attach to photojournalism is over its use of pictures which appear to illustrate some written idea, but which may have been derived from elsewhere to do so. Thus there could be a picture of the Queen looking glum, next to a story accusing her of being uncompassionate about Princess Diana - but published during the week Her Majesty was secluded in Balmoral it can be deduced that the picture as used was taken on some other occasion. It appears that this kind of misrepresentation has occurred not infrequently but that it has been noticed hardly at all, if ever, by those who write about the press.

WRITTEN JOURNALISM: SOME
ACCOUNT OF ITS RANGE AND CONTENT

To give greater depth to a description of the discourse in the press it is necessary to examine what was written. What follows here is obviously selective - but it has been chosen to represent range rather than weight of sentiment. Thus the focus is on the themes that were on offer and not on the other matter - which is an important one - of the extent to which, in terms of some possible count of the number, repetition or force of the ideas expressed, one theme could be demonstrated to have been developed more often and another less so.

In what follows, the quotations are drawn from daily national newspapers published in the week after Diana died, and will be referred to by initials of the name of the paper, the date of the item's appearance and the page on which it appeared; thus 'DM, 3, 14' would refer to an item in the *Daily Mail* of 3 September, on page 14[164]. A distinction has to be drawn as between imagining that each newspaper was in contact with and thinking along the same lines as others, so that themes in each paper could be said to be a part of some consciously integrated and jointly produced narrative - and what is more likely the truth which is that a reading of all the papers can claim to discern some network of themes, appearing to such an eclectic reader as a grand narrative. Few members of the public will have thoroughly read more than one paper a day, and extremely few will have read them all; so the grand narratives are not composed in very many minds at all. That said, there are two evident grand narratives, with each of which most people will have connected through the press with several ingredients, spread across several days.

These narratives can be called the Republican, and the Royalist accounts. In the first, Diana Spencer entered the limelight as an innocent girl manipulated by a coldly calculating royal family. The move in her fortunes was ostensibly 'up' from the status of commoner to that of Princess (a true republican would presumably construe this as a negative move from reality to dangerous fantasy - but the press treatment at the time gave hardly any space to such an interpretation; most accounts were star-struck). The next substantial stage in her life, in this account, was to be rejected, forced into sickness and alienation, to attempts to console herself through friendships - some of which may have meant sexual affairs - in all of which she moved 'down' into the experience of a victim. In both cases the promotion and the victimisation are implied to be the work of a royal machine that is essentially exploitative.

After the second stage move down, comes the third phase in Diana's public life in which her own efforts move her back 'up' to a condition in which she grasps control of her fortunes. She enjoys triumphs of adulation and happiness, but then in a dramatic fourth episode of calamity, dies. A mild republican narrative version of the royal role in this calamity is to suppose that it was royal rejection that brought about the life style in

---

[164] The other initials for papers are T for Times, DT for Daily Telegraph, I for Independent, E for Express, ES for the (London) Evening Standard, St for Star, S for Sun, M for Mirror, DM for

which Diana died; a strong republican version emerges in conspiracy theories. These were floated on the internet and only reported second hand, clearly without any explicit endorsement in the daily press, but nearly all implied that the death was not accidental but murder, with the Establishment - which whether in business, military or even ecclesiastical form supports the monarchy - at fault. Thus the *Times* on Thursday 4 September (p. 6) ran an item headlined:

> *Arabs are convinced car crash was a murder plot* The report indicated that "a poll in the West Bank showed that 47 per cent of readers of Palestinian papers were certain that the Paris car accident had been engineered. Anis Mansour, in Al Ahram alleged 'she was killed by British intelligence to save the monarchy ... the brakes of the car were tampered with by British agents paid by your Queen'. Other writers in Kuwait and Jordan echoed this notion".

There may be social and political merits, or flaws in a republican case, in either the weaker or the strong form; however, the fabric of such a narrative is available in elements spread across the week's daily press, which will be quoted below. The Royalist account can equally be shaped with a first part in which Diana Spencer (like Cinderella) is raised from being a loyal acolyte of the system, to the glory of being a princess, a glittering role both justified by and justifying a system of monarchy. This is clearly a move 'up'. The next stage was a collapse, in this account through inherent flaws and features of her mercurial character. This move 'down' was not, in this version brought about by royal malignancy or neglect, but alongside a dismayed detachment, or in spite of efforts to alleviate the difficulties. Thirdly, an emergence of Her Royal Highness Princess Diana and then, after her divorce as Diana, Princess of Wales into well targeted charitable and welfare activities was her conspicuous move back 'up', into a space created by royal glamour and permitted by palace protocols.

After her calamitous death, the Royalist narrative would hold that the royal family were themselves in a state of shock in which they grievously needed all their nation's support (rather than its criticism for apparently being aloof), while they coped with arrangements for the funeral as well as with the pastoral care of the two princes. Finally, some degree of catharsis was experienced for Diana-in-her-sons, and for their father and grandparents; the sons' experience of public grief for their mother before and at her funeral, and of support for their own future roles as king and his brother (which Diana herself said she wanted to see come about) unavoidably reinforce a royalist narrative ending on an upbeat, obviously severely qualified by the suffering that had to be endured to reach this position.

Aside from two alternative narratives concerning the monarchy, discernible in the week's press, there are two important narratives about the mass message systems themselves. The first can be called market justification in which the volume and nature of coverage of Princess Diana and of the monarchy are held to be so irresistibly interesting to the public that the press and broadcasters have to satisfy this external

---

Daily Mail; where relevant, the initial S stands for the Sunday version of the paper.

demand. Evidence has already been explored above, that helps to quantify the extent of such demand; but what will follow below is text that expresses the belief, drawn from the press itself. The second narrative about the mass message systems concerns the notion that there was, or may have been a universality both of personal experience and of mass conveyed expression about Diana's death and its context. The evidence for such a narrative of universality is again found in the press; but there is also counter-evidence of very important disparities of treatment within the press (some newspapers developing a different perspective from one important other), as well as of dissension between the press and broadcasters.

THE REPUBLICAN NARRATIVE: THE FIRST ASCENT

We begin with the notion that Diana Spencer was an innocent pawn, carelessly cast by the monarchy for the calamity ahead.

"she came to all this hopelessly unprepared ... plucked from nowhere at 19 ... in the sort of transmogrification one doesn't expect outside of bedtime stories". (G, 1, 11).

"one thing is certain ... and that will be her lasting impact on the royal family ... this retiring girl would reduce the family to a state of agonised self-doubt ... (she) ... had served the House of Windsor's dynastic needs. But she rebelled against the hypocrisy ...". (G, 1, 19).

"Diana seemed to find it hard to understand she was such a public figure, almost a goddess to many ...". (M, 1, 16).

"A few days before the wedding ... Diana 'broke down' at a polo match ... she was comforted by Lady 'Penny' Romsey ... (who with) Lord Romsey subsequently became two of Diana's greatest detractors. They told friends at the time that the marriage was quite wrong ...". (M, 1, 8).

"She was robbed of her dreams before the honeymoon was over ... she was utterly and completely alone". (Anne Robinson, E, 5, 15).

"... There is a male chauvinism about ... scapegoating ... Diana is portrayed as a mere puppet, created by royalty and manipulated by the media ... she is regarded as without free will, without responsibility for her actions". (Simon Jenkins, ES, 5, 11).

THE ROYALIST NARRATIVE: THE FIRST ASCENT

The *Times'* obituary set the scene:

"For many generations (the Spencers) served their Sovereigns ... The Princess's father was equerry to King George VI and to the present Queen. Both her grand mothers, the Countess Spencer and Lady Ruth Fermoy were close members of the court of Queen

Elizabeth the Queen Mother, as were no fewer than four Spencer great-aunts ... she also descended through several lines from the Stuart Kings Charles II and James II who were not ancestors of the Prince of Wales". (T, 1, 27).

The *Mirror* journalist James Whitaker contributed on the same day to a 48 page tribute to Diana in which he saw her as an autonomous person:

"Diana assured me that marrying into the Royal Family would not be a problem for her ... brought up next to Sandringham House, ... she was used to the Royal Family ... Diana, I firmly believed, had always wanted to become an actual member of this family, not a servant to them ... Yet in reality, she found the transition to her royal role a great strain". (M, 1, 6-7).

At the *Express*, Ross Benson (who had been a contemporary at Gordonstoun, Prince Charles' boarding school) offered a similar view:

"When she was 16 she had declared that she was 'out to get Charles' ... She started spending as much time as possible at the cottage on the Balmoral Estate with her sister, Lady Jane, who had recently married the Queen's future private secretary Sir Robert Fellowes". (E, 1, S9).

"Diana ... must have been influenced by the sight of her sister's (Jane Fellowes') happiness and the feeling that the Fellowses were part of a closely integrated community. Besides, her family had been brought up to serve the Sovereign ...". (DM, 1, 34).

"Diana's maternal grandmother Ruth, Lady Fermoy was a close friend and Lady-in-Waiting to the Queen Mother". (and she had given testimony in Diana's parents' divorce against her own daughter Frances, leading custody to be awarded to Diana's father Earl Spencer, who married again to Raine). (S, 1, 20).

"Prince Charles kissing Diana's hand in such a romantic shot ... I can't believe he never loved her. This is such a tender moment - he could not possibly fake it". (Jayne Fincher, photographer, St, 3, 18).

(Diana said) "I loved Charles. And he loved me - very very much. To say that he didn't is wrong, totally wrong". (St, 3, 20).

"Here it is, the photograph that left me convinced Charles and Diana were definitely in love. I took it during their successful 1983 trip to Australia". (St, 5, 8).

"If it is true that Charles only married Diana to fulfil his destiny as future king, then there is something deeply sad at the root of our culture. I think Charles should now marry Camilla ... then at least something good can come of this sorry tale ...". (Boy George, E, 5, 34).

THE REPUBLICAN NARRATIVE: SOURING OF THE DREAM: BAD FAITH AMONGST THE ROYAL FAMILY

Not long after the first and positive transposition a downturn in fortunes is reported to have begun. A republican narrative (which does not necessarily spring from explicit republican ideologues) is one in which the text contains ideas that imply criticism of the behavior of, or which reduce the dignity or motives of the monarchy.

"Dutifully, she quickly gave birth to an heir, one of the few events in their married life that appeared to bring deep and genuine pleasure to both". (Alan Hamilton, T, 1, 10).

"in her last interview (in Le Monde) Diana "contrasted the 'unnaturalness' of life within the Royal Family with her spontaneous relationships with ordinary people around the world.". (Ben McIntyre, T, 1, 19).

"... 'shy Di' the teenager ... single-handedly rejuvenating the creaky old institution of the Monarchy ... was not given the support she needed by either the Royal Family or their courtiers ... Diana was the victim and I said so in print ... Diana was grateful for the support and was pleased to say so. In 15 years as a positive and unpaid public relations man for the Prince of Wales, I had never had such thanks. ... her story is a deeply unhappy one: traumatised by her mother's departure from her life when she was six ... by her husband's love for another woman, trapped in a gilded cage ... as the shock of her death sinks in, The Queen and Charles may well rue the day they braved public wrath by depriving Diana of her title of HRH and expelling her from the Royal Family".[165] (Anthony Holden, E, 1, 28).

"The most significant legacy of Diana Princess of Wales will be the manner in which she changed our perception of the House of Windsor, largely to its detriment. The House of Windsor has never really recovered from the revelations ... which I serialised ... in 1992 ... For an institution that has spent the past 50 years marketing itself as a "family" Diana had dealt it a devastating blow ...". (Andrew Neil, G, 1, 20).

"Diana hated the stuffy formality of the royal palaces ... (she) longed for informal suppers, sunshine holidays and shopping trips ...". (S, 1, Tribute Section).

According to James Whitaker, following the birth of Prince William Prince Charles was asked about married life and replied:

"Its all right, but it interferes with my hunting ..."; then, too, in early 1983 on the Australian tour "seeds of disaster started to stir in Prince Charles. She was a star and he wasn't. He had never been used to this. ... crowds would groan when they ended up with Prince Charles on their side of the road". (M, 1, 11).

---

[165] Ambiguities in Mr Holden's text include the capitalisation of the terms Royal Family and the resentment, which a headlong republican might not reveal, at the expulsion of his heroine from an institution to which an admired person should not wish to belong.

"A sunshine holiday in the summer of 1986 first publicly exposed the cracks in the marriage ... (on a day's cruise) ... for seven hours the couple did not exchange a single word ... newspapers asked 'Are Charles and Di still in tune?' Buckingham Palace insisted everything was fine. ... (M, 1, 17).

"Charles continued to see Camilla who coincidentally is the great grand daughter of Alice Keppel, mistress of Charles's great grandfather Edward VII". (M, 1, 24).[166]

Whitaker alleges further, in his *Mirror* tribute (p. 39) that "in Dimbleby's authorised biography ... Charles said he never loved his wife ... (this) sent shock waves through the palace by blaming his parents, his upbringing, his school as well as his wife"[167]. In another polemic Paul Johnson wrote:

"Properly helped and guided, Diana's gifts could have transformed the relationship between royalty and the public ... making it almost invulnerable. But her royal husband betrayed her, and his family then closed ranks, robbed her of her status, downgraded her ... her death, far from being meaningless, was full of meaning ... she was a martyr to a combination of evils: the coldness of royalty, the prurience of the public in demanding even the most intimate secrets of her heart, and the cruelty of the media in supplying them...". (DM, 1, 14).

Paul Johnson's colleague Keith Waterhouse echoed the words 'betrayed', 'downgraded' ...

"there was an inner urge to keep on going in that madcap restless way. And the credit for that treadmill drive of hers will go ... to her bolting mother, her deceiving husband, her deceiving husband's mistress, and the ruthless Royals who so unceremoniously dumped her". (DM, 1, 16)..

Elsewhere, on the same day, a similarly harsh view was offered, under a headline "storybook marriage, hideous betrayal and divorce, illness, suicide attempts ..."

"This could Bankrupt the Buck House Firm ... the Royal Family ... expected her to provide children ... and then be a comforting consort ... a mere ornament, while Charles still loved and lusted for Camilla, made her literally throw up ... then rebel ... people will still think the Firm is using Di yet again for its own ends. No, Diana's death will be the body blow to the present generation of royals ... Charles will certainly never be able to marry Camilla now ... I doubt if he can ever successfully become King ... Charles comes across as a cold, remote figure ... now he will be seen as the callous betrayer who drove the most wonderful woman in the world to despair ... the only hope ... is Prince William. He is the image of his mum and just like her, he will be a superstar ...". (Peter Hill, S, 3, 8).

---

[166]Dimbleby's book denies that Charles was still seeing Camilla.

[167]It is not easy to find a passage in the book that gives this impression.

The *Evening Standard* thought it a good idea to reprint some republican rhetoric from Tuesday's *Guardian*:

> "she showed up the House of Windsor for what it was: a dumb, numb dinosaur ... she made it clear that loving one's country and loving the sorry bunch of dysfunctional Graeco-Germans[168] stuck on as an afterthought at the prow were two entirely different and sometimes contradictory things ... we have seen Diana the Good ... but we have not yet seen the other great Diana - the Destroyer. And destroyer she has been, gloriously so, with bells on; the greatest force for republicanism since Oliver Cromwell ... more subjects of the House of Windsor are against it than for it ... Windsors ... the biggest bunch of bastards who ever wore the crown ... the sickly bunch of bullies who call themselves our ruling house ...". (Julie Birchill, ES, 3, 8).

Less virulently, but from the respected person of Ludovic Kennedy came:

> "Some have asked if the media coverage is overkill. I do not think so. What can the Royal Family do? - in asking them to show a humanity that they do not instinctively feel, we are asking the impossible". (E, 4, 14).

THE ROYALIST NARRATIVE: SOURING OF THE DREAM: INHERENT WEAKNESSES OF CHARACTER AND COMPATABILITY

There is not a great deal of text that portrays the royal family's role in this phase, sympathetically. However:

> "It is the conventional wisdom to blame Diana's bulimia on Charles's on-going association with Camilla Parker Bowles. In fact, she had fallen victim to the disease long before Camilla reappeared". (Ross Benson, E, 1, 16).

Benson implied that the bulimia had occurred before the wedding, out of which Diana had said she would opt. It was, in this account her father who:

> "talked her out of her decision. Duty, he insisted, must always come before self ... (later) Charles interrupted their honeymoon to call a psychiatrist up to Balmoral ... Diana had at first refused point blank to pose for the gathered photographers and then, just when her husband had surrendered to her will, changed her mind. In the pictures ... Charles, still smarting from the argument, looks sullen ... while Diana, her mood behind her, appeared to be the very portrait of a loving wife ... it was the start of a pattern that would continue throughout all the years the couple remained together ... . (E, 1, 19).

---

[168]This epithet would probably be censured as racist, had it been applied to commoners. Although it could be argued that Oliver Cromwell bored society into yearning for a Restoration (a lesson which most British people other than the vituperative Birchill have internalised) and that the assurance about public opinion lacks verification, this passage is probably worth reproducing as the most raging piece to have appeared during the week in which much of the focus was on Diana as a purveyor of love.

The anti-royalist *Guardian*'s obituary may be seen as lending some support to Benson's account, of what happened when Diana's mother took up with:

"the lively and witty Peter Shand Kydd - a contrast to her father, whose friends and pursuits she found dull ... thus, classically ...was to emerge the bulimia ...". (G, 1, 22).

The *Daily Mail* explored the sexist convention that sexual experiences on one side could be taken for granted, but not on both sides of such a royal pair; the important point is also made of what was thus a 'necessarily' large age difference, and the difficulties that might entail:

"... in those more strait-laced days a prince could marry ... only a girl whose moral character was unimpeachable, which by the beginning of the Eighties meant someone very young indeed ... In those early days (1984) Diana ... would tease her husband, buy him clothes that ... would give him a more youthful image (she made him change his barber and tailor - and she got rid of many of his servants and friends who she felt belonged to the time 'before her'". (Anne de Courcy, DM, 1, 36, 42).

THE REPUBLICAN NARRATIVE: EMERGENCE FROM VICTIMHOOD

There are several subsets to this section of the republican narrative. We might agree to refer to each of these subsets as a theme; so there are the themes of **Diana as Saint**, or if not quite that certainly a metaphorical Angel of Mercy, including several instances of provision of a healing touch[169]; there are the themes of **wickedness,** of **dysfunction** and of **obsolescence** in the royal establishment; there are the themes of '**Dianism**' or a sort of modernism involving the display of deep and honest emotion, its endorsement within the segments of society whose ethos is gaining the upper hand, and finally of an insistence that sovereignty resides not in the monarchy but amongst the people. This **"people power"** theme takes the forms either in the weaker case, of asking the royal family to do something or other, and in the stronger case of insisting, and then of noisily pointing out that royal actions have occurred under coercion by what the press describe as the people's will.

There is a considerable amount of material on the theme of sainthood, or quasi-sainthood; several of the dicta here spill over into **the theme of the healing touch**. On the 31st of August, the London *Evening Standard* gave away a special edition including many comments by members of the public, one of whom said:

---

[169]The healing touch has been overtly associated with the powers of the British sovereign, several reigns back, and less overtly has cropped up more recently. In Diana's case it is debatable whether the repeated instantiation of healing acts would reinforce (through the second stage of the republicanist narrative in which the separation between Diana and the Royal Establishment was underlined, to the detriment of the latter) a republicanist interpretation of events; or whether the currents of subconscious feeling might link back, via the theme of Diana's support for her son's succession, to support a royalist narrative. I am inclined to think the latter is more

I think she will be turned into a saint. She deserves nothing less". (ES, 31, 7).

A much quoted contribution by a member of the public, on a bouquet was:

"Born a lady, became a princess, died a saint". (T, 1, 4).

This appeared in the same form in the *Guardian* and the *Mirror* (as a headline), while a variant was reported in the *Sun*:

"Born a Lady, Became a Princess, Died a Legend. God Bless". (S, 1, 4).

Later in the week a columnist Jane Moore observed:

"It's easy to forget Diana was a human being ... princess Diana made of flesh and blood? Surely not. Surely she was immortal like other fairytale princesses? Untouchable. Invincible even ... 'Will she wake up again like Sleeping Beauty did?' asked my daughter ...". (I, 4, 8).

Victor Adebowale, chief executive of the homelessness charity, Centrepoint said:

"the young people ... can spot a liar at 200 paces. They knew she was genuine ... we were grateful that our patron thought it important that the future King knew the reality of life for some of the people he would be representing ...".

To this, Sandra Chalmers, of Help the Aged added:

"she would pick out the oldest, probably least attractive to our eyes, to the camera's eyes ... the hand would be into that older hand and she would form a link that no other person in my experience has been able to do ...". (both T, 1, 12).

Two other luminaries, in the same newspaper contributed:

"she changed the public view of Aids sufferers when she shook hands with one a decade ago". (Peter Riddell, T, 1, 18).

"I hope" said the historian and royal biographer Ben Pimlott "that Diana will be remembered as a human being and not some sort of goddess. One is appalled by the way the imagery develops ...". But yesterday it was evident that the mythology was beyond the control of ordinary historical record ... The Princess was ... an intensely romantic figure, and around such figures myths accumulate". (Jane Shilling, T, 1, 20).

Diana's aide Patrick Jephson, who clearly knew her extremely well, made a connection with the myths of chivalrous gentility, which go back to the tales of Arthur's - royal - court when he wrote:

---

likely, though the former is theoretically possible.

"Her courtesy was of the purest kind ... it sprang from her inner conviction that those she was seeking to serve ... deserved nothing but the best".

and Nigella Lawson, a journalist reported that:

"The American shock-academic Camille Paglia once wrote that ... Diana's ... role ... was that of mater dolorosa, with all the religious and symbolic connotations involved". (both: T, 1, 23).

Paglia's statement of an opinion, well before Diana's death, does not automatically mean that what she says is true; however, many people drew on well corroborated evidence to fortify the image. Thus the broadcaster and press journalist Libby Purves reported:

"Again and again and ever more surely, she produced the same effect: she lit people up, made them confide, offered them little bits of herself, alleviated sadness with a human touch ...". (T, 1, 24).

The *Times* behaved itself as a recognisably monarchist newspaper, during a difficult week, but the same outlook was not needed at the *Guardian*, whose columnist John Ezard presciently wrote:

"Frailty, the apparent brave frailty of a candle in the wind was always Diana's supreme public quality in life. She will, as Dame Barbara (her step grandmother) said "reign forever as the Queen of Love". (G, 1, 6).

Elsewhere, the same paper reported:

"Diana ... was photographed shaking hands with seven Aids patients. People were shocked that she had worn no gloves and she was even attacked as the 'patron saint of sodomy' ... Nick Partridge, chief executive of the Terence Higgins trust said 'Diana took the stigma away from Aids". (G, 1, 6).

The *Sun* at first chose to bask in the glow of a star greater than itself, providing two headlines:

"Her almost saintly powers brought a smile to the afflicted"; and "Her Star Will Shine Forever She was the nearest thing we'll get to an angel on earth" (by her amanuensis Andrew Morton) who continued: "often bed-bound patients burst into tears in her presence and she would spontaneously put her arms around them to give them a hug ... Her guiding light was her grandmother Cynthia Spencer, whom the Princess believed watched over her from the spirit world ... the Princess was convinced that in another existence she had been a Christian nun. Perhaps this is why she utterly adored Mother Teresa of Calcutta". (S, 1, 14, 18).

The *Mirror* employs an 'agony aunt' Miriam Stoppard, whom few may remember (and she was gracious enough not to point it out) had, as a well known presenter of a television medical show kissed an AIDS patient in 1985, preceding Diana's more publicised actions. Alongside her generous comments, Lord St John of Fawsley noted that Diana had a

> "real and charismatic gift for healing ... she did not have much love in her marriage. But that did not embitter her in the sense of turning her into a person who hated. it turned her into a person who loved more". (M, 1, 18).

The newspaper followed this with a large section titled Queen of All Our Hearts, filled with many stories adding to the record:

> "when she toured a hospital or met children of courage, she was never the haughty royal. The warmth she radiated was there for all to see. She was interested in what they were doing and had to say. She listened to them, encouraged them ...". (M, 1, 20).

In the *Daily Mail*

> "Diana was in some ways a lady from the early Christian past, a fun loving princess-turned saint ... to whom only a Fra Angelico or a Donatello could have done justice ... . (DM, 1, 14).

The *Star*, hardly normally an echo-chamber of a Christian resonance declared in an editorial:

> "Diana was quite simply the most famous person the world has ever seen. The most photographed. The most talked about. The most loved. The most used. And abused". (St, 1, 8).

The *Mail*'s writer Piers Paul Reid reported from Kensington Palace that

> "There were prayers among the messages of condolence ... and a sense that here was a crowd of pilgrims in search of a shrine". (DM, 3, 17).

On the next day one could read that:

> "The Deification of Diana has begun. 'Appearances' of the Princess at St James' Palace have become the gossip of mourners who saw - or thought they saw - her image in an oil painting ...". (Claire Garner, I, 4, 2).

The blunt words of a tabloid headline declared: "Di's goodness like Christ's says top Rev" (S, 4, 25); another paper produced a telling anecdote:

> "Roger Appleby ... lay desperately ill - with chronic heart problems ... Mr Appleby heard Diana tell him about ... Prince William's idea to auction her dresses. Then he told her of his crushing illness, but even as he spoke he seemed to transform. 'He was home the next day and I couldn't believe the difference' said his wife". (DM, 4, 21).

A London School of Economics Professor's article was provided with a headline he may not have written himself, over a piece explaining that the structure of Diana's career with its astonishing and deep reversals of fortune was recognised by the Greeks (and named by them Peripateia) as the model for high drama:

"She was touched by a natural sense of divinity". (E, 4, 14).

Journalists were not unanimous in their accounts of Diana as an angel of mercy, as will emerge in the section below. However, two comments may be entered here to indicate some ambiguity:

"She was rootless, baseless, wallowing. Dinner parties would shriek with cynical laughter at her ambulance-chasing and shalwar-kameez[170] wearing. I shrieked myself ...". (Vicky Woods, G, 1, 18).

And

"How will we remember her? Saint, mother, martyr, royal, victim, heroine, legend. All labels. Some accurate, some false. They don't tell us much". (Mary Riddell, M, 5, 13).

The (pseudo)canonisation of Diana evolved from an initial "yes she is/well we shouldn't really be talking like this" to a quieter phase, dotted with occasional reports of phenomena such as that plastic figures of her were selling well in Naples amongst others of more established holy figures such as Padre Pio. During the first week of mourning, several instances of assertion cropped up moving towards a formulation that Diana stood for emotive honesty, spontaneity and opposition to stiff protocol as the things which helped push her to destruction. Her legacy, if nothing else would be to change the institution that was represented - in her experience and in the thoughts of those who felt for her - as caging a free spirit.

"Diana ... set out to be the perfect mother ... She introduced the novel conception of openly expressed affection into the Royal Family ... The depth of public shock and grief ... is precisely because she humanised an institution and let the fresh air of real feeling and sympathy into what had become a dusty old portrait gallery". (ES, 311, 12).

"Alone in the Royal Family, Diana saw that the monarchy must adapt to survive". (T, 1, 24).

"There have been, until now, two streams to the little Princes' lives: the more formal stream of life with the royals and the more unconventional, warm, spontaneous stream of life with their mother ... they will do things the way their mother would have wanted ... In

---

[170] The *shalwar-kameez* is the outfit of trousers and long-shirt worn by Pakistani women and followed by Diana's friend Jemima Goldsmith, who married the famous Pakistani sportsman Imran Khan.

that sense, those religious souls who left flowers ... saying Diana would exercise her mission from heaven were not entirely wrong". (E, 1, 11).

"when sober historians come to examine this great national tragedy ... they will see ... a huge chasm opening up between the reality of a small troubled offshore island in the grip of a steep moral decline, and the global imperial grandeur of its monarchy. And they will see Diana, a child of the new era, colliding with the whole institution of monarchy, whose rules and precepts she never accepted ...". (E, 1, 17).

"'She had reinvented royalty in recent years in perhaps the only direction it can go in and survive' said royal biographer Anthony Holden ... In her interview with Panorama, Diana mentioned that she thought the monarchy should walk hand in hand with the people more than it does. 'I think that is the only kind of monarchy that can survive in Blair's 21st century Euro-Britain' said Mr Holden". (G, 1, 8).

"Her genuine affection for people, her vitality ... were qualities rarely seen in public figures, let alone members of the royal family. Inside the Palace her hands- on appeal was at odds with traditional white-gloved formality ...". (G, 1, 19).

"While Charles opted for the blazer and slacks approach, Di preferred the baseball cap and jeans style, determined that her son would not be engulfed by the stiff and stuffy formality of the House of Windsor ... Princess Diana made sure they knew how the other half lived. With their dad, they hunted and fished in Balmoral".[171] (S, 1, 8).

A "constitutional expert" writing in the *Sun* opined

"Diana's ... influence on the monarchy, this breaking of the mould means the security of the throne is so much in doubt. Her death means the monarchy really appears to have no function ... The reaction to Diana's death from the public shows that Britain has changed utterly. Diana damaged the royal family and their traditional way of doing things. ... the family monarchy worked in a deferential society in which a common set of values applied. Diana created a new sort of magic for our new, real, radical democracy". (S, 3, 10).

On the same day London's evening readers were reminded of what the *Independent* wrote on Tuesday, that

"what would do the monarchy good and show that they had grasped the lesson of Diana's popularity would be for the Queen and Prince of Wales to break down, cry and hug one another on the steps of the Abbey ... that such an event is unthinkable shows how great is the gap between the people mourning 'their' princess, and the Royal Family". (ES, 3, 3).

Fancy also flowed at the *Express*:

---

[171]This writer had evidently not read Jonathan Dimbleby's biography of Prince Charles, or discounted what she would have found there in Chapter 17, reporting that Prince Charles "had visited a hostel for the homeless at King's Cross, and ... spent time with the adolescents rescued from the streets by the charity Centrepoint ... .

"... imagine that it was Prince Charles ... who had died. Would the Princess have hidden herself away in a stuffy royal palace ... Of course not. She would have come out to talk to the people and allow them to share her grief". (E, 4, 14).

Deeper in the paper one could read that

"... when it came to sheer numbers, her army was bigger than anyone else's". (E, 4, 15).

The next day a similar theme was sharpened in an Editorial titled "Family that did not understand"

"Diana was ... the Royal Family's only contact with the real world, their link with grassroots feeling and emotion ...". (S, 5, 10).

Beyond this **Dianism** theme of emotional honesty portrayed as in detrimental contrast with the ways of the royal family, emerges the theme of **people's (princess's) power**; in the milder form, this power is considered to alter the royal family and monarchy, presumably to the regret of those who support the stronger version that this people's power would somehow be the end of monarchy. Here, it becomes very clear that the "republican" papers such as the *Independent*, *Guardian* and for the time being at least even the *Sun* (starting on the Wednesday) gave space to quite anti-monarchist sentiment. This contrasts sharply with the stance of the *Mirror* which took an impatient though perhaps grudgingly loyal position, and the Express which presented people writing on both sides of the issue.

"'The monarchy might be in danger' said social affairs commentator Polly Toynbee, speaking on BBC Radio 4. There may be a sense of public indignation against Prince Charles. The poor man may find that where he goes he is not much liked and that he is blamed for the tragedy of Diana's life. Prince Charles flew home with the body of the woman he had rejected ...". (G, 1, 8).

Contrast:

"Diana's closest friend urged the Royal Family to posthumously restore her HRH status "I think it was very petty to have removed it and I think it would be something that the nation, who love her, would hope would be a very simple thing to do". (M, 1, 2).

And presaging a major flurry that was developed over the week:

"Crowds at Balmoral noticed that the Royal Standard was not being flown at half mast, but a Palace spokesman explained ... The Standard is the flag of the sovereign and is never flown at half mast, even when the monarch dies". (M, 1, 4).

In this narrative the seeds of popular pressure upon the monarchy germinate in a medium of the following kind of belief:

"history will remember her as the woman who changed the way we regard the Royals. Alone, she took on the might of the royal establishment and trumped it again and again and again. Diana discovered that her husband loved another woman. In her grief she became ill and made a cry-for-help suicide attempt". (M, 1, 14).

In some cases a hypothetical popular or modern formulation is projected into a respected exemplar:

"William and Harry are both old enough to have strong opinions on what they'd like to see happen now, and how they interpret their roles. The Royal Family must listen to them and respect their wishes ... It's time, now to throw away the Royal rule book".[172] (M, 1, 18).

The combative image of making the royal family kneel was to be found in the otherwise establishmentarian Daily Mail

"how the Royal Family ... can re-establish its popularity ... will not be easy but it might begin with a few words of much-needed repentance". (DM, 1, 14).

By the second day of this long mourning week papers had to find new perspectives with which to remain with and even intensify the story. One way was to have a debate between two columnists and the *Express* pitted the republicanist case by Anthony Holden against the royalist one of Geoffrey Wheatcroft. Holden chose to ignore the palace spokesperson's explanation, well known to any journalist such as himself and to find a needle with which to belabour his victim:

"they must swallow their pride and run the monarchy her way ... (apropos the flagpole empty at Buckingham Palace) "when I said so on US TV I was cheered ... by the crowds. 'Thank you' they said 'for speaking on behalf of the people'". (E, 2, 1, 4).

Prince Charles' personal future was also under pressure in this mood:

"So, what now for Charles and his Camilla? ... to marry ... must now be put off ... some of their circle are actually using the words 'for ever'". (DM, 3, 15).

The next day there was a headline in the *Express*: Camilla Will Never Be Charles' Bride.

"Camilla ... would always be seen as the woman who drove Diana away by wrecking the marriage ... all this talk of 'tears of grief' ... is cheap and vindictive at a time when people are bitter and looking for scapegoats". (E, 4, 11).

---

[172]It presumably did not occur to Miriam Stoppard, who wrote this, that one or both of the Princes might choose to support an old-fashioned formalist position. She seems to assume that their strong opinions will concur with the 'Dianist/modernist" formulation to be found in the anti-royalist narrative.

London's *Evening Standard* appeared with the banner headline "What We Need From Charles Now" and an article explaining:

"The public is waiting for some kind of gesture ... signs of physical affection between the Prince and his sons ... a public recognition from the Prince of the value of his former wife's work ... the stiff upper lip has had its day[173]. It simply isn't modern. It is not that we want to see public figures sobbing all over the place ... Prince Charles must reveal his humanity"... (ES, 3, 11).

Having prepared its campaign on the Wednesday, the *Sun* blazed forth on Thursday with a front page: The Sun Speaks Its Mind WHERE IS OUR QUEEN? WHERE IS HER FLAG?. Page 2 inside this shouted THE FINAL INSULT, accompanied by a glum picture of the Queen which must have been trawled in the library (as she was not available to be photographed on this day this surely raises a question of journalistic honesty), and three pictures of flags elsewhere at half mast. The text offered:

"Thousands of people ... accused the Royal Family of insulting Princess Diana's memory by refusing to fly a flag at half mast" (S, 4, 2).

Fifteen anti-royal remarks from people in the crowd were provided, with the conclusion offered that

"the nation pays for the royals - they should do as we bid". (S, 4, 2).

Just in case the *Sun*'s readers missed the point being made, page 3 provided thirteen photographs of other flags at half mast. The *Sun*'s great competitor the Mirror was much more circumspect on the day. The banner headline read YOUR PEOPLE ARE SUFFERING SPEAK TO US MA'AM. Two large pictures of boys crying were accompanied by one of the Queen evidently in tears, though with a somewhat quizzical look - again not recorded on the day to accompany the text. The editorial declared

"Your people have spoken ... now YOU must, Ma'am ... the Queen must show she has learnt from Diana ... By any standard, this is the most supreme display of emotion this country has seen ... and the more time passes, the greater grows the grief". (M, 4, 11).

The *Mail* bannered LET THE FLAG FLY AT HALF MAST with the text that:

"The Queen faced a growing clamour ... MPs of all parties led the criticism at Westminster ... dismayed crowds yesterday around the palace ... echoed the view. By last night 750,000 had queued for 11 hours and more to sign the books of condolence". (DM, 4, 1).

---

[173] At the end of the year, when a Royal Victorian Medal was awarded to Sidney Clarke, who drove the hearse carrying Princess Diana to Althorp, the Evening Standard's front page story quoted him as saying "If I had got too emotional I wouldn't have got there".

Neither the *Mirror* nor the *Mail* had quoted expressions of anger as had the *Sun*, and this was conceivably because they followed a loyalist tradition of keeping such things quiet. However, this would be an unlikely explanation in the context of a bitter circulation war in which one competitor had taken a dramatic line, and in the further context of the flavour of a report from the crowd outside Buckingham Palace:

"'The Queen should have done something' ... has she said anything? 'No' a kid (replied) The girl who asked stopped chewing gum 'well, what's the point of having a Queen then, because isn't she leading the country what's she supposed to do?' You didn't have to dig deep for stuff like that in St James. ... it came to you anywhere you stopped". (DM, 4, 5).

This sounds like tiredness and disappointment rather than anger, and even if there was some anger, it had not evidently inflamed the whole crowd as the *Sun* was suggesting. However, next day some journalists did take the movement of emotion more seriously. Ross Benson wrote:

"It will be seen as a defining point ... They used to tell us what to do. Now we tell them ... The Union Flag will fly over Buckingham Palace for the first time, replacing the Royal Standard ... All this week a wave of emotion that was fast turning to anger has been building. It threatened to engulf ... the monarchy itself". (E, 5, 3).

In the voice of the *Times*

"'Diana's Army Cheers Victory'. Many were exultant ... that they had apparently forced the Queen ... into a public demonstration for their 'People's Princess'. Those who ... call themselves 'Diana's Army' are convinced they have dictated the way the Monarchy should honour the Princess of Wales ... Applause rippled along the ribbon of people ... when those with radios passed on the news that the Queen was to address the nation. Zoe John 15 said 'The Queen is only doing this to save face with the people. We loved Diana more than she did' ...". (T, 5, 5).

The *Express*'s commentator already quoted, Anne Robinson capped her hostile remarks about the royal family with

"- Welcome, your Royal Majesties, to People Power. Your not-so-loyal subjects are now demanding that their wishes be taken into account ... To hell with protocol. To hell with the done thing". (E, 5, 15).

The *Sun*, for its part, was pleased, with its banner QUEEN CAVES IN AFTER SUN CAMPAIGN. This piece of lese majeste was then redressed with a picture caption DAD'S HAND OF LOVE and the claim that CHARLES FORCES QUEEN TO CAVE IN ON FLAG TRIBUTE TOO LATE. The text supported this with

"106 hours to do decent thing. Verdict of furious SUN readers. Nearly 46,000 readers bombarded our You The Jury lines to demand ... a show of respect". (S, 5, 2).

For the two previous days the newspaper had solicited such oppositional messages but although 46,000 did evidently call, the *Sun* did not care to show whether any, and if so how many (though in the circumstances this was likely to have been a small number) may actually have "voted" NO. The lower key 'campaign' in the *Mirror* was closed with the banner IN SAFE HANDS accompanying a picture of Princes Charles and Harry (M, 5, 1) and inside the paper YOU SPOKE, THEY LISTENED with the text:

"the royal standard has not flown at all, causing widespread upset. Because of the Queen's absence at Balmoral the public, without fully understanding the protocol - and more to the point, not really caring - believe Diana has been snubbed. Claire McLaughlan, 23 ... said (about Princes Andrew and Edward's walkabout) 'the crowd were lifted. All day they have been talking about the Queen's absence and the bare flagpole but that doesn't matter now' ...". (M, 5, 5).

These themes of Dianism and people's power changing how the monarchy works and even in the view of some writers undermining it towards abolition could not exist were there not already three related themes in the air of the public discourse, which we can term a **supposed wickedness**, a **dysfunctionality** of the royal family and (hence, though it is structurally a non-sequitur) an **obsolescence** of the monarchy. Evidence of these themes was in plentiful supply during the grieving week. It started on the Sunday evening

"the congregation (at Crathie Church) were asked to pray for the Royal Family, but no direct mention was made of the princess" (ES, 31, 5); and the Prince's ... private phone calls to Camilla Parker Bowles suddenly became public property ... and it was clear to all that the heir to the throne was in an adulterous relationship ... the Windsors' popularity plunged to an all time low ... Charles and Diana ... both took to using the media to snipe, swipe and snarl at one another". (ES, 31, 18).; and

"Millions of pounds and centuries of tradition had served to make our royalty the most impressive in the world, and, in return it served up a diet of stiff waves and fixed grins". (ES, 31, 31).

One paper chose to report from the street in Paris:

"Bernard Bidow, 36, gained some nods and some disapproving shakes of the head when he said: 'my idea, ... is that maybe there were figures in perfidious Albion who thought her an embarrassment. Now that is replaced by tragedy'". (T, 1, 4).

The biographer of the Queen obliquely raised a spectre in writing:

"people are inevitably looking for culprits ... they are asking how this may affect the lives of the remaining Royals and the survival of the monarchy itself". (E, 1, 12).

The *Guardian* was the natural source of obsolescence theory so we found:

"her death solves no problems for the monarchy ... The royal family has creakingly and belatedly embarked on a programme of modernisation. In response to Diana's high profile crusades on heart-rending issues ... Prince Charles has begun to emerge from under a pile of architectural drawings and demonstrate his own humanity". (G, 1, 8).

The editorial in that issue offered:

"the British monarchy ... once apparently unassailable is so badly eroded today that it looks beyond repair ... Where has she left the monarchy? Changed beyond recall ... she showed it up as dull and remote and even ... not far from malevolent. The fact that so many committed royalists now talk of skipping Prince Charles ... creating, in effect, a sort of pick'n choose monarchy, is one mark of that. Falling support for the whole institution, especially among the young, is another". (G, 1, 18).

Justifying this disparagement one needs the thought that

"a quiet retreat to obscurity would be bowing ... to the will of the Establishment which had wronged and damaged her and now wanted her out of the way". (G, 1, 18).

One of the team offered:

"twenty is almost old enough to dress up as a virgin sacrifice (her uncle vouched for her virginity, remember?) ... by the time she was 30 ... (she was) too old to play the gamine ... but too damaged ever to grow and mature as a woman. She had been inside the Royal box too long". (G, 1, 18).; and her colleague added:

"Even after death ... Diana will continue to make us all question the ethics of the family that rejected her ... the machinery attempted to intimidate Diana, who had said that all she wanted was to be a good wife, and then when she failed ... pushed her as far as it could from the centre of national life ... People will say that, if she had been found a proper role in British life, she would not have been ... in Paris dodging paparazzi without proper protection ... If the future head of state can make such a mess of his personal life, and be supported by ranks of courtiers in his attempts to extricate himself, then people are entitled to wonder about the principles of inheritance on which the monarchy is based". (G, 1, 19).

A letter in the correspondence section asks:

"the nation (to) reflect on the scale of personal sacrifice which is now demanded from those close to the throne ... whether it is reasonable to expect one family to make this sacrifice simply for the convenience of providing us with a head of state". (G, 1, 21).

A female reporter quoted a gay florist who said angrily:

"between the paparazzi and the monarchy they killed her; and I hope this is the end of the monarchy, because she was the only good thing about it"; and for herself wrote that "the Queen tours a factory or a hospital ... as a tourist ... those on whom she bestows ... the friendly word can never remember later what she said. But Diana ...". (G, 1, 21).

Finally, the paper showed its colours with:

(after the Andrew Morton book) "the Prince and the Palace were perpetually on the back foot ... which is where, after yesterday, they will perpetually remain". (G, 1, 22).

The *Mirror* which we have seen had not been anti-royalist through the week began with:

"the Princess's (Panorama interview) launched republican elements of the Labour Party into a discussion of the need for a debate on the future of the monarchy ... several opinion polls showed falling support for the royals ... In Australia, Charles was named 'Republican of the Year' by anti-monarchists". (M, 1, 44).

The *Mail*'s editorial observed on:

"issues for another day. As is the question of how Prince Charles and Buckingham Palace cast this lonely woman into a semi-royal limbo without advisers and the apparatus to protect her ...". (DM, 1, 14).

The *Star* believed that:

"Diana ... did battle with the stiff-collared mandarins of Buckingham Palace. Publicly referring to these courtiers as 'the enemy' she blamed them just as much as Charles for her troubles". (St, 1, 28).

Anthony Holden (a past biographer of Prince Charles) the next day said

"A year ago last week the Queen and her son decreed that Diana's name be removed from the Sunday prayers ... I lodged a protest on all our behalves ... I am angry - over the Windsors' shabby treatment of their unthanked unacknowledged banished-into-outer-royal-darkness superstar who single-handedly restored their lost stature around the world". (E, 2, 15).

He followed this up with:

"... the mood of the nation changes subtly ... among the crowds I sensed a shift in the direction of that anger. People were speaking of their resentment towards the Windsors ... People were appalled at the stiff-upper-lip pictures of (Prince Charles) taking the Princes to church ... 'why didn't he have his arms around them? ... why were no prayers said for Diana at Crathie?' ... The queen ... has issued no expression of regret ... this will be attributed by her courtiers to royal protocol and tradition". (E, 3, 7).

Holden's colleague Mary Kenny added:

"Prince Charles is said to be racked with guilt and remorse ... So well he might be ... Surely the Prince of Wales could have devised some sort of arrangement which ensured properly organised protection for Diana, including 24 carat safe and sober drivers, and inveigled her to accept these standards for the sake of her safety ...?". (E, 3, 17).

Wednesday was the day when what one journalist called "The Royal Hunt of the Sun" began in earnest. We have seen that they began their "flagpole" campaign then, and that was underwritten with copy that developed the themes of the Windsors as cold, unpleasant and even worse:

> " ... the grief turned to anger ... Palace officials refused to fly a flag at half mast ... the tradition sparked fury among crowds ... 'whoever is responsible for this deserves a slap' ... 'it's absolutely outrageous' ... 'it beggars belief ...' ... 'the Royal Family should hang their heads in shame' ... 'an empty flagpole is a disgrace' and 'the missing flag is the final insult to Diana' ... (S, 3, 5) followed by: "not one tear has been shed in public from a royal eye ... we know that ... Charles did love Diana ... the Queen Mother is heartbroken ... the Queen and Prince Philip are in a state of shock ... But from the outside looking in, the House of Windsor seems a cold, compassion free zone ... how out of touch the cobwebbed courtiers are ... it proves ... that the Royals are not like us ... all the good work that Diana did to modernise and popularise them has been ruined ...". (S, 3, 8).

The constitutional historian David Starkey came to a quick evaluation of the situation:

> "Diana's death may have signalled the end of the Monarchy. Charles ... lacks instinct. In trying to do the right thing and his duty he has always done the wrong thing and broken his pact with the Royal House and the British people ... there is no way we can go back to the family monarchy ...". (S, 3, 10).

Not only public figures but also members of the general public echoed this theme

> "'Shame on the Windsors for letting this happen' said one note". (ES, 3, 6).

Two letters in the *Independent* expressed similar recriminations:

> "it was ultimately the Royal "Family" who destroyed the Princess of Wales ... the House of Windsor ought to be quaking. No wonder they hide at Balmoral ... to a democratic society all monarchy is dysfunctional". (I, 4, 2).

Their social affairs correspondent Polly Toynbee, who had also expressed republican attitudes in the past joined in:

> "The kindest thing would be to set (the Princes) free from our unreasonable, insatiable emotional demands on them ... time to put away childish things ... The anger of the people on the streets against the monarchy may be unfair, but perhaps ... it will ... set us all free". (I, 4, 19).

Occasional comments were "overripe", such as this from the prolific novelettist Barbara Cartland (who also happened to be Diana's step-grandmother) "forget about the monarchy. This royal family ... is a family of Germans. The Princess of Wales was English, but not them. She is the one who will be missed". (E, 4, 3).

The *Mail* offered thoughts on dysfunctionality in the royal family:

"Friends of the couple have seen piles of flowers grow by the hour ... and realise ... how badly the Palace got it wrong by being perceived as spiteful to Diana, especially in stripping her of her royal style HRH. Camilla's friends insist she did not break up the marriage ... but ...". (DM, 3, 15).

The 'but' might generally be taken to imply that most people would believe Diana's interpretation, in Andrew Morton's book and in her Panorama programme, that an unbroken relationship between Charles and Camilla sank the marriage; however, another interpretation of the 'but' could be that Diana's interpretation was wrong about Charles in the same way that Othello was wrong about Desdemona, and that such a situation was too complex to make into a good press story. Most people outside the family itself (and even they themselves) are not in a position to establish the true dynamics of what happened, though that does not prevent some journalists from being quite firm in their interpretations of events.

Extremely few texts pointed out or explored something that Ross Benson mentioned:

"... it must have been a particularly trying moment for Sir Robert Fellowes, the brother-in-law Diana came so heartily to detest".[174] (E, 5, 3).

Sir Robert was not only married to Diana's eldest sister but also was Private Secretary to the Queen, and thus will have played some part in how the drama was handled from the Palace's side. Presumably Diana could have had a 'friend at court' but this was clearly not how matters turned out. While some writers excoriated courtiers, others hit at the royal family itself:

"The Windsor family are like Dr Frankenstein: they took a rudimentary, half formed person, put her on a slab, gave her a public life ... Instead of rising up and creating terror and mayhem, she spread sympathy and delight. Their tragedy is that they couldn't cope with that either". (Simon Hoggart in the Guardian, quoted next day) (ES, 5, 8).

THE ROYALIST NARRATIVE: EMERGENCE FROM ENTANGLEMENT

While much of the available narrative has written in terms of being the only true version of reality, there is a partly separate and partly interwoven narrative which supports a Royalist perspective. This emerges from the perceptions that Diana said she

---

[174]Sir Robert was awarded a senior decoration in the end-of-year Honours list, which is compiled for the most part by the Prime Minister and in which the Monarch's own preferences would most probably be 'run past' him.

wanted her son to be a future King, in which sense she was quite clearly a monarchist herself, that the Princes her sons were innocent and needed protection and nurturing (to which the public and its self-appointed spokespeople the journalists were keen to contribute emotional support), and, in a few places, that this (generally exemplified as England, but occasionally acknowledging the very different Scottish Welsh and Northern Irish perspectives) is a Christian country. Such a country would not be well served by a future Queen Mother's potential marriage to a Muslim. In exploring this theme, it will be important to note not only that a few commentators made explicit remarks about this direction of religious conversion; but it was not possible to find any commentator who considered the possibility that Diana Princess of Wales may have inspired her potential spouse to become a Christian.

It may also be recognised that some writers had reached a view of Diana's personality and behavior, that held that she had individual adult autonomy and responsibility from the start of her marriage, was thus not a helpless pawn, but quixotic, mercurial and (in ungallant terms) a loose cannon. These critical voices were not much in evidence during the mourning week, but some of the resonance of their case came through in places in the published discourse.

The themes of **loose cannon**, **King's mother**, **innocent Princes** and a **Christian country** are thus recognisable as ingredients of a royalist narrative that, though in second place, was still detectable in public expression during the week of mourning. The fact that the first two themes are in some ways contradictory illustrates some of the tensions she experienced, and may appear in some of the following extracts.

The *Evening Standard's* special memorial edition pointed out:

"the effect on sensitive adolescents of knowing that their private life was the subject of universal speculation can only be imagined ... what work will it do in the imagination of an adolescent boy to know that the men who so often reduced his mother to tears were the cause of her violent, untimely death?". (ES, 31, 12).

The paper made some attempt to understand the marital rift:

"It was two and a half years after Prince Harry's birth that ... the marriage was effectively over ... Charles had struggled to understand and cope with his wife's distress as best he could. Yet his attempts were translated by her as rejection and indifference". (ES, 31, 18).

The *Times* recognised that:

"She showed she believed in and was a defender of the Throne that her son must one day inherit. That is how ... she must be remembered". (T, 1, 1).

Inside the paper its leading columnist Lord Rees-Mogg wrote:

"her story ... is shaped by great and tragic events ... The Princess hoped for a renewal of the monarchy and she did not want to wait for her son's time. She wanted it to be a strong institution, compassionate and contemporary". (T, 1, 24).

Another paper put it this way:

"... The argument over what really happened was to do untold damage to the good name of the Royal Family ... Diana firmly laid the blame at the feet of her husband ... she had been driven to the point of suicide by the callous adultery of her husband ... Charles's friends ... insisted ... (he) is a man of the highest integrity who remained faithful to his wife until the marriage had irretrievably broken down - and that Diana was the one responsible for that". (E, 1, 20).

The *Times* made its attempt to guide public opinion in its editorial, thus:

"Her legacy should help to protect the monarchy. The spontaneous outpouring of grief ... shows how ... she continued to play a royal role, drawing significance from the family and institution which she never quite took as her own - and enhancing it. ... She hoped to ensure that the public identified the monarchy with social purpose rather than simply Society. And, in affirming that specifically royal role ... she communicated her own sense of the enduring importance of the Crown. By her public activities she showed she was a true defender of the Throne that her son must one day inherit". (T, 1, 25).

The paper also explained that:

"In the summer of 1992 ... a biography by Andrew Morton, a journalist from the lower echelons of the trade, caught the attention of Andrew Neil, the Editor (of its sister paper) the Sunday Times. Several weeks of serialisation damaging to the monarchy followed. ... It could be seen as a major destructive force in the Princess's life[175] (At her wedding) Lady Diana chose her favourite school hymn *I Vow To Thee My Country*". (T, 1, 27).

The image of connection with emblems of traditional value was signalled with a picture of two village cricket teams lined up for silent respect to the Princess. It was a rare journalist who would write anything on the first day of mourning that would tarnish Diana's memory, but Joanna Bale could say:

"Her self-proclaimed role as 'Queen of people's Hearts' was built up through skilful manipulation of the media. When she visited a hostel for the homeless or an Aids ward ... she made sure that mainstream newspaper photographers were tipped off". (T, 1, 16).

Support for continuity came from Mary Kenny:

---

[175]The writer is almost certainly aware that the Morton book was engineered by Princess Diana herself and thus implies that there was an element of self-destruction in the episode. Ben Pimlott, the Queen's biographer pointed out in the Guardian (1 Sept, p. 19) that "by sanctioning the Andrew Morton exposure ... she acutely embarrassed not only her husband but the institution into which she had married".

"Our thoughts and prayers go out above all to William and Harry ... the spotlight of public interest ... will shine with great intensity on (William) all that ocean of devotion which was directed at Diana will now transfer to (William) ... Prince Charles has had position thrust upon him by virtue of dynastic accident. Diana's role as a sort of symbolic universal sovereign almost appears as though by divine mission. (William) is her living embodiment. Through him, Diana lives ...". (DE, 1, 10).

Occasional inelegant and less than saintly behavior into which Diana was forced was noted by Gerard Greaves:

"in her last days she had settled on one stock response to the paparazzi - 'why don't you go and rape someone else?'". (DE, 1, 15).

The Chief Photographer at the *Mirror*, Kent Gavin saw Diana as

"A woman who lived through the camera's lens. A woman whom (sic) it seems, has died because of it ... She, better than anyone, realised the power of pictures. They were the means through which she led her life. The way through which she could convey her messages, her passions ... herself ... I remember that sad message she conveyed sitting alone in front of the Taj Mahal". (M, 1, 16).

Diana's work for deserving causes occasionally brought her close to politics:

"During the days of her impending divorce, Diana told friends Mr Major was the only person she could trust ... but relations with the Tories soured in December 1995, when she appeared to back Labour criticism of Government policy on the homeless ...". (E, 1, 27).

Assembling (reporters') "words to regret for a lifetime" Peter McKay noted that:

"(in) reactions to Diana's recent Le Monde interview in which she was said to have praised Labour and criticised the Tories on the landmines issue ... Bernard Ingham called Diana's behavior 'disgraceful ... does she realise she may be part of Labour's plot to wreck the monarchy and ruin William's chances of being king?'". (DM, 1, 19).

It is not easy to say how dealings with the occult may influence public opinion; astrology is a common feature offered by tabloid newspapers for their readers, but it is possible that some might look askance at a prominent politician or leading figure who looked to the stars for advice (as allegedly did Adolf Hitler and Nancy Reagan). So in a piece examining similarities between Marilyn Monroe, Princess Grace of Monaco and Princess Diana the *Star* noted that:

"Diana may have received a warning about her fate when she met her psychic pal Rita Rogers 17 days ago ... Di left visibly shaken after the crystal ball session". (St, 1, 14).

The Princess had arrived noisily, with Dodi in a helicopter and was photographed by teenagers, which appeared to have worried her. It is not possible to judge whether it may have been anxiety about being photographed on such an errand, or the content of the session itself that may have produced a visibly shaken appearance. A psychic person in Wales had, however, (it was reported in the *Sun*, and elsewhere) had a dream premonition that Diana would die. His credentials included having reported, before the events, premonitions of assassination attempts on the Pope and President Reagan. This may also have been known to the Princess.

The notion of Diana as a 'loose cannon' implies that she may have hit an unintended target by one or another of her actions. Yet some such as Anne Robinson approved what they believed she had done:

"That she took on the monarchy and triumphed remains for me her greatest achievement". (E, 5, 15).

While some pointed to the damage (they believed) Diana had done to the monarchy, the anti monarchist *Guardian*'s writer Matthew Engel on the contrary suggested:

"It is possible that Diana, whose life nearly ended the British monarchy, might in death lead to its rehabilitation". (G, 1, 1).

His colleague Linda Grant observed, however, that

"she continued to remain personally immune from the republican mood in the country that she had done almost as much as anyone to foster". (G, 1, 23).

For some, there was no contradiction as declared by the Royal hunting *Sun*:

"The monarchy is at a turning point. If it does not see the need for change, it will become irrelevant. Diana - the woman who dragged royalty into the 20th century - would not want that for her sons". (S, 5, 10).

This reported republican mood presumably came about during the last decade and a half - when some writers claimed that Diana had re-energised the monarchy. If she had re-energised it that implies that a slump in enthusiasm had occurred before she arrived on the scene. Few if any writers can be found who based their interpretations on a systematic examination of well conducted polls, and some such scrutiny is carried out here in Chapter 5. We can now see that many writers did provide variations on this theme of Diana as a light, even a vulnerable one:

"like a candle in the wind, the flame that burned so bright will burn no more ... (Diana) brought a sparkling personality to the Royal Family and kept the Monarchy alive". (S, 1, 10).

"she almost single-handedly saved the Royal family by adding glamour and down to earth personality to the ailing House of Windsor". (S, 1, 15).

Even Andrew Morton, whose book had done so much to externalise the marital conflict wrote:

"there is comfort in knowing that her children will carry on the legacy of her work, particularly Prince William when he becomes King". (S, 1, 19).

Penny Junor, labelled a Royal Author added:

"She was responsible for bringing them back to the nation ... for long periods Diana WAS the Royal Family". (S, 1, 21).

The editorial in the *Mirror* supported this diagnosis:

"If the monarchy survives, it will be more thanks to Diana than anyone". (M, 1, 15).

Ingrid Seward, the Editor (In Chief!) of *Majesty* magazine, writing in the *Daily Mail* said:

"al Fayed had invited her to take the boys to see the Duke of Windsor's home in Paris. She ... explained to her disappointed sons that it would cause too much upset and criticism ... Whatever her personal feelings were, she assured me she would never taint her children's relationship with their father or indeed the Queen ... she was extremely relieved that William had, in recent years, forged such a close relationship with his grandmother ... . (DM, 1, 20).

It took a dry article by Frank Prochaska to make an arcane but quite fundamental point:

"It should not be forgotten that the Princess, despite her difficulties with the House of Windsor, became a presence on the world stage because of her royal status". (T, 5, 18).

Richard Kay, whom many including he himself described as a friend as well as a reporter introduced this question:

"She asked me why the media were 'so anti-Dodi. Is it because he is a millionaire ...?' She didn't talk too much about Dodi ... she was afraid that the moment too much was read into the relationship it would end. ... 'Who would have me with all the baggage I come with?'". (DM, 1, 5).

Instead of reflecting and testing the question by asking what the evidence was that the media were anti-Dodi, he suggested that it might have to do with Dodi's father's controversial image[176]. Some contribution to this little discussed matter came from the *Mirror*'s discussion of Diana's alleged affair with a heart surgeon Hasnat Khan:

---

[176] Mosts British people know of Mr Mohammed al Fayed as the owner of Harrods store which he rules in maverick manner. He has been known to eject an American woman customer,

"Although Diana had become fascinated by the Muslim faith, his family would expect ... an arranged marriage and that would obviously be impossible in this case. In the end he ... decided the best thing to do would be to break off...". (M, 1, 38).

The image of a Christian country of which Diana was an essential expression was not explicitly made, but was probably evident in one letter to the *Mirror*, which can hardly be construed as something which would have arisen in a Muslim, or other religious context:

"God waited hundreds of years before choosing a Queen of Hearts and that person was you". (M, 4, 27).

On that day the *Mirror* published 22 letters and verses of tribute, the *Mail* had 31, and the *Star* had 5; out of these 58 expressions from members of the public 22 contained explicit core religious words such as God, angels, heaven, prayers. These suggest that at times of bereavement there is widespread feeling that connects with religious formulae and in this case the tradition is recognisably Christian. This is a nexus in which the powerful Christian signs of buildings such as Westminster Abbey and the forms and contents of the funeral service recall the Princess to, and reaffirm the nature of her and of the country's essence.

Though there are several other themes which relate to the two grand narratives of republicanism and of monarchism, it is important to attend to two minor narratives about the mass message systems themselves. One is simply the belief, which has already been mentioned - and examined with the aid of real data - in **market justification**. This is the notion that the market for "news" about stars such as Diana is mechanistically simple: people want to see such coverage, they will buy newspapers they do not normally read, or watch programmes they might not normally view if they expect there is a story (of the kind that the journalists believe is in this kind of demand) covered by the special edition. Since papers compete with each other, as they feel it, for survival even more than for prosperity, and since television channels also compete for audiences as do broadcasting and the press, it follows in this model that an outlet which has the chance of publishing what they believe to be highly demanded material, virtually can not avoid doing so.

Touching on the meanings of some of the treatment offered in mass message systems, the second minor narrative contains the themes of **universalism, false inference syndrome** and when taken to an extreme, what one journalist termed **feeling fascism**. Universalism is found in statements of the kind that some perception or feeling actually is widespread or even wholly pervasive in society. False inference syndrome takes certain explanations for granted as true. Feeling fascism is an implied or even an explicit pressure that every person should perceive, feel or act in some particular way. Examples of these themes have already occurred in the passages above (though they have

---

apparently because he did not approve of her clothes. Fayed senior tried to acquire British citizenship which (at least up until the millennium) has not been granted him, eveidently on the grounds that he is not a person of sufficiently good character.

not been pointed out, as the purpose had been to point to other themes that will have been woven in with one or another of these). Fresh examples now follow, beginning with ones that illustrate the notion of market justification.

Early in the week the focus of blame for Diana's death was being debated - the chain involving paparazzi, editors, sales, and readers was in focus. The *Times* quoted Massimo Sestini, a leading paparazzo:

> "we do the job because newspapers and magazines want to print the pictures we get, and newspapers want them because their readers want them. Readers have a right to see whatever they want to see ...". (T, 1, 16).

This apparently noble account of selfless service was not questioned in the article, regarding the possible part played by vanity, greed for money, the thrill of the chase and a mildly psychopathic lack of care for the concerns of the people photographed. Indeed, a high prestige source, no less than Cardinal Hume was found, on page 20 to agree that "photographs ... sold newspapers". This was echoed by Simon Jenkins (an ex editor of the paper), who asked:

> "who buys these products ... if not readers? ... Nowadays nobody dies by accident. Blame is sovereign lord to every misfortune and demands swift recompense ...". (T, 1, 24).

Ben Pimlott, the historian turned media scientist for the day averred:

> "it is we, the public - who insisted on a daily diet of royal scandals and royal bodies and souls stripped bare - that in the end share some of the responsibility for getting our grim reward". (E, 1, 13).

In actuarial detail, the journalist Gerard Greaves explained:

> "recent photographs of her kissing Dodi Fayed earned £1 million but the Sunday newspaper which first featured them sold more than 250,000 extra copies ... They satisfied a public craving ...". (E, 1, 15).

The editor of the *Guardian*, Alan Rusbridger mentioned that pictures of bodies in the smashed car were being hawked for prices around £200,000 to $1 million. Steve Coz, editor of the *National Enquirer* asked for an international boycott of these. The *Mirror* group had previously paid £250,000 for the pictures of cuddling and kissing on a yacht. Rusbridger added:

> "millions of readers every day buy the newspapers to gawk at this and similar morsels ...". (G, 1, 20).

Peter Preston, a previous *Guardian* editor served to head off any bandwagon for a ban on publishing - or taking - intrusive photographs of celebrities:

"You bought more newspapers and switched on more television news bulletins five weeks ago when the first pictures of Diana's romance were snatched and sold. Action in one country (he refers here to a ban) is utterly irrelevant". (G, 1, 20).

Roy Greenslade who previously edited the *Mirror* and subsequently analysed the press for the *Guardian* assured his readers:

"Lloyd Turner (then editor of the *Daily Star*) made a declaration: his paper would no longer pursue the royal family. That pledge collapsed as he watched rivals increase sales ... magazines increased sales every time they put the princess on the cover - even news bulletins featuring Diana reported high audiences". (G, 1, 21).

Towards the end of the week the *Standard* had gained confidence in the notion that the press was not as guilty of "push" as probably were the readers of "pull".

"Day in day out the Diana fan club lavished its custom on any newspaper prepared to serve up any nonsense they could find about her. They ignored papers that showed restraint. Now they seek to make the Press a scapegoat ... this is hypocrisy". (ES, 5, 11).; and "Earlier this week *Scotsman* editor-in-chief Andrew Neil denounced Sky News as 'an organisation which never lost an opportunity to intrude upon Princess Diana's privacy'. It must have been another Andrew Neil altogether who was chairman of Sky TV from 1988 - 1990". (ES, 5, 11).

At least three kinds of questions should be asked about this; one is whether there is other evidence of a "public craving" for such material - do people say in systematically carried out polls with well designed questions that they want to see such things? And are people physiologically set back if they have to live without such stimuli? The other kind of question is to calculate the earnings on the quarter of a million extra copies and to make it clear that these exceed the cost of the enterprise. Thirdly, the culture of leadership and of down-the-line behavior in the press - and broadcasting (which is regulated to minimise disruptions of good taste and decency) should be honestly described. None of these kinds of questions have been adequately raised, let alone properly discussed in the press. All that we are given is yet more affirmation of the case, in some cases of a romantic sort. One bouquet at Buckingham Palace was reported to have carried this anonymous poem:

"I killed her. I hounded her
to death. I followed her
every movement.
I gave her no peace. For I
bought the papers. I read the
stories and
I looked at the photographs
they did this for me.
How can I live with that?". (G, 1, 1).

One way to live with these thoughts is to realise (one hopes) that had there been no such photographs the author would still have bought his newspaper - to read about more important matters; and that without such pictures he would live just as happy a life as he did, with them. The paper's journalists did not open up such enquiries; instead, John Ezard wrote:

> "More than 16 years ago ... the media discovered that almost any cobbled up material about her raised newspaper sales and TV audiences". (G, 1, 6).

Considerable evidence exists about patterns of viewing of television news, and little of it suggests that particular ingredients beyond an everyday kind do much to increase levels of viewing.[177] It is necessary for the press itself to produce the detailed, and well controlled sales-related-to-content evidence for the case as regards the press, before the public's responsibility in the form of prurient interest is simply accepted.

Universalism can be thought of as a belief that some perception or feeling is shared by all. The 'all' refers in the first place to everyone in the nation but may exceptionally be extended to mean everyone in the globe. Most of the examples below exemplify the first perspective but some go broader than that. Fewer quoted remarks will be provided explicitly to illustrate the drawing of false inferences but some of the universalist examples probably do spring from an untrained view of how to generalise, or how not to do so from certain kinds of evidence. The false inference in some of these cases is to take 'lots of people' to mean 'everyone'. The process began during the first day of shock in the week of mourning, led by the Prime Minister.

> "Tributes flooded in from around the globe, led by Prime Minister Tony Blair. A stunned public flocked to Kensington Palace and Buckingham Palace ... Blair pours praise on the 'People's Princess' ... I feel like everyone else in this country today, utterly devastated. We are today a nation in a state of shock, in mourning, in grief. People everywhere ... regarded her as one of the people".[178] (ES, 31, pages 1 and 6).

A less universalist form of Mr Blair's thoughts appeared next day in the *Mirror*:

> "The Royal Family is good for us. Diana travels the world and is well known, well respected and well liked by people". (M, 1, 8).

The Prime Minister's role as a conductor of an orchestra in unison appeared later in the week:

---

[177]Studies of the Falklands and Gulf wars indicate that news viewing levels increased briefly and by a small amount, before stabilising again. Experimental control is not easy to arrange with live news broadcasting, by which one could assert that one particular ingredient of a news programme was instrumental in increasing viewing. (Wober, 1988).

[178]Nigella Lawson, a journalist on the *Times* wrote (1, p. 16) that the term People's Princess was coined a decade ago, by the polemicist Julie Burchill (who during this week used the term Graeco-Germans to imply an insult to the Windsors).

"A quiet word from Tony Blair and the nation gets its wish". (DM, 5, 2).

It was, apparently, the more universalist version that took hold during the mourning week. Like other newspapers, the *Standard* printed messages of admiration from well known people across the world - Nelson Mandela, Luciano Pavarotti, Henry Kissinger, Mother Teresa, Elton John, Imran Khan, the Australian Prime Minister John Howard, the outgoing Irish President Mary Robinson, and Jacques Chirac were all found for early comment. In Britain the paper located Viscount Tonypandy, Alex Salmond and Diana's one-time lover James Hewitt's mother. The diversity of witness may well have contributed to a perception, at least in print, that everybody feels the same way. Most of these appeared again next day in the *Mirror*, which had also added King Juan Carlos of Spain. The *Times* quoted from newspaper headlines in America, and added Presidents Clinton and Yeltsin and Cambodian King Norodom Sihanouk to the list of top to bottom affirmation of loss.

"tens of thousands of illiterate Afghans, hobbling on crutches, knew her name. ... the New York Post ran a black bordered front page: 'World in Shock. Diana is Dead'. ... People Magazine had used Princess Diana on their cover 43 times - more than any other celebrity in its 23 year history ... a Bosnian landmine victim said "my whole family is crying ... she came here to help us. She was a beautiful woman who did great work for mine victims ...". (T, 11, 6).

The *Express* coached its readers in a similar direction of perception and feeling:

"Our love was so great that we all feel guilty". (E, 1, 12).

Deeper in the paper, a visitor from Dallas was quoted saying:

"I feel almost intrusive being here as a foreigner but Diana was a Princess for the world, not just Britain". (E, 1, 24).

The *Guardian* at first allowed some detachment to appear, but several of its writers joined the universalist throng:

"often the grief was mixed with a mood as surreal as Diana's own life and death. ... At Buckingham Palace ... some people, mostly elderly, were in tears. But more were eating ice creams". (G, 1, 1).

"She was probably the most famous ... person of her time". (G, editorial, 1, 18).

"Whoever else deserted her - Charles, the royal family, her dreadful lovers the people never did". (G, 1, 21).

While the *Guardian* might pride itself on being a journal of discrimination and independent views the *Sun* drives for a popular or universalist readership. It is natural therefore to read there that:

"today the people ache to their bones with grief". (S, 1, 10).

Then, under a minor headline, the universalist theme emerged:

"Elton: I lost my special friend. Nations united in sorrow ... From superstars to presidents ... whole world weeps for Di". (S, 1, 12).

Queen of All our Hearts". (S, 1, 16).

The implied pressure on everyone to recognise similar feelings in themselves was expanded further down with an affirmative explanation (which may, without further supportive investigation turn out to be a false inference) of a process:

"it was her very vulnerability and her courage in publicly admitting to her failings that endeared her even further to the public so that ... she had truly become a people's princess". (S, 1, 18).

It may be another false inference that is embedded in the account of Diana's interview on BBC television's *Panorama*:

"minutes after the interview it became obvious she had won the heart of the nation. The BBC switchboard was jammed with messages of love and support". (S, 1, 24).

The *Mail* reminded its readers of what many will have seen on television:

"BBC TV prefaced its news with that Union Jack symbol and the playing of the national anthem". (DM, 1, 14).

Two days later some press writers were beginning to demur from an unquestioned universalism:

"Throughout Sunday the BBC cleared all but one of its radio and television channels ... many to whom I have spoken and thousands who telephoned the BBC found the response excessive. They felt they were being corralled by the media into a certain sort of grief". (Simon Jenkins, T, 3, 3).

These demurrals were however in a minority. The *Mail* provided interviews with people at different places in the realm, in all cases emphasising the tears and grief people reported feeling. Other editorials concealed inferences which may have been completely true - or not:

"Princess Diana's death has brought together the nation ... for the first time since the Second World War we all know the same grief and sadness". (E, 4, 14).

"At the Queen's Coronation, the streets were lined with cheering crowds ... at the Silver Jubilee, almost every street in the country threw a party ... the reaction to these occasions can be understood. But not this astonishing overwhelming emotion ... It isn't mass hysteria ...". (DM, 4, 11).

The *Star* broadened the constituency:

"The world wept as Prince Charles brought Princess Di's body home from Paris yesterday". (St, 1, 2).

Some of the messages were administrative directives:

"Britain will be united in an official one minute silence ... it was announced by Buckingham Palace yesterday ...". (DM, 3, 6).

The notion of a **feeding frenzy** borrows from the field of cybernetics; a situation arises in which signals are put out by an emitter, which are picked up by a sensor and fed back into the amplifier and emitter; the result is a rapid escalation of the transmission into a screaming howl.[179] In the present case it was at least possible that initial messages about the universality and intensity of grief were believed in the first place by newspapers and broadcasters who continued to write and talk in such terms - without fully listening, to whether the assumptions were really true. A sign that the phenomenon might exist was given at the start of the week:

"there are now so many newspapers, magazines, TV and radio stations disgorging material ... fuelled by an apparently insatiable public appetite, that the demand for information and entertainment of every kind has become almost limitless ...". (ES, 31, 13).

To the hypothesis of public demand one may add one about competitiveness amongst providers:

"Justifying his pursuit of the Princess in a recent interview (Jason Fraser, agent for paparazzi) said: 'I think she is entitled to a certain degree of privacy but she abdicated a certain amount of that when she started briefing journalists ... if you are going to forge these close relationships with journalists ... other(s) ... will want to correct the imbalance'". (T, 1, 16).

---

[179]This is why callers in to a radio station are asked to switch off their receiver. A good example of a feeding frenzy in the press occurred when the film *The Day After* was shown in America; the story concerned the nuclear bombing of Lawrence Kansas and it was feared that fear would grip the nation (Kubey, 1988). Boards of psychiatrists sat ready to receive anguished calls; the

This idea of reinforcement of a particular form of expression was expressed in several papers:

"Did Diana Touch Your Life?" (the paper made an invitation to call or write) but also reminded its readers "she was the most important woman in the world and was symbol of everything that is good about Britain". (M, 1, 11).

There is one relationship in which reinforcement was not wholly at work, and that is the one between the press and broadcasting:

"... The BBC was most mediocre in its coverage ... I listened for two hours to Today ... before James Naughtie even mentioned where, in Paris, the accident had taken place ... Sue McGregor ... allowed herself ... to follow the same cul de sac of soliciting commentary and opinion before facts were established". (E, 1, 17). yet:

"By 3 pm the BBC had learnt ... what viewers want and what they will not tolerate ... At first the calls were complimentary about the unified coverage ... on both (TV) channels. But then the complaints started and by 3 pm the normal, though carefully chosen programmes resumed on BBC2". (T, 1, 23).

It has been pointed out that the *Sun* had begun a campaign pressing on the royal family to show emotion and fly a flag at half mast (which George Walden had memorably labelled in the *Standard* The Royal Hunt of the *Sun*); this was certainly not wholly taken up in all newspapers, but the stridency (and circulation) of positive feedbacks exceeded that of braking advice: "SHOW US YOU CARE" bannered the *Express*, together with a large photograph of the Queen, clearly not taken during the selfsame week, let alone the day before the headline, showing her screwing her eyes up against the light, thus producing an oppositional expression. Yet:

"The Prime Minister's office said the press could not expect the Royal Family to 'jump in and be extras in a media event'". (I, 4, 1).

Towards the end of the week a few writers stood aside from the avalanche. Rhoda Koenig, an American met her neighbour and started with:

"'Isn't it dreadful'. 'Oh yes', she replied 'disgraceful, all this hysteria. Rushing around ... crying your eyes out on television - I've never heard of such a thing! What an American way to behave ... I blame Rupert Murdoch' ... ... (concerning the 'stiff upper lip' now derided in the tide of Dianism) the idea that calm is the same as coldness, that the surface is the same as the centre is too simple for truth. Barbara Walters wipes her eyes on prime time TV and, social climbing into a coffin, says she has lost a friend ... the unelected guardians of our heartstrings can also use their emotions as a club with which to beat the rest of us. Far from promoting sensitivity, which is ipso facto an awareness of the differences among people, feeling fascism insists that other people are just like us, and, if not, they ought to be". (ES, 5, 8).

event passed by with hardly a murmur - the press had wound itself up beforehand.

Naming feeling fascism is a powerful act; others did not pick up the term, but echoed the perception:

"...As the emotional barometer has risen, so has a disturbing sense of menace in the atmosphere ... newspaper columnists, sensing the family's isolation, have been fighting their poisoned arrows ... everything about Diana's life is being recast as legend, as the first step in conferring upon her a secular sainthood". (ES, 5, 11).

"a punk republicanism now perches on the memory of ... the image which one of the most pitilessly efficient media machines in the world pumped in and out of her". (T, 5, 18).

OVERVIEW

The Chapter began with a map of various themes which were likely to be embedded in the overall story of the death of Princess Diana. In the perspective of the overarching interest in the connections between mass message systems and the monarchy, two questions of influence arise: does the monarchy work through and influence the press and broadcasters themselves and through them, the public? And in the other direction, do the media influence public opinion and through that impinge on the monarchy - either to reinforce or to undermine it? Several propositions were set out which appear to be connected, but whose validity should not be accepted unless and until evidence can be shown that each proposition contains some empirical truth. The task of the chapter is to seek evidence concerning these propositions, and to point to the need for a tailored survey with which to test some of them, with evidence from opinions amongst the public.

Two grand narratives have been detected, which can be seen as a pro and an anti-monarchist standpoint in each case. Neither narrative is presented in a comprehensive and coherent way in the sources examined here - that is a project for weekly or monthly newsmagazines, which have done such work; to examine them is a task separate from that tackled here, which is to focus on the material in front of the British public during the week of mourning for Diana Princess of Wales. This material has been chosen because of its quantity and intensity, unavailable at any other place and time. Each narrative emerges as a series of connected ideas, feelings and expressions, found in different places but, when considered, recognisable as having an underlying unity. Each narrative can be seen as constructed with a number of themes, and these themes overlap to a considerable extent with the propositions set out at the start of the chapter. Other themes forced themselves into focus in the process of examining the material.

The first notion (a) that press pictures of Princess Diana would significantly increase sales of a periodical, and the related notion (b) about broadcasting were investigated with the aid of published industry data on newspaper readership and viewing audiences. It does seem to be true in each case, that a blitz of treatment such as witnessed in the week of mourning attracted reading and viewing. Two reservations are, however, considered advisable. One is that the argument (market justification) that the press had to publish certain material because they had to satisfy a public demand needs to be scrutinised in much closer detail than has been offered in available sources. If a paper pays a considerable amount for scoop material, it is by no means certain that the extra sales it achieves thereby, cover the cost of the investment or handsomely exceed it. There may be long-term gains, or losses in terms of changes in public esteem of a paper which publishes something hugely controversial in this way. Neither the short term nor the long term gains have been tightly documented, while the treatment here has begun to point to ways in which such a documentation should be carried out. The second reservation is that though short term gains do probably reward publication of exceptionally dramatic or interesting material, these fluctuations are but small in the context of the overall figures of consumption of mass message material, which tell of relative stability and of a general loss of performance amongst the traditional message sources across the years.

The notion that Princess Diana was desperately seeking to mend her life in which she had been the principal victim in a divorce was certainly supported by a large amount of admiring print. Writers about divorce itself might often emphasise that not just one person but several parties are victims - including the children and both spouses, and probably their parents and other blood relatives. In the present instance, because so much of the writing was in mourning of Diana very little drew attention to the notion that Prince Charles and his Windsor family may also have been victims - of a situation brought about by a complex interaction of all the people involved. It did seem that the weight of attention focused on Diana as victim of the divorce.

One alleged quotation of what Diana is supposed to have said, to paparazzi, to go and rape someone else suggests that she felt at least in part a victim of these photographers. Her very human frustration with the burden, to ask it to be shifted to someone else also detracts from that universalism of compassion which characterises a truly saintly figure. It is certainly realised here that this dictum may not have been true; Diana may not really have said these words. Much else in the discourse quoted above may have fallen short of being true to source. While untruth of that kind is much to be regretted, the material remains important here because this is what is available to the public, and which may influence what people think and feel.

Much writing pointed to Diana feeling that she had enemies at the Palace, though far less specified exactly which member of the royal family was supposed to have been particularly unhelpful or oppositional, or which member(s) of the courtiers or Palace bureaucracy may have been similarly troublesome for her. All the other themes it was conjectured would emerge (from d to j in the list at the start of the chapter) did crop up in the printed discourse. This does not mean that all the propositions were true, or indeed any of them. It first means that the propositions were put forward in the press. Thus for example, propositions i and h, that there was widespread shock and a feeling of bereavement were both asserted in print; and by much of the quoted evidence, were true. That the shock and bereavement were universal was not, through the evidence thus far presented, demonstrable.

Proposition j, that the nation's personality structure had changed was asserted, but by no means proven. Indeed, theory in psychology which holds that something like 40 per cent of any individual's personality structure is genetically influenced suggests that it is extremely unlikely that any social trauma, however severe, will change personality structure in the population. Personality can be thought of as similar to physique, so if a population contains many tall blond people it will be most unlikely that even the largest of emotional shocks will alter physiques to becoming short and dark, neither in the present generation nor in the next. Little or nothing was developed in the press about the situation that Diana's own sister and brother in law were part of the society of the court, and that she had been brought up as a child as quite familiar with the Windsor family. So how the relationships between Diana and her in-laws had deteriorated, and if so why; and whether anything could have been done, or was done to try to mend such relationships and use the resulting bonds to rescue a marriage, tended to be ignored.

Such elements of family life and relationships within the Palace are, of course, known only at second hand (if that) to journalists; but they often do not acknowledge this distance in what they describe. On the contrary, they often adopt a *verité* approach implying that the journalist was a 'fly on the wall' (thus, Robert Jobson in the *Express* of 1 September wrote: "finally, at 5:15 am Charles stepped into his sons rooms" (to tell them of the tragedy); it takes an exceptionally diligent and detached reader to realise that this does not give exactly the same picture as available in the *Sun* (same date, p. 3) which wrote: "Charles decided not to tell his sons until they woke up". The *Sun* (same date, p. 4) assured its readers that "Princess Diana had never looked happier or more beautiful than in recent weeks. and it was all down to the delicious feeling of romantic love that had eluded her for so long"; if that interpretation was true, then another, offered in the Express the same day (p. 18) could not also have been so: "whatever personal contentment she found with Dodi Fayed, she was not happy".

These phenomena have been referred to in the main text as examples of "**false inference syndrome**" (FIS) - or what one might more simply call, making it up. Sometimes this behavior is at a conscious level - writers must realise they are operating as playwrights rather than as quasi-legal witnesses. Other examples of FIS occur when writers seem not to recognise that the projections they are making (like so many about the universalism of the emotional reactions during the mourning week) arise from ignorance about the phenomena of sampling in representing public opinion. It is easy to suppose that because some thousands of telephone calls complain about blanket coverage of an event on two television channels, or about absence of a flag on a flagpole, that this means the whole society thinks and feels the same way. Such an assumption may be true - and it may not. The best way to try and explore and possibly confirm the merit of what should really be presented as hypotheses, or guesses, is to put the right questions to as well distributed a sample of people as it is possible to find, and to analyse the replies in some detail. This is what has been done for our enquiry and the results will be presented in Chapter 8.

Chapter 7

RESOLUTIONS OF THE PROBLEM OF
DIANA: IN THE PRESS

The funeral of Diana Princess of Wales took place on Saturday September 7th. Had she married, or even become engaged to Dodi Fayed as some newspapers had conjectured had been their plan, it is possible or even likely that she would (like her friend Jemima Khan) have adopted Islam. Had that happened she would have been buried as Dodi was, as soon as possible. There would not then have been a week in which hundreds of thousands of people participated in an elaborate and protracted mourning rite that was devised in part by themselves and in part influenced by the press. There would still clearly have been massive press attention, but it would have taken a different shape. If the funeral had been a private one focussing around the Fayed family Diana's sons would certainly have attended but Prince Charles and even more so the Queen and the older members of the Windsor family would have had far less prominent roles than those in which they were in fact cast by the events of the real week which was lived out.

A grand scenario had been constructed amongst various national newspapers, in which the first component was that the Windsors were partly to blame for Diana's alienation (which shades psychologically into the greater alienation from this life, of death). Behind that it was said by many that the Windsors were dysfunctional as individuals and as a family, and behind that hypothesis (though several writers dealt with it as an established fact) there was a prior view of their family style, of alleged emotional restraint and social discipline, and a belief that this was now obsolete as a model for society and indeed as a form of practice. This whole model of "Windsor style" jarring against that of the lost heroine would have had much less space to have been developed had Diana been buried swiftly, as a Muslim.

Two other aspects of the week which were important in the development of this anti-Windsorian model included the way in which the royal family's position in Balmoral was portrayed as a lack of care (for the nation, ignoring whatever it entailed for the boys who had lost their mother), and the way in which the patience of the public who stood in queues to contribute their messages in books of remembrance was drawn upon by sections of the press. When people come from some distance and then have to stand for some hours in a queue they must talk to each other and amongst the topics that will arise are some that are given prominence in the press. The empty flagpole above Buckingham Palace was a very salient focus for such attention and it is wholly understandable that people could see this as a sign of lack of care, in stark contrast to what they were doing themselves by giving their time and emotional energy. Both of these elements, the absence of the royal family from London (and very few 'national' newspapers transcended this London-centred view, that Balmoral was an 'away place', not a home) and the amplification of dissatisfaction over the symbol of the empty flagpole would not have occurred had there been a prompt funeral.

In fact however, Diana had remained a Christian; her funeral took the best part of a week to arrange - plans were modified as it was realised that huge numbers wanted to line the route, and the press (in particular, but also the national television channels in their news and discussion programmes but also radio stations with their 'phone-in programmes, of which records are mostly lost other than in participants' minds) thus had their time in which to pose a problem. The problem, as evidenced in the last chapter was this: to what extent was the anti-royalist or republican grand narrative now well developed and to the fore; and to what extent did the traditional royalist narrative still hold sway in the minds of the public; and thus, which of these doctrines would win the day? Was Britain to become a republic - presently, or in due course? Would it remain a monarchy, and if so on what terms? These were questions, or themes which elements of the press had orchestrated during the discourse of their hectic week. Now, after the funeral, readers (probably) but certainly journalists wanted answers. The problem had to be resolved.

Who was to resolve this problem, and how? One way - and the one most likely to be used by journalists, who are not for the most part social scientists trained in empirical enquiry, is to turn one's mind to the problem, to use one's intuition based on one's own circle of evidence, in effect to pronounce judgement as a verdict in the tradition of literary criticism rather than of social science. The other option was to carry out social research and to base one's predictions of the likely shape of the future mood of the nation on empirical findings. This process, however, takes time; and journalism is in a hurry. So what happened was that elements of the press went ahead and decided on the result of this contest of ideologies; some writers made use of the results of public opinion surveys, while others did without. In effect, one grand arena in which a great deal was said, as during the week before the funeral, was that of the press; and the press offered a resolution of the problem that it itself had set. It is this resolution (or resolutions - there were more than one) that is the topic of this chapter.

Before setting out what was found in the press, it is acknowledged that there is no such homogeneous entity. Some newspapers said one thing, others something else. Some newspapers even offered opposite analyses from contributors, even if they also came down on one side editorially as well. There was thus diversity of analysis. Another important matter is that apart from daily and weekend newspapers there are respected weekly news magazines which had paid a good deal of attention to the matter. Three of these titles are the *New Statesman*, and the *Spectator* in Britain, and the *New Yorker* in the United States. The first two have sales of around thirty thousand each and readerships of some four times that figure; their readerships of some 120,000 each (including some unknown proportion in common) are not (as they would be in the world of daily newspapers) negligible, for these readers are the intelligentsia, opinion-leaders (they think) or perhaps mainly opinion-staters. Attention will therefore be paid in this chapter to ideas and judgements offered in these weeklies.

The period covered by this chapter runs from the Sunday immediately after the funeral, to the end of the year. Sunday September 7th contained the big news of the funeral itself, most of which was planned and anticipated except for the content of the speech by Diana's brother Earl Spencer, and the reception this had. Other elements in the news on that day included the comportment of the members of the royal family, the invited mourners in the Abbey and of the crowds outside. At the end of the year there were memorial reviews of Diana's life, deeds and death, and several television programmes which had their own audiences and secondary audiences amongst readers of newspapers' accounts of these programmes. Relevant events between September and December included a royal tour by the Queen and Prince Philip to Pakistan and India, one by Prince Charles with Prince Harry to South Africa and particularly the unseemly proceedings of the divorce in the South African courts of Earl Spencer and his (ex)wife Victoria. Most importantly there was also the celebration of the Golden Wedding anniversary of the Queen and Prince Philip, with another service in Westminster Abbey followed by a walkabout by the royal pair amongst modest-sized but clearly well-wishing crowds, and a people's lunch at the banqueting hall in Whitehall to which the guests were drawn from a wider circle of eminent people than the civil dignitaries from whom some previous banquet's guests might have been drawn. There was also the completion of the major repairs to Windsor Castle, reported in the press and in a magnificent television programme as a triumph of British craftspersonship, and ready just in time for a ball with which to celebrate the Golden Wedding anniversary.

Quotations will now be made, as in the previous chapter, of examples of themes in the discourse. Some of these themes unequivocally belong to a monarchist grand narrative, others to a republican one; but some could be harnessed by either side, or are relatively neutral and it is these with which we may start. One of the elements of the discourse is not a theme in itself, but a contradiction between interpretations of events. Another theme that was not prominent in the texts of the week of the funeral and thus in the last chapter was that of the press and of broadcasting reflecting on their own roles.

A SPENCER WINDSOR RIFT

The first theme that can be identified and illustrated is that of **Spencer versus Windsor**. This was sparked off particularly by the funeral oration by Diana's brother Charles, which was reported in the *Observer* under the headline "The nation unites against tradition"[180]:

> " ...despite the most bizarre life imaginable after her childhood, she remained intact, true to herself. ... we, your blood family will do all we can ... so that their souls are not simply immersed by duty and tradition, but can sing openly as you planned. We fully respect the heritage into which they have both been born, and will always respect and encourage them in their royal role ...". (O, 7, 2).[181]

Elements among these words were taken up by journalists McKie and Kemp as follows:

> Earl Spencer's dismissal of the 'bizarre' royal life struck a resonant note across the nation yesterday, uniting the views of constitutional experts and the public ... Anthony Barnett, from the constitutional reform group Charter 88, said his remarks showed 'Britain's traditional power was cracking' ... critics of the monarchy were articulate while the Establishment was tongue tied". (O, 7, 6).

Clive Goodman, the 'Royal Editor' in the *News of the World* also took a combative view, under the heading "Earl's speech shows rift with House of Windsor":

> "Charles Spencer ... (made) a bitter attack on the Royal Family - and left the Queen outraged ... David Starkey said ... Earl Spencer had made William and Harry 'the victims' of a public tug of war' ... Spencer also made a bitter attack on the media ...". (NOW, 7, 10).

These extracts are shown to illustrate not just the theme of a battle between the Spencers and Windsors, but also the grand narrative of anti-monarchy. There is the possibility of claiming that there is a contradiction, inasmuch as the Earl's words were of a "bizarre life" - which could be held to include the Princess's own misalignment and bulimia rather than being thought to be mostly a description of the royal life and thus by implication only of the Windsors. There is also the possibility that there is an example of **False Inference Syndrome** (as noted in the last chapter) in assuming that the nation and the public were at one with (all) constitutional experts.

---

[180] As often in the press, headlines do not faithfully reflect important elements in the stories they introduce. Here, the sub-editor's aspirations conveniently ignored the Earl's "full respect" for heritage.

[181] O: *Observer*; NOW: *News of the World*; NS: *New Statesman*; NY: *New Yorker*; EOS: *Express on Sunday*; Sp: *Spectator*; IOS: *Independent on Sunday*. The central number in all parenthetic references indicates the date within September - unless specified otherwise, while the final number denotes the page.

The next day the *Express* took a similar view. Under the overall headline BATTLE ROYAL came the sub-head "The Queen is facing growing pressure for radical reform of the monarchy after Earl Spencer's bitter assault ..." (E, 8, 1), though this was followed more conciliatingly by their analyst Robert Jobson who wrote, mentioning Diana's sister Jane that the:

"... Spencers are a more dysfunctional clan than the Windsors. ... Lady Jane Fellowes is obviously perfectly placed to influence what is happening. Her daughter, Laura, is a playmate of William and Harry ... if anyone can heal the wounds ... it is Prince William". (E, 8, 4).

For its part the *Times'* editor Peter Stothard wrote under the caption: Sad Captain of Diana's Army:

"was this day to be the end of the battle between the people and the House of Windsor? ... he had thrown down a graceless gauntlet to his Sovereign - and one that must damage his best hopes ... True leadership is not the ability to tell people what they want to hear but to make people want what is best ...". (T, 8, 20).

A weekly weighed in when Mary Riddell wrote, with what may be another instance of False Inference Syndrome, and which itself pointed to a contradiction:

"As the hours passed, and the days, it became clear that Earl Spencer's funeral oration had united a congregation and a nation swaying robotically to his tune. ... There are ... inconsistencies in his theories ... also ironies. The monarchy has lurched from Jurassic to Pleistocene in the space of days, precisely because the media, on behalf of the people, applied boot to dinosaur rump ... We are now not subjects, but citizens[182] ... Earl Spencer ... appeared to drive a wedge between the orphaned children and a father who patently loves them". (NS, 12, 11).

In the same paper a Labour MP Clive Soley held that:

"the applause for Earl Spencer's speech indicates that the royal family must change, or wither away". (NS, 12, 15).

The English novelist Julian Barnes offered a different perspective on the alleged relations between the Spencers and the Windsors, to his American readers:

"The received opinion is that it was the misfortune of Diana and Fergie to marry into a cold, unhuggy, tight-assed family of Germans; they were fresh, hopeful girls broken on the wheel. But perhaps it was the Windsors' greater misfortune to marry into the

---

[182]This was not, incidentally, an accomplishment by Princess Diana but a consequence of a Conservative government endorsing the Maastricht Treaty through which the Queen herself becomes a citizen of Europe (though it is to be determined, legally, whether this nevertheless means that British people remain subjects of the Queen).

dysfunctional Spencers and Fergusons ... You can hug and still be barking mad". (NY, 15, 78).

Part of the portrayal of an alleged Spencer/Windsor rift referred to the report that there had been one disagreement about the nature of the funeral, and another about the princess's title. The *Express* of 8th September said that the palace had offered the Spencers, on the Saturday afternoon immediately after the funeral to restore the title Her Royal Highness to Diana. Lord Spencer was said unequivocally to have turned this down. The newspaper also said that Buckingham Palace's "firm view was that the Princess herself would not have wished for any change".

Over the next two days the *Times* rejected reports of a conflict. On the 9th the paper noted (p. 9) "Palace denies royal dispute" but mentioned that the news presenter Jon Snow had claimed on Channel 4's respected seven o'clock news hour that there had been a Spencer-Windsor row. On the 10th Princess Diana's mother Frances Shand Kydd entered the fray. The *Times* (p. 7) reported that in a hand written statement released to the Press Association she said "There is no division, nor has there been, between (the Princes') paternal and maternal relations. Earl Spencer earlier denied he had clashed ... to suggest that there were divisions ... is so far from the truth as to be laughable ...". It may be opportune here to recall the Earl's words, spoken in the Abbey and evidently neglected by some among the press "we fully respect the heritage into which they have both been born ...".

Some journalists noted the formal connections between the Spencers and the Windsors. Dominic Lawson - whose own daughter had Princess Diana as a godmother - his wife Rosa Monckton was a good friend of the princess - pointed out in the *Evening Standard* (16, 6) under the heading: "Family says 'stop' but the flowers keep coming" that Charles Spencer was himself the Queen's godchild. The *Daily Telegraph* however, on the same day returned (on p. 1) to a story on "The Queen denies rift over funeral" noting that Jon Snow stuck to his claim that his story alleging conflict had been correct, from a credible source "understood to be a minister close to Tony Blair". More on this emerged at the weekend from Marianne MacDonald in the *Observer*:

> "The Queen had no sympathy for Diana in life and has no reason to mourn her now ... Jon Snow ... offered an answer ... the Queen had barred the use of Diana's name in her presence ... Diana stuck the knife into the Royal Family in the most public way on *Panorama* ... she divorced Charles against the monarchy's strongest wishes ... (she quotes Lady Colin Campbell in her biography *Diana in Private* who reported of the Queen): 'she was really anxious to keep her happy. The possibility of having the Princess of Wales leave the heir to the throne filled the Queen with unspeakable horror ... yet the Queen did, it seems, go to great lengths to keep Diana happy ... Diana was even allowed to revolutionise the royal dress code by leaving off her gloves". (O, 14, 19).

One might find the conclusion that the Queen had no reason to mourn Diana somewhat excessive; however, more than one journalist interpreted matters unidirectionally.

Take Anne Robinson, in the *Express*:

"The Queen, head of the Church of England, was condoning the infidelity of Prince Charles. The Windsors deliberately chose to ignore the unhappiness this was causing ... the blue blooded Sloane they had ruthlessly picked out to produce an heir and a spare ...".(E, 1 Oct, 11).;

but then, seemingly offering an element of contradiction:

"out of all her schoolfriends she was the only one without a boyfriend. As she explained 'I knew somehow that I had to keep myself very tidy for whatever was coming'". (E.3Oct, 3).

Within this argument about whether the Windsors misused Diana Spencer, or indeed whether she made what she wanted of the Windsors it is relevant to note the claim of a journalist Roy Greenslade, in a story on 'A Royal Marriage Made by the Media':

Who picked this shy girl to be princess? We did ... He quotes the Sun's photographer Arthus Edwards saying "she once stopped him in the street and asked 'why all this harassment'. He replied 'because you're going to be the prince's bride'. She laughed. At the time Charles had not proposed marriage, but the papers had made up their minds ...". (G, 20 Oct 3).

The *News of the World* ran a piece by Richard Stott (ex editor of the *Mirror* newspaper) which was very uncompromising:

"Now we know that she virtually wrote the Morton book herself in spite of her direct denials ... Buckingham Palace cries foul and tries to use her two sons as a moral blackmail ... If the Palace had shown half the concern for the boys and their mother's welfare years ago, things might have been different ... the sooner we know the full dreadful story of Diana's tragic life and death, the better we will be able to form a judgement about who was to blame. And when we do I have a strong suspicion that paparazzi ... and tabloid newspapers will be a long way down the list".[183] (NOW, 5 Oct, 7).

It seems from these journalists' reflections that Earl Spencer's remarks had some of the nature of a Rorschach inkblot - different people could read different meanings into what he said. Some focussed on his phrase 'blood family' and on his caution about being 'not simply immersed by duty and tradition' to infer hostility to the Windsors and possibly to his Godmother in particular; others offered stories of alleged conflict over the form of the funeral and over the possibility of restoration of a full royal title. Some journalists went as far as to infer that the whole nation agreed with a reading of the Earl's speech as specifically targeting the royal family as to blame for Diana's misfortunes and death. Some journalists were however aware that part of the press

---

[183]This is a challenge that will be taken up in the next chapter.

wanted to deflect attention from its own role in publishing intrusive pictures taken by paparazzi, and that the royal family presented an easy alternative target. Clive Soley, a politician pursuing measures to instil some respect for privacy in press behavior wrote:

> "Circulation goes up at most 300,000 when sensational pictures are used and the core readership still buys the paper for sport, television listings and light news or entertainment. Throughout the past week we have had the unedifying spectacle of editors trying to apportion blame ... to everyone except themselves, and then claiming credit for provoking a response from the royals ... a privacy law has its place, but only if matched by a freedom of information act". (NS, 12, 15).

Libby Purves in the *Times* (9, 18) believed that Earl Spencer had spoken well and judged that "there is no need to look for a spark of hostility, still less to fan it with our wind-machines". *The Evening Standard* had commented more combatively, however, under a heading of "the hidden text of the tabloids":

> "'after talking of the pressures faced by Diana in dealing with the huge interest in her life' was how the *Sunday Mirror* precised (Earl Spencer's) words ... the People continued to avoid any mention of the passage (in which he had then attacked the intrusiveness of the press) ... these two newspapers are unusually cheap and spiteful rags, even by the standards of their proprietor David Montgomery". (ES, 8, 13).

In the same paper Max Hastings wrote:

> "When I edited the *Daily Telegraph* ... we did our utmost to support the Royal Family ... for six months after its publication we made no reference at all ... to Andrew Morton's devastating book which inflicted such harm on the Prince ... I was astounded when the prince ... offered interviews ... to the Murdoch titles ... most of the material, including the ... valuable Dimbleby book was never even offered to the *Telegraph*. The Murdoch papers profited greatly, and the palace seemed not to care a jot. ... henceforward, if there is really a desire ... for a new contract between society and the media, there is no more assured way to achieve it than to favour those newspapers which try to behave responsibly, and to shun those which do not ... We were reminded (by every readership study) that today's generation are the children of the TV sound bite, for whom 100 words at one go is a big read ...". (ES, 8 11).

In spite of this last caution, Hastings had provided an article over 1700 words long, possibly not intending to be read by younger people. Hastings' remarks also indicated that he did not believe that a public relations approach akin to that of appeasing a bullying opponent would work. Some weeks later the *Guardian* reported the Queen's former private secretary Sir William Heseltine opining about one of his compatriot Rupert Murdoch's papers that:

> "The Sun has a good deal to answer for in the way the coverage of the members of the royal family degenerated in the late eighties ... other tabloid newspapers felt they had to do the same to compete". (G, 20 Oct, Media, p. 5).

A columnist who is not usually pro-Monarchy may have lent this idea some support arising from his evident dislike of some papers' behavior:

"A year ago, the *Sun* ran a telephone poll asking its readers whom they would prefer to date - the Duchess of York or a goat ... Stuart Higgins[184] argued ... Sarah Ferguson ... was fair game and was begging to be ridiculed ... this kind of habitual assault had become many degrees too corrosive ...; the tabloids in the Murdoch stable have done more than most to cauterise our sensibilities and introduce a withering harshness into public life ... the red-top readership[185] ... demanded a harshness of tone against the Royal Family ... there was a demotic insistence that the family should address the nation's grief before the princes'. No one appeared to see the wild inconsistency involved in berating the press for its invasion of Diana's life at the same time as insisting that the Royal Family's own privacy should be abruptly brought to an end to satisfy the people". (ES, 10, 55).

Apart from these longer perspectives, thoughtful observers reflected on the possibility that the public's behavior during the mourning week might not have taken the form it had done, had there not been a press to tell it what it was, and perhaps should be doing. The television journalist Jon Snow reported:

"On Thursday night ... I went ... to Kensington palace ... up to 15,000 people walking across Kensington Gardens ... it was curiously serene - hushed tones, no raised voices, purged of cynicism ... Every single day last week I found myself asking 'have we got this right? Are we exaggerating, leading, massaging the national mood?". (G, 8, 7).

It is not easy to find any journalist who has reflected on Snow's first question, in depth, at least until some weeks had elapsed. Adam Gopnik, in the distant *New Yorker* considered that:

"... there was a sense among many intellectuals that what the ... Americanised media were reporting as a liberation from centuries of emotional frigidity was in fact a rejection of deep (and equally 'emotional') national traditions of mourning, while what was being touted as a more "feeling" replacement was a kind of media-induced autism ... the idea that the country of Lady Macbeth and Little Nell and Johnny Rotten had a hard time 'dealing with emotion' was bewildering. It's as if Dunblane[186] never happened". (NY, 29, 36).

Even later, Ian Jack focused an article on Those Who Felt Differently and recollected his experience in the mourning week, and some of his ideas about it, in the *Guardian Weekend Magazine:*

---

[184]Then editor of the *Sun*.

[185]This readership has been reducing steadily over a number of years, raising the possibility that not all previous, present or potential readers approve of the trends in such papers.

[186] Dunblane is a small town in Scotland where a shooting of primary school children took place, prompting nationwide horror and the passing of an anti-gun law.

"We crossed the Mall and went into the park ... it was normal ... People were arriving with bunches (of flowers) every couple of minutes ... men in T-shirts had begun to set up scaffolding for television ... September was not a good month for those who imagined that human society is, or might one day be, governed by reason ... As of Sept 15 Buckingham palace had received 500,000 letters and 580,000 email messages of sympathy ... There was an oppression of grief. People had not only to grieve, they had to be seen to grieve, and in the most pictorial way, by hugging and kissing. New Britain was the princess, the prime minister, flowers, compassion and the therapeutic benefits of touching and crying ... Old Britain was the Queen, her son and heir, pensioners with 'stiff upper lips', reticence and the neurosis brought about by repression. My guess is that ... it was recreational grieving, that it was enjoyable, that it promoted the griever from the audience to an onstage part in the final act of the opera". (GWM, 27Dec).

This was a daring and radical suggestion, fitting the interpretation into a perspective spoken about currently as "post-modernism". The barrier between sender and receiver may, at least for some, have been dissolved and even reversed; but if in London and a few other centres a part of the crowd had become the makers and tellers rather than just the receivers of the tale, it has to be remembered that the majority even of the urban population as well as those in other parts of the country were still seeing these sights on television and reading such stories in the press in the role of receivers. An echo of these points arose in two letters in the *Times' Saturday Magazine* in January. An article had appeared by an actor Jeremy Irons, speaking of his feelings of genuine grief, and universalising them to apply to the nation at large, to which two rejoinders were made by private letter writers:

"Jeremy Irons ... does oversimplify ... London is not the same as England ... The country was not united in grief ... a large part kept quiet ... they are loyal to the Queen...". (Rev John de Chazal, T, 17 Jan, 99).

"A clue ... to the Rev ... Chazal's question was provided by last week's *Any Questions?*[187] Apparently no one in the Manchester audience had contributed to her memorial fund ... responses were driven by the media, which is predominantly London-based". (J.E.Scott, T, 31 Jan, 97).

Other papers had occasionally allowed such sentiments to appear, more forcefully expressed by private letter writers than by journalists:

"I have been consumed with fury ... all week at the cruel and unjustified attacks on our royal family ... the media is more powerful than any monarch or government and they have been abusing that power". (JMM Upson, E on S. 14, 42).

One press baron, however, took up the cudgels. Conrad Black of the *Telegraph* weighed in to the *Mail*. Black wrote a letter to the paper he owns in which he called on Sir David English, editor-in-chief of the *Mail* to 'repent or resign' as Chairman of the

---

[187] A BBC Radio 4 weekly program.

Press Complaints Council's Code of Practice Committee. The evidence allegedly was the *Mail*'s:

"infamous conjuring up of the Prince of Wales's "tears of guilt" front page headline on September 2 ... the *Daily Mail* led the baying hounds in pursuit of Diana ... the gnashing of teeth in grieving for her; the defamation of the Royal Family when the nation was in mourning for her ...". (T, 16, 19).

The *Times*' Brian MacArthur wrote of this as "Fleet Street's biggest brawl in living memory" and said the Mail had been wounded by the criticism. MacArthur cited the *Mail*'s front page in the days before Diana's death:

"Monday: Diana and Dodi: Amazing New Pictures (from paparazzi) Tuesday: Charles and the Indian 'Rasputin' Wednesday: Why Diana is such a Poor Mother to her Boys (Lynda Lee Potter) Thursday: Diana's Fury at 'Stick Up' Friday: Diana and Dodi, on a jet ski made for two (from paparazzi)". (T, 17, 39).

This spat seems to have submerged fairly swiftly. Another was referred to in the *Independent* (25 Sept, p. 7) which reported that postal subscriptions to the satirical bi-weekly *Private Eye* had doubled. The satirical weekly's editor Ian Hislop said we took on the hypocrisy of the public, which was risky. But most of it was the overwhelming bilge being pumped out by the media; what he had done was to print items such as Lynda Lee Potter's words before Diana's death which contrasted shamingly alongside what was written afterwards. The main newsagents W.H. Smith had felt this behavior was insensitive and withdrew the issue from the shelves, losing many counter sales. This rather unusual press censorship by retailer did not draw much, if any censure from the rest of the press, in defence of free speech. An accusation of craven behavior then arose from a review of the book by the American Kitty Kelley - which was not available openly in Britain. Referring to Kelley's hate, the columnist Ros Coward observed:

"such sustained ... hostility does ... throw up real questions, in particular about the role of the press. No wonder they don't want to read it ... She exposes the British press regularly mouthing palace denials of things which turn out to be true, exercising extraordinary degrees of self-censorship to hide unpleasant aspects of royal behavior ... it raises questions about whether sections of the press colluded with the royal family's vicious discrediting of Diana simply out of deference". (G, 13 Oct, 17).

Before leaving this rather untidy theme of a conflict between two behavioral stereotypes marshalled under the titles of Windsor and Spencer, two further comments are worth including to make its ambit even wider. Adam Gopnik suggested that

"French media are in many ways thirty years 'behind' the Anglo-Americans ... French television, with its strong dose of Anglo-American imports, still looks like a medium instead of a substitute for life; it's harder to mistake the tube for life when people's lips don't always move in time with their words". (NY, 29, 34).

Many seemingly plausible hypotheses turn out to be difficult to substantiate when evidence is sought about them, and this is a more subtle suggestion. Nevertheless, Gopnik alerted us to a way in which viewers, and perhaps readers may be made more aware, by an unsuspected feature of the message, of the difference between reality and representation, which raises the possibility that the social perceptions of both journalists and public developed a view of the nation's' feelings and behavior which may not have been accurate. Finally, Salman Rushdie contributed a thought as to why Diana's death overwhelmed the press, in particular - a thought which was picked up elsewhere and ridiculed, but which should not perhaps be dismissed too lightly:

> "In our erotic imaginations, perhaps only the camera can rival the automobile. The camera, as a reporter, captures the news and delivers it to our door ... often looks upon beautiful women and offers them up for our delight. In Diana's fatal crash, the Camera (as both Reporter and Lover) is joined to the Automobile and the Star, and the cocktail of death and desire becomes even more powerful ...". (NY, 15, 68).

It can now be seen that the press has paid some attention to the functioning and qualities of its own roles, illustrating a theme of **the role of the press**. The account is, however, patchy, quite likely because the press considers its agenda is generally to look outwards at events among and the behavior of others, rather than to be introspective, especially when this may produce some discomfort. In all this there is the overarching possibility that practices in the press may have influenced the perceptions, attitudes and even behavior of the public. Some allege that the press have been over protective of the monarchy, hiding its alleged misdemeanours, and others that there has been unfair criticism; if anything, the latter may have more recently gained the upper hand, as several writers claim that the tide of feeling has been turning, against the monarchy. Drawn into the discussion have been allegations by and about newspaper owners, that they have pressed on one or the other of the grand narratives. These matters can not be resolved without much more information being drawn in, both about contents of the page, and of readers' minds. The latter will be explored in the next chapter and this one will continue with further examples of the great themes present in mass message system content.

THE GRAND NARRATIVE OF ANTI-MONARCHISM OR REPUBLICANISM

Without needing to spend time on political theory it should be recognised that the two 'isms' in the title are not necessarily identical. One may be anti-monarchist in a limited sense of disliking the royal family personally, and or their court and some or many of its practices (such as protocol and hunting), but that is not the same as a positive republicanism which springs from particular perceptions of human nature and needs and believes, even sometimes with reluctance, that it should supplant a monarchy. Some of the themes that can be discerned, which undercut or oppose the monarchy include stories alleging **anti-monarchism of the Labour leadership**, others revealing **anti-monarchism in the press itself**, and a view asserting **the sovereignty of the people**. Ancillary themes include one of a growing **multiculturalism in society**, which (if it is true) may dilute a historical British regard for its monarchy, and a notion that an approach to life associated (paradoxically) with Princess **Diana undercut the monarchy**, and that **the nation had changed** psychologically and culturally during the decade of Diana's influence, loosening its allegiance to the monarchy. These last two themes, that the Nation has Changed, and that Diana Undermined the Monarchy provide some kind of rationale for explaining how a monarchy may now be obsolete, and a look at them will precede an examination of the broader case of alleged obsolescence.

Starting an editorial, the *Observer* began to explain this notion that Diana herself, simply in her image, undermined the monarchy:

> "The end is approaching. Indeed the Royal Family itself may wish it, so Britain becomes the first republic brought into being from above rather than by revolution from below ... it continued ... the crown tarnished before our eyes. The Prince of Wales ... had to maintain his dignity against the reproach of an audience running into billions ... Every slow step ... could only enhance Diana's claim on the nation's affections even as it weakened his own ... the cool anger Diana's brother directed against the Royal Family and press was stunning ... In 1997 people ... are now sovereign; the Crown must follow where they lead". (O, 7, 7).

This extract provides a rich lode of other themes, possibly including a massive case of False Inference Syndrome, and the idea of Popular Sovereignty, before apparently lapsing into a contradiction in the final clause which suggests somehow that after all the steam may have been let off, even such harbingers of change as the writer of these lines, eventually succumbs to the habit of accepting the Crown (complete with its capital letter).

The *Evening Standard* quoted two other newspapers airing the themes that Diana changed not just the monarchy, but also the nation. First, the latter:

> "(The Guardian) ... 'last week ... we realised that - at some emotional level we cannot yet fathom - we had changed ... there appeared to be a glimmering recognition that we are, after all, citizens rather than subjects. Diana, said her brother, "needed no royal title"'. ... Then: (from the) *Express* ... 'the people are visibly renegotiating their contract with their rulers. We need the monarchy; without it Diana would have been nothing ... but we need a monarchy which listens to its people and derives its strength from listening'". (ES, 8, 6).

These germs of change were further pointed out by Anthony Holden in the *Express*:

> "It is certain that last week changed the country in some fundamental way ... As far as the monarchy is concerned it was the end of the aloof, imperial style, the beginning of a new bonding with the people which they must now deepen to survive. As long as William is Diana's living legacy, republicanism can return from the barricades to its bedsits ...". (E, 8, 11).

Two weeklies explored the notion of national change catalysed somehow by Diana's presence or example. Derek Draper in the *Spectator* wrote:

"...Despite the wrapping of Diana's body in the royal colours it is by no means certain that her myth will be harnessed to the royal cause. As her brother said in Westminster Abbey 'she needed no royal title to generate her particular brand of magic'...". (Sp, 12, 10).

In the same week in the *New Yorker* the historian Simon Schama believed that:

"When Maggie barked and commanded, the country stood at attention; when Di smiled ... the same country melted in a warm puddle of admiration. Both women were necessary for the rebuilding of national confidence ... Diana's allure gave the lie to the hoary jibe that where other nations had sex Britain had hot water bottles ... she was Peter Pan's Wendy, ministering to an entire nation of Lost Boys ... To the morning coats in the Palace, Diana the Martyr was an even bigger nightmare than Diana the Pop Idol. Hence the desperate tactic of Prince Charles's making an end-run around his wife's mastery of the media and giving the notorious interview that effectively ended the experiment begun in St Paul's Cathedral. Diana's response was to out- confess her husband ... And the great British public ... now Felt Her Pain". (NY, 15, 64).

The scenario resurfaced at the end of September when the *Times* chose to publish extracts from Andrew Morton's retitled *True Story* biography of Diana. The front page, and two inside pages gave prominence to the new reports that Diana had not just fed Morton with the material but had read every word he had written down and annotated the text in several places, so one might say it was a ghosted autobiography. Aside from tricky questions of copyright (which was not contested by her estate) Morton as "author" and his publisher said they had donated a sum of undisclosed size to a charity. The *Sun* (6 October, pp. 2-3) however reported that the Halo Trust, an anti-landmine charity had refused donations from Morton's profits, and that Harrods the mega-store owned by Mohammed Fayed the father of Diana's friend Dodi had refused to stock the book. Several papers, such as the *Standard* (29 Sept, p. 7) reported that "Buckingham Palace today condemned the re-release ... it was 'particularly sad so soon after her death'". The *Express* said that "Charles accuses author Morton of 'callous commercialism', and expanded:

"amazing is the disclosure that she developed (bulimia) only a week after the engagement - not, as was previously believed, during the marriage. On her honeymoon ... she finds herself dreaming about Camilla. She was, 'obsessed by Camilla totally. Didn't trust (Charles), thought every five minutes he was ringing her up' ... Although Diana is fiercely critical of Charles, it is obvious that she was in love with him and that he did respond". (E, 3 Oct, 3).

The demarche between "the Diana camp" and the Palace sprang considerably from the act of publishing the book rather than from the implications of all of its contents, some of which do not wholly support the case, made by her most zealous supporters, that a 'wicked' Windsor family unreservedly victimised her. The black writer and television programme maker Darcus Howe saw national change from a different, multi-cultural perspective:

"In the recent general election we failed to identify the massive shift in public feeling. ... We swallowed ... the myths of how the British people were: conservative, gradualistic, instinctively right wing ... royalist. And racist to the core. We were monumentally wrong. Blair is well advised to go for thorough reform. Abolish both the House of Lords and the House of Windsor as the first step ... Tony Blair ... announced a new Britain. He has got much more than he bargained for ...". (NS, 12, 13).

Another black source, the *New Nation* produced an image of a demographically and culturally changed nation - but one in which the black people were by no means deficient in loyalty to the established order.

"Hip hop lovers ... in West London were stunned when ultra-militant rapper McD, who once sang 'The Queen Mum's a slag' broke off his Sunday night stage show to admit 'I ain't ashamed to say I'm touched by Diana's death'. ... Seymour McLean of the Ethiopian World Federation ... sent a letter of condolence to the Queen, urging her to include a reading from the Ethiopian Covenant of Mercy at the funeral ... A New Nation straw poll identified various factors (to explain Diana's appeal to the black community) ... an outsider kicking back against a stiff-necked British establishment ... her relationship with an African Muslim, and ... her status as a two-timed Mum ...". (NN, 8, 2).

In their editorial the newspaper said:

"... Britons, both black and white, made their way to Buckingham Palace ... in order that we could somehow tell Diana how much we cared for her. ... This tragedy has brought the country closer together. With Diana's death Britain became, however briefly, truly a united kingdom". (NN, 8, 10).

In one respect the film actor already quoted, Jeremy Irons, agreed with Darcus Howe, however much their analysis of public feeling at the election may have developed an exaggeratedly false view:

"England has gone through a quiet revolution ... In May ... the Tories were routed, sent packing, dismissed as totally anachronistic[188]. ... Sinead (his wife - readers are supposed to know) ... thinks the British were grieving ... for what we felt we had become over the past 20 years ... we had begun to believe we were what the media told us we were ... lager louts, road rage, urban decay, child molesters, the lost empire, yuppies and Essex girls -

---

[188]In fact the New Labour party of Tony Blair received fewer votes in 1997 than John Major's Conservatives had, when they won the previous election in 1992 'on the slide' from Margaret Thatcher's larger parliamentary majority. The Parliamentary majority is not to be confused, because of the electoral system, with the extent of the plurality (more votes than the next ranking party) in the country, let alone with the notion of an actual popular majority (more than half the votes cast). These distinctions were not recognised by most journalists who merely translated their own euphoria into descriptions of an overwhelming national consensus (False Inference Syndrome).

the monarchy stained, our position in Europe sidelined, our place in the world unnoticed ... And suddenly, the boil, it seemed, had been lanced ... through the guilt which recognises that the media only mirrored our own appetites, there is a growing feeling that we want England to do and to be better ...". (T.Magazine, 27Dec, 26).

Irons thus seems to have conflated political support for Prime Minister Blair with emotional support for Diana; there is an implied theory (to stray into sociological terms) that a previous Britain four or five decades ago had noble values underwriting a cohesion that was manifest in the street parties of the Coronation; then followed two materialist decades ending in Thatcher's regime of a denial of society and a cult of competitive individualism that produced a state of (reluctant) anomie. This anomie would not have given rise to cohesive behavior at some great national occasion but, in Irons' view "the boil had been lanced", so presumably we were catalysed by Diana's death into a return to a psychological nirvana. There are a number of logical and empirical problems with this view; but at this stage we are not concerned with debating this analysis, rather than with quoting it as an eloquent - and perhaps influential, as it comes from a source with a presumed high status - ingredient in the available discourse.

We have seen several expressions of the theme that the Nation has Changed, to which another theme, describing **Therapeutic Catharsis** is relevant. Corinne Sweet wrote in the *Independent:*

"The popular criticism that people ... were being manipulated by an overheated media machine doesn't quite wash ... I'm sure I was prey to media hype, we all were. But I was crying all the way to the funeral and all the time there. There was permission to do this - and in public. It was a way of letting my own feelings be heard - and, I can tell you it was such a bloody relief". (I, 14, 1).

That weekend, the sister paper carried a related piece by Joan Smith (under the heading Why Do We Pretend We've Forgotten Diana's Faults?):

"To whom (are all the cards) being addressed? ... condolence cards are normally sent to surviving relatives, not the person who has died ... a reader wrote to explain that 'Diana's death gave us the right to mourn our own losses' ... genuine grief for Princess Diana is being used as a way of releasing other, previously unexpressed feelings ... some of the women who scribbled heartfelt messages to Princess Diana ... have also been writing to themselves ... and it explains why nothing can be allowed to disrupt the perfection of her image". (IOS, 14, 13).

Libby Purves realised a very special instance of a person whose own experience may have coloured her feelings on this occasion:

"As an army of private, neurotic, phantom, symbolic Dianas rose around us, Frieda Hughes more than anyone felt for the boys whose father and family were being vilified, and whose mother's grave had perforce to be hidden from mawkish intruders on an island in a lake". (T, 20 Jan, 17).

Purves had previously noted that:

"Spencer's taking Diana's body to safety on the lake island ... was a brotherly act; ... the parallel ... is not with Churchill's grave but with that of Sylvia Plath which to this day is still regularly claimed and ideologically defaced by those who think they revere her, but never knew her and care nothing for her living children". (T, 9, 18).

Frieda Hughes is the daughter of the poet laureate Ted Hughes, and of Sylvia Plath the famous poetess who took her own life; Plath's death was blamed by zealots on Hughes' presumed oppression, which is their reason for their aggressive behavior. This harsh component of what was in Diana's case heralded as a wave of positive and open emotionality connects with the theme of **Feeling Fascism** which will be illustrated presently. The genuine grief of a large number of people must however be recognised and respected and attempts have been made to understand it, sometimes involving the notion that the nation has changed, and in a way that at the very least destabilises the monarchy. The *Evening Standard* discussed the matter:

"The wave of public emotion ... drowned out the few voices that lamented the loss of traditional British reserve or - even worse - suggested that Diana was perhaps less than a saint. Two months on, is the national mood changing? Nigel Rosser talks to a family ... Mrs Smith thinks the Queen should retire ... opinion polls support Mrs Smith ... (but) Quentin Letts (writes) The dissent that dare not speak its name begins to brave a whisper. People who were ambivalent about Diana feared to speak their minds. To do so was to risk physical assault ... normal rules did not apply that week. London was a dissent-free zone and it was stated that Britain had changed for ever". (ES, 27 Oct, 15).

Aside from judgements that the shock of Diana's death may have rocked the monarchy, several pieces focused on the idea that prominent new Labour leaders and activists are anti-monarchists and, when not simply reporting such allegations as observations, in several cases agree with the standpoint. Thus we have two related themes, of Labour's anti-monarchism, and of the (journalist's) own anti-monarchism. This is sometimes explicit in a commentary, and sometimes implicit in a news story. Let us start with the intimations of Labour's anti-monarchism. Peter Hitchens wrote:

"The British people probably do not know how many senior figures in the Labour movement privately despise not only the monarchy but the Union Flag, symbol of a nation they wish to break up. Such people wisely keep their thoughts to themselves most of the time". (E, 8, 17).

This was followed at the weekend in the sister paper:

"... a few weeks before Princess Diana's death Mr Blair declared 'the monarchy is not constitutionally significant' ... Mr Blair has been given the credit for saving the Royal Family over the past two weeks. The irony is that no Prime Minister this century has cared less about the monarchy ... the monarchy, our greatest unifying symbol for more than 1000 years, has no place in (the New Britain)". (EOS. 14, 41).

We will see, below, that there are some quite different views of Mr Blair's loyalties, and this range of analyses is a suitable warning to treat all other journalists' judgements as just that (though there may be a tendency among some readers to accept what they read as 'objectively' true). The *Guardian* however ran a piece by Anthony Barnett, the Founding Director of Charter 88, a constitutional reform pressure group, and he said:

"On Saturday we invested the first President of the Republic of Britain ... The Sanctification of Diana has permitted the demystification of the monarchy. It has been undertaken with loyalty but with an unmistakable will to be modern, that connects to the electoral landslide of May 1". (G, 8, 8).

A week later the *Guardian*'s diary referred to a writer whose work has been quoted several times above:

"As well as a royal watcher, (Anthony) Holden is a founder member of the Common Sense Club, a group that meets every month to plot something akin to the downfall of the monarchy. Guests ... have included ... Kitty Kelley". (G, 16, 12).

This was reinforced a few weeks later in the same paper's Media Magazine by the ex-tabloid editor Roy Greenslade, with:

"... the general view of senior tabloid executives ... was unsympathetic to royalty. As part of an increasingly confident post-war working class, we abhorred inherited privilege ... tabloid deference to the monarchy was long past ... the key to treating the royal family as just another branch of show business lay in the indifference towards them by Rupert Murdoch". (G, Mag, 20 Oct, p. 22).

Reflecting on Andrew Morton's re-issued (auto)biography of Princess Diana, which had been translated into 29 languages and was published in 80 countries, selling 5 million copies, Sarah Courtenay wrote in the *News of the World*:

"He calls himself a serious historian ... but (sic, !?) he works in a former brothel above a curry house ... (she quotes Morton) 'It will take 20 years to bring down the House of Windsor - and I'm very happy to live off the collapse ... (then, seemingly at odds with what he has just said) 'some of what I was told I left out deliberately ... the down-side I didn't mention - it would have smacked too much of attacking Prince Charles". (NOW, 5Oct, 44).

Morton's alleged motives are not construed here as part of an explicit Labour movement, however, if true about himself, they would reinforce any such organised tendencies, which had more fully been described a few weeks before in the Spectator by Derek Draper, an adviser to Peter Mandelson, himself an adviser to Tony Blair. Draper explained:

" ... deep in the Oxfordshire countryside the annual Young Fabian weekend school ... were scathing about the behavior of the House of Windsor and not one of them expected the monarchy to survive the death of the Queen ... Abolishing the monarchy is not top of the political agenda, but that is for practical reasons - and a sense of inertia - not because of any royalist sympathies. ... We do not know the current state of government back-bench opinion because Labour MPs are now instructed not to participate in polls, but a 1995 survey showed 41 per cent of Labour MPs expressing republican sympathies ... in 1996 ... two thirds wanted the future of the monarchy 'put up for discussion' ... Blair talks of his 'third way' a new form of republicanism from a new brand of the left ... it comes from an understanding of the modern media and a deep belief in democracy, citizenship and meritocracy ...". (Sp, 12, 10).

Reports of politicians' ideas may be less potent than news stories which derogate the monarchy, and attitudes amongst columnists which range from outright hostility to the institution as such, to sympathy for its incumbents. Salman Rushdie was found in the *New Yorker* conjecturing that:

"Diana herself seemed far happier once she'd escaped from the Royal Family. Perhaps Britain itself would be happier if it made the same escape, and learned to live without kings and queens. Such are the unthinkable thoughts that have become all too thinkable now". (NY, 15, 68).

For its wide domestic readership the *News of the World* provided both hostile news stories, and hard hitting opinion from an ex-tabloid editor:

"Diana's Staff Told To Leave Palace. Household members ... will be given three months' notice ... The move will save Prince Charles - who funded the princess's office expenses ... the equivalent of £400,000 pa". (NOTW, 7, 1).

"PM Forced Queen To Act Charles uses Blair to Twist Palace Arms". (NOW, 7, pp. 2, 3).

"Princes teach Charles to love again". (NOW, 7, 23).

Then, from the columnist Richard Stott:

"Did HM - looking through mink lined blinkers - see only a woman who spelt trouble for her cosy, privileged family, a woman to be banished at all costs, a woman to be isolated and humiliated by the loss of the title Her Royal Highness? Has the dreadful truth at last revealed itself to the House of Windsor that the country now loves another who is no longer here more than the family that is left behind? We have lost not just a jewel in the crown. We have lost the crown, orb and sceptre ... If Buckingham Palace had not been so spiteful over insisting Diana lost her HRH, she would possibly be alive today ... the VIP Protection Squad ... would have been at the Ritz ... Inside the Palace today there is some simpering courtier who dreamed up this bitchy humiliation. He is probably the same beribboned half-wit who decided the only two places in Britain without flags at half-mast would be Buckingham palace and Balmoral". (NOW, 7, 38).

The *Guardian* next day ran an item titled Media, Monarchy and the Earl, followed by nine letters from readers, all (chosen to be) republican, under the title "A speech that shook the monarchy's foundations" and rounded off with a piece by the ennobled Labour politician Roy Hattersley, headed "The First nail in the royal coffin"(G, 8, 6). The *Independent* took its opportunity later in the month to show its attitude, in an interview by David Usborne in New York, with the writer Kitty Kelley, on "the irreversible crumbling of the monarchy" (22 Sept, p. 4). The rumbling against, certainly, and possibly (though this is contested) the crumbling would continue as long as anti monarchists remained writing for and even in charge of some newspapers.

One interesting situation arose in February 1998; the crumbling *Independent* newspaper had come under severe pressure from the *Times* which cut its cover price on two days a week. A motion in the House of Lords attacking predatory pricing succeeded. Pieces were written saying that Rupert Murdoch, who opposed the monarchy and would have been pleased with an Australian Constitutional Commission's advice for that country to sever its links with the monarchy, wanted to drive the *Independent* out of business. The *Independent* may have approved Murdoch's politics while fearing his aggression in business, but chose to devote its editorial to the former theme (15 February), telling the Queen to "get on your bike - ma'am" which combined the hostility to a monarchy of sovereignty and magnificence with a resignation to the idea that the institution itself would continue. These then are some signs that some politicians, some journalists, some newspaper owners and thus some newspapers (most notably the *Sun* and the *News of the World* in Murdoch's popular stable, and under different ownerships the *Observer*, the *Independent*, the *Guardian*) were either republican and against the monarchy, or at least lent themselves to dilutions of the institution or of damage to it, if such developments were seen as under way. In other words, kick it if it is down.

THE GRAND NARRATIVE OF MONARCHISM - COMMUNICATIONS LIKELY TO REINFORCE THE MONARCHY

Before we come to expressions of ideological support for the monarchy, there are numerous events which take place in the life of a nation and which, when reported may automatically reinforce acceptance of the given order. I call these **penumbra stories** since they lend shade and colour to the discourse on the monarchy without connecting with the ideological struggle at the centre of the discussion about its value.

At an early stage in the discourse the sociologist Roy Foster wrote:

"... around the story accumulate satellite anecdotes ... Princess Anne ... was allegedly spotted ... buying two black hats ... in her local British Home Stores. This seems to me to demonstrate the common touch, but the general reaction was sniffy. Diana ... would probably have flown in a milliner from Milan, and thus demonstrated ... what her public really like - or how they would really like to be". (NS, 12 Sept, 12).

Under the headline: "Kitty Zipper. Kitty Kelley's sack of sleaze makes the Royals look good", the British novelist Julian Barnes told his American readers the tale of

"Sardinian, Fabio Piras who lifted a Teddy bear left by a girl called Regina. Gerry Moorhouse, a forty-three year old Londoner, unfuelled by the new compassion punched him in the face and said afterward, 'she was the queen of everybody's hearts. Why should an Italian get away with this? It's disgusting'". (NY, 15 Sept, 78).

The resonances of this cameo are extremely rich, hinting that "British (and its institutions and behavior, including that of its monarchy, represented in the amazing coincidence of the name Regina) is, as British was". On the 26th of September the *Times* ran an item (p. 14) saying "The man born to be Emperor Napoleon IV ... has become a most unlikely cult figure in France". This son of Napoleon III went as an observer to a war in South Africa, where he was killed by Zulu warriors. France is the stereotypical republican country in modern Europe and one might expect that symbols of an obsolete system would have no appeal there. Yet here is a suggestion that some kind of positive feelings for such icons survive. Nobody would be rash enough to carry the story a step further, in print, to look for other signs of a re-emergence of support for monarchy in France; instead, such stirrings are left to arise, if they will, at a subconscious level in readers' minds and feelings.

An intriguing penumbra ingredient arose in a feature in the *Sun* on 6 October (pp. 2-3) which reported a holiday in Barbuda several months before her death, in which Princess Diana had befriended a Belgian girl, Marion, aged 11, even suggesting that "I would like you to be my daughter" and be a playmate for her sons. This is not in itself the potentially pro-monarchic ingredient it may be worth noticing, but an incidental observation was that Prince William spoke French to Marion most of the time. Here is information about a still unusual skill in a young English man, which is likely to produce admiration for him - an ingredient which may weigh, however slightly, in people's estimations of a likely future king.

On 18th October the *Times* discovered a letter to the paper written by Queen Victoria, after her husband Albert's death in 1861, in which she had rejected notions that she might soon emerge from mourning back to public life. This showed that a monarch did - occasionally - communicate directly to the press, even if it was to require what was even then, and would much more so now be considered an extreme degree of withdrawal into privacy. Early in the next month several broadsheet newspapers (the *Times*, the *Observer*) carried major obituaries of Harold Albert. The strange feature of this man's life had been that he had written two dozen biographies of royal family members, under the name of Helen Cathcart. Requests before the second world war, for interviews with 'her' had been dealt with by his wife, or in other ways deflected, so that his nom de plume remained undisturbed. The image conveyed by this episode is of a layer of secretiveness that helps insulate members of the royal family - even when their lives are ostensibly being described - and in marked contrast to what had filled the press in recent years.

At the end of October some papers (e.g., the *Times*, 23 October, p. 1) ran pieces on a new portrait of the Queen "reflecting her advancing years ... chosen to appear on coins from next year". An item like this underlines one of the symbolic functions of the monarch which has been accepted as a sign of sovereignty for nearly two thousand years (coins in Roman Britain carried portraits of the then Roman rulers). This is also an underlying concern of those who worry about the advent of a European currency, whether the coins for use in Britain will depict the national sovereign. The story reinforces a "business as usual" association with the monarchy. At the other end of the spectrum another item in the *Times* (Internet section, p. 15) on 21 January 1998 reported that the Queen and her family used e-mail and the internet (and it is widely known that the Palace has a website), depicting the royal establishment as a modern monarchy[189].

While the notion of the British sovereign ruling by "Divine Right" has been obsolete for over three hundred years, there remains something **numinous about the royal entity** or connected with a non-everyday sphere of existence, which often crops up. Although Earl Spencer had said that his sister needed no royalty to achieve what she did, others did not agree. Hugo Young, in an anti monarchical daily echoed the opinion of Frank Prochaska (mentioned in the last Chapter) that:

> "... only accoutred with royal status did (Diana) gain access first to the people's fascination, then to their adoration, finally to their imagined love ... She was the best of the royals but what mattered, miles ahead of everything else was the royal. Only royalty reaches the millions and ties bouquets to railings up and down the land". (G, 8, 7).

This notion of royal numinosity was hinted at by Damian Thompson, soon after Diana's funeral:

> "... to a remarkable degree (Diana) personified this unpredictable public craving for the numinous, consulting a clairvoyant one day and lighting candles in a Greek Orthodox chapel the next". (T, 13, 22).

One way in which secular experience may be seen as different from something beyond it is through the realm of music. The editor of *Private Eye*, perhaps normally thought of as stirring baser emotions, reflected on Diana's funeral service:

> "... the one emotion which popular music can not convey is awe. Elton John may be sad in the face of death but Verdi, with the Dies Irae, scares the life out of you ... the Requiem ... is at odds with so much of the sentimentality of recent weeks". (S.Teleg.Magazine, 28 Sept, 7).

In Adam Gopnik's view (and he was writing from Paris after a hugely successful papal visit there):

---

[189] In addition to the Palace's website www.althorp-house.co.uk receives some 3000 visits a day accessing a guide to and history of Althorp House Diana's ancestral home, and to the exhibition dedicated to her. www.royal.gov.uk is an online magazine devoted to the royal family.

"The Princess's funeral was in many ways a triumph of the popular, intuitive version of the Old Religion ... Popular Catholicism - the appetite for a cult of saints and their symbols, for emotional ritual, for a charismatic center - remains one of the most potent forces left in Europe at the end of the century". (NY, 15 Sept, 36).

It took a historian Simon Schama, in the same journal to explain:

"... (when) the Princess touched people ... she was, perhaps without knowing it tapping one of the most ancient rituals of royal magic: thaumaturgy, or touching for the king's evil. Mediaeval kings, at their coronation ... would extend their hands to those suffering from ... scrofula. It was believed that ... they were able to absorb the evil of the disease into their own body and exorcise it ... But of course, it was for the Prince to exercise thaumaturgy, not his wife ... But even as Diana was becoming an adept at healing the wounds of the British body politic she was secretly doing hurt to her own". (NY, 15 Sept, 64).

Within the overall house of a monarchy whose members have somewhat more than normal human natures, princesses have two options in fairy tale and myth, in which they are either extremely bad or superlatively good. Several writers have identified Diana as a good princess (which tales usually connect with the youngest sister - just as Diana was, among three Spencer girls). A private letter writer Ben Couldry soon pointed out that:

"Now Princess Diana rests as the Lady of the Lake, will King Arthur return? Would any curmudgeon deny Prince William that right? This young man need not draw a blade from a rock: his composure gives evidence of an inner strength and fortitude". (DM, 17, 53).

Money is to be made from such perceptions however, and Roger Boyes of the *Times* Weekend magazine introduced a book by Austrian writers Elizabeth, Eva and Robert Menasse and their illustrator Gerhard Haderer, called *Diana, The Lost Fairy Tale Princess*. An extract runs:

"the Old Queen never much liked the Princess. Now she had to do all kinds of things to honour her, because otherwise the sad people would have chased her out of her palace". (Times Magazine, 22 Nov, 1).

These assimilations of Diana into a role of a good fairytale princess and even of the Queen into a predatory person may on the surface appear to hit at the royal family and at the monarchy. It could be otherwise, however, that identifying these ordinary humans with such larger-than-life roles reinforces perceptions of the "hyper-real" character of monarchy and possibly also reinforces the awe in which it is held.

How can it be determined, which way the influence (if any) of such writing would go? One way is to look at opinion poll results. Given the importance of the situation, it may be noteworthy that not many polls were commissioned and reported in the few weeks after Diana's death; this may be, partly, because many among the press decided they knew what the public felt, so did not have to spend money on finding out. Nevertheless, on the day after the funeral Peter Kellner, an extremely experienced pollster was poorly served by a sub-editor who headed his story "Two in three say the monarchy is damaged". This seems to represent the (whole) public's opinion but the text then explains:

> "A random (sic?) sample of 433 people *who had queued to sign the books* (emphasis introduced here) of condolence" ... gave the Queen an "approval rating" (on a 1 - 10 scale) of 5.2 and Prince Charles 5.0. 68 per cent thought the monarchy would be weakened (by the events of the mourning week) while 13 per cent actually thought it would be strengthened; 72 per cent thought Prince William should inherit the crown and only 21 per cent thought Prince Charles should do so. Kellner pointed out "it is possible that last week's mourners represent an atypical self-selecting group[190] ... who have long thought more highly of Diana than (of) the rest of the Royal Family". (O, 7, 14).

It is democratic and accords with the people's rhetoric of the time to suppose that individual members of the public are good judges of the aggregate public mood. We shall see that individual journalists may have been wrong and there are reasons to be cautious about relying on a lay judgement about how press coverage may affect opinions. Nevertheless, this first assessment of public opinion, described with some of the jargon of systematic procedure, seemed to indicate that feelings were running against the established monarchy. The impression was reinforced at the next weekend. The *Express On Sunday* reported an NOP poll (for *the Sunday Times*) undoubtedly with a properly sampled selection of the public, that included the following findings:

> "58% considered that the 'monarchy in its present form' would no longer exist in 30 years' time; 23 % believed the Queen should step down now; over half thought she should abdicate (seemingly at odds with the previous item); 42% thought the Queen should reign as long as she lived; over 40% felt William should succeed the Queen. Unsurprisingly, given the press coverage during the week, over 70% thought the Queen was 'out of touch'". (E on S, 14, 3).

The *Independent* on the same day referred on its front page to the NOP results and also to an ICM poll for the *Observer* in which "over 80 per cent thought the royal family had lost touch, while 53 per cent thought William should inherit - compared with 38 per cent who thought Prince Charles should do so". Detailed attention may suggest that these results are less negative for the monarchy than they had been made to seem (Derek Draper, in the *Spectator*, 12 Sept, p. 10 referred to the same poll noting that "support for the royal family" dipped below 50 per cent - to 48 per cent "for the first time"). Discrepancies in the proportions of those who think that Prince William should inherit the crown point not just to the differences between a true sample of the public, and one representing a crowd that has gathered for a particular purpose; they also may mean that in a labile situation interviewer effects might have some bearing on what people say. The

---

[190] This is why the headline should not have implied a finding about the general public; the Market Research Society has guidelines which discourage the reporting of its members' work in such ways.

question item "monarchy in its present form will no longer exist" is fraught with potential to mislead: if someone agrees with this it can mean that the monarchy will continue to exist -but in an amended form; or it can mean that the monarchy will no longer exist (in this - or in any other form). "Support for the royal family" is not the same as for the monarchy, so the ICM result, though certainly unfriendly, does not go as far as justifying some anti-monarchists' hopes. Steve Richards' assessment was that:

> "National moods are easy to misread. In the short term what will follow Diana's death is stylistic change to the monarchy, which may well have happened anyway. The closer ties now established between Downing Street and the palace will greatly benefit the monarchy". (NS, 12 Sept, 7).

The *Evening Standard* tried to sum up polling evidence towards the end of the next month, pointing out that:

> "a recent ICM poll said seven out of ten believe the Queen should 'consider retiring', one in three thought she should step aside in the next 2 - 3 years, while 44 per cent said the crown should pass straight to Prince William. A MORI poll a week after Diana's death showed that one in three believed the monarchy would last 50 years. (However) Gallup found huge support for a monarchy but (for) a more democratic and approachable institution". (ES, 25 Oct, 7).

We have seen that several voices amongst the press supposed and hoped that the republic's moment had come, or at least reminded readers that republicans were busy thinking about such a future and felt that there was support for such ideas amongst the public. Yet it would not be correct to refer amorphously to 'the press' (and certainly not to 'the media' - the BBC functions under a Royal Charter and could be thought to be required to reflect this aegis in its overall content and style) to describe its opinions; indeed after the emotional turmoil of the week of mourning many papers and writers declared themselves monarchist, and even believed that the leadership of Tony Blair supported the monarchy as well, even if it spoke of "modernisation".

The theme of **Blair supporting the monarchy** runs counter to that which believes that (New) Labour's elite are anti-monarchist. Whether this means that the Labour hierarchy is split on this most important constitutional matter, or whether one group of writers is as wrong as the other is right, can not be determined. What matters here is what effect journalists believe has been distilled out of the events of Princess Diana's death. Two weeks after the event a *Times* editorial wrote:

> "If (the Prime Minister) mirrors the public mood and presses for the Princesses kind of monarchy, he risks undermining the institution and inflaming republican opinion on his own benches". (T, 15, 17).

The *Guardian*'s Hugo Young had previously written:

"the royals have the right prime minister on hand. Tony Blair ... is a social and political conservative. No particle of him has even the smallest leaning towards anything so radical as the end of the monarchy". (G, 8, 7).

Robert Hardman writing in the *Spectator* seemed to agree with this:

"The man who had coined the phrase 'the People's Princess' ... leapt to the defence of the royal family against preposterous charges by 'the people' that the Windsors were somehow indifferent to the Princess's death ... Mr Blair's behind-the-scenes support was crucial in bolstering royal morale ... Despite some reports that the Queen was urging a private funeral, it was the Spencer family whose initial wishes ... were for a quiet affair. The Prince, with the Prime Minister's backing, persuaded them otherwise. Last week has taught Tony that the country is really deeply monarchist but not deeply Windsorist ...' explained a Blair lieutenant ...". (Sp, 15 Sept, 18).

Explicit support for the monarchy (rather than third-party reporting that the public seemed to support it) was offered by several journalists. Clive James, the Australian based in England wrote in the *New Yorker*:

"... the man who knew her most intimately of all, Prince Charles, he is a man as good and honest as any I have ever met, and I know him well enough to be sure that today he is on the Cross ... he was impeccably sensitive, courteous, and just plain thoughtful - a quality of his which is continually underestimated, and which will make him a great king when his turn comes, as come it must. (Diana's declaration, in her Panorama interview that Charles might never reign was the single biggest mistake she ever made)". (NY, 15 Sept, 50).

Adam Gopnik offered the same readers:

"Americans also seem to believe that the monarchy is a kind of mediaeval hangover, encumbered by pre-modern notions of decorum; the reality is that the British monarchy is ... a modern political institution ... a servant of Parliament, having been reinvented to perform a particular role. That role is ... to resist popular emotion ...". (NY, 15 Sept, 36).

A quite different analysis was offered by the Rev Dr Ian Bradley in a letter:

"The monarchy is not a democratic institution, but rather a divinely instituted symbol and mystery ... our kings and queens ... are ... accountable first and foremost to God and not to a fickle populace so easily manipulated and swayed by the mass media ... Many of the courtiers and commoners (at the Abbey service) were caught by the television cameras chattering, giggling or maintaining a sullen silence through the great hymns of the Christian faith. They might care to reflect ... God will save the Queen, not public opinion and certainly not the media". (T, 22, Nov, 15).

The Oxford academic Frank Prochaska wrote a piece more dispassionately under the title: "Why royalty thrives on republicanism"; while he did not explain this apparent paradox very clearly, he did suggest that:

"Popular rule requires symbols of legitimacy, never more so than during periods of reforming zeal ..." He quoted Lord Brougham writing in 1837 'far from dreading the policy which would strengthen the people's hands by confirming their liberties and extending their rights, we ought to pursue this course for the sake of the monarchy itself, which we shall thus better entitle to the people's affections, and render, because more beloved, more secure' and continued: Contemporary republicans have failed to notice just how much the monarchy has adapted already. Britain (has) become a 'republic with a hereditary president'". (T, 13 Oct, 20).

Steve Richards grappled with the same conundrum, in the *New Statesman:*

"The criticisms of the Windsors have actually reinforced the basic legitimacy of the royal family rather than undermined it ... In particular "the people" wanted to hear from the Queen. She was born to reign over us and "the people" wanted her to do some reigning. How pleased they were when members of the family appeared in London earlier than planned". (NS, 12 Sept, p. 7).

British journalists at the time seem to have delved less deeply in political theory, but there were possibly unexpected discoveries of personal emotions, such as one offered by Matthew Norman:

" how deeply moving the national anthem was to those of us who have scorned it as a tedious and irrelevant tune, who thought ourselves staunch republicans ... for reasons buried too deep to be displaced by logic ... the monarchy continues to exert a powerful symbolic hold over us all ...". (ES, 8, 13).

Less unexpectedly, the same newspaper's licensed rogue commentator A.N. Wilson offered:

"the whole essence of Lady Di's character was caprice, whereas the whole essence of a constitutional monarchy is continuity, sameness and what some would call dullness ... the republicans who think that the crowds are 'demanding' a new type of monarchy ... are simply using these events as an excuse to further their ends ...". (ES, 10, 11).

More bluntly, a letter writer in the *Times* put it:

"the death of Diana Princess of Wales was unbearably tragic, her funeral intensely moving. But I have also found the behavior of the British public and media unbearable. The response and its coverage were totally excessive, the style for the most part mawkish, vulgar, self-indulgent and hysterical. And the conclusion that we are at some kind of national turning point is presumptuous arrogance". (T, 11, 21).

The next day the *Times* ran a lengthy interview with Lady Mountbatten, expanding on the compassion and warmth, combined with self-control shown by leading members of the royal family. It may be the case that the popular press has a short memory; when the events of Princess Diana's death and burial recede, they are replaced by others which the papers need to present as being of equal impact and gravity, simply in order (as they appear to believe) to continue to sell as many copies. Thus the continuing symbolic service of the "senior royals" (the Queen, and Prince Charles) in the national interest, and of the Queen mother in the national esteem and affection (as when she recovered, early in 1998, from a broken hip) proceeds to reinforce those feelings and perceptions, laid down in history in which the monarchy is affirmed in British life. Events of this nature in late 1997 and early 1998 included the Queen's tour to Pakistan and India (in which she rose above the political squabbles in which the British foreign minister became involved), Prince Charles's tours to South Africa, Sri Lanka and Bhutan, the Queen and Duke of Edinburgh's golden jubilee of their marriage (on which occasion Prime Minister Blair described the Queen as "quite simply, the Best of British") and, to please the monarchy-modernisers, the appointment of a black Briton (the first ever) to the Prince's staff and an article, on the anguish of homelessness by the Prince in *The Big Issue*, the magazine sold by homeless vendors.

The aftermath in the press, then, of Princess Diana's death is thus richly varied; but though there are voices of republican dissatisfaction with the established system, and hopes for major change, most people with such opinions appear to have limited themselves to urgings towards reform rather than revolution. On the other hand, there are two kinds of support in view for the monarchy: One is a reflection on the trauma and its digestion by the press and the public - coming up with support for monarchist continuity; the other is a coincidental support arising from the conservative reporting of major events requiring symbolic national leadership.

As an endpiece to this process of conspicuous personal evaluation (by experts and professional writers) of the standing of the monarchy after Diana's death the *Times* reported (5 January 1998, p. 4) that The Palace "asks the people to point monarchy in right direction". The story referred to the commissioning by a think tank of focus groups conducted by the pollsters MORI. Such groups do not represent the whole of public opinion, however much they may be useful in deriving ideas about why feelings exist as they do. They should complement a representative and 'architectural' study of public feelings of the kind which we will examine in the next Chapter.

Chapter 8

WHAT THE PUBLIC FELT AFTER DIANA DIED: AN ARCHITECTURAL ACCOUNT?

Ian Jack was quoted in the previous chapter, reporting what he took to be a neglected strand of opinion:

"In September ... the public mood, as relayed and reinforced by the media became vindictive towards dissension ... Letters began to appear in a few newspapers which suggested another kind of community ... the people who were not quite sad enough. How many of these were there - were we? No reliable quantification can exist". (GWM, 27 Dec 18).

We can be more positive than that; one can take up questionnaires against a sea of problems and, by analysing, solve at least a few of them. For the last two chapters we have joined with the press in reporting feelings among the public in the remarkable first week of September, and what the various people amongst the press made of the patterns of all this experience. I say "feelings among the public" and not "what the public felt", for several strong reasons, connected with care over the impressions distilled from different means of knowing. In emotionally charged circumstances it is not certain that a better account will be achieved by "systematic" methods of detached and preferably representative questioning, or whether a truer account is delivered by immersion, as was practised by the journalists. Immersion runs the risk of a dominance of the personal over the public perspective and that the feelings of the journalist-observers, very few of whom are trained social anthropologists, will have biased their accounts. Attempted systematisation runs the risk of losing touch with authenticity. The best solution is probably to use both approaches. We have explored the first and now come to the second and quite different manner of enquiry

The survey now to be reported was devised in September and posted out and returned, largely in October. Over 400 replies were received, from throughout Great Britain. People were asked to reply to multiple choice questions about their actions, their perceptions, and feelings and they had space in which to (and many did) write further comments. The sample was not obtained by orthodox methods of opinion polling[191]; so the results must be presented, and studied, with care. We are not in a position unequivocally to assert "x per cent of the public felt this, or did that"; we are however quite close to that position, as the sample was modestly large, touched on all major segments of the population and showed relatively little internal differentiation in its profiles of response. This means that although there were more women in the sample (60%) than were needed to represent the population (51%) and far fewer people aged 65 and over (7%) compared with those in the full population (21%) this probably does not matter greatly, as the *profiles* of replies on important questions were not markedly different amongst women or men, or between younger and older people. Note, this statement concerns the profiles of replies - and what this means will become clearer presently.

The first purpose of the exercise was to come usefully close to representing the population at large, normatively; but the real intention was to go beyond that. This idea was to examine how behavior, perceptions and attitudes knitted together. This is like deducing the internal architectural plans of a building, of which the profile is what is seen from the outside. Again, what this means will become clearer as we go along; but for this purpose the sample, even in its unorthodox origins, is probably quite valid.

How Fast Did the News Spread?

The first item in the questionnaire tackled a matter that had first been noticed systematically by students of modern society at the time of the assassination of President Kennedy. The news spread like wildfire, modern means of communication by telephone and broadcasting to the fore. The current shock was of equal, some boasted of greater seismic strength, the means of communication over three decades more developed (portable telephones, more radio stations, 24 hour television) and so it might be expected that the news of Diana's death was diffused as quickly, if not more so than was the case with previous shocks. We have some observations from two other news traumas in this decade, with which to compare the speed of diffusion of the news about Diana's death[192].

---

[191] One segment of questionnaires was sent, in packs of five each, by students to their parents around the country, asking them to urge their friends and acquaintances to return completed forms in the envelopes provided. Other segments were obtained by asking friends, in Scotland and in Manchester, to distribute copies to acquaintances and to gather them for return. Yet other individiual respondents were found by appeals put out on radio and on the internet.

[192] See: Wober, J.M. (1995) The Tottering of Totems on TV. Some Implications Of The Diffusion Of News In Britain. *Communications*. 20. 1. 7-24.

Table 8.1: Speed of Diffusion of News of the Death of Princess Diana

	Diana's Death People Aged				Thatcher's Resignation*	Soviet Coup against Gorbachov**
	<=24	25-44	>=45	All	All	All
Number:	120	154	129	403	2860	2894
	%	%	%	%	%	%
Report hearing the news:						
pre: 6 am	8	9	16	11	37	36
7 - 8 am	17	21	23	21		
8 - 9 am	28	20	18	22	25	
9 - 10 am	16	15	10	14		
10 - 11 am	4	7	5	5		
11 - 12 am	4	4	1	3	15	16
12 - 2 pm	6	1	2	3		
2 - 4 pm	0	0	2	1	10	
4 - 6 pm	0	0	0	0	3	4
6 - midnight	0	0	1	1	0	7
after Sunday	1	2	1	1	0	6
Not sure, No reply					12	23

*the specified time slots here were: 9.45 - 10.45am, 10.45 - noon, noon - 3pm 3 - 6pm, 6 - 9pm, 9 - midnight all on Thursday, Friday, Saturday or later.

**the times slots here were 6-9am, 9am - noon, noon - 3pm, 3 - 6pm, 6 - 9pm, 9 - midnight all on Monday, Tuesday and later.

News of Margaret Thatcher's resignation came on a Monday morning just after 9.30; that of the Soviet coup came through in the UK at dawn. The questionnaire structure was not exactly the same in each case, but it is possible to make a reasonable comparison between the events. Essentially, in the case of Diana's death the whole sample report that they heard the news on the same day, over half of them by eight in the morning and ninety per cent by eleven in the morning. The first five hours saw 95 per cent of the sample aware of the news; in a similar span of time around 80 per cent of the population had heard of Mrs Thatcher's resignation. The differences are not huge, and may be influenced by the arrival of the news of Diana's death on a Sunday, when most people are at home. The Soviet coup also became known to a majority of the population (62 per cent) within nine hours; one may be entitled to say that that news of that event diffused recognisably more slowly in Great Britain, and less widely too, with over a fifth of the sample not answering definitively.

In brief, an event of major structural significance to the whole world, namely the Soviet coup, became known to the British population very rapidly, but not as quickly as an event of similar significance within the British polity, namely Prime Minister Thatcher's resignation. Princess Diana's death was in itself of little structural significance either to British or to world society - unless it was made to be so by the way in which the population was determined to experience it. For some, it was an event to shake the monarchy and in that regard of structural importance. If the monarchy does change, especially with reference to this event and the way in which it has been experienced - not necessarily by the people, but for the people by the press - then the event will turn out to have been of national, and ultimately of some international structural significance.

Though not shown in the Table, age appears to make some difference to the diffusion speed of news about Diana's death. Those aged 24 or under included 41 per cent who had heard the news by 8 am; in a middle bracket aged 25 to 44 50 per cent had heard the news by the same time while the oldest segment aged 46 and above contained 67 per cent who had already heard of the event by then. The likely explanation is that younger adults, more socially active at weekends were still in bed when some of their elders began to discover the news, and that older people tend to listen more to news-as-genre while younger people spend more time with music. On this day, however, all stations will have carried the news. It is important that the providers of broadcast and print news should be aware that with an event of this gravity they can take it that either directly through the mass message systems or in connection with them, the whole population knows about the bare facts within the first full day. Newscasters' job then has to turn to other aspects of the situation. An impressionistic recollection of the newscasts on the second day after Diana died is that they had indeed realised that there was nobody who had yet to be informed of the basic facts of the event, and had moved on to portraying events in a wider context.

SOURCES OF NEWS

Everyone in Britain is likely to have learned of the event, on Sunday 31 August. By what means did people get this news[193] - and how may these sources compare with those in the other two important events earlier in the decade?

---

[193]The question on this occasion was simply "from what source did you get the news" but coming immediately after the question "when did you first get the news" clearly focuses on the mode of discovery.

Table 8.2: Sources of Traumatic News Events

	Diana	Thatcher	Soviet Coup
Number	403	2860	2894
	%	%	%
Television	46	26	38
Radio	24	23	34
Newspapers	1	1	1
Word of mouth	33	39	11
Other	-	1	1
No reply	-	9	14

The patterns are clearly established in all these events, as regards the newspapers being only a minority source for breaking the news. The word of mouth source for news about Princess Diana was subdivided into 7 per cent hearing by telephone and 26 per cent by personal contact (most likely within the home). It is tempting, though possibly misleading to take these results to mean that television has been gaining on radio as a news source, in general. On this occasion television, as not one but two "media" (sight and sound) may have been switched on by the first household members awake and learning about the matter, some of whom may have heard it first on radio; but then others entering the room will have been presented with a set switched on.

BEHAVIORAL REACTIONS TO RECEIVING THE NEWS OF DIANA'S DEATH

Short term. What did people do when they got the news? Respondents could cite more than one action within a list on offer. The question was, for the news about Diana: "Which of these things, if any, did you **do in the 10 minutes immediately after** getting the news?". In the other two instances the time scale was less clearly specified, with "When you first heard about (...) did you ...?"

As will be seen, the present study split up the possible activities in a different pair of questions, so the figures above from the previous events should be read in connection with the next set.

Table 8.3: Initial Behavioral Reactions to Traumatic News Events

	Diana	Thatcher	Soviet Coup
Number	403	2860	2894
	%	%	%
Spoke to family/friends nearby	35	66	53
Felt sad		37	53
cried	26	-	-
Telephoned someone	10	9	2
Carried on viewing/listening	65	( )	( )
Listened to special music	3	( )	( )
Read something special	2	( )	( )
Felt pleased	( )	51	7
Listened to broadcasts/ read papers which mostly had the same feelings as you	( )	40	40
Found a TV ... straight away	( )	31	34
Found a radio ... straight away	( )	17	22
Got a paper with the news	( )	15	21
Spoke to strangers	( )	13	7

Longer term reactions In the new study respondents were asked what they did, amongst a range of options listed, in the week after getting the news. It will be useful to see whether replies differed amongst the different age groups in the sample.

Table 8.4: Longer Term Responses to Traumatic News Events

	People Aged			
	<=24	25-44	>=45	*ALL*
Number:	120	154	129	403
	%	%	%	%
Watched extra TV	72	79	74	75
Spoke to relations	64	66	60	63
Bought extra newspapers	38	34	40	37
Spoke to strangers	23	24	**39**	28
Signed a memorial book	**18**	30	30	26
Listened to extra radio	29	22	29	26
Placed flowers in a public place	18	18	14	16
Visited a place where the public gathered	**19**	14	11	14
Turned away from media news	**19**	14	10	11
Went to a religious service	11	9	16	12
Gave to charity	13	6	15	11
Wore a ribbon	13	7	10	10
Wrote and sent a memorial message	11	10	9	10
Wrote a message I did not send	7	5	6	6
Did something I regret	3	2	0	2

(particularly high, or low scores are shown in bold)

There are huge differences in the extent to which people reported carrying out these various kinds of behavior. In comparison with this major source of difference, age is barely if at all a discriminator in most of the kinds of behavior examined - another sign of reassurance in the efficacy of the sample as an indicator of the whole public's pattern of reactions. What one means by this is that giving to a charity, at around one in ten people is almost certainly, on a population scale going to be less than half as frequent as signing a memorial book, at around a quarter of the population. While hardly anyone had first learned of the news from a paper, nearly four in ten said they bought extra newspapers; this clearly exceeded - and in all three age groups - the proportion who reported turning to radio as a sounding board. As the figures in a previous chapter support, from a different source, three quarters of the sample here reported watching extra television.

A great deal of personal communication occurred, however. In hindsight the question on speaking to relatives is not very informative - unless one had further information on who had how many other people in the household - but well over a quarter saying they spoke to strangers is likely to be a fair indication of an opening up of discourse, beyond normal levels. This is one of two items - the other is signing a memorial book - in which the older segment included more people reporting that action[194]. If there has been a notion that the "Diana phenomenon" is one in which young people see and feel the world in a new way, the findings here that older people were more likely to speak to strangers and to have signed a memorial book suggest that at least these ways of joining in the occasion have been older rather than younger modes of action.

The number of people saying they had been to a religious service is not any more than would have been expected, given that to a later question a similar proportion said they do normally go to services. The other kinds of activity characteristic of mourners at a personal level, placing of flowers (reported by 16 per cent), signing a memorial book (one quarter) visiting a place where other people gathered (14 per cent) and wearing a ribbon (one in ten) were not reported by a majority section of the population, but nevertheless were carried out by very substantial minorities. Other than in signing the memorial books these participatory mourning activities were not really any more commonly reported by young, middle aged or older people.

---

[194]Statistical tests of the differences in proportions reporting these two actions have been calculated. In the case of speaking to strangers, Chi Sq = 7.69 which exceeds significance at the level of $p = 0.01$; in the case of signing a memorial book Chi Sq = 4.19 which is significant at a level of $0.05 < p > 0.01$.

ATTITUDES: THE MONARCHY

Without a doubt the major question underlying the engagement of the press in the last quarter of the year, and which was explored in this survey, was the matter of the public's attitudes to the monarchy. This questionnaire went about the task of tapping respondents' opinions in a contextualised way. What is meant by this is that while some opinion polls might present two or three attitude items about the monarchy either quite by themselves, or amongst a longer list of questions about completely different topics, this questionnaire presented twenty three items all connected with the experience of the nation after the death of Princess Diana, asking for respondents' levels of agreement or disagreement with each item. They had a seven point scale within which to make each reply and the ends of the scale were labelled strongly agree and strongly disagree; the mid point was labelled not sure/no opinion. The items dealt with attitudes towards the broadcasting, the blame for the accident, the leadership roles of "media", the prime minister and the monarchy, and to the durability of the monarchy itself.

Three items focussed on attitudes towards the monarchy and before we come to see how these take their place amongst the other attitudes and behavioral reactions measured, we will examine the results they evoked.

Table 8.5: Attitudes to the Future of the Monarchy

		N	Strongly Agree			Not Sure			Strongly Disagree
The	Y*	120 %	14	7	5	22	12	9	32
Monarchy	M*	154 %	18	8	10	15	3	8	38
should be	O*	129 %	13	2	4	17	3	5	55
ended, soon	All	403 %	15	6	7	18	6	8	41

* in this and subsequent Tables Y = 24 or less; M = 25-44; O = 45 or over years old.

To show a pro-monarchy attitude a respondent had to 'strongly disagree' with a proposition - a step that is sometimes regarded as more difficult than merely agreeing with some statement. Within this difficult context for the idea of monarchy, 21 per cent, one fifth, agreed to a swift end to it. Opposing them, 49 per cent or just around one half dismissed a swift end for the monarchy. A compact way of taking account both of those who oppose and others who support the proposition is to subtract the proportions agreeing from those disagreeing; this reveals that amongst the younger sector there remained a 20 per cent margin of those who stood for a monarchy, over those who opposed it; amongst the oldest sector there was a 45 per cent margin of those who preferred the monarchy, over and above those who opposed it. It may be asked whether this is a real difference between the two age groups, or might just be an outcome of a sample that is not huge, and not fully representative; the results have been put to a statistical test and the outcome is that the difference is indeed very significant - younger people were less (though still net) in favour of the monarchy[195]. The non-representativity of the sample does not undercut the reality of the difference in response between ages; this illustrates an 'architectural' aspect of the study, for which the sample works well. We may also infer that the population at large, which contains a greater proportion of old people than did the present sample, would be more in favor of the monarchy than was the sample.

Even with the current respondent sample there is a comfortable net support for the continuation of the monarchy. We know that there is a shortage of older members in the sample and that older people are more likely to support the monarchy. A fully representative sample would thus have been more supportive than the present group. As has been explained, the purpose for which this sample is more apt, than trying to represent the public fully accurately, is to establish the relative strengths of attitudes to items in comparison with each other, and that kind of analysis is to be provided, presently. Before we reach that, we may examine results on the other two 'monarchy' items:

Table 8.6: Predictions of the Longevity of the Monarchy

		N	Strongly Agree			Not Sure			Strongly Disagree
The Monarchy is	Y	120 %	25	24	20	21	2	2	7
likely to continue	M	154 %	31	20	15	18	5	3	10
for many years to	O	129 %	51	10	8	23	4	0	4
come	All	403 %	36	18	14	20	4	2	7

While 49 per cent opposed the removal of the monarchy, 54 per cent considered that it will likely continue. The proportions thinking it would likely continue were clearly much greater among the older segment (a 57 per cent 'plurality' of those who agree, over those who disagree) than among the younger segment (a 40 per cent plurality). As explained in the footnote, this is a significant difference. As with the first item, the population at large would be yet more expecting the monarchy to continue. While the monarchy may be tolerated, however reluctantly, by those who might prefer it to go, some of these "evolutionary anti-monarchists", especially in the wake of the affection for Princess Diana discussed the notion that the inheritance might pass directly to Prince William, for some reason omitting a King Charles[196]. What was this sample's response to this notion?

---

[195]Calculations of Student's t show a value for this first item of $t = 2.44$ (the means were 4.64 among the young and 5.31 among the older groups) which has a probability level of $p<0.02$; the difference of means in the second item (young: 2.82, old: 2.34) has a t value of 2.29 for which $p<0.05$; and for the third item (young: 4.03, old: 3.68) $t = 1.16$ for which $p>0.10$.

[196]We may infer the reason is, to punish Charles for his role in the breakdown of his marriage and

Table 8.7: Attitudes towards Prince Charles's Inheritance

		N	Strongly Agree			Not Sure			Strongly Disagree
Prince	Y	120 %	22	13	11	13	4	13	24
Charles	M	154 %	23	11	6	20	5	10	26
should reign	O	129 %	34	9	4	20	4	1	29
after QE II	All	403 %	26	11	7	18	4	8	26

The youngest sector were by a tiny margin less in favour of Charles' succession (35 per cent) than opposed to it (37 per cent); the oldest sector were more recognisably in favour of Charles' succession (43 per cent) than against it (30 per cent) and though this difference is statistically significant, and of socio-political importance inasmuch as the coming generation did not for the time being show support for the monarch designated by the system, it will be borne in mind that the population at large contains many more older people than did the study sample. It is a problem that has cropped up in analyses of attitudes across generations in more than one sphere, but two different possibilities present themselves: one is that we are looking at a true cultural shift and the younger people will carry their current attitude with them as they age, changing the overall pattern of opinion. The other possibility is that people will change their attitude as they age and the culture will remain not greatly altered. An analysis elsewhere of survey results on religious belief, and one reported in Chapter 5, on desirability of the monarchy, suggest that the second option is closer to what will happen, and it remains to be judged how the climate of wider opinion may bear upon the current attitudes amongst younger adults.

ATTITUDES: THEIR STRUCTURE AND LEVELS

If this heading seems difficult to understand by itself, its explanation should become clearer by reading what follows. The items about the monarchy dealt with above are only three among a list of twenty three statements, to each of which people showed their levels of agreement or disagreement. We would intuitively expect that somebody who believes Prince Charles should inherit the monarchy, will also disagree that the monarchy should be ended; in technical terms we would expect a large, but negative

---

to look to a (half) Spencer on the throne instead of a full Windsor. The implied genetic algebra of those who take to William as a Spencer (his swimming prowess is greeted in the press as acquired from his mother rather than from both parents) should recognise that Charles is by inheritance a quarter a Bowes Lyon. Virtually nothing in the public discourse identifies him thus, instead labelling him as though he is wholly 'Windsor' (though some add in the Battenberg component, thus in their eyes justifying the atavistically derogatory epithet 'Graeco-German').

correlation between scores given on these two items, as worded. People who disagree that Charles should inherit are likely, in common sense, to agree that the monarchy should be ended. These two items may then turn out to be opposite sides of the same coin, or closely linked in such a way that we could reasonably predict a person's attitude on one by knowing their answer on the other item.

It is quite possible that all twenty three items are really related ways of expressing opinions on a central core concept of some kind (say, monarchism as an alternative to republicanism). If that was the case there should be significant correlations between each and every one of all twenty three attitude statements. Another possibility is that the items fall into groups within each of which there is some recognisable common meaning; in that case, the correlations in amongst replies to items within each group would be high, while the correlations between replies to items from separate groups should be much smaller, or even insignificant. The question now is, how in fact did all the patterns of agreement and disagreement with the twenty three statements turn out?[197]

The answer is that the calculations showed there was not just the one factor binding each of the items into a single conceptual family. There were six readily recognisable factors. We can now look at which of the items belonged to which factors, and begin to map out the architecture or underlying plan of the **attitude structure** amongst the public. We will also see scores that show the strength of support within each of three age groups, to each item. It is vital to bear in mind that the scoring system gives a mark of 1 for strongly agree through 4 for not sure/no opinion along to 7 for strongly disagree.

The first factor that emerged clearly expresses disapproval with broadcasting during the mourning week.

The figures in the first column are all 44 or over, showing that people who agree to any one of these items are likely to agree with each of the other items; this applies most strongly for those three items with loadings of over 80, and least strongly for the other two items. Nevertheless, the extent to which these items cling together and do not ambiguously share common fraternity with items in other groups is shown by the low average loadings, in the second column, on the other five factors.

---

[197]The procedure for calculating the correlations between every single pairing of each of twenty three items, to confirm whether there is one single underlying conceptual structure, or more than one, is called Factor Analysis. In particular, the SPSS computer package calculates a "Varimax Rotated" factor analysis within which items have 'loadings' (which can have values anywhere from -.99 to +.99) on one or more factors. The loading for an item on a factor shows the analyst whether that item is thought of and responded to in a predictably similar way to other items within its family or factor, while having little or no bearing on how responses are structured in other attitude groups or factors.

Table 8.8: Attitudes towards Broadcasting during Princess Diana's Mourning

	Loading of item on this factor	Average loading on other factors	Extent of Agreement among:		
			Young	Medium	Old
In the week before the funeral, there was too much coverage, overall	82	09	3.6	3.7	3.6
BBC TV 1 and 2 should have taken it in turns, more, to carry on with their normal, published programmes	90	06	3.2	3.2	3.1
Satellite & Cable channels did well	44	11	3.6	3.7	3.9
Channels 3 and 4 should have taken it in turns, more, to show their normal published programmes	91	05	3.2	3.2	3.2
TV coverage had too much of celebrity comment and opinion, not enough of everyday people's contributions	51	07	4.1	4.1	3.8

There is no outstanding tendency for the youngest subgroup to have a different opinion from the oldest subgroup (with the mid-aged group in between as to the **levels** of opinion); respondents regardless of age most clearly agreed that there should have been more opportunity to see normal programming; then, there was recognisable affirmation that there had been too much coverage and (though there were more 'don't knows' on this item) that satellite and cable channels had done well. Younger respondents were perhaps more likely to agree with this idea, than were older people, whose replies clustered closer to an opt-out position. The age-pattern was reversed in the case of the perception of 'celebrity loading' - older people were more likely to agree that this had happened, younger people less likely to agree with this statement; but still, those who thought there was too much celebrity representation were likely also to agree with each of the other four items in the list.

It may be considered acceptable to label this group of items, or factor, *TV Over The Top* or TVOTT for brevity. We will be examining, later on, how the attitudes on this collectivity may have related, or not, with other measures - such as what we know about how people behaved, or their patterns of newspaper readership, or their sex, age, income or religious attendance.

A small factor, consisting of two items, brings together perceptions of blame. Each of ten role-players in the story were asked about, preceded by the phrase: "Some part, at least, of the blame for the tragic car accident should be shared by: (and then each possible actor was listed)", to what extent respondents agreed or disagreed in each case.

Table 8.9: Perception of Shared Responsibility for the Crash: Victims

	Loading of item on this factor	Average loading on other factors	Extent of Agreement among:		
			Young	Medium	Old
Princess Diana herself. for taking the risks of the 'jet set' lifestyle	82	10	5.1	4.8	4.6
Dodi Fayed, for involving Diana in the 'jet set' lifestyle	79	08	5.4	5.1	4.7

The few people who thought Diana had some responsibility for the event, also tended to say that Dodi Fayed was in part responsible; whatever people thought about the responsibilities of these two had relatively little to do with their patterns of opinion on the other factors (such as TVOTT) and the other attitude clusters which will be described next. It is worth noticing that people of each age group refuted these statements (full refutation would earn a score of 7.0); however younger people refuted these two statements more so than did older people. We can call this factor *Blame Victims* or BV in abbreviation.

Another blame-perception factor is more complex:

Table 8.10: Perceptions of Blame: Collective Responsibility

	Loading of item on this factor	Average loading on other factors	Extent of Agreement among:		
(to blame are):			Young	Medium	Old
the paparazzi behind the car	63	16	2.0	1.9	1.9
newspaper editors, who buy pictures taken by paparazzi	81	04	2.7	2.3	2.2
readers of papers with paparazzi photos	77	10	3.4	3.3	3.0
me, for following any such coverage	58	18	4.6	4.1	4.5
the Royal Family, for disturbing Diana	52	17	4.4	4.0	4.0

There seems to be a more complex concept here that we can call *Collective Blame* or abbreviate to COLBLAME. There is a clear implication that the circle of behavior connecting the paparazzi with oglers of press photographs is identified as a perceived structure. The levels at which people respond to each of these items are, however, very different. There is strong agreement (2.0 is not far from 1.0 which would indicate strong agreement from every respondent) that the paparazzi bear some blame; editors are next, followed by 'readers', while ones own self is actually rejected, on average, within each of the young and old age groups as bearing blame. The presence of these items, differing in level of average response, in the same factor is explained by the fact that (s)he who takes a stronger agreement on any one of these items also takes a stronger agreement on each of the others.

What, then, is the royal family doing within this factor of collective blame? What this must imply, surely, is that there is some identification between respondents themselves, and each of the parties, including the royal family, in the larger scheme of pressures that brought about Diana's death. It is important to note that the level of response on this item about the royal family is at a point of equivocality (some say yes, a similar number say no) amongst middle and older age groups, but it was the youngest group who more clearly rejected the notion that the royal family shared responsibility, just as the young age group more clearly rejected the notion that they themselves might share responsibility ("not me, not the royal family").

This conjunction in blame-perception is probably one of the least expected features of the whole structure of attitude and perception factors. Much of the press coverage set up a disjunction between the royal family, portrayed as separated cold and remote, and the people, vividly portrayed as assembled in crowds, warm and present. The outcome here does little to validate that picture and indeed refutes it in a subtle analysis of the pattern of connections between responses. There is a third set of bearers of blame; this consists of three parties all of whom were part of the Ritz team.

Table 8.11: Perceptions of Blame: The Ritz Group

(to blame are):	Loading of item on this factor	Average loading on other factors	Extent of Agreement among:		
			Young	Medium	Old
the driver of the car	68	08	2.0	2.1	1.9
the bodyguard in the car	70	08	5.0	4.5	5.0
the management of the Ritz, in whose car the accident occurred	64	10	4.1	3.9	3.2

There are clearly different levels at which blame is attached to the three parties in the Ritz team. People generally rejected the idea that the bodyguard was responsible for the accident; those, however, who rejected this less firmly tended to point for blame at the driver, who it was widely agreed was responsible for the accident. He shares the position of principal perceived agent of the mishap, with the paparazzi. As to the management of the Ritz, younger respondents as a group were uncertain about its responsibility but older people did identify the hotel management as culpable.

The negative elements in the questionnaire have now been dealt with; they show how perceptions coalesced into four recognisable groups of items, revealing a mild degree of dissatisfaction with excessive television coverage, and identification of blame for the accident to various groups of actors. This leaves all the remaining items expressing positive features of the situation, which the same process of calculation shows are grouped into two 'factors'. One factor assembles role players who have been considered to have helped the nation to make something positive out of reaction to the tragedy (PULLING TOGETHER).

Table 8.12: Perceptions of Contributors to Positive Reaction

	Loading of item on this factor	Average loading on other factors	Extent of Agreement among:		
			Young	Medium	Old
Prime Minister	58	10	3.5	3.3	3.2
Broadcasters	84	05	3.5	3.6	3.1
The Royal Family	68	11	3.8	4.0	3.7
The Press	80	04	4.1	3.9	3.5

Having found an earlier factor of attitude items describing television coverage as excessive in amount, we now see that not only was that not very heavily agreed with, but in this new grouping of thoughts about a positive contribution it was mildly agreed that broadcasters did help the nation to some positive resolution. In this, broadcasters came second to the Prime Minister, and ahead of the royal family. Least recognised as helping the nation to a positive resolution was the press. Two points about this last result that need to be underlined include that the press is probably an over-inclusive category; had the questionnaire been re-run it might well have been of interest to explore the possibility of a favourable distinction in respondents' minds between "the paper(s) I read" and "other newspapers". The same distinction does not arise so clearly as regards broadcasters, since viewing habits are generally less selective. A second result that might not have been expected is that it was older respondents who were slightly more positive about the role of the press, while younger respondents included a greater proportion who thought poorly about the press.

The final factor contains four items, all concerning the monarchy and can be labelled MONARCHISM.

Table 8.13: A Group of Related Statements on Monarchism

	Loading of item on this factor	Average loading on other factors	Extent of Agreement among:		
			Young	Medium	Old
The monarchy should be ended, soon	-76*	08	4.6 (2.4)	4.5 (2.5)	5.3 (1.7)*
The royal family should be enabled to keep their personal feelings private	49	10	2.3	2.4	2.3
The monarchy is likely to continue for many years to come	74	08	2.8	3.0	2.3
Prince Charles should reign, after Queen Elizabeth II	60	12	4.0	4.1	3.7

*the item is 'negatively' worded; so the extent to which respondents *disagree* with the idea indicates (by subtracting the score from 7.0) how much they would likely *agree* with the same idea worded in the opposite direction (... should continue)

It is noteworthy that the respondents resisted the leading question suggesting that the monarchy should be ended; those who gave strongest disagreement with the sentence as worded were also likely to want privacy protected, to believe that the monarchy is likely to continue for many years, and even to agree that Prince Charles should inherit the crown (though this item was not, overall, clearly supported). In three items the older respondents were more monarchist than the younger ones, leaving the item on privacy, which younger people upheld as strongly as did their older counterparts. A summary of the results on these six attitude and perception factors may be helpful:

Table 8.14: Support for Each of Six Attitude Factors, by Respondents' Age

		Extent of Agreement among:		
		Young	Medium	Old
	COLBLAME	3.4	3.1	3.1
"Negative"	TVOTT	3.5	3.6	3.5
perceptions	BLAME RITZ	3.7	3.5	3.4
	BLAME VICTIMS	5.2	4.9	4.6
"Positive"	MONARCHISM	2.9	3.0	2.5
perceptions	PULLING TOGETHER	3.7	3.7	3.4

If it is remembered that a reply of "strongly agree" from everyone would produce a mark of 1.0 and "strongly disagree" from all would yield a 7.0, with 4.0 being the mid-point indicating uncertainty we can see that people were very likely to agree with the positive-meaning ideas of support for the monarchy, and that the public actors of the

Prime Minister, Press, Broadcasters and royal family helped the nation "make something positive out of reaction to the tragedy". The levels of agreement with the items in the more negatively toned factors were similar to or less than for the positively flavoured propositions. It is necessary to bear in mind that this survey has not been organised so as to accurately represent the levels of the views of the nation; however, the comparisons between people of different ages are likely to be valid. Where there are no effective differences between age groups, it is increasingly likely that the obtained results are a fair representation of those of the nation at large.

CONNECTIONS BETWEEN ATTITUDES, PERSONAL BACKGROUND AND BEHAVIOR

We have used age as an aspect of respondents' culture, to explore whether it relates with attitudes. If the overall national culture is changing, then one would expect younger people to have different attitudes from their elders, and secondly, for these newer attitudes to be enduring so that when a younger generation changes it takes its attitudes with it into middle and later age. This is not necessarily going to be true of many attitudes, as people may shed the perspectives of youth and find that as they age, so do their attitudes. As we have seen, however, age has not pointed to major differences of opinion on many of the measures we have taken. A few items revealed differences: younger people were more likely to reject the notion firmly that Dodi Fayed had any blame for the accident, than were older people; younger people were somewhat less firm in their agreement that the monarchy was likely to continue for many years, than were older people.

Age is not the only personal characteristic that may be a key to attitude differences; sex, or level of income may relate with outlooks, as may the practice - or absence - of religious observance[198]. People also replied to a question on whether they read a daily paper or a Sunday one. Only 268 replied that they read a daily and only 169 said they read a Sunday; they also said which paper they generally read, and this enabled us to code whether their reading was of papers taking a monarchist position, or lending themselves to republican opinions, or which were not conspicuously committed to one side or the other[199]. Equipped with these scores for each of the respondents we can now explore questions of this kind:

---

[198]Respondents indicated whether, in any normal ten-week period how many religious services they went to; replies were: none at all: 77%; one: 7%; two: 3%; three: 2%; four: less than half a per cent and five or more: 10%. The sample suggests the population is polarised as between a majority of around three quarters who basically do not go to services, ten per cent who go quite frequently and about 12 per cent who go occasionally or sometimes. Marks were given each person to show their frequency of religious attendance - 1 for the minimum and 6 for the maximum. These 'scores' were thus available for comparison with other measures.

[199]On a basis of the analyses reported in the previous chapters, a 1 score for a monarchist position was accorded to the *Telegraph, Sunday Telegraph,* and daily *Times*; a 3 score for a more

- Are people who are more monarchist more likely to be found amongst women than men?
- Are monarchists more likely older, of higher income groups?
- Are monarchists more likely to be religiously observant, and readers of a monarchist-supporting press?

If such connections exist, we would find *positive correlations* between the measure of this attitude. and these six other measures. If no systematic connections exist, we would not find any significant correlations between the pairs of measures.

This gives us six questions, involving the possible connections between the attitude to the factor of monarchism, and each of six measures of personal attributes. But there are six similar questions for the attitude measure of COLBLAME, and another six with PULL TOGETHER and overall, thirty six such questions examining the pairing of each of the six attitude and six other personal measures. The simplest and most efficient way to examine these thirty six questions is to perform appropriate statistical calculations[200], and to show where there was evidence for measures being related together, symbolically, as follows:

Table 8.15: Connections between Attitudes and Other Personal Attributes

	Sex	Age	Income	Religion	D. Press	S Press
TVOTT						
COLBLAME			**			
PULLING TOGETHER	**					
MONARCHISM		*	*		*	*
BLAME VICTIM	*	**				
BLAME RITZ	*					**

* shows a distinct connection between two measures
**shows a very distinct connection between two measures

---

republican position was accorded to the *Sun, Guardian, Independent, Sunday Times, Observer, People* and *Independent on Sunday*; other papers, daily and Sunday, were each accorded a score of 2. These press-reading scores were therefore also available for comparison with other measures.

[200] Correlation coefficients were calculated for the matrix of thirty six comparisons; ten of these results were significant at levels that would not be expected to arise by chance; these significant results included COLBLAME x Income: $r=.13$, $N=403$, $p<.01$; PULLTOGETHER x Sex: $r=-.16$, $N=403$, $p<.01$; MONARCHISM x Age: $r=-.10$, $N=403$, $p<.05$; x Income: $r=-.11$, $N=403$, $p<.05$; x Daily Press: $r=.15$, $N=268$, $p<.05$; x Sunday Press: $r=.15$, $N=169$, $p<.05$; BLAME VICTIM x Sex: $r=.11$, $N=403$, $p<.05$; x Age: $r=-.13$, $N=403$, $p<.01$; BLAME VICTIM x Sex: $r=.10$, $N=403$, $p<.05$; x Sunday Press: $r=-.18$, $N=169$, $p<.01$.

This diagram shows which attitude and other measures were indeed connected, and to what extent. It does not show in which *direction* these significant links existed. These important features will now be explained.

Those who were more inclined to acknowledge a collective blame tended to be people with lower incomes. Those who were more likely to agree that the leadership pulled together to make something positive from the tragedy were more likely to be women. People who agreed more firmly with monarchism tended to be older, and with higher incomes; they also tended to report reading both daily papers, and Sunday papers that we can describe as more monarchist. Those who tended to accept the notion that one may blame the victims were more likely male than female, and more likely to be older respondents; and finally those who were more likely to recognise some blame in the Ritz camp were more likely to be male, and to report reading the more republican Sunday newspapers. The notion that television coverage was more than required was not correlated with any of the six personal measures - this means that a similar support for this attitude pattern was found among men and women, those of any age, income or frequency of attending religious services and regardless of which papers they said they read.

How does all this evidence help us?

On April 17th the *Times* made a front page headline out of an article by a Professor O'Hear in which he was quoted as saying that the example of Princess Diana induced people to "elevate feeling above reason"; the editors of the book in which the article appeared were said to condemn Diana herself for "elevating feeling, image and spontaneity over reason and restraint". The newspaper continued that "the essays depict a morally bankrupt society in which the old fashioned values of duty and self-reliance have been replaced by a decadent and debilitating sentimentalism". These articles were discussed in other newspapers and on the radio. Our evidence helps to judge whether these allegations are to any extent true.

The survey shows clearly that not all people think and feel alike. There are distinct signs of a continuing support for restraint in certain important matters. We have seen, for example, that the concept of monarchism was still, even among the young, supported by a comfortable majority and that the notion that the royal family should be enabled to keep their personal feelings private was strongly supported. This does not indicate that the society was polarised into a majority monarchist camp and that the surge of sympathetic activity did not occur or was false. Over a quarter of the sample reported that they cried on hearing the news of Diana's death. Over a quarter of the sample reported signing a memorial book and around one in six said they placed flowers in a public place. One in ten wrote and sent a memorial message and another one in twenty wrote a message which they did not send. Over one in ten went to a religious service, but the indications are that just this number reported in any case that they often attend services, so that no particular 'new' attendance at services is likely to have arisen.

A few months after Diana's death British military forces could have been mobilised to bomb Iraq, and a poll at that time indicated that over half the public would have supported such action. This is not a sign of a sudden mellowing or sentimentalisation of society. The *Times* of April 15th, 1998 reported an unusual accident at an amusement park in which sixteen "thrill seekers were trapped for almost an hour in the freezing cold ... about 70 ft. up in the air ... overhanging a vertiginous drop into a 'black hole' obscured by clouds of mist". What was the reaction to this potentially hysteria-inducing threat? "Stephen Barber, the ... manager ... said 'There wasn't a panic ... none of them were in shock and they were given a complimentary cup of tea before leaving the park'". Certainly, there are occasions in Britain of rampant exhibitionist hooliganism, for example at football matches[201] but the anecdotal news evidence just cited adds colour to the survey indications that in substantial sectors of society a reasoned restraint to potentially inflammatory stimuli is still very much in evidence.

The ratings of a newspaper's position vis a vis the monarchy did not relate significantly with each of five attitude complexes - but they did relate with personal attitudes to the monarchy. Is this a case of influence? Single correlations are usually taken as too ambiguous to interpret: they may either mean that people with certain predilections choose to read certain newspapers, or that positions taken in the newspapers that people read slowly begin to influence the attitudes that people have. The first kind of interpretation - selective choice of message system use - does without the need to acknowledge that "media have effects"; the second kind of interpretation, accepting effects is vigorously rejected in one controversial realm, that violent images may induce violent behavior, with the general assertion that simple correlations can not resolve the problem of direction of causality. There is however a third model - that of assortment and reinforcement. In this, people who prefer a certain point of view, be it monarchist or the opposite, move towards reading certain newspapers and there, their attitudes are continuously reinforced by what they find to read there. This seems more likely to be what is happening.

There are reasons why a society's culture may have a considerable degree of inertia and reluctance to radical change, even in the turmoil of stirring events. Some psychologists assert that human personality is approximately half genetically determined, and others add that the formative experiences of childhood lay further foundations for the structures of personality attributes such as extroversion and neuroticism (which underlie the 'Diana syndrome' of 'feeling, image and spontaneity over reason' attributed by the *Times* to Professor O'Hear). Thus the 'architecture' of the personality-range within a society establishes something we may liken to a built environment of houses in a town. These may then experience the damage of a severe storm or an organised refurbishment with new paint and landscaping - but the underlying structure remains in existence, recognisable and continuing to exert a strong influence on how people live and what they do. A storm like the event of Diana Princess of Wales' death can thus seem, or even be made to seem by the media as having radically changed society by changing the

---

[201] The case of Eric Cantona leaping over a barrier to kick an abusive patron attracted a huge amount of comment - but initial appeals to repatriate him or exact other large punishments were smoothed down into a milder sentence of community service.

individuals of which society is composed; but this semblance is likely to turn out to have been much of an illusion. The signs are that British society, notwithstanding the political efforts to put about a post Diana-shaped cool Britannia is quite resilient and that support for monarchism and for restraint, especially over the value of privacy, remain marked features of that society.

Chapter 9

MESSAGE SYSTEMS, MONARCHY AND THE PUBLIC: A "MODEL"

It should help, to put a great deal of information into tidy and systematic order, to set up a model, or plan of the ways in which the three entities we are concerned with, interact. The simplest such model is to set up a triangle at one apex of which we place Monarchy, at the next Message Systems and at the third, the Public. The sides of the triangle give us connections between these three entities or actors. We can ask several questions about the nature of these connections and also make progress in answering these questions. A fourth and important entity we should also put on the map can be called Law, in the centre of the triangle. A line can be taken from each apex to the centre; thus the Monarchy and Law may have connections - which we can and should study, and so do the Public and the Message Systems each have contact with the legal entity.

The discussion will be primarily in terms of the British monarchy and overall society, but some allusions will be made for comparison with other monarchies or nations. One can examine many aspects of the nature of connections between the actors on the model, but for convenience I have decided to concentrate on four such features. The first is Information Flow, the second Influence (including power and authority), the third is Cohesion (including constancy and change) and finally I will look at Payoff - or benefits, of a connection either to the Self, or to Others on the model. The discussion can look back to material in the previous chapters but can also examine more recent information. Hopefully, this systematic approach will help to get a better understanding of the avalanche of discourse - and events - concerning the monarchy which continues to inundate not only the British system but which is also very prominent in other nations.

MONARCHY AND PUBLIC - INFORMATION FLOW

Does the (British) monarchy itself provide the public with information (aside from what the message systems want to distribute)? It certainly does, in a variety of ways. One way is **symbolic**. By its mere existence a monarchy 'speaks' to its public of the history of its constituency - the state. There will often be legends (or indeed true stories) of the foundation of the state and of its coherence under a supreme leadership. Earlier chapters have pointed to examples of such stories of 'scripts' (as it is fashionable to term them, in current social science) which set out why a nation has a valid separate existence.

It may be asked, if this is a book about "media" carrying messages between parties why we are going to consider direct flows between the monarchy and the public? The answer is that I have considered it better to think of the idea of "medium" to refer to the nature of the gap between sender and receiver, in particular with regard to the sense organs involved. So light is a medium and engages the eye, and when one sees someone or something a meaning can be generated from that vision; that is an example of information flowing in the visual medium. We do not need to consider the case of press and broadcasting yet, and they are thought of here as message systems - some of which do indeed use the visual medium and others sound, some both. Such mass message systems can not readily use touch as a medium, but direct encounters do give scope for impressions to be put across by touch. Likewise, mass message systems have not (yet) learned in any sophisticated way to use the medium of smell[202] but direct encounters do involve transmission of meanings by smell, even if the coding of meanings in this medium is not particularly well controlled or understood. Odor has been part of a set of meanings relating monarch and people; for example in the time of Elizabeth I of England her court often based itself in the estate of some noble, but their lack of toilet facilities meant that the atmosphere grew so nauseous indoors that the ensemble packed up and moved on after a while (leaving the aggrieved noble's servants to clear up, and his kitchen budget some chance to recover).

In some cases a monarchy symbolises to a public its continuing and future identity; the case has been discussed of Britain's King George VI and Queen Elizabeth who, during World War II remained in London to share the life of the population under bombing. Quite apart from anything they may have explicitly said it seems to have been the active presence of the symbol that was taken to mean a support for national stamina and a will to win. Whether a presidential leadership could have had a similar symbolic strength is an open question, but one reason which made this monarchic symbol important is likely to have been the depth in history which is brought to bear on the present. Presidential leadership to some extent symbolises the degree of support it had at the last election (or coup), and takes the risk of rejection at the next election, while it is a constitution which embodies a history of a republican nation. It is less possible for an abstract constitution than it is for a monarchy symbolised in a person either visibly to endure life in a capital under bombardment, or to retreat to a place of safety.

Another example of monarchy symbolising the historic identity of the nation is seen in Japan. The American victors of World War II in the East had the option of removing the Emperor of Japan or even of trying and executing him as a war criminal; instead,

---

[202] It may be argued that tear gas used in crowd control is an example where smell carries a message; but the articulation in this medium is crude.

they focused on the civil leadership (even though the Prime Minister was a general) as responsible for the catastrophe; and the Emperor (who may more precisely be regarded as a high priest than as a monarch) remained in his position. An example where a republican polity actually uses its shallowness in a positive way is in France, where after one upheaval or another the state moves from designating itself as a Third Republic to a Fourth Republic (and so on) precisely to shake off any encumbrance that a previous identity is felt to have had.

It has been said (leading from observation of the British monarchy - but obviously applying to that in other states as well) that a royal wedding is "the brilliant edition of a universal fact". A recent Danish royal wedding is an intriguing example. Louise Phillips[203] reports that the proceedings involved drives in gilded carriages - the fairy tale staging - with a banquet and a ball. The Prince Joachim was marrying Alexandra Manley a young woman with one Chinese grandparent, but who, though her mother tongue was not Danish had taken the trouble to learn the language.

Denmark's two main TV channels ran extensive coverage of these events, which were watched (indirectly) by nearly the whole population. Both channels constructed ingenious programming to promote feelings of involvement. TV2 set up a panel of experts, dressed in gala clothes, sitting at tables resembling those at the actual wedding banquet and eating a meal consisting of three of the four courses on the official menu; these experts provided discussion of the ongoing broadcast, and fielded questions from telephoners-in. Phillips emphasises that the Danish population evidently considers itself as a (giant) family, and immigrants who wish truly to belong and be fully accepted in this community learn to speak Danish - as Alexandra did and demonstrated. DR1 showed archive film of previous royal celebrations such as the silver wedding of the Queen and Prince Henrik. Phillips writes that Danish television did what it could to convey to viewers that they were in the 'front row' and present (unlike any of the actual participants and crowds lining routes) at all phases and places of the proceedings. As with BBC broadcasts of such events presentational devices promote intimacy, including narrators keeping themselves off screen and speaking little and quietly.

Denmark's royal wedding maximised real personal interactions, including the couple meeting officials at the town hall, and the family going on several drives to see and be seen by the public. The mass message systems behaved in as personal a way as possible and the whole event evoked a trust in the couple's cohesion and a fairy tale feeling (not far beneath the surface in the country of Hans Andersen). A contrast was realised between this Danish wedding and that of Prince Charles and Diana Spencer (though that had been much more widely televised and dramatised as a fairy tale in the making). That may be why, when that marriage failed and the spell was not just broken, but seemingly trampled in the dirt, the disappointment and rejection was all the more widespread and more deeply felt. A royal wedding then offers information to the public about marriage as a desirable institution, even without the royal family actually saying so in so many

---

[203] Phillips, L. (1999) Media discourse and the Danish monarchy: reconciling egalitarianisn and royalism. *Media, Culture & Society*, 21, 221-245.

words. Presidential marriages seldom occur in office and even weddings of presidents'
sons and daughters do not have the same weight as do royal ones, one reason being that
monarchy is usually hereditary while presidential offspring are unlikely to have similarly
important public lives.

Other occasions on which the British monarchy displays symbolic information
include the *Trooping of the Colour* where the monarch reviews splendidly uniformed and
disciplined troops, and *Opening of Parliament* (at Westminster). The Trooping is a
particularly interesting phenomenon; at one level there is an explanation in terms of
military history and administration - a flag has to be given to a particular unit; but that
does not explain why it is done with such splendour, in the centre of the capital city, in
early summer when glitter can be at its greatest. Televised every year since this message
system became widespread, nothing is said at the Trooping by the participants (apart
from some barely intelligible military commands) and certainly not by the monarch.
Although the television commentators keep talking it is a fair guess that little of what
they have said has had much substantial content or has been retained by viewers. So is
there a message, a symbolic one? The matter is open to interpretation in the way that art
critics happily decide on the meanings of pictures, but such diagnoses should really be
put to a further test of systematic public enquiry. This, however, is difficult and has
probably not been done yet for the particular case of the meaning of the trooping of the
colour, for the British public.

What are possible meanings conveyed by the trooping of the colour? One is that the
monarch is not there in Britain, to say things, but merely - or more accurately
magnificently, to be; to BE. The monarch, seen on these occasions, is upright, colorful,
surrounded by tremendous, and entertaining support (though potentially armed, the
firepower is not to the fore, rather it is a brass-band musical extravaganza - contrast the
Presidential parades in the Soviet Red Square and in other dictatorships, but also in
democracies such as India where camouflaged rockets and tanks trundle past). None of
the dazzling support-cast at the trooping steps out of line. The event is witnessed by a
sizeable crowd, but there is no cheering (let alone booing) - this is not a carnival, where
public participants take an active part. The uniforms and staging are archaic, old-
fashioned; they say that what happened years ago - the nation's history - is glorious. The
fact that the ceremony is annual is enough to connect with the present and the near-
future; this is no rebranding or future-promotional effort such as may be tried at the
Millennium Dome. Indeed, such exercises would be hostages to fortune as the future
often fails to resemble what is forecast.

What of the Opening of Parliament? At Westminster, the Queen reads out what "her"
government (though she had no part in choosing it whatsoever - it was chosen for her by
"her" people) plans to do. There is a considerable ambiguity in the display. On one hand
it might be thought that a monarch with real power, wearing a dazzling crown and
sumptuous robes is really "telling" a House of Commons what it will do; it remains true
that (some people think that) Sovereignty is embodied in the monarch; others perceive
that Sovereignty is embodied in Parliament where, though that body is voted in and thus

has public validity, that public power is - as it were - "switched on" when the symbol of the monarchy, that is the Mace, rests on its support on the table in front of the Speaker and in between the leaders of the two main parties. The situation is different in Scotland where the tradition held (until the Parliament suspended action in 1707 and was taken up again in May 1999) that sovereignty inheres in the public - to whom the Scottish parliament is presumably thus subservient.

Aside from these less frequent grand ceremonials - and others include occasions when the monarch invests new members of the Order of the Garter - again much glitter, though this time at Windsor Castle, or when she receives foreign potentates, there are literally hundreds of other occasions when the monarch and her close family visit institutions all round the country. On these occasions royal family members do speak, but they do this to individuals. The wider public - there may be larger or smaller crowds - are not addressed directly, but they still receive a message. This time one may suggest (with a little evidence) that one of the messages is that the monarchy cares about the subjects. We have seen something in earlier chapters of what Billig and Nairn have reported (interestingly, it seems with reluctance, as neither of these scholars puts himself forward as a monarchist, rather in fact the opposite) of unexpectedly loyal responses of public members to royal visits. People are often tongue-tied, somehow taken out of the mode of ordinary discourse and impressed (more often than not, favorably) by the charisma of such encounters.

A recent account to hand of symbolic meanings coming across from a monarchy (in the person of the heir) to the public occurs in three articles written for the London *Evening Standard* by an astute journalist Allison Pearson. She had written a witty column for several years as a television critic, thus sharpening her perceptions of messages and meanings; she had not conspicuously lined up as a republican but was no royal sycophant either. First we can see that she has her doubts[204]:

> "I'm still not sure whether a Prince of Wales should exist, but I think we're lucky to have him" ... .

Her story is based on a day in which she followed the Prince on a visit to the North East (an area politically left-wing and possibly therefore less pro-monarchist).

> "As the Royal Train pulls in, the receiving line visibly stiffens ... and here comes the man himself. It is the first time I have seen him in the flesh and it is riveting ... He has a fierce high colour ... impeccable in a grey suit ... with that wiry build and ascetic fervour you see only in long distance runners or mediaeval saints ... (they visit the Tyneside Foyer) ... they are staging a discussion for his benefit ... it's like conducting the interview from hell. He must ask questions and have endless supplementaries ready, because the people he talks to are either speechless with nerves or in a state of mild hysteria. John ... has dishwater grey skin that tells of bad diet ... (HRH chats away to him gamely ignoring the photographers wedged three deep in a corner) ... John turn to the bookshelves and a

---

[204] Allison Pearson Charles at 50 The Man Behind the Image. *Evening Standard,* 6 November 1998, p. 4.

volume on the parachute regiment which John hopes to join ... I do hope you manage to get in all right ... .

It has been a strained five minutes ... but, to my surprise, John is chuffed to bits ... 'I spent about three days tidying my room ... but he was canny. He takes time out to be bothered with people ... I think he'll be a really good king'. In the communal kitchen the man who may indeed be the 63rd occupant of the English throne is making another brave stab at modernity 'Is that a ... microwave?' 'Yes, sir!' Everyone beams at this encouragingly as if he were a toddler taking his first steps (the entourage then visit the National Glass Centre) ... walking through the permanent display of glassware HRH spots a 'Mirror Mirror on the Wall' exhibit and practically breaks into a run. No fool, he can see the headlines 'Who's The Fairest of them All?' Last year, the Prince of Wales carried out 513 engagements ... It was hard not to be impressed by his blend of pragmatism and idealism, he has more of both than any politician. The next day, it is the photograph of the Prince caught in front of the Playboy poster in John's bedroom which makes the papers. Hours of earnest grind reduced to a smutty footnote: how could he not despair?".

The public who saw the prince on that day most likely did not know of the other 512 visits that year, and many have had meaningful conversations which function aside from the symbolic register. Some will have disparaged the whole endeavor but others - according to the impression distilled by the journalist - were impressed. Many toilets - according to Pearson - had been polished to gleam and not only was this preparation some sign of a special respect, but even the fact she reports that none of the facilities were used, seemed to indicate a perception of something beyond a normal humanity in the royal figure[205]. Prince Charles is a complex character whose many facets may include some with which a person may agree and others they might disapprove. The reaction we are trying to sense or to claim here is not a logical one to his stance on modern architecture, organic farming, shooting as a hobby or to his life as a lover, husband or parent, or to some package containing all these potentially conflicting items, but a response to his very being, his existence, his manifestation as a member of the monarchy.

Allison Pearson also mentioned something that provides evidence for a meaning moving in the opposite direction to what we have been discussing, from the public to the monarchy. Members of the public may speak or write to the royal family, which is a

---

[205] Billig M. ((1992) *Talking of the Royal Family*, London: Routledge, p. 70) had tackled these mysteries a decade beforehand: "a journalist ... commented that 'everyone knows that it is the lavs that get done up, first and sumptuously, when the monarch intends a visit ... carefully arranging the lavatory, polishing the seat and obtaining the softest of soft paper would seem to be acts of pure devotion. But these acts reduce regal dignity to the basest level ... the royal seated defencelessly, ludicrously upon the toilet. Of course, 'their' bodies function like anybody else's. Or do they? That is the mystery; or, rather, it is the continuing joke". The opposite of these occasions of burnished mystery is the exposure of royal bodily functional privacy - which some consider was a quintessential reason for the choice of a virgin bride for Prince Charles (though not, correspondingly, of a virgin husband for her, which is one reason why the rupture of the marriage caused such hostility especially amongst feminists) - that occurred when infidelities and carnal expressions were publicised in Britain in the "Squidgygate" and "Camillagate" publications of 1992. To some extent the repetition of such, and other material in the book by Kitty Kelley could be looked down upon, or away from in Britain, as an 'obscenity' (literally, 'off scene') inasmuch as it was foreign.

channel by which complex ideas and feelings can be carried. Out in the street they can cheer or boo - very occasionally throw things - place flowers or react in some collective way which represents a current of feeling. On this, Pearson writes that Prince Charles "told the journalist Byron Rogers that, until the Queen's Jubilee in 1977 he had not believed in the monarchy, but the cheering crowds had persuaded him it was worth something".

One way in which the monarchy "speaks" to the public with iconic brevity is by the existence and use of royal warrants. In the anti- or at least non-monarchist newspaper the *Independent* Nick Lezard caters for readers who must presumably only profess an anthropological interest in the monarchy (10 February 1999, p. 7) pointing out that there are over 1000[206] royal warrants for products giving their manufacturers the right to print on the label "By appointment to her Majesty the Queen" (or the Prince of Wales, or whichever member of the royal family agrees to cite use of a product or service). Included in the list was a brand of silver polish which gave Mr Lezard the idea that "it really is the Queen who polishes the silver on Sunday evenings while watching the telly. It was the idea that the Queen was human - in express contradiction to her constitutional position as head of state[207] - that made the royal warrant appealing even to republicans like myself". The companion in anti-monarchy the *Guardian* (11 February 1999, pp. 4-5) took up the story writing that the thousand odd suppliers "offer a unique window on royal life ... there are some splendid inclusions: W. Forbes of Aberdeenshire, taxidermists by royal appointment. Who, apart from the press, does the Queen want stuffed?". Those with a smattering of history (and some of children's literature) will recall that some past monarchs did indeed apply an "off with their heads" response to impertinent offense.

The *Independent's* Lezard joked that "Anton Laundry in Andover, Hants, washes the Prince's underpants ... (employees make a 100 mile round trip to and from Highgrove, which either means that they are superb at their job - or else HRH should get a copy of the Yellow Pages)". The curiosity about this is the use of the term HRH (His Royal Highness). Even though used sarcastically, its appearance may well reinforce just that which this author seems to want to reject (or does he, really?), that is, respect of Majesty; for the point of the story, almost submerged in frivolity was that the royal warrant was being denied to the tobacco giant Gallaher. Prince Charles was also said (see Lean op. cit.) to have considered denying his warrant to companies that sold Genetically Modified Foods. We can see, then, that the royal warrants have both positive and negative functions. What is more, having been shorn of direct political power in centuries of

---

[206] In the same newspaper (10 January 1999) the environment correspondent Geoffrey Lean was more exact, counting 1180 *companies* carrying the Queen's warrant; Lean also said 170 carry the Prince's warrant.

[207] Lezard is not right about this supposed contradiction; his remark is of value here inasmuch as it hints at the awe with which he, even in his "people's" surroundings appears to regard the monarch.

constitutional development this institution, of warranty, implies that there is scope for judicious development of influence through the use of status in patronage.

Lezard mentioned that "one area ... (in which) ... the royal warrant is becoming highly troubling ... is the case of purveyors of creative imagination to the Royal Family (note the capitals); in other words the Poet Laureate". The appointment of (Professor) Andrew Motion as the new Laureate, in May 1999 provoked squeals of not very articulate hostility from those who were passed over for the title - some of whom had taken the precaution of stating in poor doggerel why they did not want it (the episode reminding one of bored children in a game of pass-the-parcel who holler when a present passes them by). Francis Wheen (not himself a monarchist, writing in the *Guardian* (26 May 1999, G2, p. 4) found himself in a cleft stick, being a friend of Motion. When mentioned that "'a bag of shite' was the considered reaction of one angry young poet ... denounced ... on the left for his conservatism. Motion was simultaneously attacked (by) the *Sunday Telegraph* for having 'republican sympathies'. All he had said was that 'there are bad examples of monarchy and good examples'".

The poet laureate is actually chosen by the Prime Minister (and hopefully truly agreed by the monarch) and the original rewards given to the first incumbent John Dryden of an annual fee of £100 (a majestic sum in mid-seventeenth century) plus a butt of wine (126 gallons - larger than US gallons) have been updated to a £5000 honorarium and a case (12 bottles, maximum) of claret. There is no formal requirement to produce verse to a certain amount, or quality (unassayable, in any case, these days) but merely an expectation, or hope. Wordsworth held the title for seven years, producing nothing specifically for it. It seems difficult for a modern mind trained in a supermarket culture and stuck to a 'price tag' approach to assessing value to realise that the seemingly no-show poet can nevertheless have been of huge value; not by a grovelling and false homage in verse to the monarchy, but by distilling an essence of a sensibility tuned to the particular culture, expressed in his other output, s/he may cast his/her lustre upon all, monarchy included. This way of considering value might have been more readily understood in the Balian culture briefly mentioned in the first chapter.

The monarchy encourages and celebrates industry and commerce not only through its practice of awarding warrants - which recognises services and commodities which the royal family use themselves, but also in its Awards (of the right to carry an insignia, like a medal) for Industry. These are assigned by the central government's Department of Trade and Industry and the decisions are "made known to Her Majesty" by the Minister; these awards recognise merit in performance and can be given not just for manufacturing but for other institutions such as universities. There is also a wholly separate organisation concerned with the Duke of Edinburgh's Award Scheme in which if a range of performance specifications (physical, social, intellectual) are met, a youngster earns a level of merit recognition. Awareness of these Awards is spread very widely throughout society (for example, a local newspaper may run a story on a teenager who has won a Duke of Edinburgh's Award; and the classified ads from companies will tuck in the corner the insignia of an Award to Industry, if the company has that). The unstated message of these signs is not just that the youngster or the company has merit, but that merit has more recognition for having been noticed by a symbolic, pervasive royal eye. The royal entity is thus a kind of sun whose brilliance is reflected best by those in its environment who have the gem-like quality to shine with this lustre. The lustre thus paradoxically works to the merit of both parties, the recipient, and the - royal - bestower of such recognition.

Moving into the next millennium the monarchy is developing the fashionable way in which to provide direct information to (an increasing proportion of) the public. Buckingham Palace has its own website, as has the Prince of Wales (www.Prince of Wales). There are "minor" websites such as www.royalinsight.gov.uk, and others created by private enthusiasts (www.royalarchive.com - news snippets assembled by one Aaron Gilmer) and even satirists (www.royalnetwork.com). The verbal contents of these websites are not symbolic in the sense being discussed above, but the heraldic motifs and pictures of crowns and other regalia most likely do convey an impression of a substantial difference in the contact between the commoner at the computer and the 'other' in this case.

Aside from symbolic meanings conveyed to the public there are **simple verbal exchanges** which can potentially be of considerable importance. Prochaska[208] has examined archives from the first three decades of the century and says that palace advisors "told the monarchy to reinvent itself as a caring, unostentatious institution which could relate to the aspirations of working class people"[209]. The concern was that after the fall of the German and Austrian monarchies (and the Russian one) and some firebrand expressions in Britain (Bob Williams, secretary of the powerful Transport Workers' Union declared during the General Election of 1918 that he wanted to see the Red flag flying over Buckingham Palace) a Bolshevik-style upheaval could occur in Britain. The King was advised to meet more often with Labour leaders who were then "regularly invited for tea" so that Britain's first Communist Member of Parliament observed "never has there been such a rush on court tailors and court dressmakers". During Armistice week the King and Queen toured east London five times and had a tumultuous reception (symbolic communication).

It only involves simple back of the envelope arithmetic to explore the possibilities that exist with direct communication, alongside those attached to symbolic interaction. If the prince makes visits (or receives delegations) 500 times in a year, and on each occasion can manage a minimum of 5 minutes' contact either one-to-one, or in small group meetings thereby reaching 40 people on each day, this would amount to some 20,000 people who could thus feel they had met the prince personally, in a year. It must be realised that this involves a major output of intellectual and physical stamina on the part of the prince, and of careful staff work by a small team. This circle will be expanded by the work done by the Queen and other members of the royal family and could thus

---

[208] Prochaska, F. (1999) *Twentieth Century British History*.

[209] Marie Woolf. "How the Royals headed off revolution" *The Independent on Sunday*, 28 March 1999, p. 7.

amount to 60 or 70,000 people reached in such ways. Alongside such an estimated 70,0000 personal (and judging from a sample of reports probably favourable) impressions a year the non-verbal and thus symbolic direct penumbra consists of those who, without talking to a royal person nevertheless attend garden parties, witness motorcades and visits and who help prepare for and clear up after such encounters. The number reached via these means is likely to exceed that of those who do speak to (senior) royal family members. However both these circles of contact, achieved by considerable hard work are dwarfed by the size of the public reached by the daily press which is estimated to produce well over 30 million readers each day, who see messages many of which are far from favourable.

In May 1999 the son of Camilla Parker Bowles, who is also godson to Prince Charles and said to be a good friend of Prince William was trapped in a cocaine-taking sting. This led to conjectures that Prince William might one day be accused of such or related misbehavior and an immediate imperative for Prince Charles to read the riot act both to his godson and more especially to his own two sons. This reported disciplining was not only a verbal message from Prince Charles to his own boys, but through them to the country. On a matter such as this, therefore, his words and through them his real personal thoughts could be communicated to tens of millions of his future subjects. Often, however, his speeches inhabit a formal register and mediated words may not have the positive function that is more likely to develop with direct personal contact, or through symbolic communication, which is why this mode remains hugely important.

The public provides both symbolic and explicit verbal messages to the monarchy, in many ways. The number of people who attend royal processions and who respond however the mood dictates show that there is either support for the institution, and or what has been written about as affection or even 'love' for particular royal family members. This shows itself positively in support for occasions of national and royal celebration (anniversaries of the end of World War II, and weddings being examples in the last two decades) and of royal tragedy (unambiguously when King George VI died and, as the previous chapters indicate, with ambiguities after the death of Diana Princess of Wales). Many reporters noted that early in the marriage of Prince Charles and Princess Diana there might be walkabouts in which a larger, denser and more enthusiastic crowd lined the side of the road along which the princess walked, leaving a thinner and less warm response for the prince. He may well have felt hurt by this (or proud of his wife) but it might well have been the best course to have understood and felt these responses to have signalled support for the institution at large rather than as a sign of personal affections.

We have already seen, in previous chapters with instances of letters sent to the Palace (this could include items personally addressed to a royal family member, or displayed in a number of public places) that there is a large volume of verbal expression from the public directly to the monarchy. There is no well known study of the contents of such messages though impressionistic assessments suggest that the feelings contained are largely positive.

There is no "message system" of flags in the UK, as there is with the Stars and Stripes in the United States, which could serve to express feelings about the monarchy. To exhibit a British Union Flag (popularly known as 'Jack") is to say something about feelings for the nation rather than for its sovereign; it is extremely widely debased by incorporation into clothing and advertising, and often wrongly depicted (indicating that few among the public know what the correct configuration is). Flags of Scotland and Wales are increasingly common, and may even be stimulating the English to field the St George's flag of a vertical red cross on a white ground, and it is extremely unlikely that showing a Scottish Saltire (diagonal white cross on a blue ground) as some do from flagpoles or as stickers on cars says anything positive about the monarchy; indeed some who show this flag as a symbol of Scottish independence are known to feel republican, though systematic survey evidence (in previous chapters) does indicate that such feelings belong to a minority.

The monarch has her own flag, flown above buildings where she is in residence (and whose absence brought forth all that orchestrated resentment reported in previous chapters, when the royal family were not in Buckingham Palace in the days soon after Diana died), but no commoner or civil institution would exhibit this flag even as a sign of loyalty. It is conceivable that a flag could be devised and sold which would express support for the monarchy as such (rather than to any one or more members of the royal family) and it is an unknown market as to how many would buy and use such a device. Many monarchist supporters would be reluctant to make a display of their sentiments, reticence being a characteristic of such loyalties. It is easy therefore to interpret an absence of symbolic approval as an absence of approval, an interpretation which many social commentators adopt and reflect.

MONARCHY AND PUBLIC - THE OPTION OF INFLUENCE

This section is here as a conceptual possibility and will be remarkable for its brevity. The questions are, does the monarchy today try or manage, by explicit or implicit ways to influence the public? And does the public try or manage, by explicit or implicit ways to influence the monarchy? Mostly, the answer to these questions is NO. Centuries ago a monarch might exert direct military leadership - Henry V stirred his troops to victory at Agincourt, Elizabeth encouraged resistance to Spanish invasion, Charles I led troops in a civil war and the last British king who went to battle was George II at the battle of Dettingen. George III tried to exert his will via his ministers in government but increasingly monarchs had less and less political power. The monarch herself is now a-political in her role; no longer does she express or lead foreign policy in standing at the head of military endeavours. We have seen in a previous chapter that whatever her opinions as a human being, on apartheid in South Africa and on how it might or should be dealt with, it was not the monarch's business to use her status as leverage to effect a particular kind of policy. That was why, when a national newspaper suggested the Queen was exerting pressure on the Prime Minister on that issue, that kind of disclosure (which the Palace could neither combat nor affirm, otherwise it would have entered the political process) was not just unfair but technically treasonous.

The attitudes of royal family members to matters which do become politically controversial are sometimes perfectly clear. Thus several royal family members join in fox and other kinds of hunting and in shooting birds where there is little hunting involved, more a case of carnivorous harvesting (the birds mostly go to the shops, for sale to be eaten). Political sides are taken and though royal family members may not enter the explicit argument their known practices show what they would prefer. There is some element of discourse which can be construed as addressed to the monarchy, though indirectly so through newspaper letters and articles, or opinions expressed on the radio, in which commoners are in effect asking the royal family not to hunt or even to lead by example in the move against hunting. There has been no explicit royal gesture of "hanging up the shotgun" or putting one's hunter out to grass which would no doubt cause much clamor - and even approval - if it occurred; public opinion is known to oppose foxhunting by a wide margin and to be generally opposed to owning and using guns, even if only for seeking food.

What is open to royal support is the world of organised charities, and those of the arts. Many of the hundreds of annual royal engagements consist of supporting charities and arts bodies and these efforts are spread across such a wide spectrum that it would be difficult - and churlish - if anybody chose either to detect and demonstrate any gap, or to claim that such a gap denoted disapproval and thus some kind of covert political statement. A departure from the broad-band approach occurred in the last year of Diana Princess of Wales's life, when she focused her efforts on fewer than a dozen charities, leaving herself exposed to the perception that there was a detectable political preference in her selection of beneficiaries.

Alongside this general account that royal support for arts and charities is not political Prince Charles has made a careful selection of topics on which he has taken up a quasi-political stance. He is known to support organic farming methods (though he is also a keen shot - the highly publicised photograph of himself with a friend, armed and carrying a few brace of grouse, when his mother and Prince Andrew were battling the aftermath of the fire at Windsor Castle, struck a jarring note) and a corresponding approach to architecture. Modern and post-modern architects, favoring glass steel and concrete materials in rectangular (modern) or more recently irregularly shaped (post-modern) designs were known or thought to displease the prince (though in late 1999, with the move of his architecture school to a retrieved warehouse location it was suggested that he had liked the Bilbao museum by Frank Gehry, a leading post-modern design). Along with a considerable irritation at what is seen as his conservatism, in professional circles, there is also a significant element of support there, and more (to the former group's chagrin) amongst the public.

In suggesting that he might, as King change one of his titles from that of Defender of The Faith (the 'The' meaning the established Church of England - equivalent to the Episcopalian Church in the United States) to Defender of Faiths Prince Charles has sent a message both to institutions and to the public at large. He has said by this message that he supports religions, but all valid religions as systems of principle as bases for a good quality of life. This message has had a mixed response and it can be said that the suggestion is still being considered or digested. Representative surveys have shown that a substantial majority of the public consider that Britain is (still) a unicultural country (rather than a multicultural one, as is argued in many intelligentsia newspapers and broadcasting discussions) and that culture is a Christian one, and that moreover, steps should be taken to retain this identity, even though there is also support for services of other faiths to be held and even televised nationally. Seeing the country as Christian - in heritage and current culture, if not in daily or weekly institutional practise - may or may not mean that the public is saying to the Prince that it wants him to continue as head of an established Church, or to evolve towards being a figurehead of support for all main religions. These are sensitive matters which remain to be explored by tactful and skilful enquiry (rather than with the dogmatic assertion they more often receive).

MONARCHY AND PUBLIC - COHESION AND PAYOFF

During the twentieth century the British monarchy has often been the focus and catalyst of national cohesion, though it has also contributed to dissent less frequently. Episodes of dissent can be examined compactly, while those of cohesion could be expanded to fill a book in themselves. When Edward VIII fell in love with the American divorcée Mrs Simpson two deeply felt and opposing positions developed in public life. Some led with their affections for the new King who had impressed people with his feelings for the welfare of the unemployed in Wales, while he was Prince of that Principality. His supporters were willing to accept his choice of bride and wanted some way to be found to combine marriage and some suitable status (the Church at that time did not marry divorcees) so he could remain King. Opponents recalled his playboy style of life and did not want as King a man whose wife had a previous love life so that people could talk intimately about her personal charms. The Prime Minister consulted with his Dominion colleagues and the upshot was an abdication which shocked the nation, whichever outcome the opposed factions had wanted.

The three previous chapters provide an extended case study of the disturbance to cohesion which arose from the troubled marriage of Prince Charles. The purpose here is not to look to the roles played by the mass message systems in picking at this sore in itself but to remain aware that the direct and the symbolic personal relationships between monarchy and public were disturbed. Diana Princess of Wales symbolised the commoner who had acquired royal status so on any occasion (and there were many) when she was shown uncomfortably together with the prince there was opportunity for many among the public who identified with the princess, to feel estranged from the next monarch. "Diana's body language is our body language" is an equation that may have reinforced discomfort with the prince, and that had been shown in many opinion polls over several years in which the percentages admiring or liking him or expecting him to be a good King or indeed a King at all had fallen markedly.

Beyond discomforts associated with mass disseminated pictures there will have been all the personal contacts between the prince and private people, and the princess and the private people in which an unspoken element of the interaction will have been a knowledge of the marital difficulties and of the embarrassments of disclosures about affairs and "secret" correspondence. Thus for a hospital patient, an aid worker or any other person who met the princess and reacted warmly to her, an implication may have been that "I know about your troubles and I support you" - and thus a second implication remains unspoken "I think the prince has been behaving badly". A similar scenario will have affected implications generated during encounters with the prince even though by all accounts many of these were positive on the surface. Only after tragedy had put these conflicts in the past could people settle down to meetings with the prince which could glow with the charisma received of contact with monarchy, without at the same time covertly cancelling such effects through unstated support for "the opposition".

The implications for relationships between the Queen and her subjects, of this marital breakdown were serious in similar ways. Had she visibly tried to salvage the marriage she would run a danger of being seen to support one side or the other; to appear aloof seemed heartless. Perhaps in the tradition of remaining impartial in the political world the Queen tended not to play marriage counsellor as a piece of public theatre; any private people she met - and there were as we have seen, hundreds and even thousands each year - will have kept their perceptions of the Queen's family difficulties out of the conversation; but this will not have excluded them from the interaction. Again, only when divorce and then death intervened could these ambiguities be left in the past.

Of the central royal trio - the present Queen, the King-to-be and the previous Queen (Mother) the only one to escape from unspoken expectations that she was herself living out a disaster, or undiscussably involved in it as a third party was this third person. It has been a truism in the 1990s that the Queen Mother's popularity has remained intact. The Queen's own historian wrote after a politician's posthumous diaries had made various allegations about the Queen Mother's political ideas[210] "after George VI's death in 1952 the Queen Mother continued to talk happily to all comers about the misdeeds of communists and Left wingers in the Labour Party and the BBC - and probably still does. It has never occurred to anybody to shut her up; or, indeed, to any newspaper editor to break ranks and print what she said, even though her views were so widely known that the white Rhodesians in the sixties, fantasising about their direct link to the Crown, believed she was interceding with the Government on their behalf".

Pimlott argued that a robust system should be glad of a "non-robotic" ruling family and "as for the antediluvian opinions of the ever-charming Queen Mum, the commonsensical British public will take them in its stride"[211]. In contrast to these

---

[210] Pimlott, B. *Daily Express*, 5 October 1998, p. 11.

[211] More people may have welcomed these disclosures about the Queen Mother's attitudes, than who were disturbed by them, feeling that 'she can say the kinds of things I would like to say but

observations it was reported in late May 1999 that Prince Phillip was approached in Cardiff, during the royal visit in connection with the opening of the Welsh Assembly, by an official of an organization representing the deaf. The report in the paper suggested that the prince tried to make a joke about the likely cause of deafness being the kind of pop concert he had just attended. Having made a brief remark, the prince was said to have turned abruptly away. The official was reported as having taken offence at the remarks and at the gesture that followed them. None of this may be true, or only partly so; or all of it may be true. Not long afterwards Prince Phillip remarked during a visit to an Edinburgh factory that a suspect-looking piece of equipment "looked as if it was put in by an Indian". Whether or not he really did say this, it was taken as real by the Palace which issued an apology for any offence it may have inflicted. At least one newspaper remarked that, the xenophobic proportion of the public being as large as it is, his implied disparagement of a minority community in Britain may have been welcomed by more people than who disliked it. At the least, these examples suggest that royal figures have to be extremely careful not just in what they say to individuals, but especially also in how they are seen to say it. The medium here is the visual and kinaesthetic body language, aside from a verbal component (which truly qualifies for the term language).

MONARCHY AND MASS MESSAGE SYSTEMS - INFORMATION FLOW

The communication between the monarchy and mass message systems is at the moment quite professionalised. The Palace has its public relations staffs - one telephone number at Buckingham Palace gives access either to the Queen's or to the Prince of Wales's staff, the latter a separate small group at St James's Palace. In the previous reign, of George VI, a quite different corps and style of professionalism was involved in contrast to what is in place now. Previously courtiers drawn from families of the aristocracy ran the royal household and dealt with the newspapers. The owners of the press were magnates who may have worked their ways up from humble origins, but whatever their original backgrounds they will have been able to meet with courtiers in the district of "clubland" that exists in the streets just north of St James's Palace, and at the estates of the aristocracy. Information about royal activities, thoughts, intentions, and feelings could thus be transmitted along channels of personal contact between people who were in positions of wealth, power or both.

Until the emergence of the Labour party in the early years of the twentieth century, the political elites were well connected with palace and press circles, giving the opportunity for information flow and content to have been managed in support of the monarchy. Extramarital affairs of King Edward VII and the allegedly acquisitive behavior of Queen Mary (wife of King George V) as well as the finances of the monarchy could be dealt with between palace and politicians, often with the press in the know, but without the pressures of the market tempting the press to play for scandal.

---

can't, in today's more careful public space'.

When George V died the nature and timing of the medical procedures that occurred, and their announcement were carried out in such a way that the death and its announcement were dignified. Even when the present Queen Elizabeth was crowned the news of the first ascent of Everest by a British-led Commonwealth climbing team was delayed a day or two so that it was given out on the morning of the great day, intensifying the positive feelings amongst the crowds lining the processional route. We have already seen, above, that when the Labour party became prominent the monarch George V was advised to extend and improve his contacts with its leaders, and that he did so quite successfully.

During the 1930s radio emerged as a mass message system not only linking the monarch with the British people but also with those of the (then) empire world wide. There was only one institution (not a commercial company, indeed its ideological antithesis) running radio - the British Broadcasting Corporation. The BBC's first Director General John (later Lord) Reith was a royalist who used the BBC as an important instrument in moulding several aspects of the nation's consciousness. At a domestic level broadcasting for children used texts - and accents and speech styles - that stood for an ideal (if not for a norm) of how the world was to be seen. One of the texts that radio will have helped popularise was A.A. Milne's Christopher Robin story - one episode of which was the visit to (the railings in front of) Buckingham Palace, then held in the highest regard, even awe.

At an opposite pole to the domestic, BBC radio broadcast and thus fortified as national institutions such sporting events as the Oxford-Cambridge boat race, the Grand National (horserace) and the annual Final of the Football (soccer) Cup and such ceremonial events as the Opening of Parliament, the Lord Mayor's Banquet, the Trooping of the Colour, the service of Remembrance (for the fallen in World War I) at the Cenotaph, and Christmas messages spoken - live - by the sovereign, the first of these having taken place in 1932. Royal broadcasts on radio continued with the launching of the Queen Mary liner by Her Majesty and the wedding of the Duke of Kent and Princess Marina at Westminster Abbey. The broadcast of the state funeral for George V was preceded by those of a Thanksgiving Service at St Paul's and the lying-in-state at Westminster Hall. These were followed some months later with the Proclamation of Edward VIII's accession in 1936 and then his own abdication message early in 1937.

The BBC's outside broadcast of the coronation of King George VI and Queen Elizabeth was a tour de force. Continuous broadcasting went on from ten in the morning when the gilded coaches left the Palace until half past five in the afternoon for the end of the service in Westminster Abbey. The special wiring used 427 miles of cable, there were 58 microphones including 11 along the route to catch crowd sounds and many of the 60 BBC engineers had to wear full morning dress with gloves and top hats. Two commentators catered especially for the USA and there were also commentaries in Czech, Danish, Dutch, Finnish, Flemish, French, German, Hungarian, Japanese, Norwegian, Spanish, Swedish and Serbo-Croat; 78 rpm shellac records were sold as well as newspapers, books, souvenir plates, mugs, cigarette cards and a further array of quasi-holy mementoes of the occasion.

The BBC was fortunate to have the commentator Richard Dimbleby[212], whose words echoed some of the more romantic resonances of the language and history of England. Dimbleby's word pictures were a form of poetry and it has not been formally recognised that the platforms on which poets of earlier ages held forth, Chaucer's tavern tales, Shakespeare's rough theatres and the print of Keats and Wordsworth, and based on which the office of the poet laureate has for over three hundred years expected its incumbents to produce commemorative verse on suitable occasions, had now been replaced by broadcasting. Had this been recognised in 1999, when a new poet laureate was appointed to succeed Ted Hughes - who we have already seen fulfilled his laureateship innovatively, more through the form of a social anthropologically informed literary criticism than by his verse, which had its own heroic momentum and quality - the office might have been translated into one of a "broadcasting laureate"; his or her commentaries would have carried on the momentum (not necessarily the tradition) of Dimbleby, who had found a way to evoke for the nation some of what it considered its best qualities, and who did so in what came across as live and unscripted and above all sincere.

Dimbleby's spoken poetic prose succeeds also in print. As an example, this is some of what he said at the lying-in-state of George VI:

"It is dark in New Palace Yard at Westminster tonight. As I look down from this old, leaded window, I can see the ancient courtyard dappled with little pools of light where the lamps of London try to pierce the biting, wintry gloom and fail. And moving through the darkness of the night is an even darker stream of human beings, coming, almost noiselessly, from under a long, white canopy that crosses the pavement and ends at the great doors of Westminster Hall ... they are passing, in their thousands, through the hall of history while history is being made. No one knows from where they come or where they go, but they are the people, and to watch them pass is to watch the nation pass... .
It is very simple, this Lying-in-State of a dead King, and of incomparable beauty. High above all light and shadow and rich in carving is the massive roof of chestnut, that Richard II put over the great Hall. from that roof the light slants down in clear, straight beams ... There lies the coffin of the King. ... The oak of Sandringham, hidden beneath the rich golden folds of the Standard; the slow flicker of the candles touches gently the gems of the imperial Crown, even that ruby that King Henry wore at Agincourt ... the ghosts that must be here in the shadows ... the men and women of those tumultuous days of long ago, of Chaucer, Essex, Anne Boleyn, Charles and Cromwell, Warren Hastings and those early Georges ... .
I thought when I watched the Bearers take the coffin into this Hall yesterday that I had never seen a sight so touching. The clasped arms of the Grenadiers, the reverent care with which they lifted and carried their King. But I was wrong. In the silent tableau of this lying-in-state there is a beauty that no movement can ever bring. ...

---

[212] It was also lucky to have the services of Antony Craxton - who died in June 1999. Craxton was the major producer for all royal ceremonial occasions after 1951, including the Queen's first television Christmas broadcast, the Duke of Edinburgh's *Round the World in 40 Minutes*, and all the royal marriages; they included the Lying in State of the Duke of Windsor, the investiture of Prince Charles as Prince of Wales, 10 state visits abroad and 19 visits by foreign heads of state to Britain.

In 1955 the BBC's hold on broadcasting was broken with the arrival of a commercial channel, "ITV" (Independent TV). ITV had to abide by controls exercised by a body[213] that was more intrusive than the FCC is in its functioning, and both BBC and ITV at first broadcast the Queen's Christmas message simultaneously as well as offering simultaneous coverage of many major ceremonies. These did not, however, include some such as the Trooping of the Colour and this change from a single channel situation which on appropriate times showed only royal events meant that demotic entertainment ran alongside these more formal ones and, especially with the subsequent proliferation of channels, side-tracked them from the centrality they had, for a few brief years, experienced.

As has been said, above, the administrative hub of the monarchy at the Palace provided not only a public relations interface with the mass message systems, with press officers, releases and conferences, it also provided those occasions of State Theatre that Dimbleby so eloquently described. Toward the end of the millennium Dimbleby's able successor Tom Fleming continued commentaries in a similar vein, but this began to attract satire in some quarters. Crossing the millennium, with the establishment of a Scottish Parliament after a gap of nearly three hundred years, and a Welsh Assembly, the United Kingdom of which the existing monarchy is a principal symbol is subject to divisive strains. The Scottish Parliament was opened with the Queen in attendance, but not wearing her robes or regalia. Verses of an anti-royalist nature by Robert Burns were recited. The Welsh Assembly was opened also with the Queen in non-regal dress, with Princes Phillip and Charles seated, as she was, on simple chairs rather than on an obvious throne.

Meeting the monarchy's professional news staff are the many court and royal correspondents employed by the newspapers and broadcasters. Their duty is to make the most of royal stories; but the duty is ultimately to the company's owner in a profit tending market, rather than to the readers-as-subjects (a term which itself has come under criticism) or to the nation in its trajectory through history. (Contrast the case of Japan, discussed briefly below). The large corps of royal reporters include many who are dissatisfied with the institution they are reporting. It is as if many, even half of the corps of sports reporters were bored with or even antagonistic to sport. These monarchy watchers include many who do not take well to heirs and graces, whose own knowledge of history is shallow, who sometimes wish to punish royal family members for what they see as inconsiderate behavior (as with the incidents involving Prince Phillip mentioned

---

[213] At first called the Independent Television Authority (ITA) it later grew to become the IBA (B for Broadcasting) when is also supervised the start of commercial radio. Eventually in 1992 the IBA became the Independent Television Commission (the logo designer evidently wished to de-emphasise the independent element of the organisation and provided the format iTC) with a shift in its duties from proactive control of broadcast schedules and content, to retroactive scope either to approve or to punish (by fines or ultimately, removal of franchise) contractor companies feeding the three UK-wide commercially funded terrestrially broadcast channels. The iTC had no link with commercial radio which was supervised in a similar fashion by the Radio Authority.

above) and who may see the royals themselves as subjects - of the reporters' opportunity to exploit them as "dinosaurs on display" who inexplicably, perhaps disappointingly (to that republican cast of view) provide the opportunity for what are thought to be profits to be made from a prurient public whose tastes, sensibilities and loyalties remain stuck in an ancient mold.

Amongst the message system staffs there is a competitive ethos in which one reporter will wish to scoop others and be the first to bring a story to his or her paper or broadcast channel. They therefore expect the news provider, in this case the royal establishments to provide equal access to all, otherwise there is a feeling that favorites get better and fresher material, which reinforces resentment. An analogy is that of a lion enclosure in a zoo; the lions expect the keepers to put out meat enough for all, at the same time and equally accessible to all; each lion would nevertheless want to grab not only its own but also others' shares, and also to mount independent raids on the meat store. The lions would be angry if the keeper cut down the supply and only put it in front of certain lazier or less ferocious beasts. Illustrating this awareness, the non-monarchist *Independent,* on 2 February 1999 ran an item (The Man Behind Operation Ritz - when Prince Charles and Camilla Parker Bowles provided a "photo-op" - see below) which described Prince Charles's "royal spin surgeon" (Mark Bolland, his deputy private secretary). The item complained that "his information, when supplied, is like a golden nugget falling from the sky for the hand-picked assortment of editors and reporters he chooses to entrust ..."; the newspapers the *Sun, Mail* and *Telegraph* were mentioned as favoured and supportive titles.

This illustrates a dilemma for the royal public relations approach. If they target information at selected loyalist outlets the others may resent not only this, but allow the feeling to spread to that for the monarchy as a whole. On the other hand it can be argued that serving the anti-monarchist outlets on an equal basis will make no difference to them but lead to a different kind of frustration amongst the loyal papers and broadcasters who could think that they should get better treatment on account of their positivity. The presumed optimum strategy for royal public relations practice would be to reinforce loyal papers and broadcasters by feeding them newsworthy information somewhat earlier and more fully than is made more widely available, but also to try to increase the circle of those thus favoured. Another approach might be to select news stories to match outlets the establishment wished to befriend. Two examples may illustrate these dilemmas.

Early in 1999 newspapers assumed that Prince Charles was wanting to develop a positive public reception for Camilla Parker Bowles. The idea was that the couple should emerge from a function at the Ritz Hotel (in London - the name was noticed as not altogether a tactful option, seeing that the Ritz in Paris was where Princess Diana had her last supper), publicly to depart together for their night's rest. Mark Lawson, in the *Guardian* (30 January 1999 - "Language of Love") criticised the timing of the photo-op; at midnight, there would only be minority news channels on air, and it would be too late for early newspaper editions. Wrote Lawson "as well as restricting the immediate distribution of the pictures, this clear reluctance about the enterprise limits the success ...

by being apparent in the body language. The sense ... that this short walk is an ordeal ... unavoidably gives the images the feel of scandal ... some may enjoy the echoes of Cinderella in ... an exit from a ball at the stroke of midnight. But what is it that Charles and Camilla hope to turn into?". Here we see an anti-monarchist writer, in a republican paper being scathing at this opportunity - though it is not easy to suppose that he would have been more friendly had the exit taken place at 9 pm.

The notion that the public might come to accept a marriage between Prince Charles and Camilla Parker Bowles, possibly aided by a better reception elsewhere than in the *Guardian* took a sharp knock when the press revealed itself in 'lion as hunter' mode: a tabloid established a scoop when, at the Cannes Film Festival it reported that Camilla's twenty-something son Tom, a publicist by trade, had taken cocaine. Although the press widely acknowledge that large proportions of their own profession had indulged in "leisure" drug taking, they nevertheless assumed that the stain was a real and a deep one. Not only would Camilla be tainted but so too would the friendship between Tom and Prince William. This scoop, obviously not press released by the royal establishment was thought to have damaged the progress being made by Prince Charles, and acceptance of his projects and ideas, in terms of positive public opinion.

At the end of May, 1999 Prince Charles took an initiative in the form of bestowing a scoop, this time in the *Daily Mail*. This is the widest-selling middle-brow (not "red top" tabloid, and neither a broadsheet) and generally a monarchist paper. For them the Prince wrote a highly controversial article setting out his cautious ideas on genetically modified foods. The GM food issue had become a scare; a large majority amongst the public were known to oppose introduction of such foods, at least until several years of intensive research may have shown that their planting and use was harmless. An undertone to the controversy was an element of resentment that the company mainly identified with GM foods, Monsanto, is an American-based multinational, the kind of outfit perceived as gaining power if not also sovereignty over a functional rather than a territorially-defined 'realm' cross-nationally, and thus eroding the sovereignty contained in conventional nation states.

For Prince Charles to take up this position was a risk in at least two ways. First, time might reveal that his anxieties lacked substance, in which case he would be revealed as scientifically naive; secondly, his position brought him in conflict with that taken by the government, for whom their chief scientific adviser had just been quoted as saying that the organic farming movement was "theological ... It has nothing to do with biology ... some of the stuff they use is really nasty but is deemed OK by the ayatollahs who run the Soil Association". According to he *Times*[214] it was this ayatollah barb which goaded Prince Charles to make his reply. Not only did this involve him in media politics because the article appeared in one paper which the others had merely to follow but also in national politics. It has been a principle of British practice that the monarch does not intervene in matters of political controversy. Yet here was the next monarch doing just that; and because, notwithstanding the support among scientists for GM food development, the public were widely against it the Prince was on solid "people's" ground and the government reacted with conciliatory noises.

In between the dubious event outside the Ritz and the (initially, at least) successful thrust over GM foods we can look at a 'micro-event' which occurred within a larger and well-staged initiative which was the visit early in 1999 of Prince Charles to Argentina. The latter country, still sensitive about its failed attempt to take over the Falkland Islands (in 1982) provided a stage for some positive diplomacy, even though there were hostile demonstrations which were shown (briefly) on British television. During the visit the prince attended a function at which he was partnered by a vivacious and evidently mischievous tango expert; at one moment during the dance this attractive woman wound her right leg round Prince Charles's left side, her dress revealing a good deal above the knee and his left hand hovering in the air above and clearly as far as possible from touching her leg as he could manage it.

This scene made several newspaper front pages as well as being shown on television, and offers a challenge to semeioticians. What were the "meanings" of this image? How did (different) people interpret it? Did such interpretations work positively for Prince Charles's image, or negatively? One might suggest that, quite by accident, this image may have worked extremely well. The two undercurrent themes it displayed were of bonding and of control. The couple were evidently moving closely together, with smiles on both their faces, the United Kingdom and Argentina in harmony. At the same time, the seductive 'takeover' attempt - which evoked the Argentinean war on the Falklands, but also the pressure by the Spanish government on British sovereignty over Gibraltar - was resisted. The Latin tide may rise upon the British shore, but that shore would remain rock firm and resist erosion. If these may have been politically undercurrent themes, there was also a personal-relations theme that may have been touched. In this, the Prince who has endured several years of being perceived as an uncaring sexually exploitative person who may well have thus "driven Diana Princess of Wales to her death" could be seen as a desirable person who, nevertheless (with thoughts of partner and family at home) showed that he would resist temptation.

The Prince of Wales, who conceivably might never be King (should he, or the regime itself meet with an accident), probably has more freedom of action than has the Queen. Her activities are stage managed (it might be more appropriate to say state managed) for her by the royal household, but clearly the government has a hand in the form of many of these appearances. The openings of the Parliament in Scotland and the Assembly in Wales were performed without royal robes and leaving most of the possible ceremonial in wraps, possibly for later use. The Scottish regalia in particular would have made a very rich connection between the new present and Scottish history. The Scots hid their regalia from Oliver Cromwell and after the Act of Union (between Scotland and England, in 1707) everything was locked in a chest in Edinburgh until Walter Scott had the package opened (a great crowd outside the Castle applauded loudly when the moment of discovery was announced by the raising of the royal standard). Scotland's "Honours

---

[214] Valerie Elliott, (1999) The *Times* 2 June, p. 6.

Three" comprise the Crown, the Sceptre and the Sword of State, which are among the oldest Crown Jewels in Europe. The Crown dates from Robert I in the early 14th century; the Sceptre was given to James IV by the Pope, in 1494 and is the emblem of the royal person. The Sword of State was also given to James by a later Pope and signifies justice and the right of peace and war.

The incoming Labour administration in Scotland, having recovered from a fright delivered by the republicanist Scottish National Party (SNP) which had earlier drawn level in polls but which later lost ground, was nevertheless cautious about too demonstrative a monarchism. Scottish history had most recently been evoked by the (not wholly accurate) movie *Braveheart* with a 'people's power' and thus anti-monarchist tone. The story focused on the popular leader William Wallace, executed by the (thus wicked) English monarchy, and managed to gloss over the presence of a similarly rough Scottish monarchy, whose England-beating champion in those times was King Robert 'the Bruce', victor of Bannockburn. The SNP, when trailing in the pre-election polls called on its most famous movie-star supporter, Sean Connery, who had recently not been knighted (it was said, because the Labour administration in London was displeased with his support for the SNP); he did his best for the independent - and thus also for many people republican cause, but more than one Scottish newspaper taunted him that he was not Scottish enough actually to live there, and the SNP remained a distinct second. The whole episode of the downplaying of monarchic symbolism in Scotland involves a rich matrix of pressures and rivalries including screen, press, palace and party - and also the people. Recent representative polls have, however, continued to suggest a majority support for monarchy in Scotland, a sentiment that was not allowed to be symbolised visually at the opening of the new parliament but which may (nobody has tested the matter with studies of the type seen above in Chapter 5) have had something to do with the fading from parity with Labour that the SNP had enjoyed just a few months before the election.

Welsh history has not left that country with its own crown jewels, but the royal event which comes to mind when engaging with this matter is the presentation of the Prince of Wales to the people of the country (there is now some opposition to the term Principality), by the Queen, when he had come of age (that was twenty one, in 1970). A ceremony was devised for the occasion which took place in Caernarvon Castle and which was televised. Some had feared that Welsh separatists might show violent opposition, but that did not happen; a writer Andrew Duncan had a sceptical view of the event:

> "Only the most audacious and gifted antiquarians could succeed in transporting several hundred of the country's important men on a damp Tuesday afternoon to a limestone ruin partially covered with fifty tons of turf specially imported for its uniform greenness on colour television, and sit them on uncomfortable red chairs for four hours ... to watch a twenty year old Prince with a French fleur-de-lis of African feathers as his badge and a German phrase as his motto pay medieval homage of a Roman Catholic Duke in a Nonconformist country whose subjugation was being celebrated, largely for the benefit of American tourists ...".

We have seen, in a previous chapter on the matter of *Spitting Image* that it is difficult to demonstrate that cynical satire damages loyalty to the monarchy. It may be that a majority of people smile at scurrilous iconoclasm but then return to their basic attitudes.

Away from the world of satire the monarch makes, or allows to be made pictorial statements about the monarchy, in the form of portraits. These may be paintings, photographs or sculpture. Sometimes these are kept quiet until they are unveiled, usually at the institution which has commissioned them, but on other occasions there are "photo-ops" for the press who come to report work in progress; occasionally there is discussion of something which may not even have been commissioned, such as the idea that Lucien Freud 'Britain's greatest portrait painter' (as newspapers are all to ready to label someone, without much ability to substantiate such judgements) who is known to produce naked and often harsh portrayals may paint the Queen, with the implication that the result would be controversial in its "penetration of its *subject*".

We should pause here to give thought to these metaphorical terms. It is often considered that artists develop a physically intimate knowledge of models whom they often portray, and that would be utterly unthinkable in the case of representing the Queen. The notion of subject is recognised in describing the status of each of the people vis a vis the monarch, who is sovereign. Americans are not subjects of the President, nor of the constitution - they are citizens in whom (or perhaps jointly with the constitution) sovereignty resides. At the moment British people are subjects of the monarch - though all, including the monarch are co-citizens of Europe. It is often held by radical critics that the role of subject is lower in status and thus demeaning. However, there are other shades of meaning of the word subject.

One definition of subject applies to the one who is active in a sentence or statement while the 'object' is that person or thing upon whom or which the action is performed. This is the way in which the word subject is used in the (now fading) world of grammar. The subject has a positive status. In the relation between artist and 'subject', too, while the artist is the one who performs an action, the subject is not merely passive for it is the subject who is being served by the artist. The most widely encountered portraits of the Queen are certainly those silhouettes encountered on the coins and postage stamps. Another painting, released in 1999 has also proved interesting to serious critics and is the work commissioned by the Royal Society of Portrait Painters and shown at their annual exhibition in the Mall galleries.

A 'radical' newspaper piece on this painting was given the 'spun' title by its subeditor: "Putting the Queen in her place" (*Independent*, 11 May 1999). The text's author Philip Hensher had to pay homage to the paper's self-regarding ideology by starting, "... portraits of the Queen are not normally anyone's idea of interesting art. ... Most of the paintings here are richly self-satisfied paintings of richly self-satisfied people ..." (but would he equally dismiss, for this reason, so many memorable images of the Italian renaissance rich?). He decided, however that this painting is a "serious and profound statement about the future of the country, and its past". Hensher felt the work is "an excellent likeness, and the composition is both complex and grand". It also packs in a "substantial, and rather devastating, volume of radical ideas". The Queen is shown in the "outfit (not 'robes' - this is the *Independent*) she wears for the State Opening of Parliament ... an occasion customarily (sic) derided for the archaic and intricate symbolism of its ritual". Interesting here is the connection Hensher felt he had to make with the (dis)loyalties assumed to animate the *Independent*'s readers; but the writer is drawn by the painting to have to add, against the grain "what its critics rarely understand, however, is that many of those apparently quaint rituals express a fundamental truth about the constitution, that the monarch and the upper chamber are ultimately subject (that word again - with its meaning turned 'upside-down'!) to the wishes of the elected house".

Behind the Queen stand two Chelsea Pensioners (retired soldiers, in scarlet uniforms, often used as symbols of loyal service to the monarchy) holding spears, behind the tips of which are shown the heads of the executed King Charles I and his wife (not executed, and mother of a subsequent king) Henrietta Maria, as portrayed over three centuries ago by Van Dyck. Hensher 'reads' the picture to depict that the soldier over whose spear the executed Charles is shown is the only (live) subject looking at the viewer, and is a person who has fought in a war to preserve democracy, the same democracy that killed the king. This interpretation makes the portrait palatable for readers of the *Independent*. Hensher quotes from the seventeenth century intellectual Francis Bacon, saying that "one of the reasons that we flatter princes is to teach them how they should behave" from which he draws an implication that in the new portrait "an important statement is being made about the future of our political institutions ..."[215]

On rare occasions the Palace sends tough communications to the press. In January 1999 lawyers acting for the Queen, Princess Margaret and the Prince of Wales wrote to the editor of the *Mirror* over the publication of extracts from private letters (reported in the *Guardian*, 21 January 1999). The letters in themselves were not scandalous and purported to show, amongst other things[216], that Charles really did love Diana; the issue was the breach of privacy entailed (and in earlier chapters it has been shown that the public contain large majorities who agree with statements that royal privacy should be protected). The same report continued that the editor said "we have given ... an undertaking that we will not publish any more letters: primarily for the reason that we

---

[215] It would be interesting to have Hensher's notion tested out - by showing the picture to many people and asking them either in an open-ended way what they think it is saying about the future of our institutions, or by prompting them with a list of items - does this picture make you think about the past? about the future? to what extent do you connect each of these terms with what you see: arrogance, bravery, caring, determination, fear, graciousness, etc. Art critics with decided opinions might be surprised at what they would find.

[216] One point was that Charles had written (some years previously, and dealt with in Jonathan Dimbleby's biography of the Prince) that he was "terrified of being King". The *Mirror* argued that the Queen had tried her best to welcome Diana to the Palace ..."her affection for Diana was understandable. She had known her for years ... one of the youngster's nannies ... recalled walking into the drawing room at Sandringham to find the Queen playing hide and seek with six year old Prince Andrew and five year old Diana ...".

have no more". Such amoralities characterise much of the stance of the press. In May the *Sun* tabloid ran a ten-year-old picture of royal bride-to-be Sophie Rhys-Jones, with a breast exposed. There was much seemingly moral horror vented by competing newspapers and the Press Complaints Commission (a self-regulatory body) began to look into the misdemeanour. What happens in most such incidents is that the newspaper promises to behave itself, and does so - until the next time it sees fit (and believes profitable) to offend again.

The *Mirror's* offense followed hard upon that of the journalist Penny Junor whose book *Charles: Victim or Villain?* had been serialised in the *Mail on Sunday*. The book claimed that Prince Charles's main feeling on hearing the news of Diana's death was of relief; he had not, Junor claimed, felt guilt. Junor claimed that Diana had made late night death threat telephone calls to Camilla and that she had been the first to have been unfaithful. The claim was made that Princess Diana had slashed herself when told that her ex security guard, alleged to have been her lover, had died in a motorbike crash. Other suggestions were that the Queen feared a Muslim death threat and that Camilla only succumbed to an affair with Charles because of her own husband's philandering. It is impossible for the public to judge the veracity of such claims and many might want to respond by not wanting to know - exercising an old fashioned British habit of minding one's own business.

Junor was attacked from two directions - according to Kamal Ahmed (in the *Guardian* 27 October 1998 pp. 2-3) "Buckingham Palace said that 'significant parts of the book were a gross misrepresentation of the truth'; (however, he also wrote), ... long in the future ... someone will judge Charles ... Is Charles to blame for the loss of public faith in royalty? Is Charles a cad? ... Charles has a fear. History will answer in the affirmative. And so the fight goes on ...". Andrew Neil, whom we have met before, wrote in the *Independent* (27 October 1998, p. 14) "Prince Charles's camp ... (manages) ... to have it both ways by demanding that the press cease ... from such unsavory revelations, while being privately delighted that Miss Junor has socked it to Diana ... I find it bizarre that the limits of a free society should be set by the need to keep two teenagers (he means Princes William and Harry) in the dark about their parents ... (and) ... some powerful people in our society have decided that this is what we should now think ... to their advantage if not necessarily to ours" (he means the monarchists have gained some momentum, with the anti-monarchists taken aback). One of the latter, (David Aaronovich, *Independent* 27 October 1998 p. 3) chose personal vilification: "speculating about other people's tragedies has helped her (i.e. Penny Junor) send her son to Eton (where he can swap parental tales with ... Prince Harry) ... Also benefiting are ... the venal editors and the nosy, Springer-fed, voyeuristic, stupid, ethics-free multitude, who buy this stuff because it is so much easier to have an opinion about than, say, the Health Service or Welfare Reform. God, how it all makes me, previously a constitutional agnostic, yearn for a republic".

The Junor episode illustrates a phenomenon amongst the press, which is that on certain occasions, not infrequently concerned with monarchy stories, there is a vicious fight amongst themselves. Junor wrote (*The Biter Bit - Guardian*, 23 November 1998) that the Press Complaints Commission Code item that "the use of long lens photography to take pictures of people in private places without their consent is unacceptable" had been breached - it had happened to her! Press person Junor admitted "for the first time, I understood what it was like to be on the receiving end of the media ... to have the tables turned was a very sobering experience ... I had not bargained for the ferocious onslaught from the tabloids that branded me as 'vile', 'villainous', 'cruel', 'spiteful' and 'wicked' ... there were calls to ban this 'evil' book ... no one had read the book, of course ... - but when have the red-top tabloids allowed the facts to get in the way of a good piece of prejudice?". At a concert "a drag queen in the next box tried to assault me - condemned for defending the 'wimp of Wales and his whore' ... I did more than 50 interviews ... and then ... in New York ... much the same. I had expected America to be much more threatening than London. To my complete surprise it was not. New Yorkers were actually interested in what I had to say ... and they ... wished me every success".

By now it should be clear that much of the content of the press is display of opinion. It has been shown that newspapers have become larger over the years but this has not been principally so they can carry more information; a great deal of the added volume consists of articles by columnists, analysts, commentators[217]; they do not by any means always reflect public opinion, as discovered in polls and, more recently, in the increased number of correspondence pages and 'phone in programs on radio. These writers have two advantages over ordinary mortals: they do have expressive skill and they have a great deal more room in which to deploy it. The columnists can be classified for our purposes into three groups - those who support monarchy, those who oppose it and the remainder who have either uncertain opinions (in which case they tend to turn to other topics, as professional opinionisers) or whose expression of what they claim are firm opinions turns out to contain oppositional strands. What these columnists say is sometimes directed more towards the public - but would be pleased to reach royal circles for consideration, is sometimes directed to royal circles and would be pleased enough with public attention and sometimes is directed both ways.

One self-proclaimed monarchist is Tim Hames, who teamed up to produce a pamphlet with a young man who seems more of an opponent of the institution. Hames had written a piece in early 1998 assuring his readers that President Clinton's level of opinion poll support would soon collapse, leading to his resignation or successful impeachment. Armed with this credit to his name he ventured forth (the *Times*, 28 July 1998, p. 20) with the prophecy that he disagreed that the monarchy "can be preserved in its present state (merely) with the assistance of a smoother communications strategy". Why? In Hames's view the monarchy was "trying to straddle a number of increasingly incompatible functions: (establishing) a significant formal role in the political sphere, leadership of an established Church and conduct of numerous, essentially philanthropic public engagements". Hames did not show how the third of these is incompatible with the second, or in what ways the first role is incompatible with the others; however he perceived that "the actions of Buckingham Palace during the past year have focused on sharper public relations rather than a substantive reconsideration of the monarch's functions. We believe that this strategy is undesirable and unsustainable. Mark Leonard of Demos and I will argue for a radically reconstructed monarchy that is more relevant to modern Britain and ... the next century".

Presently, Hames (*Times* 7 September 1998, p. 20 *"How To Save The Monarchy"*) revealed his ideas released in the Demos pamphlet. The current outdated and cumbersome political functions of the Crown need to be abandoned (this mainly refers to the fact that if and when there is an inconclusive general election the Queen can choose one of the prominent leaders and ask him or her if he or she can form a government). The difficulty is that if the Queen does not do this someone else would have to, and nobody has come up with an outstandingly more convincing option. Hames says the Royal Household needs to be replaced with a meritocratic, open and professional alternative. Thirdly the "obscure financial arrangements ... should be more accountable"; fourthly the "archaic link between the Crown and the Church of England does not suit contemporary Britain" and finally, the monarch should embrace a more diverse and dynamic symbolic role. Hames and Leonard declared that the "court that matters today is that of public opinion ... the new monarch would recognise the supremacy of public opinion ..." and called for a referendum shortly after and in order to confirm, or not, a succession. This would not just take the monarchy out of politics, it would hugely import politics into the monarchy (whence, having arrived, it would be difficult to remove from the monarchy).

What does Hames mean about the Royal Household? He feels it is too narrowly appointed and should be replaced by "high flying civil servants and some specialist personal appointments ... (might this mean 'me'?) ... an advisory council drawn from all walks of life". And what does he mean by a more diverse symbolic role? He spells out "predominantly philanthropic activity at home and the promotion of Britain abroad ... (including) adopting previously troubled schools at an early stage of their transformation and directing energy, time and resources (politics, politics!) towards supporting their efforts to improve ...". Hames agreed a scoop release of the story of his pamphlet in the (anti-monarchist) *Independent on Sunday* and followed this up with scores of interviews not only in Britain but for audiences in Canada, Australia and New Zealand.

Polly Toynbee the anti-royalist columnist in the *Guardian* considered that "historians may look back and mark (the) pamphlet as one of the stations on the road to abolition ...". Brian MacArthur in *The Times* (11 September 1998, p. 40) reported that "Hames, a leader writer in the *Times* ... is now a sadder and wiser man. Hames ... is no left-wing radical but a Conservative. Yet all the tabloid reports said that 'plans' for the 'virtual abolition' of the monarchy had been unveiled by a think-tank 'with strong links to Tony Blair'". It is conceivable that all that Hames achieved in this episode was to have cast doubt on the value of think tanks.

With friends like these one might well prefer enemies and one of these was the founding editor of the *Independent*, Andreas Whittam Smith to which he returned to

---

[217] See Negrine, R. (1996) *The Communication Of Politics*. London: Sage.

write (3 February 1998, p. 21) of his participation in a debate at Oxford University's Union Society to support the motion that "this house believes that the Monarchy has outlived its usefulness". Whittam Smith reported that the debate was influenced by the argument that the monarchy already was outside the world of political competition and "can represent the whole nation in an emotionally satisfying way". Although that may not have happened just after the death of Princess Diana, it remained more often true and influenced those present to defeat Mr Whittam Smith and his motion.

Another kind of support for the British monarchy takes the form of favourable reports on monarchies elsewhere, or favourable comparisons with presidencies. One whole discourse is about the Japanese monarchy which Alan Hamilton pointed out in the *Times* (25 May 1998) had been fixed in a Constitution written by the victorious Americans after World War II. Hamilton explained that the Japanese imperial budget was far larger than the British one; the Japanese supported a much larger circle of royal family than the British do, with generous grants, and there was no opposition to this in the Japanese press or public opinion. Not long ago it was clear that the Japanese monarchy were behaving with a great deal more formality than was being pressed upon the British monarchy by those who decided that modernism was necessary. Joanna Pitman (*Times*, 16 October 1992 p. 9) told readers:

> "as emperor and empress assumed their thrones ... reporters rose to their feet and performed a deep and lingering collective bow. A senior journalist pronounced in exquisitely polite tones that all present were painfully aware of their impinging inexcusably on the busy schedule of their honourable emperor. The emperor moved his head down half an inch in acknowledgement ... questions are submitted in advance to be vetted by the Imperial Household Agency ... the emperor commits his answers to memory and, in the event that he strays from his official script, reporters attend a post-conference conference at which the 'mistakes' are 'corrected' ... any breach of protocol brings instant ... withdrawal of all access to the palace ...".

No room there for a Japanese Tim Hames; but that is partly because there had been no perceived flaws in imperial behavior, as there had been in Britain. The previous emperor Hirohito had at one time tried to be a citizen monarch throwing baseballs and touring factories and mines. On one occasion a miner addressed him as "Ten-Chan" - roughly 'Empy-Baby' and tried to shake his hand. "Let's do this the Japanese way" said Hirohito. Emperor and coalminer bowed solemnly in the lamplit tunnel. In the last half of his life, reported Murray Sayle (*New Yorker* 10 May 1993, pp. 43 - 52), Hirohito had "stepped back a thousand years, reviving the ancient Confucian idea of a monarch who rules by setting a good example in his public and personal life". The present emperor Akihito had been brought up with the assistance of an American Quaker tutor and had modernised, but assumed no political powers. Murray Sayle pointed out that over 90 % of respondents approved the Japanese royal family (while only 18 % did so for the cabinet, and only 1 % disagreed that all politicians were crooks and deserved to be in jail). Sayle also described Masako Owada (meaning feminine elegance) destined to wed the heir apparent. A selection committee had worked on a list of 300 eligibles, narrowed to 100 "perfect women" (who had no scandals in their families). The Japanese Newspaper Publishers and Editors Association (JNPEA) agreed to a 3-month news blackout in the search for a crown princess and had to renew this blackout three further times.

Masako accepted in December 1992 barely a week after Charles and Diana announced their separation. Masako declared she would "be of service to Your Highness". The couple were married in 1993, the wooing having spanned 7 years and included three refusals. One could understand that, as Masako speaks four European languages, studied at Harvard and Oxford and had been destined for a high flying diplomatic career. Having married she dropped out of sight, getting to know the intricacies of court history, poetry and imperial etiquette. She performed demurely at state occasions, always positioned three paces behind her husband. There was no question, as there had been with Diana's public appearances, of upstaging the heir. Manners were antique and what westerners would consider sexist, though the anti-sexist critique - as we shall see below - became much more acute in Britain than in Japan.

Press behavior in Japan is seen as much more deferent toward the monarch than is its counterpart in Britain. Terry McCarthy (*Independent* 11 June 1993) noted that "the 'surprise announcement' on Japanese television stations (of the imperial engagement) ... was a vast sham since the leading newspapers had known about the engagement for weeks. And yet ... everyone co-operated in the make believe theatre of the happy moment declaring with one voice how overjoyed they were ... (the news having been leaked to Japan from an American source), the JNPEA had decided that ... 'self restraint' ... could no longer be maintained ... but far from being embarrassed ... the Japanese press proceeded to congratulate itself on keeping the story quiet for so long".

These matters are not reported in this chapter to illustrate a 'better' Japanese way of doing things, but to illustrate that some British - and American periodicals considered it worth reporting good manners in a non-disparaging way. Other 'good press' from beyond Britain was underlined for Prince Charles again by the (monarchist) *Times* correspondent Alan Hamilton (5 November 1998, p. 6) when the Prince visited Romania (headlined for the story: 'Land of Bloody Villains'); "Romanians well remember the Prince's speech of 1989, in which he raised his voice in protest at Ceausescu's destruction of villages. ... Romania's Deputy Culture Minister ... said it was an extraordinary hope for us when we heard that speech on the BBC. He was the first to raise his voice against destruction ...".

Prince Charles has also had very positive reporting of his visit late in 1998 to South Africa - where he took his son Harry and met not only Nelson Mandela but also Spice Girls, another trip to Bhutan where he painted water colours, and to Argentina (mentioned above) where he resisted the temptations of the tango dancer. Aside from the Prince the *Times*' Paris correspondent (21 May 1999 p. 12) ran a small piece noting that "In France, It's Chic Again to be a Royalist" focusing on the success of a sound and light show celebrating an uprising: - not one hostile to the monarch but a less known one involving it is said some 100,000 peasants in the Vendée region who tried to stop the Revolution and beheading of King Louis XVI in 1793. A television documentary *Sagas* was positive about European royalty; but the show's presenter was quoted as saying that the French had adopted "two royal families, the Windsors and the Grimaldis of Monaco ... who give us the pomp and circumstance that we lack". This observation is interesting inasmuch as it suggests that a foreign monarchy is not felt as a burden if its members are accused in their own countries of misdemeanours (and serious allegations occurred in both Belgium and the Netherlands), but only the glitter comes across (not much from the Low Countries, compared with what has been available from Britain - unless the new administration drabs it down). It is not recognised in Britain that the British monarchy is at least in some small sense and for some of its functions valid for non-British countries; the Queen may have lost (?) imperial and Commonwealth domains but apparently may be gaining others - not as domains but as some new form of constituency as yet unlabelled by political scientists.

MONARCHY AND MESSAGE SYSTEMS - OPTIONS OF INFLUENCE

The monarchy does not set out to influence the structure of the mass message systems; for example, though the BBC is empowered by a Royal Charter it is not the monarchy which would set out to lay down rules about how the BBC could report - or even satirise - it. However, the monarchy may and probably does try to get favorable material published or broadcast and it acts 'anti-negatively' in combating or trying to avoid unfavorable content. Unfavorable content means first the action of prying into privacy - which can be done by telephoto cameras or, as we have seen above, by the press obtaining private correspondence and publishing it. Unfavorable content also means revealing non-admirable aspects of behavior alleged to have been carried out by royal family members. Britain has a Press Complaints Commission which becomes vocal after some marked abuse of decent disclosure - as in the example of release of a photo of Sophie Rees Jones shortly before her marriage to the Queen's son Prince Edward; the PCC leader plays for time, says the press will exercise restraint (in future - until the next transgression), and has no powers of punishment other than to express disapproval. Very occasionally the royal establishment will seek legal action to restrain publication, or damages; but these actions are seen as demeaning the monarchic role - which stands above the common struggle for existence and quality of existence. To squabble is the plight of the commoner; to stand above abuse (however painful it may be) demonstrates the dignity of majesty (which some commoners, acknowledging no superior status than the common humanity - resent).

The relative passivity of the monarchy, or at least its tendency to try to exert influence on content by informal representations ('backdoor diplomacy') contrasts with the efforts of some mass message vehicles (e.g. newspapers) and operators to try to influence not just the behavior and status but the very existence of the monarchy. We have seen evidence above in this and in previous chapters, of publication of anti-monarchist contents. These range from portrayals of royal family members (rightly or wrongly) as badly behaved in various ways - arrogant, extravagant, exploitative, outdated, to discussions of the institution of monarchy. Such messages are directed in two ways - one towards the public who it is implied will come to accept these negative portrayals and eventually turn against and thus at second hand impact upon the institution, and also directly at royal family members who may wish to take account of criticisms; thus Princes Charles and Philip may decide to shoot fewer grouse, or the Queen may decide to open the Scottish Parliament not wearing robes but a special outfit designed with tartan decoration by an Orkney couturier. However, by deflecting criticisms through taking them as advice the monarchy adapts to the changing ways in which it may be supported.

One of the hostile discourses in Britain about the monarchy has been that offered by feminists. In many cases such writers address each other, or the public; but one in particular, Beatrix Campbell appears also to be facing the monarchy direct. She has written several articles and appeared on several broadcast shows offering her analysis as well as providing her ideas in a book.[218] Campbell argues that Prince Charles should have changed the "patriarchal principles of royal marriage". By patriarchal principles Campbell means that the monarchy - and aristocracy - convey their titles down through the male descendants - where they exist, in preference to females, who only receive titles when there are no sons (or grandsons). The latter case was how Queens Victoria and Elizabeth became monarchs. Linked with this institutional rule are an informal perception that women are inferior, and a double standard about sexual behavior. The latter means that royal men can or are expected to be promiscuous before marriage (and, as Kitty Kelley the American author insists, after it too), while their women are expected to be virgins at marriage and faithful thereafter[219]. Thus it was, after the 1970s that the thirty-something Charles had to find someone ten years his junior to be sure she was a virgin. This meant that Diana was too immature to take the strains of her role - which Campbell claims was not helped by the Queen and Prince Philip - and that her problems of adjustment contributed to the divorce.

Campbell has several other dislikes about Prince Charles, his parents, and his uncle and advisor Lord Mountbatten[220]. Mountbatten is excoriated because he "enjoyed acting as a royal procurer" (or, it could be put less acidly that he encouraged the young Charles to have affairs with women). In Campbell's terms Mountbatten's "princely project ... has been ... discussed by a biographer as if it were the bungling sport of a benign old buffer. It was not - it was malign. The royal relatives ... were all implicated in a Machiavellian

---

[218] Campbell, B. (1998) *Diana, Princess of Wales: How Sexual Politics Shook the Monarchy.* London: Women's Press.

[219] The undiscussed reason for this is surely male insecurity and lack of esteem in one's gender, in that the royal men do not wish to risk the existence of other males who had sexual knowledge of a royal bride, and who might betray details of that knowledge to other - unseemly - men; such male discourse, in this model of a sexist society, improves the esteem of such males in their circles. The flaw in this argument is that there are women who have carnal knowledge of the royal male - but they are expected not to discuss it; and if they do, it damages their esteem in the same male-sexist society.

[220] Campbell, B. (1998) The Man Who Would Be King. *Guardian Weekend* 13 June pp. 10-29.

ordinance to the prince: 'Thou shalt be married to a WASP virgin. Thy wife shall know no better'".

The parents are vilified because they "appeared to break with royal tradition - by sending (Charles) to school instead of employing tutors ... but ... selected exclusive institutions that would protect the boy from the people". In this, Campbell fails to recognise that Charles' education in the late 1950s was indeed radically open for that era, in which he met many middle class people - many of whom gave him a particularly hard time; he also went to college in Australia and to a non-Ivy-League school in Wales. If that is not sufficient to satisfy Campbell she rails at Charles's "participation in bloody sports which, towards the end of the century, became increasingly besieged by popular dissent (from) ... the elite tradition of murderous manliness ...". This stereotypes one particular form of animal killing for pleasure, ignoring the plebeian forms (albeit uncommon) of dog-fighting, badger hunting, and most commonly (and practised across all classes), fishing.

Another platform on which some journalists address the monarchy is that of fatigue - the idea that "it's too much bother, some of us (we won't say how many) don't want you to continue, why not just quit". As part of the *Guardian's* discussion of the wedding of Prince Edward to Sophie Rhys Jones their columnist Jonathan Freedland (16 June, 1999) was given a whole page on which to write a speech he would have liked to have heard from the Prince after his wedding - though he knew it would not happen. Some of the words he devised for this fantasy speech included: "you, mum are the official sovereign ... those people ... who watched our wedding on cable, satellite and terrestrial TV, are our 'subjects'. I mean, come on. This is 1999! It's ridiculous; it causes misery to us and diminishes them ...". The argument that it causes misery to the royal family is supported by saying that the burden of intrusion into privacy is excessive; the notion that it diminishes the public is not discussed at all, unless it has been done under the umbrella idea that the year 1999 is so modern - infused with science, technology, rationality, that there is no place at the turn of the millennium for an institution that was set up in pre-modern times.

Not all newspapers provide platforms for anti-monarchist rhetoric, indeed the majority in terms of readership are supportive, even if some often give in to opportunities to tease the Queen. The press thus presents a picture of a wide variety of opinions. Those which support the monarchy are generally not trying to tell it to change its ways except perhaps to relate better to the people at large; this is not all that easy when modern - especially youth culture has moved far and in many ways from the morals and aesthetics of the world into which the Queen was born. Those titles which do oppose the monarchy do tell it what they would like it to do, touching upon the royal family's finances, styles of child rearing, vulnerability to intrusion, sporting and cultural preferences and activities; these titles also in the same breath tell the public what they believe the public should demand of the monarchy.

This anti-monarchism involves an ambiguity in as much as it often says "change radically (though you may continue)" but also says "go away - like the kings of Portugal,

Italy and so many other countries". The royal family and those who support it and the monarchy are thus given the option of two strategies of response - one which tries to oblige the complainers - and the others which are more radical: either for the monarch simply to refuse to change, or to set down the sceptre and go. Refusal to change has not been much discussed in the press, partly because the British way has been to seek compromise; it also leaves unexplored the possibility of developing opposition to 'rebellion'. Thus for example there are a few life-Peers who sit in the House of Lords, having accepted ermine and a Royally-signed warrant, who nevertheless give support to disloyal sectors; the Queen could try cancelling one or two of such peerages and see what happened. There would likely be a major fuss - and it would be dramatised that most if not all peers want to hang on to their privileges - the corollary to which is that they are expected to perform their roles with dignity in public service, within the existing (unwritten) constitution. It used to be the case that the monarch would discipline infractious subjects by murdering them and of course no such thing can now be imagined. However, symbolic punishments could be applied, though this has (virtually) never been broached in public discourse. One knight had his title removed, for having been a communist agent (he was also the keeper of the Queen's art collection), but the disgrace was seen as emanating from the Prime Minister's wrath rather than from outrage to the Queen.

The other radical option in response to disloyalty is voluntary abdication, not just of the Queen in favor of a successor, but of the monarchy as a whole. It is safe to say that the immersion of the Queen in British history (and present life), the commitments she made in her upbringing and coronation and the training she has imparted to her children, all are likely to be diametrically opposed to any form of abdication, which would be seen and felt as failure and defeat - not just for a family, but for the continuity of national history that that family has symbolised. We are back, here, to the notion of the monarchy as in itself a 'medium', a conduit through which the messages - desirable or not - of the nation's history and current development are expressed.

Aside from the major foreground status of the British monarchy - in Britain but also in other countries - there is a ground bass of sounds raising the notion that monarchy might be a resort for countries which had long been without it. After the Serbian collapse against NATO there were at least some demonstrators who raised the royal flag (the Karageorgevich dynasty in Serbia had disappeared well before the second world war) suggesting a return of monarchy there. The sentiment would seem to be not very well justified in Balkan history, more so by the northern European example of constitutional monarchies in which the people seek a symbol of national dignity which has not been available, or has been grossly let down in civilian leadership. Similar monarchist demonstrations have been seen in several Eastern European countries including Poland, Romania and Estonia. Other articles, several quoted above, detail how Japan loyally sustains its monarchy as do Thailand, Brunei and other countries, while the republican South Korea, India and other countries visited by British royalty make it clear enough how the institution and its symbolic exponents are admired. All these themes are to be found in the press, not necessarily as parts of an explicit argument about what Britain should or should not do, but as quiet service to the discourse in which the nation decides how it wants to act about its feelings.

Broadcasting in Britain affords less of a rumbustious discourse than is found in the press. One reason may be that the BBC - whose services are still at the end of the century being used weekly by well over 90 per cent of the public - is as we have seen established under a Royal Charter; the Independent (i.e. commercial) broadcasters are established under Acts of Parliament which are also couched in terms that these are protocols devised by Her Majesty's minister and validated by her signature. It is extremely doubtful that satirists and political commentators on the airwaves bear these royal statuses in mind, or whether if they did they would serve as reminders of loyalty or as instigations to more vociferous opposition, but the culture of broadcasting contains major elements that are loyalist and which tend to depict outright opposition as something negative - evidence of inadequate socialisation, personal sourness or other formulations that are marginal or even malign.

MONARCHY AND MESSAGE SYSTEMS - OPTIONS OF INFLUENCE

There is a huge and obvious benefit for the monarchy if it can influence the mass message systems. To do this it needs not only good public relations operators but also effective intelligence in the form of insightful social science, and influential creatives such as writers, musicians and artists. We have seen much attention to the arts, with the appointment of poet laureate (and, some years back, a Master of the Queen's Music) and the commissioning of numerous portraits of the Queen. This does not mean that the arts are required to be sycophantic, providing works that adore the monarch or her family; rather, they should have the insight that they have the opportunity to celebrate or develop positive themes in the cultural self esteem of the nation and of its many strands of membership. It should not be considered, either, that the use of public relations personnel implies a demeaning and new descent into dishonest manipulation of information ('spin'). Monarchs over the ages and monarchs everywhere have employed the equivalent of public relations professionals in their own time and the modern forms are considerably more elegant and humane than many of their frankly murderous predecessors.

The monarchy includes the heir apparent Prince Charles, and he has publicised his position in the fields of architecture (opposing non-human scales and idioms, favoring decorative elements such as pillars and their capitals which, he says, are derived from nature's trees) and organic farming; both of his ideological positions are increasingly widely supported. Occasional press articles suggest that Charles' positions are opposed to the Queen's, but 'Buckingham Palace' (the press's term for the position of the monarch) avoids rising to the bait of such leads, which would reveal and underline any differences of perspective that may exist. The monarchy can thus influence message systems either by planned activities or statements (for an ingenious example that may not have entirely succeeded, see the case of the Queen's tea with the Commoner, below); or by riding oppositional waves; or very occasionally by formal restraints as when the Palace has either taken or intended to take legal action, say about publication of material that is derogatory, untrue or 'merely' extremely unpleasant[221].

It is suggested, below, that there is no particular payoff for mass message systems or for those who operate within them, if they succeed either in bolstering or in abolishing the monarchy. If they weaken it drastically, it becomes so much less interesting for the public at large and so much less vital in its symbolic life that it would constitute a loss of negative payoff. This does not deter some operators who believe, altruistically, that regardless of increased power or profits for the message system they use, it would benefit the public and the culture if they could succeed in changing the monarchy, some by seeking to strengthen it, others by wanting to weaken and yet others to abolish it. The monarchy is thus a highly contested 'site', to use the jargon of post-modern discourse analysts.

MESSAGE SYSTEMS AND THE PUBLIC - INFORMATION FLOW

Mass message systems have as their prime business to pump out information to the public. Much of this information is about the monarchy. Members of the public probably often realise - when they think about it, which is not always - that the pattern and contents of information in the press and broadcasting does not wholly represent reality. What is relayed has been selected, and to realise that instead of taking it as a template of the truth requires a degree of intellectual energy and vigilance that can not be expected of a reader, viewer or listener in ordinary mode. We have seen a number of studies, in Chapter Five that have looked for any connection between amount of reading, or of viewing, and perceptions regarding the monarchy; and more often than not, and perhaps surprisingly so even in the case of viewing television satire that is extremely harsh on members of the royal family, it has been difficult to show that more viewing connects with more critical feelings about the monarchy.

An example of something that has a very low profile in message system content is the fact that the Queen is an amusing and skilful mimic. She can imitate ministers and other exalted figures, with wit and intelligence, to considerable effect. One such person is the public relations official Simon Lewis whom Prime Minister Blair provided her with as part of a drive to modernise - or at least to portray as modern - the institution whose most important brand attribute might be considered by others to be its

---

[221] Intrusion into privacy is perhaps the commonest heading under which the monarchy wishes to restrain mass message operators. An episode that might assist the monarchy's case occurred in July 1999 when Prime Minister Blair took action to restrain the *Daily Mail* from comments about the education of his daughter who had been placed in what was considered a privileged school. The Prime Minister's case was that such intrusion did not serve any public interest, and this is exactly the ground which he thus shares with royal family members who often have to put up with intrusive stories.

timelessness. On one occasion the Queen was taken to have tea with a woman living in a council estate (municipal subsidised housing). Pictures were taken of the scene and published in many papers. The *Guardian* (9 July 1999, G2, pp. 1-3) devoted much space to analysing the meanings of its picture; 'the' picture showed the Queen sitting primly though with a most happy smile, facing the householder. Amanda Foreman (which analyst might dare to lay down the meanings of *her* name, against what she may feel about it herself?) first recognises that "the palace and the press have interpreted (the picture) in different ways". The picture is nevertheless "one of the most important artefacts of the Elizabethan reign ... it is a complex statement about the simultaneous decline of Britain's monarchy and the apotheosis of Elizabeth II[222]". Perhaps Foreman speaks more convincingly for the jury of public perception when she writes: "it depicts the truth of Bagehot's insistence that the monarch must be, and is, different from the ordinary person[223]. In trying to be different from the ordinary, the Queen only manages to be surreal ...". Foreman also thinks that through "royal participation in the public's way of life" the Queen's "tacit acceptance of her new role is little short of a revolution ... it may even ... give back the Queen her dignity".

After an (informative) excursion into the history of royal interaction with commoners Foreman returns to the "hostess" of the occasion. "Although the photograph suggests a different story, Mrs McCarron insists that the Queen was relaxed and friendly ...". In the end, though the Queen "has given up much more than any of her predecessors ... she has sacrificed the battle to win the war". What a *Guardian*-only reader will not realise is that their picture was not the only one. The *Independent*, at least, offered an extremely similar one but there are two important details of difference: while the *Guardian*'s has son James McCarron on a seat behind the Queen, apparently picking his nose (and what are the rich semantics of that gesture?) the *Independent*'s icon has the boy not seemingly picking his nose; but importantly it has caught the Queen at a moment when she is not smiling; perhaps feeling uncomfortable.

The point of this example is that it is common for the press to offer interpretative accounts, diagnoses, statements about 'the public's perception' - but without really having consulted the public. The *Guardian* journalist and picture are here telling the public about Mrs McCarron and the Queen - or perhaps not telling all, or getting it partly right or not getting it wholly right - it is not possible to tell better without having been there; but the press (and so were other papers - the *Mail* captioned its picture 'Tea for One') is also telling the public about what it - the public - thinks. Interestingly, it was the non-monarchist *Guardian* which gave so much space to analysing the "meaning" (does this mean: the feelings and thoughts that viewers will take from the image?) of the picture.

---

[222] A complex detail here is that the Queen, pictured in Scotland, is not the second Elizabeth to reign over that country but the first, which some Scots would like to emphasise. The seemingly insightful article has thus missed at least one element of (public) perception - in Scotland.

[223] Each one of whom is, of course, different from each other one ... .

The *Independent* carried a jesting comment to the effect that the Queen is now being forced to do things which are against her nature and that of her position, by the intending populariser Simon Lewis; but rather than leave its non-monarchist readers with the feeling that the Queen is left at a disadvantage by the episode, the columnist reminds them that she can get her own back by her artful mimicry, to her family, of Mr Lewis, thus, on her own ground, making him a laughing stock. We, the public, who are treated by the press to all manner of secrets do not hear or see the Queen's own satire; it would certainly be a devastating coup for television, simply in terms of entertainment to obtain some such footage, and it might also be devastatingly effective politically to see fun made of politicians, say, or other celebrities.

Historians have discussed the roles of court jesters in which a witty commoner's jokes at the expense of the monarch were tolerated, perhaps as a defusing mechanism (what a sport his majesty is, to put up with this, when he could easily have the man executed); should the Queen's own mimicry of commoners be televised this would create a new and potentially extremely powerful meaning for the term court jester. In Shakespeare's representations monarchs could joke with commoners, but that was in a pre-print era when sensibilities were more collective, constructed in a different way from what became conventional in the centuries dominated by print and mass literacy, in which a sense of private individuality was more widely constructed. In this newer modern sensibility, the rounded identity of the monarch was withdrawn or hidden, replaced by an image-for-the-public, one characterised by dignity. This may make it seem that the monarch either does not make jokes, or does not do so in exchange with the public (where one risks the danger of losing an exchange - or contest - of jests). It may be argued that society is now moving into an age of post-print electronic sensibility, in which private individuality is a less dominant element and that within this new situation the monarch might do well, if she or he can, to trade jests with commoners.

To distil the relevance of the teaparty picture we can say that the press - and broadcasters - put out a great deal of information, but the extent of the completeness or validity of that information is not visible. Some information is accidentally misleading but sometimes some may be purposefully deceitful. Michael Shea who was once the Queen's Press Secretary was quoted (by Noreen Taylor in the *Times*, 28 April 1998, p. 17: In the Palace's Shadow) as claiming that "one highly respected editor of a broadsheet telephoned ... to tell me that the Queen Mother was on the point of death. He knew for certain, they were clearing the front page ... Happened all the time, these stories. Works of fiction. We live in a media age where reputations are brutally slaughtered by a headline. Like the one alleging that Prince Phillip told British students in China they'd get slitty eyes if they stayed on much longer. He was referring to ... the effect the sun's brightness would have on their eyes ... Prince Phillip is ... far too sophisticated ... to insult people".

MESSAGE SYSTEMS AND THE PUBLIC - OPTIONS OF INFLUENCE

It has happened that several successive message systems (film, children's 'comics', broadcast television, video games) have been accused by some analysts of having a bad influence on their users. Such harmful effects have included prompting aggressive behavior, distorting individuals' perceptions of society, and of their body images and ideals to the extent that people damage their own health, and fostering aggressive nationalism or inter-ethnic tensions. Some of these malfunctions may have been true, and the criticisms led to both self discipline amongst message makers and to some external regulation of their efforts. It is rare to find newspaper articles blaming the press - as a system - for harmful effects; however it may be more true that press articles accuse television as a phenomenon in itself, for various troubles. Television programs do not have much occasion to accuse the press of producing harms, and may develop even fewer occasions on which to turn against their own system. British radio carries discussion programs and 'phone-ins in which there is much unfettered discussion, including some which consider television and the press as sometimes being harmful; but the influence of such radio material is hard to assess. It is more in the realm of academic research that evidence may exist that suggests that one or another message system affects social institutions, sometimes for the better but sometimes in a way that could be considered harmful.

For example, there is some discussion that televising courtrooms might negatively influence the quality of justice - itself - or its perceived quality (others argue for positive effects). A similar discourse explores the possibility that televising parliaments may enhance - or damage democratic institutions. Each mass message system is much more likely to address the public - whom it courts as users - with the idea that what they are offered - will be of benefit rather than harm: "we are going to educate you" or "entertain you". It is unnatural to expect or to find a mass message system saying to users "come to us and we will harm you". It is more common that individuals address message systems with complaints about harms; in Britain there are several institutions that exist to deal with complaints, especially about broadcasting, and supervisory bodies (the Governors of the BBC, the Commission of the independent television system, the Press Complaints Commission, the Advertising Standards Authority) all of which to an extent forestall and dissipate concerns about harms.

With regard to the monarchy it is a matter of opinion whether reinforcing loyalty is considered a harm, or a benefit. Most of the mass operators follow public opinion which they know broadly supports the monarchy and either give it wholehearted support or, if journalists are against it (and we know - see Chapter 5) that a slight majority of them are opposed to it) they try to keep their feelings to themselves. We have seen in previous chapters, nevertheless, that in normal times opposition to monarchy seeps through management's protective screens and on occasion - especially shortly after Diana Princess of Wales died, it erupts in full flower. To what extent any of this produces effects in the direction of the opinions on offer is doubtful - as previous chapters indicate. All of this concerns explicit content - programs such as the BBC's documentary EIIR which 'say' "the monarchy is magnificent (implying) let's keep it" or articles explicitly against the monarchy such as described above, by Toynbee, Campbell and others.

This leaves an area of discourse in which it may be that what is said is not ostensibly in any way about the monarchy but which may affect perceptions of it. This area of possible incidental effects includes the reporting of the conflict in Northern Ireland. There, the Unionist faction proclaims loyalty to the British state and crown; this in turn provokes the republicans (who have most skilfully grasped the label 'nationalists' - evidently a term of approval - as applying to them) to agitate for detachment of Ulster from the United Kingdom and its assimilation into Eire. The fighting and terrorism that the conflict has produced has caused much disgust and fatigue on the mainland, where substantial minorities think territorially and believe that Ireland should be for the Irish and accept the republican case. This perception in turn sees the Unionists as the source of conflict.

Unionist public relations are internally strong but externally poor. They carry out apparently militaristic marches in which they wear suits and bowler hats - garb considered outmoded on the mainland and, moreover, carrying overtones of psychopathic terrorism as depicted in the movie *Clockwork Orange* and in punk, hard rock and the more strident musical oppositional sub cultures. What may happen therefore - and this has not been the topic of any systematic research - is that mainland UK readers and viewers who consider the Irish conflict and the role of Unionists in it, come to dislike the term loyalist and quite likely, with it, the concept royalist. In short, Ulster Unionism - or at least the way it has been portrayed in British mass message systems may have had an indirect and unintended effect of souring mainlanders' feelings about the monarchy.

Another field of discourse which less indirectly spills over on to that of the monarchy is that of the future of the House of Lords. The Blair-led Labour administration has ended the right of hereditary peers to vote in the Upper House of Parliament, thus cutting the iconic links the peerage claims or appears to or really does have with British history. Lord Cranborne is an example of such links; he is a scion of the Cecil family whose distant ancestor advised Queen Elizabeth I of England (see the movie *Elizabeth*), and whose less remote ancestor was a prime minister but who now faces being the last of his line to have any unelected influence in British affairs. Peers have a largely rural rather than an urban image, whose aristocratic features include foxhunting and ownership of tracts of countryside which they wish to defend from the right to roam for the people at large. The Blair administration has established an Act which provides a right to roam (on lands belonging, among others, to peers) and by the time this is printed may already have banned foxhunting. These changes may not visibly intend to undercut attitudes that support the monarchy together with its supporting peerage and rural affiliations, but they may turn out to have that effect; and indeed they may have covertly been intended to have that effect (the administration which also supports openness may not be quite so open about it if an anti-monarchist intention has been connected with such changes).

These examples suggest that operators of mass message systems do realise they have a chance of influencing the public by directing particular, explicit suggestions about and criticism of the monarchy to the consumers. There are also possible mechanisms whereby discussion of matters not ostensibly primarily connected with the monarchy may also influence public attitudes. These attitudes are very often the topic of polls and mass message operators know that the public remain monarchist, a feeling that the message operators realise they have to respect, ultimately, if they want to preserve their audiences. This provides a channel whereby the public - without knowing it or intending it coherently - influence the mass message operators.

MASS MESSAGE SYSTEMS AND THE
PUBLIC - COHESION AND PAYOFF

As already demonstrated and discussed there is no overall cohesion amongst the press, as regards its direction and degree of support for or opposition to the monarchy. The majority of the press by readership reflects what it takes to be its customers' opinions and behaves in a more or less monarchist manner, sometimes with visible reluctance. While the monarchist papers may carry some hostility or innuendo, the anti-monarchist papers often include material which fail to deny a feeling for monarchism. In a single issue of the *Guardian* (17 July 1999) there are two substantial stories, one about the refurbishment of the Kremlin including many symbolic touches of regal splendour in the shape of thrones and crown decorations, the other about the squabble amongst the descendants of the French Bourbons, the second last of whom evidently disinherited his son (leaving open the cliff-hanger of who - and there are many other biological heirs - would indeed be the object of quasi-monarchist attentions in the glossy society magazines).

Broadcasters in Britain are either enabled by a Royal Charter (the BBC) or an Act of Parliament (commercial TV and radio) that is countersigned by the monarch, so are less likely to behave anti-monarchistically. They nevertheless give way from time to time to temptations to provide antimonarchist satire and discussions. These are far outweighed by the mainstream material which remains monarchist; in recent years however there have been elements of content which might indirectly - as in the Northern Ireland and foxhunting examples given in the previous section - detract from cohesion of ideology in a different way.

It remains for philosophers, historians, political scientists and a wide range of disciplined critics to judge whether, for the public, there is reward in remaining monarchist, in altering the character of the monarchy or in abandoning it. This last option is rejected by all but a minority of future thinkers, if not on the grounds of affection amongst all upholders then because of a preference for caution. The press and broadcasters could probably have it both ways. If the monarchy remains there is endless scope for scrutiny and copy; if it is abolished, not only would there be a new order to examine but the retired royals would remain - as the French and Germans treat the British monarchy - as a starry object of interest; though the star quality would ultimately wane. If the monarchy is demoted to some minor entity the mass message systems would lose out on a phenomenon which, especially if it remains potent, provides such an object of interest, loyalty or dispute, in all cases delivering readers, viewers and listeners for the discourse.

INDEX

C

D

N

O

P

Q

R